C0-BPL-311

SOUTH ASIAN CHRISTIAN DIASPORA

The South Asian Christian diaspora is largely invisible in the literature about religion and migration. This is the first comprehensive study of South Asian Christians living in Europe and North America, presenting the main features of these diasporas, their community histories and their religious practices.

The South Asian Christian diaspora is pluralistic both in terms of religious adherence, cultural tradition and geographical areas of origin. This book gives justice to such pluralism and presents a multiplicity of cultures and traditions typical of the South Asian Christian diaspora. Issues such as the institutionalization of the religious traditions in new countries, identity, the paradox of belonging both to a minority immigrant group and a majority religion, the social functions of rituals, attitudes to language, generational transfer, and marriage and family life, are all discussed.

South Asian Christian Diaspora

Invisible Diaspora in Europe and North America

Edited by

KNUT A. JACOBSEN
University of Bergen, Norway
and
SELVA J. RAJ
formerly Albion College, USA

ASHGATE

© Knut A. Jacobsen and the Estate of Selva J. Raj 2008

All rights reserved. No part of this publication may be reproduced, stored in a retrieval system or transmitted in any form or by any means, electronic, mechanical, photocopying, recording or otherwise without the prior permission of the publisher.

Knut A. Jacobsen and Selva J. Raj have asserted their moral right under the Copyright, Designs and Patents Act, 1988, to be identified as the editors of this work.

Published by
Ashgate Publishing Limited
Wey Court East
Union Road
Farnham
Surrey GU9 7PT
England

Ashgate Publishing Company
Suite 420
101 Cherry Street
Burlington, VT 05401-4405
USA

www.ashgate.com

British Library Cataloguing in Publication Data
South Asian Christian diaspora : invisible diaspora in Europe and North America
1. South Asians – Europe – Religion 2. South Asians – North America – Religion
I. Jacobsen, Knut A., 1956– II. Raj, Selva J.
270.8'3'089914

Library of Congress Cataloging-in-Publication Data
South Asian Christian diaspora : invisible diaspora in Europe and North America / edited by Knut A. Jacobsen and Selva J. Raj.
p. cm.
ISBN 978-0-7546-6261-7 (hardcover : alk. paper) 1. South Asians—Europe—Religion.
2. South Asians—North America—Religion. I. Jacobsen, Knut A., 1956– II. Raj, Selva J.

BR737.S68S68 2008
270.8'3089914—dc22

BR
737
.S68
S68
2008

2008015399

ISBN 978-0-7546-6261-7

Mixed Sources
Product group from well-managed forests and other controlled sources
www.fsc.org Cert no. SA-COC-1565
© 1996 Forest Stewardship Council
FSC

Printed and bound in Great Britain by
MPG Books Ltd, Bodmin, Cornwall.

Contents

List of Figures

Preface

Knut A. Jacobsen

A month after Selva J. Raj and I had mailed the manuscript of this book to the publisher, Ashgate, I was in Puducherry (Pondicherry), one of the great places of religious pluralism in India. I had been lecturing for two weeks and was ready to leave, had packed my things in a backpack and suitcase, and used the last minutes while waiting for the car that would take me to the airport in Chennai to check my e-mails. I opened an e-mail message, and thus I learned that Selva J. Raj had died of natural causes in his home in Albion, Michigan on 14 March 2008, at only 55 years of age.

Selva was one of the world's foremost scholars on Christians in India and in the South Asian diaspora. His interest was in the popular traditions, in rituals and what people do. He was a gentle and creative intellectual and a warm human being. He had many friends and good colleagues. I had seen Selva at a few international conferences and had listened to a few of his vivid paper presentations but we made contact only in 2005. We had a common interest in religious pluralism in South Asia and the South Asian diaspora, which led to our meeting at a conference in 2005 in Tokyo.

In our conversation, I pointed out that during my studies of the Sri Lankan Tamils (who are Hindus and Roman Catholics) in Norway and Europe, I had noticed the almost complete absence of the Roman Catholic Tamils in the research literature on religion in the Sri Lankan and Indian diaspora. It was almost as if they were non-existent. Much had been published on the Sri Lankan Tamil Hindus in Europe and North America, but hardly anything on the Sri Lankan Tamil Catholics. They were an invisible diaspora. Selva observed that this invisibility was also the case, although not as dramatic, in the research literature on Christians in India and South Asia.

We thought we would co-operate in an attempt to make the South Asian Christian diaspora more visible in the research literature, and decided to co-edit this volume. I would take care of the contributions on the diaspora in Europe, and he those in North America.

We are thankful to the contributors. It is our hope that this book will lead to an increased interest in the religious pluralism of South Asia and in the South Asian diaspora, and that this interest will generate new research in the future.

Many people had known Selva for much longer than me, and some of them are contributors to this volume. I therefore asked one of them, Rachel Fell McDermott, to write a Contributor's Memorial.

Contributor's Memorial

Rachel Fell McDermott

The outpouring of grief at Selva J. Raj's death on 14 March 2008 from those at Albion College, where he had taught since 1995, extending to all of us in the fields of South Asian, Catholic, Indian Christian, Hindu-Christian and Comparative Studies, attests to the enormity of Selva's gifts. A man of great gentleness and kindness, Selva was a constant facilitator of intellectual projects: he joined colleagues together, encouraged them in new consultative ventures, and prodded his friends to think in creative directions. He always believed in the potential of projects, of people.

At Albion College, he was absolutely beloved. He was twice given an endowed professorship, every summer offered funding for research projects in India, and six times awarded the Outstanding Male Professor, Professor of the Month and Most Dedicated Professor awards by students. Indeed, Selva's death has interrupted so much. In addition to the 27 articles, chapters, and encyclopaedia entries, and six co-edited books he had already published or prepared for publication – and the current volume is only one of four that will appear posthumously – Selva was in the process of writing books or articles on vernacular Catholicism in South India, his experiences with Mother Theresa, Indian wayside shrines, tribal indigenization, women in rural India, and even cyber-cemeteries.

His intellectual curiosity was boundless, and so was his energy for involvement. At the time of his death, he was planning two panel presentations for the 2008 American Academy of Religion meetings. He was being sought as an applicant for prestigious positions in Catholic Studies in the United States. So much is lost by this loss. So much productivity. So many opportunities for even deeper friendship, as well as for new friends to be touched by this warm, ebullient, wonderful man.

Among the many, many things for which I feel grateful to Selva is my chapter in the present volume. He essentially commanded me to write it. He waved away my protests that I am not an expert on Indian Christianity, or the diaspora, or Dalit Studies. 'You can do the research,' he said. 'We need a chapter like this.'

However the outcome is judged, my life has been deeply touched by the men and women whom I interviewed in order to write the chapter. My scholarly life has a new dimension now, and I have Selva to thank for it. This sentiment, in innumerable unique ways, is being echoed all over the world by well-wishers and mourners. From whatever religious perspective we come, we pray for his peace.

List of Contributors

Freek L. Bakker studied theology and Indology. His thesis dealt with Balinese Hinduism, but he later wrote about Surinamese and Caribbean Hinduism. He is involved in the dialogue between Hindus and Christians in the Netherlands. Since May 2003 he has been a senior lecturer and researcher in Hinduism and Buddhism and Asian Christian Theology at the Department of Theology of the Utrecht University, The Netherlands. As such, he is Managing Editor of the journal *Exchange*. Nowadays, he is also active in the fields of cinema, religion and theology.

Elizabeth Cameron Galbraith received her doctorate from the University of Cambridge in 1992. She is the author of *Kant and Theology: Was Kant a Closet Theologian?* (International Scholars Publications, 1996). In the past ten years, she has become increasingly involved in Japan and India Studies programmes and has burgeoning research interests in Asian Christianity. Her most recent contribution to this area of studies, 'Christian Imperialism: The Case of Indian Christianity', is to be published by *Religion* in 2008.

Urmila Goel is a postdoctoral researcher in social and cultural anthropology affiliated to the European University Frankfurt/Oder in Germany. Her research interests cover mainly strategies in dealing with experiences of racism and the interdependency of racism and heteronormativity. She conducts her ethnographic work among those marked as Indians in Germany. More information is available at <www.urmila.de>.

Nori Henk is a PhD candidate at Loyola University Chicago. This chapter emerged from her master's thesis on Christian Indian immigrants. Her doctoral research is on a religious social movement in the Catholic Church. She teaches at West Los Angeles College.

Knut A. Jacobsen is Professor in the History of Religions at the University of Bergen, Norway, and author or editor of 15 books and more than 60 articles in journals and edited volumes on various aspects on religions in South Asia and the South Asian diasporas. Recent publications include *Kapila: Founder of Samkhya and Avatara of Vishnu* (Munshiram Manoharlal 2008) and the edited volumes *South Asians in the Diaspora: Histories and Religious Traditions* (with Pratap Kumar) (Brill, 2004), *Theory and Practice of Yoga: Essays in Honour of Gerald James Larson* (Brill, 2005) and *South Asian Religions on Display: Religious Processions in South Asia and in the Diaspora* (Routledge, 2008).

Brigitte Luchesi teaches in the Department of Comparative Religion at the University of Bremen, Germany. She is a trained sociologist, historian of religion and social anthropologist, having worked for many years on forms of local religion in North India and on religious practices of Hindu immigrants from South Asia in Germany.

Damaris Lüthi, a social anthropologist, focused her PhD thesis, 'Washing off Sin: Cleanliness in Kottar, South India', on the relationship between everyday hygiene and so-called ritual notions of im/purity, and its relevance for the Indian caste system. It was based on 16 months of fieldwork in a South Indian Tamil town neighbourhood in 1995–96. Recently, she has conducted research on social change among Sri Lankan Tamil refugees in Switzerland (2001–2003). She is also a documentary filmmaker (*1000° Celsius*, 1993; *Silk, Muthappar and VHS*, 1998; *Hippie Masala*, 2006), teaches Visual Anthropology at the University of Berne, and is responsible for women empowerment programmes in India for a Swiss development agency.

Eleanor Nesbitt is Professor of Religions and Education in the Institute of Education at the University of Warwick, UK, and a founder member of the Punjab Research Group. She writes on Hindu, Sikh and Christian communities and religious socialization. Her recent publications include *Sikhism A Very Short Introduction* (Oxford University Press, 2005), *Intercultural Education: Ethnographic and Religious Approaches* (Sussex Academic Press, 2004) and *Interfaith Pilgrims* (Quaker Books, 2003). With support from the Arts and Humanities Research Council, she is currently researching the religious identity formation of young people in mixed-faith families.

Rachel Fell McDermott is Associate Professor and Chair of the Department of Asian and Middle Eastern Cultures, Barnard College, New York. She is the author of *Mother of My Heart, Daughter of My Dreams: Kali and Uma in the Devotional Poetry of Bengal* (Oxford University Press, 2001) and *Singing to the Goddess: Poems to Kali and Uma from Bengal* (Oxford University Press, 2001), and co-editor, with Jeffrey Kripal, of *Encountering Kali: In the Margins, at the Center, in the West* (University of California Press, 2003).

Selva J. Raj was Stanley S. Kresge Professor and Chair of Religious Studies at Albion College, Michigan. His research interests were in the areas of ritual exchange between Hindus and Catholics in south India, Indian Christian diaspora in the United States, Hindu women saints, and contemporary women's movements in India. The author of numerous articles, he co-edited three volumes: *Popular Christianity in India: Riting between the Lines* (SUNY Press, 2002), *Dealing with Deities: The Ritual Vow in South Asia* (SUNY Press, 2006), and *Miracle as Modern Conundrum in South Asian Religious Traditions* (SUNY Press, forthcoming).

Helena Maria Mauricio C. Sant'ana teaches social anthropology in the Higher Institute of Social Sciences (ISCSP), Technical University of Lisbon, and belongs to the research team of Centre for Research and Studies in Sociology (CIES), developing research in processes of social recomposition and cultural reconfiguration. She specializes in gender relations, ethnicity, colonialism in Africa and India, and identity formation of Indian diaspora in Portugal.

Brigitte Sébastia is a researcher in social anthropology at the French Institute of Pondicherry and a member of the École des Hautes Études en Sciences Sociales (EHESS), Paris. She has conducted research in South India for many years in the field of the Indianization of Catholicism, especially through the study of the shrines at Velankanni and Puliyampatti, and more recently on the religious approach to the treatment of mental disorders. She is now concentrating on the theory and practice of Siddha medicine in Tamil Nadu. She is the author of several works, including *Māriyamman-Mariyamman: Catholic Practices and Image of Virgin in Velankanni* (FIP, 2002) and *Les rondes de Saint Antoine. Culte, affliction et possession en Inde du sud* (Aux Lieux d'Etre, 2006).

Farha Ternikar, who received her master's and doctorate degrees from Loyola University, Chicago, is Assistant Professor of Sociology at Le Moyne College. Her primary areas of interest include gender, Islam and South Asian immigration. She has authored articles on South Asian immigrants and Islam in the USA. Her ongoing research projects pertain to American Pakistani immigrants, gender and marriage.

Raymond Brady Williams is the Charles D. and Elizabeth LaFollette Distinguished Professor in the Humanities emeritus at Wabash College. He founded and directed the Wabash Center for Teaching and Learning in Theology and Religion and the Wabash Pastoral Leadership Program. He was founding editor of the journal *Teaching Theology and Religion* (Blackwell). Among his books are *Williams on South Asian Religions and Immigration* (Ashgate, 2004), *An Introduction to Swaminarayan Hinduism* (Cambridge University Press, 2001), *Christian Pluralism in the United States: The Indian Immigrant Experience* (Cambridge University Press, 1996), *Religions of Immigrants from India and Pakistan* (Cambridge University Press, 1988) and, as co-author, *Buddhists, Hindus and Sikhs in America* (Oxford University Press, 2008). He has been Visiting Scholar at universities in Madras, Gujarat and Cambridge.

Introduction

Making an Invisible Diaspora Visible

Knut A. Jacobsen and Selva J. Raj

The closing decades of the twentieth century witnessed a new and growing interest in diaspora studies. The growing number of doctoral dissertations on various South Asian diaspora communities attests to this new trend and interest in the academy. The numerous regional, national and international conferences as well as the steady flow of new literature on South Asian diaspora suggest that South Asian immigrant communities in Europe and North America are not only here to stay, but diaspora studies is a legitimate and important sub-field in South Asian Studies. However, all such scholarly efforts focus almost exclusively on Hindu, Jain and Sikh diaspora communities, with little or no attention to Christian immigrants from South Asia. Christian immigrants from diverse ethnic, linguistic and cultural backgrounds have largely been overlooked by academics. Consequently, this important constituency has largely been a silent and invisible community, under-represented in scholarly literature and public academic discourses. We believe that diaspora studies and scholarship on South Asia ought to truly represent and mirror the true complexion and the rich internal plurality and diversity of the South Asian religious landscape. The present volume is therefore a response to the serious current imbalance in diaspora studies, not unlike the imbalance in the field of Religious Studies and South Asian Studies in general that to date have privileged Hindu, Sikh and Jain immigrants from South Asia. Through a careful study of a select number of South Asian Christian immigrant groups in North America and Europe, the present volume is a first step in remedying the current lacuna in South Asian diaspora studies.

In our view, several factors account for the current scholarly disinterest in and the consequent paucity of studies on South Asian Christian communities settled in the West, whether in Europe or North America. First, South Asian Christians look Hindu, indistinguishable in their physical appearance, speech, dress, and to some extent even customs and habits, from their South Asian religious counterparts. While understandable, this has led to the homogenization, however mistaken and false it might be, of South Asian immigrants. Second, Western scholars of South Asian religions, most of whom have strong cultural and/or religious ties to Christianity, seem less interested in the study of Christianity and Christians, whether at home or abroad, and more interested in such exotic South Asian religious groups as Hindus, Jains and Sikhs. An underlying yet mistaken assumptions here is a homogenized understanding of Christianity, namely that Christianity is the same everywhere, irrespective of cultural and geographical differences. However, a close look at the ritual life of these traditions would convince us otherwise. For example, animal sacrifices so popular in South Indian Catholic devotional life are by no means a universal Catholic phenomenon.[1] While widespread among non-specialists, even serious academics subscribe to this assumption, a related second, again unspoken, assumption is that there is nothing interesting or exotic about South Asian Christianity. However, the religious life of the practitioners tells a different story. For example, the complexities of Indian Christianity that include numerous Eastern Orthodox churches like the Syro-Malabar and Syro-Malankara churches and their liturgical traditions that have found North American and European homes challenge any such simplistic constructions.[2]

A third reason is related to the influential perspective of Louis Dumont, who interpreted an upper-caste version of Hinduism as the ideology of India and defined caste as its essence.[3] Although caste is found among Muslims, Christians, Sikhs, Jains and Buddhists in South Asia, it is in Hinduism that caste is given a religious justification, and the other religions were therefore seen as peripheral to the essence.[4] India was Hindu India, and the study of India therefore meant the study of caste. In the cities, caste had become less important, and researchers were therefore encouraged to do fieldwork in village India. In the villages, the caste system was thought to be preserved in its original authentic state. Even if these villages had populations belonging to the minority religions, these groups were often treated as unimportant or made invisible. Or when they were studied,

---

[1]   Selva J. Raj, 'Transgressing Boundaries, Transcending Turner: The Pilgrimage Tradition at the Shrine of St. John de Britto', in Selva J. Raj and Corinne G. Dempsey (eds), *Popular Christianity in India: Riting between the Lines* (Albany, NY, 2002), pp. 85–111.

[2]   A new generation of emerging scholars is helping to nullify even the 'exotic' argument. See Corinne G. Dempsey, 'Lessons in Miracles from Kerala, South India: Stories of Three "Christian" Saints', in Raj and Dempsey (eds), *Popular Christianity in India*, pp. 111–39; Eliza F. Kent, 'Redemptive Hegemony and the Ritualization of Reading', in Raj and Dempsey (eds), *Popular Christianity in India*, pp. 191–209; Eliza F. Kent, *Converting Women: Gender and Protestant Christianity in Colonial South India* (New York, 2004); Margaret Meibohm, 'Past Selves and Present Others: The Ritual Construction of Identity at a Catholic Festival in South India', in Raj and Dempsey (eds), *Popular Christianity in India*, pp. 61–83; Selva J. Raj, 'The Ganges, the Jordan, and the Mountain: The Three Strands of Santal Popular Catholicism', in Raj and Dempsey (eds), *Popular Christianity in India*, pp. 39–60; Mathew N. Schmalz, 'Charismatic Transgressions: The Life and Work of an Indian Catholic Healer', in Raj and Dempsey (eds), *Popular Christianity in India*, pp. 163–87. See also Clara A.B. Joseph, 'Rethinking Hybridity: The Syro-Malabar Church in North America', in Knut A. Jacobsen and P. Pratap Kumar (eds), *South Asians in the Diaspora: Histories and Religious Traditions* (Leiden, 2004), pp. 220–39, and Anna Lindberg, 'Transformation of Marriage Patterns in the Kerala Diaspora in the United States', in Jacobsen and Kumar (eds), *South Asians in the Diaspora*, pp. 203–19.

[3]   Louis Dumont, *Homo hierarchicus: An Essay on the Caste System*, trans. Mark Sainsbury (Chicago, IL, 1970).

[4]   Rowena Robinson, *Christians of India* (New Delhi, 2003), p. 17.

it was with the question, 'Is there caste in non-Hindu communities?' Robinson argues that scholars as well as politicians have collapsed the 'Indian philosophical outlook' with a Hindu or Brahmanical one, and as a consequence the Christians were perceived as representatives of traditions that were alien and foreign to the land of India.[5] The Indian tradition was defined in a way that made it impossible to link Christians to this tradition.[6]

Fourth, the Western academic privileging of the dominant religion of the sub-continent palpable in South Asian studies in general is also reflected in diaspora scholarship and literature. Fifth, the study of South Asian Christianity and Christian communities from an ethnographic and non-theological perspective is a relatively new sub-field in religious studies.[7] This accounts in part for the lack of academic interest in South Asian Christian immigrant communities in the West. Finally, since Christians form a tiny minority in India, it is difficult to know the numerical strength of Christian immigrants in the West since most available national statistics on South Asian immigrants in the West invariably classify them under the convenient rubric of national origin rather than religious affiliation.

The study of Christian immigrants from South Asia becomes even more complicated when we realize that the South Asian Christian community is by no means a monolithic or homogenous group. In terms of ethnic origins, cultural heritage and religious praxis, it is as variegated and diverse as the sub-continent. Christian immigrants from South Asia come in various stripes and shapes. There are Sinhalese Christians, Sri Lankan Tamil Christians, Nepalese Christians, Bangladeshi Christians, Pakistani Christians and Indian Christians. In the Indian sub-continent itself, there is striking internal religious diversity based on ethnic, linguistic, geographical, denominational and liturgical considerations and factors. A similar diversity defines the ethnic composition of Indian Christian immigrants. Thus, there are Goan Christians, Tamil Christians, Malayalee Christians, Dalit Christians, Mangalorean Christians, and *adivasi* (tribal) Christians. Not all Christian immigrants share the same religious history. While some trace their Christian roots to the first century CE, others are recent converts. In addition, while some hail from higher castes, others come from modest social backgrounds. Denominational affiliations further complicate the complexion of Christian diaspora, since there are orthodox Christians, Protestant Christians affiliated to various denominational sub-sects, and Catholics of different liturgical rites. The intra-religious plurality

---

[5]   Ibid.

[6]   Robinson also argues that because of this, Christianity in India has too often been viewed through the lens of conversion (*from* Hinduism), with negative consequences for the understanding of the Christian communities.

[7]   Corinne G. Dempsey, *Kerala Christian Sainthood: Collisions of Culture and Worldview in South India* (New York, 2001). Raj, 'Transgressing Boundaries, Transcending Turner'; Selva J. Raj, 'Dialogue "On the Ground": The Complicated Identities and the Complex Negotiations of Catholics and Hindus in South India', *Journal of Hindu–Christian Studies*, 17 (2004): 33–44.

characteristic of South Asian Christianity in the native context is faithfully replicated in the diaspora setting. These facts suggest that the diasporic experience of South Asian Christian immigrants is, to say the least, quite complex and complicated, defying any simplistic conclusions. A minority group in South Asia, Christian immigrants in Europe and North America share a common religious faith with the majority group. In this regard, their diasporic experience is quite distinct from that of other South Asian religious groups. None the less, like other South Asian immigrants, they too wrestle with a sense of religious liminality and alienation, leading them to carve out – through their churches, associations, and worship services – a distinctive cultural space to reinforce and strengthen their distinctive religious identity.

Inherited Identities

The largest groups of Christians from South Asia living in Europe and North America are from Goa, Kerala, Puducherry (Pondicherry), Punjab, Tamil Nadu and Sri Lanka. But there are also Christians from Pakistan, Nepal, Bangladesh, other areas of India, and also second-time diaspora Indians such as South Asian Christians from Suriname living in the Netherlands. Some are recent converts to Christianity (see Chapters 1 and 13), but for the great majority, being Christian is an inherited religious identity. It is part of the cultural heritage. Much work is invested in generational transfer of this heritage.

In the diaspora setting, religion often gains some new functions. Religion gets involved in the maintenance of linguistic and cultural identities in the minority situation. In the multi-cultural Roman Catholic churches in Norway, separate masses are performed for a number of ethnic groups and nationalities. A similar practice is reported from Lutheran churches in North America (see Chapter 12). The church space is shared between the groups, but they do not worship together. The religious tradition is identified with linguistic, cultural and ritual traditions. The weekly Tamil Catholic masses in Norway are ritual events meant for the Tamils. Tamil Catholics do not identify with the ritual performance of Vietnamese Catholics presented in Vietnamese or of Polish Catholics presented in Polish and so on. In the diaspora, religion may gain renewed importance since it becomes a marker of difference. Participation in the worship that is organized specifically for one ethnic group is important for identity formation. Participation confirms ethnic identity and belonging. Other Christian communities such as the Syro-Malabar Catholics in Chicago organize their own churches. The churches become cultural comfort zones on which members, especially among the lower economic groups, depend for cultural survival and social networks (see Chapter 10). But others might be opposed to identifying religion with the ethnic tradition. Some have left South Asia to escape oppression. Caste continues to be a problem also in the diaspora (see Chapters 2 and 13). Dalit Christians often prefer 'mainstream' congregations where they become known as Indians rather than Dalits, or mixed congregations where the effort is to unite (see Chapter 13). The level of integration and assimilation varies. Assimilation characterizes the integration of Goans in Portugal, while for Roman Catholics from Sri Lanka in Germany, Norway and Switzerland, religion is a vital part of the ethnic identity formation (see Chapters 4–7).

Christianity is a pluralistic religion with a large number of churches and sects and a large number of different ethnic and cultural identities. Being Christian might mean being Roman Catholic Malayalee in Germany, Lutheran Telegu in Chicago, Baptist from Punjab in London, Pentecostal Tamil from Sri Lanka in Oslo, Norway, and so on. Being a Syro-Malabar Catholic in Chicago or Tamil Roman Catholic in Norway (a predominantly Lutheran nation) means your religious identity lies with a minority tradition, and this is quite different from being a Roman Catholic from Goa living in Portugal, a predominantly Catholic country, and having a Portuguese name, as most Goan Roman Catholics in Portugal do (see Chapters 6, 7, 9 and 10). The religious traditions are also shaped in many ways by the features of the majority culture of the new settlement. For immigrants to secular countries such as the Netherlands or Germany, religion might lose some of its importance for the second generation (see Chapters 3 and 8). Although in the diaspora the first generation tends to give the same importance to religion than before migration, or more, the second generation may withdraw partially from church life as a function of the secular environment of the society at large.

Studies on South Asian Christian diasporas can help correct some mistaken perceptions. In several countries in Europe (Germany, the United Kingdom, Switzerland, France, Denmark, Norway) there are large communities of Tamils from Sri Lanka. The largest community of Sri Lankan Tamils is found in Canada. Much information about the religious life of the Tamil Hindus is now readily available. Books and articles have been published.[8] However, hardly anything has been written about the religious life of the Sri Lankan Tamil Christians. In this book, three chapters cover the Sri Lankan Tamil Christian diaspora (Chapters 4–6). For most Christians, religion is part of an ethnic identity and religion is important for the preservation and the transmission of this ethnic identity from one generation to the next. In the South Asian diasporas, the Christian identity is for most people an inherited identity from the country of origin that people invest much energy in preserving and transferring to the next generation. It is an obvious part of their South Asian identities. Preservation of the Christian identity is a way to attempt to safeguard the religious culture inherited from their parents and grandparents. Preservation of something old, not conversion to something new, often characterizes the situation. This preservation takes place in a number of different contexts.

---

[8]   See Martin Baumann, Brigitte Luchesi and Annette Wilke (eds), *Tempel und Tamilen in zweiter Heimat. Hindus aus Sri Lanka im deutschsprachigen und skandinavischen Raum* (Würzburg, 2003).

Strategies of Cultural Survival and Assimilation

In his landmark study of Asian Indian Christian immigrants in the United States, Raymond Williams proposes a typology of six adaptive strategies employed by Indian Christian immigrants, strategies that resemble the ones he discovered in his 1992 study of Hindu organizations in the United States.[9] These adaptive strategies are: 'individual, national, ecumenical, ethnic, hierarchical, and "denominational"'.[10] Williams argues that these strategies account for the differences in the language, types of religious leadership, general ethos of the community, cuisine and arts among Indian Christian groups. The selection of a specific adaptive strategy is itself influenced by the four variables of social location: length of residence, population density, transition from the first to succeeding generations, and majority/minority status. While Williams regards these six strategies as parameters that define the process of adaptation of Asian Indian Christian immigrants to the American landscape, he reminds us that these strategies are often malleable, since immigrants' desire to preserve several overlapping identities leads them to 'adopt elements of more than one strategy'.[11] We believe this typology can be effectively applied not only to the larger North American and European contexts, but to all South Asian Christian immigrant groups as well. While the various groups represented in this volume may not employ all six strategies, they do employ one or more of these strategies, tailoring them to their particular cultural and social context. We encourage readers to relate these 'ideal types' as they navigate through the complex histories and distinctive dynamics of the various Christian immigrant groups discussed in this volume.

As with other South Asian immigrants, religion and ritual play a pivotal role in the construction of their distinct 'South Asian Christian' identity based on regional, ethnic, linguistic, denominational and liturgical heritage. Their self-perception as 'South Asian Christian' immigrants living in the West (Europe and North America) as distinct from other South Asian immigrants of diverse religious persuasions compels and leads them to establish their own 'spaces' for social exchange and religious worship that act as locus for identity formation. 'Differentiation' is a major reason and key strategy for the establishment of churches like the Tamil Christuva Koil in New York that McDermott discusses in Chapter 13. Such efforts are aimed at two distinct audiences: a domestic audience that encompasses their second-generation immigrant children, Western religious 'others' and non-Christian South Asian 'others', and a distant, transnational audience comprising fellow Christians in their native villages and regions. The formation of religious centres and groups enables South Asian Christian immigrants who, like most immigrants, are more religious in the diaspora setting than in the native setting to maintain transnational

---

[9]   Raymond Brady Williams, *Christian Pluralism in the United States: The Indian Immigrant Experience* (Cambridge, 1996), pp. 96–111.

[10]   Ibid., p. 97.

[11]   Ibid., p. 111.

ties with native Christian communities with whom they feel a certain emotional affinity through fund-raisers for and mission trips to native churches and groups.

Even as these immigrants negotiate their adjustment and assimilation to a new, often alien, cultural and religious landscape, traditional patterns of distinctions, divisions and boundaries based on caste, linguistic heritage, places of origin and regional identities are not only faithfully replicated but vigorously reinforced and perpetuated, causing a sense of cultural ambivalence and puzzlement among their second-generation children. This is amply illustrated in the constant and ever-increasing proliferation of Christian social and religious groups in diaspora settings.

The South Asian Christian Diaspora in Europe and North America

At the very outset, we wish to state that this study is neither comprehensive in the range of South Asian Christian immigrant groups found in North America and Europe nor exhaustive in its analysis of the dynamics of these groups. An obvious limitation of this volume is the limited coverage and attention accorded to Dalit Christian immigrants even though they constitute the largest segment of the Indian Christian population. Even if we wanted to cover them more fully, we would not have succeeded given that only recently has a small group of scholars begun to study Dalit Christians in South Asia or abroad. If the study of South Asian Christianity is a nascent sub-field in religious studies, it is even more true of diaspora studies, which accounts for the paucity – nay more, absence – of literature on the subject. Hence, the selection of contributions for inclusion in this volume was guided by practical realities and exigencies in the academy. We invited those scholars we knew to have research specialties and interests in South Asian Christian immigrants to contribute their recent work. Located in two different continents, these contributors, who hail from diverse disciplinary backgrounds (sociology, anthropology, religious studies), investigate intra-community and inter-community religious dynamics from their respective disciplinary and inter-disciplinary perspectives. Our modest goal in preparing this volume is threefold: (1) to call attention to an understudied diaspora group; (2) to provide a select number of case-studies of South Asian Christian immigrants originating from fresh and recent field-research, and (3) to offer some generalizations that will stimulate further research. To use a culinary metaphor, we envision this volume as the first course in a South Asian Christian immigrant feast to be followed by other delectable studies by future scholars.

Scholars continue to debate the viability, adequacy and usefulness of the familiar term 'diaspora' when speaking of post-1960 immigrants from South Asia, whether Hindu, Christian, Muslim or Sikh. While some scholars tend to dismiss this term because of its specific historical reference to South Asians and Indians who emigrated from India and South Asia as indentured labourers, inapplicable to the educated, affluent and white-collar generation, the editors and contributors have chosen to use the common term 'diaspora'. 'Diaspora' refers to processes of maintaining and transferring cultural and linguistic identities and traditions in a minority situation associated with migration, independent of the educational success, affluence or economic integration of the group. In his seminal work on Hindu diaspora, Vertovec highlights three specific meanings of diaspora: diaspora as social form, diaspora as type of consciousness, and diaspora as mode of cultural production.[12] Vertovec's observations on Hindu diaspora can be equally extended to Christian immigrants. All three forms are discernible in the case studies documented by our authors.

The chapters in this book present the community histories, issues of identity, the links between religious and cultural traditions, the use and reinvention of religious and cultural traditions, appearance of new ritual traditions, attitudes to language, generational transfer, marriage and family life, the plurality of Christian traditions to which they belong, their relationship to non-Christian South Asians and to the Christian majority churches, and so on. The scant literature on South Asian Christians in Europe and North America also leads the authors to lament the current situation and indicate areas for further research.

The settlement of South Asian Christians in Europe, the subject of the Part One of the book, 'Europe', is related to colonial history, the division of Europe during the Cold War, and refugee laws. Those nations that had colonies in South Asia or had colonies that used Indians as indentured labour often have the largest populations of South Asian Christians. The largest South Asian Christian population in Europe is in the UK. In Chapter 1 on the South Asian Christian diaspora in the UK, Eleanor Nesbitt emphasizes diversity and the plurality of traditions of the South Asian Christians in that country, both in terms of regional background and church affiliation, and observes that South Asian Christians do not have a sense of comprising a single society. She also notes that because of the inclusiveness of the Hindu traditions, many Hindus have Christian images included in their domestic shrines, problematizing the relationship between Christian practice and Christian identity. She observes that for some Christianity is the inherited religion, for others it is a new religion to which they have converted while living in the UK. This makes a difference because as an inherited identity, Christianity is bound up with South Asian cultural and linguistic forms. But South Asian Christians are generally or mostly an invisible diaspora because they do not establish separate churches. Nesbitt notices that South Asian Christians express frustration that government grants are available for non-Christians for building community centres and other purposes, but not for South Asian Christians, and this contributes to a feeling of marginalization. Interestingly, among the South Asian Christians in the UK, shared culture and language often takes precedence over denominational divides.

The diversity among the South Asian Christians in the UK is unique in Europe so far. In other European countries that have a sizeable South Asian Christian

---

[12] Steven Vetrovec, *The Hindu Diaspora: Comparative Patterns* (London, 2000), pp. 142–56.

population, the vast majority of them often come from the same region in South Asia and belong to the same church. For example, the South Asian Christians in France are mainly Roman Catholic Tamils from Puducherry (Pondicherry) and Sri Lanka. In Chapter 2, Brigitte Sébastia discusses several cases of Indianization of Catholic rituals among the Tamils in France, and the dilemmas and difficulties involved. Sébastia shows how Tamil rituals were integrated into the Catholic liturgy in an attempt to inculturate Catholic faith. Our Lady of Health of Velankanni has been installed in many churches. Even the annual Tamil pilgrimage to Lourdes has been 'Indianized'. Sébastia argues that some families chose the Indianization or Tamilization of the Catholic Church and the rituals in order to exalt Tamil identity and to gain prestige and recognition, which, however, was opposed by others. She notes that many of the Tamil Catholics in France are Untouchables, and for many of them, affirming a Christian identity means the rejection of everything that symbolizes Hinduism.

Two chapters focus on the South Asian Christian diaspora in Germany: Chapter 3 on the immigrants from Kerala who arrived mainly in the 1960s and 1970s, most of whom were nurses, and Chapter 4 on the immigration of Sri Lankan Tamils who arrived in the 1980s and 1990s and continue to arrive.

The South Asian Christian diaspora in Germany started with the recruitment in the 1960s by the Catholic Church of young Christian women in Kerala to work in German hospitals and homes for the elderly as nurses. Many settled in Germany permanently, but had arranged marriages with Malayalee men in Kerala. Their husbands were not immediately allowed to work, and thus their activities were restricted to the household and child-rearing as well as to the establishment of an ethnic infrastructure including cultural, sports and religious organizations. Urmila Goel, who builds Chapter 3 around one person, a Christian male who arrived in Germany from Kerala in 1966, focuses on identity issues. Goel observes that even if the language and food are different, Christianity to some extent makes the Malayalees less 'alien' than other migrants.

In Chapter 4, Brigitte Luchesi reviews the Sri Lankan Tamil Catholic diaspora in Germany and analyses the remarkable Tamil pilgrimage undertaken every year by Tamil Christian refugees from Sri Lanka to the Madonna in Kevelaer, Germany, near the Dutch border. The Tamil pilgrimage, which was invented as early as 1987, has become the largest single pilgrimage event to this place. The pilgrimage has an association to the pilgrimage to Our Lady of Madhu, the main Marian shrine in Sri Lanka, and many Tamils associate Kevalar with Our Lady of Madhu. This is a good example of how Tamil space is increasingly being created within the Roman Catholic Church in Europe.

The South Asian Christians in Switzerland and Norway are primarily Roman Catholic Tamils from Sri Lanka. Damaris Lüthi's informants in Chapter 5 regularly emphasized that religiosity is an important constituent of traditional Tamil culture to be passed on to the next generation. Lüthi's chapter draws many comparisons between Tamil Christians and Hindus and the role of religion, and shows that the social values of the first generation Hindus and Christians are very similar. She suggests that a specific Tamil religiosity often transcends the traditional Christian/Hindu dichotomy. Lüthi further discusses the festival calendar, the participation of Catholics in Hindu festivals, their worship of the Madonna, caste and impurity/purity regulations, and the relationship between the first- and second-generation immigrants.

In Norway, the Tamil ritual events in the Roman Catholic churches have become important expressions of Sri Lankan Tamil identity. Tamil ritualization has been a key strategy for the Tamils in Norway to negotiate their identities, and the Catholic Church has participated in this by hiring several Tamil priests who have assisted in creating Tamil Catholic traditions in the churches in order to ensure Tamil participation. In Chapter 6, Knut A. Jacobsen argues that the institutionalization of Tamil space within the Catholic Church has paralleled the establishment of Hindu temples, and that both function to preserve Tamil religious traditions and to transmit them to the next generation. The chapter focuses on their immigration history and the various ways devised to transfer religious practice, especially the construction of Tamil Catholic sacred space and sacred time in Norway. Although not without conflicts, the inclusion of the worship of Our Lady of Madhu in the church liturgy shows that Tamil Catholicism is accepted by the church.

Helena Sant'ana in Chapter 7 focuses on the history of Goa and Daman and Diu, the process of conversion, the migration patterns between India, Africa and Portugal and Goans and Damanians living in Portugal. Goa and Daman and Diu were created as Portuguese colonies on the coastal territories of Konkan and Gujarat. Conversion to Christianity in these areas produced an ethnic and political identity different from that of other Indians. Many of these Christians came to Portugal to study or work; many also went to Africa to work in the Portuguese colonies there, and later, when the Portuguese colonies in Africa gained independence (in 1974), they went to Portugal. Change in religion caused Christian Goans and Damanians to identify with the Portuguese Catholic Church, take Portuguese names, communicate in Portuguese and adopt a Portuguese lifestyle. In Portugal, they have become fully integrated and assimilated in Portuguese society. That they are Roman Catholics in the Portuguese tradition means that religion does not set them apart.

Finally, as in Portugal, a large part of the Indian diaspora in the Netherlands, is a second diaspora. The great majority of Indians in the Netherlands are from Suriname. Referred to as Hindustanis in the Netherlands, most of the Surinamese are Hindus, with Christians forming a small minority. Due to mission history in Suriname, there are two different Christian groups among the Hindustanis in the Netherlands: the Moravian brethren (Congregation of Evangelical Brethren) and Roman Catholics. The Moravian brethren are the largest groups of Hindustani Christians in the Netherlands. In Chapter 8, Freek L. Bakker describes the creation of these communities, their organizational structures, dilemmas and different strategies.

Part Two of the book is about North America. Christians from Kerala have dominated the South Asian Christian diaspora in North America, and the majority of the South Asian Christians belong to Malayalee churches. Several of the chapters are based on research into these churches. The last two deal with the issues of evangelization, and with Dalit Christians.

The Syro-Malabar and the Syro-Malankara churches are the focus of Elizabeth Galbraith in Chapter 9. Her contribution is based on field research among Indian Catholic communities both in India and North America, and examines what might be considered the plight of Eastern Catholic traditions in the West, with specific reference to Indian Catholic communities in North America. She rightly points out that Indian Christians leave a country where Christians are a tiny majority and come to a country where they are for the first time the religious majority. But their particular religious traditions are still not mainstream, and it is the preservation and transference of these traditions that become important.

In Chapter 10, Selva J. Raj explores the role and function of religion in the acculturation of its immigrant members to the American landscape by focusing on the history of the Syro-Malabar Catholic Church in Chicago. Raj investigates this church as the locus of culture transmission, and asks whether the church functions for assimilation or de-assimilation. Since the modes of transmission of the religious tradition are language and rituals the Syro-Malabar Catholic Church re-creates the environment of the country of origin, and thus might become what Raj calls 'a culture comfort zone'. This chapter analyses further some of the dilemmas of the liminality situation of the immigrant group, being neither American when in the US nor Indians when in India.

Chapter 11 by Farha Ternikar focuses on the Brethren, Catholic and Knanaya Indian immigrants. She examines changing marriage patterns among Indian Christians (Catholics and Protestants) in the Chicago area. Religion remains an important factor when choosing mates. Arranged marriage or semi-arranged marriage is still the most common option, and it is always between persons of the same pan-ethnic and religious background. She argues that ethnic endogamy is closely linked to religious endogamy. The strong link between Indian Christianity and specific Indian cultural practices is also emphasized. Ternikar concludes, however, that there is a slight increase in inter-marriage between whites and Indian Christians in the US.

Nori Henk in Chapter 12 looks at how Christian Indians are creating a community within the larger Indian immigrant population, and how religious identity is negotiated with, and influenced by, ethnic and national constraints and opportunities. The author notes that in the Chicago area which she investigated, Indian Christian organizations both incorporate into and segregate from the larger Christian community. The tendency is for separate ethnic congregations to use the church space separately. The author investigates some Indian Protestant groups in North America which are more focused on evangelization than on the preservation and transference of religious identity, noting that for them, sharing Christ with non-Christians is a moral imperative. The interest here is to bring other non-Christian immigrants into their churches. This particular focus is in sharp contrast with many other churches and communities presented in this volume which focus almost exclusively on the maintenance of the group's religious traditions and preservation of its inherited identity.

In Chapter 13, Rachel Fell McDermott presents material on Indian Christians in New York. She raises the issue of caste, for many an uncomfortable subject, as a central concern, and laments that there is a silence about Dalits in the research literature on the Indian and South Asian churches in North America (as well as in Europe). There are several reasons for this: the lack of diaspora studies on the South Asian Christians in general; the fact that the Dalits themselves often do not want to draw attention to themselves, and the lack of exact numbers. In contrast to many other contributions in this volume that are about preservation and transference of inherited religious traditions, Dalit Christians are often first-generation Christians who have converted, often after contact with missionaries. For Dalit Christians, the migration from India can also be interpreted as an exodus from a society in which discrimination on the basis of caste is still prevalent. It is understandable, therefore, that in contrast to many other South Asian Christian communities in the diaspora, Dalit Christians feel more welcome in 'mainstream' congregations where they are known as Indians rather than as Dalits, or in mixed congregations where the purpose is to unite, not to preserve an identity of difference. McDermott notes that discrimination on the basis of caste is common among Indian immigrants in the United States, but that there are also 'opportunities for its alleviation and potential healing'.

The book concludes with a response contribution by Raymond Brady Williams. Williams is the first North American scholar to undertake a comprehensive study of Asian Indian Christian immigrants in the United States. His insightful chapter draws attention to many common dilemmas and general trends in the South Asian Indian Christian immigrant history in Europe and North America: their transnational experience, functions of religion in the immigrant situation, relations with other religious groups, and tensions and conflicts. He stresses the importance of religion in the immigrant experience, in that religion provides a transcendent grounding for identity. However, he also argues that the establishment of new congregations and organizations in Europe and North America is not an act of separation, but is important for establishing a base from which to negotiate with social political and economic structures regarding place and power in society. Interestingly, in the discussion of tensions and conflicts, he suggests that Christian immigrants from South Asia in several countries in Europe and North America occupy a position with a potential to mediate between South Asian religious groups and the majority population. Finally, Williams suggests several trajectories for future research.

References

Baumann, Martin, Brigitte Luchesi and Annette Wilke (eds), *Tempel und Tamilen in zweiter Heimat. Hindus aus Sri Lanka im deutschsprachigen und skandinavischen Raum* (Würzburg: Ergon Press, 2003).

Dempsey, Corinne G., *Kerala Christian Sainthood: Collisions of Culture and Worldview in South India* (New York: Oxford University Press, 2001).

Dempsey, Corinne G., 'Lessons in Miracles from Kerala, South India: Stories of Three "Christian" Saints', in *Popular Christianity in India: Riting between the Lines*, ed. Selva J. Raj and Corinne G. Dempsey (Albany, NY: State University of New York Press, 2002), pp. 111–39.

Dumont, Louis, *Homo hierarchicus: An Essay on the Caste System*, trans. Mark Sainsbury (Chicago, IL: University of Chicago Press, 1970).

Jacobsen, Knut A. and P. Pratap Kumar (eds), *South Asians in the Diaspora: Histories and Religious Traditions* (Leiden: Brill, 2004).

Joseph, Clara A.B., 'Rethinking Hybridity: The Syro-Malabar Church in North America', in Knut A. Jacobsen and P. Pratap Kumar (eds), *South Asians in the Diaspora: Histories and Religious Traditions* (Leiden: Brill, 2004), pp. 220–39.

Kent, Eliza F., 'Redemptive Hegemony and the Ritualization of Reading', in Selva J. Raj and Corinne G. Dempsey (eds), *Popular Christianity in India: Riting between the Lines* (Albany, NY: State University of New York Press, 2002), pp. 191–209.

Kent, Eliza F., *Converting Women: Gender and Protestant Christianity in Colonial South India* (New York: Oxford University Press, 2004).

Lindberg, Anna, 'Transformation of Marriage Patterns in the Kerala Diaspora in the United States', in Knut A. Jacobsen and P. Pratap Kumar (eds), *South Asians in the Diaspora: Histories and Religious Traditions* (Leiden: Brill, 2004), pp. 203–19.

Meibohm, Margaret, 'Past Selves and Present Others: The Ritual Construction of Identity at a Catholic Festival in South India', in Selva J. Raj and Corinne G. Dempsey (eds), *Popular Christianity in India: Riting between the Lines* (Albany, NY: State University of New York Press, 2002), pp. 61–83.

Raj, Selva J., 'The Ganges, the Jordan, and the Mountain: The Three Strands of Santal Popular Catholicism', in Selva J. Raj and Corinne G. Dempsey (eds), *Popular Christianity in India: Riting between the Lines* (Albany, NY: State University of New York Press, 2002), pp. 39–60.

Raj, Selva J., 'Transgressing Boundaries, Transcending Turner: The Pilgrimage Tradition at the Shrine of St. John de Britto', in Selva J. Raj and Corinne G. Dempsey (eds), *Popular Christianity in India: Riting between the Lines* (Albany, NY: State University of New York Press, 2002), pp. 85–111.

Raj, Selva J., 'Dialogue "On the Ground": The Complicated Identities and the Complex Negotiations of Catholics and Hindus in South India', *Journal of Hindu–Christian Studies*, 17 (2004): 33–44.

Raj, Selva J. and Corinne G. Dempsey (eds), *Popular Christianity in India: Riting between the Lines* (Albany, NY: State University of New York Press, 2002).

Robinson, Rowena, *Christians of India* (New Delhi: Sage, 2003).

Schmalz, Mathew N., 'Charismatic Transgressions: The Life and Work of an Indian Catholic Healer', in Selva J. Raj and Corinne G. Dempsey (eds), *Popular Christianity in India: Riting between the Lines* (Albany, NY: State University of New York Press, 2002), pp. 163–87.

Vetrovec, Steven, *The Hindu Diaspora: Comparative Patterns* (London: Routledge, 2000).

Williams, Raymond Brady (ed.), *A Sacred Thread: Modern Transmission of Hindu Traditions in India and Abroad* (Chambersburg, PA: Anima Publications, 1992).

Williams, Raymond Brady, *Christian Pluralism in the United States: The Indian Immigrant Experience* (Cambridge: Cambridge University Press, 1996).

PART ONE
Europe

Chapter 1

South Asian Christians in the UK

Eleanor Nesbitt

Introduction

This chapter presents a framework for exploring the history and contemporary experience of Christians of South Asian background living in the UK. Importantly, it draws attention to the near absence of scholarly research on a largely invisible and growing sector of the UK population.

For ease of reference, in this chapter the terms 'South Asian Christians' and 'South Asian Christian community' will be used. However, it needs to be emphasized at the outset that, while the individuals concerned all have family roots in South Asia and share their self-identification as Christian and certain aspects of their experience, there is none the less no strong sense of comprising a single community overriding the many cross-cutting factors such as regional origin in South Asia, family language and culture, migration history and Christian denomination.

Any account of the development of Britain's South Asian community necessitates attention to three demographically major groupings. Accordingly, in terms of states of origin in the Indian sub-continent, we will look particularly at South Indian (mainly Keralite) Christians, Goan Christians and Punjabi Christians (from the Punjab states of present-day Pakistan and India). In denominational terms, we will be looking respectively at what may broadly be called 'St Thomas Christians' (including Syro Malabar rite Catholics) as well as at Roman Catholics and at Protestants of various denominations.

The individuals and groups concerned identify with a range of religious and geographical designations. To take just one: 'Malayalee' is one preferred identification for Malayalam-speakers, including Christians, from the South Indian state of Kerala.[1] In different contexts, UK South Asian Christians express different strands – ethnic, linguistic, religious, national – of their multiple identities.[2]

This chapter's opening acknowledgement of the 400-year-old relationship between Britain and the Indian sub-continent leads into a summary account of

---

[1]   BBC, 'Where I Live: Gloucestershire' (2006), available at <http://www.bbc.co.uk/gloucestershire/untold_stories/asian/christian_community.shtml>, accessed 13 April 2006.

[2]   R.B. Williams, 'South Asian Christians in Britain, Canada, and the United States', in H. Coward, J.R. Hinnells and R.B. Williams (eds), *The South Asian Religious Diaspora in Britain, Canada, and the United States* (Albany, NY, 2000), pp. 13–34. See p. 14.

each of the groupings mentioned above, as well as an indication of the broader diversity of South Asian Christians in the UK. Comment on the current extent of relevant research and publication introduces key issues that emerge from such data as are available, plus mention of some prominent individuals.

Statistics

Statistics for faith communities are notoriously elusive and unreliable, and in the case of Britain's South Asian Christians, numbers are especially problematic. Some individuals are only nominally Christian, so do not appear in counts of congregational membership. In any case, although some South Asian Christians worship in separate South Asian congregations, many others belong to 'white' churches. Easton,[3] following the Alliance of Asian Christians (AAC),[4] suggests that the ratio of worshippers in Asian congregations to worshippers in non-specific congregations is 60:40.

After 1851, and until 2001, there was no question in the UK census on religious allegiance. In recent decades, several attempts were made to provide statistics, including, for example, research for Brierley which included, under its heading 'Other churches: overseas nationals', these three estimates of church membership for the year 2000: 480 members of the 'Syrian Church, Mar Thoma',[5] 1100 members of 'Tamil congregations' and 50 members of 'Urdu and Punjabi' congregations.[6] The fact that in 1991 I was told of approximately 60 Punjabi Christian families in Coventry alone suggests the extreme unreliability of the figures available.[7] According to one estimate, some 45,000 UK Christians are South Asian.[8]

From the 2001 Census, Christians emerge as the largest faith community in the UK (42,079 million, 71.6 per cent) in terms of self-identification, but the data do not allow for reliable correlations between 'South Asian' and 'Christian'. The available information that 77,637 Christians were born in India, 902 in Bangladesh,

---

[3]   B. Easton, 'Worshipping a White God: A Study of the Religious Experience of Young Asian Christians' (unpublished MA in Religious Education dissertation, Institute of Education, University of Warwick, 2000).

[4]   Alliance of Asian Christians, *Introducing: Alliance of Asian Christians* (Birmingham, 1999), p. 2.

[5]   P. Brierley, *UK Christian Handbook Religious Trends 1998/9 No. 1* (London, 1998/99), 9.28.

[6]   Ibid., 9.29.

[7]   E. Nesbitt 'The Punjabi Christian Community in Coventry: Its Development and Pointers to the Future' (unpublished paper presented at Punjab Research Group. Coventry University, 26 October 1991).

[8]   Easton, 'Worshipping a White God', p. 27.

9353 in Pakistan and 18,276 in Sri Lanka (a total of 106,168) is likely to include many 'white' individuals who were born during British colonial rule.[9]

Historical Background

Interaction between Britain and India can best be understood in the framework of successive periods: the activity of the East India Company, the consolidation of empire (the Raj), and lastly, the period of independent states. The present state of India gained its independence in 1947, and the simultaneous partition of India resulted in the formation of Pakistan, which itself subdivided in 1971 with the birth of Bangladesh. Although migration to Britain long pre-dated India's independence, substantial South Asian communities in the UK formed only in the second half of the twentieth century. In widespread discourse, these families are most frequently referred to as 'Asian', alongside the more scholarly and precise 'South Asian'. In order to understand the experience of South Asian Christians in the UK, a sense of the wider UK South Asian context is vital.

By religion, the majority of Britain's South Asians are Muslim (1 million of Britain's 1.6 million Muslims are from South Asia, including two-thirds from Pakistan, under a third from Bangladesh and the remainder from India),[10] Hindu (559,000, with the majority self-identifying as Indian) and Sikh (336,000, all of whose family roots are in present-day India or Pakistan), with smaller numbers of Christians, Jains, Buddhists and Zoroastrians (often known as Parsis). In terms of ethnicity or region of origin, the largest South Asian communities in the UK are from northern Pakistan (mainly from Azad Kashmir and Punjab), north-west India (from Punjab), western India (Gujarat), Bangladesh (from Sylhet) and Sri Lanka (mainly Tamils). Studies of South Asian communities correspond to this profile, and so focus almost exclusively on Muslim, Hindu and Sikh populations, whereas scholarship on Britain's South Asian Christians is almost non-existent.

Migration to the UK was triggered both by 'pull' factors, such as the shortage of labour in industry and transport in British cities after the Second World War, and by 'push' factors including the increasing restrictions on South Asians resident in East Africa, another area of the former British Empire, in the late 1960s, which climaxed in the expulsion of 'Asians' from Uganda in 1970. Along with the exodus of Hindus and Sikhs, and smaller numbers of Muslims and Zoroastrians, many Goan Catholics also came to Britain from East Africa. From the southern Indian states of Tamil Nadu and Kerala, as from Sri Lanka, migration has been smaller-scale and is particularly evident in the National Health Service.

---

[9]   The source is table CO414, 'Country of Birth by Religion' extrapolated from UK Census 2001, Crown Copyright © 2004. Crown copyright material is reproduced with the permission of the Controller of HMSO.

[10]   Tahir Abbas, *British Islam* (Cambridge, 2007).

While settlement of South Asian Christians in Britain probably began with Goan seafarers arriving in London in the seventeenth century, the history of Christianity in India goes back much further, almost certainly to the first century CE. The ensuing account of the South Asian Christian groupings that are most strongly represented in Britain follows the sequence of the history of conversion in India rather than of emigration to the UK. It also takes account of the fact that a growing minority of South Asian Christians in the UK are individuals who have converted to Christianity while living in the UK.

UK South Asian Christians' Sub-continental History

Christianity in the Indian sub-continent (in the southernmost states of Kerala and Tamil Nadu) almost certainly pre-dates the arrival of the first Christian missionaries in the British Isles. The strong belief among South Indian Christians that the apostle Thomas himself came to Maliankara village in AD 52, converted local Jews and established seven Christian communities cannot be proven, but there is no evidence that disproves it, and its possibility is strengthened by recent archaeological, geographical and historical investigations. These include a sea journey undertaken in 2000 by the British historical writer William Dalrymple, who followed the route mentioned in a Syriac manuscript, the Acts of Thomas.[11] Certainly, by the first century CE, Jewish traders were settled in South India and the sea route between South India and West Asia was well known.

In the case of Goa, further north on India's west coast, Christianity arrived almost a millennium and a half after it had reached South India, and it came from western Europe not western Asia. Following the navigator Vasco da Gama's arrival via the Cape of Good Hope at Calicut on India's west coast in 1498, the Portuguese identified Goa as particularly well suited to serving them as a port. They conquered it in 1510 and killed many Muslim inhabitants. Subsequently, the Portuguese adopted violent means of making the Hindu populace Catholic.

Sadly, the Portuguese encounter with the Christians of South India was similarly coercive, as this long-established community had had no reason to acknowledge the primacy of the Pope. As a result, the most ancient Judaeo-Christian tradition in South India was all but wiped out and the South Indian 'St Thomas Christians' fractured into separate churches ranging across a spectrum with linkages that have shifted over the centuries. Today's churches include the Mar Thoma Church, which retains a Syriac identity while maintaining close association with the Anglican Communion, as well as the Malabar Independent Syrian Church, two Orthodox churches, two Eastern Catholic churches and the Chaldean Syrian Church.

---

[11]   See Wikipedia, 'Syrian Malabar Nasrani', available at <http://en.wikipedia.org/wiki/Syrian_Malabar_Nasrani>, accessed 22 May 2006; Wikipedia. 'St Thomas Christians', available at <http://en.wikipedia.org/wiki/Saint_Thomas_Christians>, accessed 22 May 2006; W. Dalrymple, 'Indian Journeys', BBC Television documentary, 17 April 2000.

By contrast with Goan and South Indian Christians, few people from the more northern state of Punjab had become Christian before the 1890s.[12] Most of the missionaries in Punjab were British (although some came from Scandinavia and North America), so Punjabi converts learned generally British styles of Christianity. Although the missionaries had hoped to win high-caste, influential converts, most of those who responded to their call belonged to families from the Dalit (literally 'oppressed') caste that was associated with a particularly 'polluting' hereditary occupation, and so suffered many forms of discrimination. This has had continuing implications for how other Punjabis in India and (since its establishment in 1947) in Pakistan, and more recently in the UK, tend to view South Asian (or at least Punjabi) Christians.

Although, in line with respective numbers in the UK, the present chapter focuses particularly on Christians with family roots in these three areas of the sub-continent, it must be remembered that some British South Asian Christians' roots are elsewhere. Thus the Anglican theological writer Mukti Barton writes as a Bengali,[13] from a community evoked in Alison Mukherjee's novel, *Nirmal Babu's Bride*, which is set in both Bengal and the UK.[14] The Quaker Lilamani Wickramaratne, writer of a report on racism within the Religious Society of Friends,[15] is from a Singhalese Methodist background in Sri Lanka.

Moreover, an increasing number of the UK's South Asian Christians are from non-Christian families, and themselves converted either shortly prior to migration or while settled in the UK. Indeed, Barbara Easton found that most of her Asian Christian contacts in Wolverhampton had converted since coming to Britain in the late 1960s.[16] Attempts to proselytize among people of 'other faiths', and so among South Asians especially, are made by evangelical organizations such as Operation Mobilization and (from outside the theological mainstream) by the Jehovah's Witnesses. In Wolverhampton, two retired American missionaries with experience of northern India plus a Punjabi couple have conducted an intensive campaign to convert new arrivals.[17]

Nationally, there has been an increasing rate of conversion from Hinduism.[18] Reasons include the relaxed attitude which many Hindu parents take to inducting children into their faith tradition (as compared to the more widespread provision of Islamic supplementary classes) and the confusingly nebulous impression of their

---

[12] M. Caleb, 'Christian Sunday Worship in a Punjabi Village', in J.C.B. Webster (ed.), *Popular Religion in the Punjab Today* (Batala, India, 1974), pp. 119–26; see p. 11.

[13] M. Barton, *Rejection, Resistance, Resurrection: Speaking out on Racism in the Church* (London, 2005).

[14] A. Mukherjee, *Nirmal Babu's Bride* (New Delhi, 2002).

[15] L. Woolrych, *Communicating across Cultures: A Report by Joseph Rowntree Fellow 1992/93* (York: 1998).

[16] Easton, 'Worshipping a White God', p. 29.

[17] Ibid. and *East*, BBC 2 Television programme, 30 August 1991.

[18] Ibid.

faith that many young Hindus have. Particularly at times of personal crisis, such individuals are vulnerable to sympathetic evangelists. It is also likely that many converts revert to their earlier faith. Easton quotes an AAC survey's finding that 'seventy per cent of new converts return to their former faith with[in] one year'.[19]

By contrast with the active evangelism of some Christians, initiatives by, for example, the Church of England, the Methodists and the United Reformed Church are more frequently characterized by 'dialogue' and 'being alongside'. Pat Hooker, an Anglican, exemplified this approach among Sikhs in the West Midlands.[20] Annual consultations of Sikhs and Christians in the 1980s and 1990s under the auspices of the Other Faiths Committee of the United Reformed Church also encouraged a receptive and co-operative relationship between Christians and Sikhs, rather than aiming at winning converts.

Although identification as Christian (or with another faith) is usually unproblematic for individuals, the imagined dividing line between South Asian Christians and other South Asians (in the UK and elsewhere) is in practice blurred in some ways. For example, the inclusiveness of much Hindu devotion means that it is not unusual for Hindu domestic shrines to include Christian images. Furthermore, both in their country of origin and in the UK, many Hindu, Muslim, Sikh and Zoroastrian families have elected to enrol their children in Christian schools, and in many cases a Christian influence has persisted. This chapter will also be reporting areas of cultural overlap between Christians and members of other faiths from the same regional and language background.

Yet another way in which any imagined boundary around 'South Asian Christians' is blurred is the strong South Asian aspect to the Christian profession of some 'white' Christians who have lived in South Asia. So, for example, the artist Caroline Mackenzie's work celebrates Hindu as well as Christian sources.[21] Other white UK Christians acknowledge the influence on their own spiritual journeying of living among Hindus and Muslims, or the impact of Father Bede Griffiths and other European exemplars of a Christian profession profoundly affected by exploration of Hinduism.

South Asian Christians' Settlement in the UK

The first South Asian Christian community in the UK was Goan. It is noteworthy that 98 per cent of Goans in the UK are Roman Catholic and English-speaking, although in Goa itself, the (declining) percentage of Catholics is (according to

---

[19]   Easton, 'Worshipping a White God', p. 27.

[20]   P. Hooker, *His Other Sheep*, Grove Pastoral Care Series no. 37 (Nottingham, 1989).

[21]   C. Mackenzie, 'Extrait Choisi: The Hindu Sources of a European Christian Artist' (no date), available at <http://www.voiesorient.be/Bulletin/carolineuk.htm>, accessed 23 May 2006.

the 2001 Census) less than 27 per cent.[22] The majority of UK Goans are from the coastal regions that the Portuguese first conquered.

According to The Goan Community of London Website (<http://www. portcities.org.uk/london/server/show/ConNarrative.50/The-Goan-community-of-London.html>), there are over 6000 Goans in London alone, and the community has a historical association with the docks of East London. This is because, after the Portuguese acquisition of Goa in 1510, Goan seafarers became part of the Portuguese seafaring tradition for the East India Company. Goa was a favourite port, and its ships picked up Goan *lascars* (the Portuguese word for 'non-European seamen'). The Goans of Mumbai (Bombay) became British subjects when the Portuguese Catherine of Braganza married Charles II in 1661, and Mumbai was subsequently loaned to the East India Company by Charles II.

Baptism records from the end of the seventeenth century in East Greenwich show a number of Indians from the Malabar coast had come to England as servants, but it is unclear where they came from. Certainly, East India Company captains liked having Indo-Portuguese cooks, and by the mid-nineteenth century an increasing number of Goan seamen were settling in London because they had been stranded by their masters. This early Goan community, however, ceased to be a distinct community in London.

In the second half of the twentieth century, Goans arrived from areas of former British rule as diverse as Aden, Kenya and Pakistan. Many Goans had settled in East Africa, especially during the inter-war period, 1918–39, and most left for Canada (and in smaller numbers) for Britain in the early 1970s. Some Goans have married into non-Goan families – both 'white' British and non-Christian South Asian. Under Portuguese law, Goans born before 1961 (when Portugal's colonial rule ended), plus their children and grandchildren, are entitled to Portuguese citizenship, and so to work in the UK and other European Union countries.[23] As tourism in Goa drives up the cost of living, Goans are migrating to the UK: in Swindon (a town in south-west England) alone, 'up to 9000' are estimated to have settled since the 2001 Census.[24]

Probably the earliest, and certainly the most famous, Punjabi Christian to arrive in Britain was Duleep (or Dalip) Singh, the deposed heir of Punjab's maharaja, Ranjit Singh.[25] In 1854, Duleep Singh was brought to the UK, having

[22] De Souza Eremita, 'Church Worry as Goa's Catholic Population Declines' (Missio Hilfe für eine andere Welt, 2005), available at <http://www.missio-aachen.de/menschen-kulturen/nachrichten/Church_people_worry_>, accessed 22 May 2006.

[23] T. Norton, 'Goan Migrants Swell Catholic Community', *The Tablet*, 6 October 2007, p. 40.

[24] Ibid.

[25] Copious documentation of Duleep Singh's life includes P. Bance, *The Duleep Singhs: The Photograph Album of Queen Victoria's Maharajah* (Stroud, UK, 2004), C. Campbell, *The Maharajah's Box* (London, 2000), and R.R. Chakrabarty, *Duleep Singh: The Maharajah of Punjab and the Raj* (Birmingham, 1988).

been formally admitted to the Christian faith in 1853. In later years, disillusioned with his treatment in Britain, he reclaimed his Sikh faith.

Twentieth-century Christian migration from Punjab was part of the larger movement of Sikhs and Hindus, mainly from the Jalandhar Doaba region from the 1950s onwards. Punjabi Christians tended to settle in the same urban locations as their non-Christian relatives. Thus Bedford, Birmingham, Coventry and Oxford, for example, are centres of both the Punjabi Christian and Valmiki population, 'Valmiki' being a preferred self-designation of members of the 'lowest' caste who did not convert from their traditional ritual practices and who increasingly identify with the movement named after the sage who composed the Hindus' epic, the *Ramayana*.[26]

A smaller number of Punjabi Christians are from other social backgrounds – Easton provides the spectrum of Wolverhampton Christians' caste backgrounds.[27] In addition, a minority come from 'twice migrant' families, examples being Ram Gidoomal and Inderjit Bhogal (see below), who experienced life in East Africa before coming to the UK.

South Indian Christians for the most part came to the UK later in the second half of the twentieth century, and they are most concentrated and longest established in London. Here, there are members of the Syro Malabar rite Catholic Church, the Malankara Orthodox Syrian Church, the Malankara Orthodox Church, the Mar Thoma Church, Parumala Church and Orthodox Syrian Church. In the case of the Mar Thoma Church, in 1957 regular services began in the Indian YMCA, involving all the Christian communities of Kerala. From 1978 to 1986, Mar Thoma Christians had an official parish, and in 1986 two parishes were established. St John's Mar Thoma Church, Hounslow lists as members 320 families from all over the UK and is part of the Diocese of North America and Europe. The parish has services and prayer groups in Bristol, Manchester, Liverpool, Birmingham, Guildford and Peterborough, and it also arranges occasional services in Germany and Switzerland and Eire.[28] Members work in education, medicine, healthcare, IT, business, law and order, accountancy, social services and community relations. Williams especially mentions that 'Mar Thoma parishes claim a large number of physicians who were trained in India and "stayed on".'[29]

---

[26]   M. Juergensmeyer, *Religion as Social Vision: The Movement against Untouchability in Twentieth-century Punjab* (Berkeley, CA, 1982), pp. 181–92; E. Nesbitt, 'Religion and Identity: The Valmiki Community in Coventry', *New Community*, 16/2 (2001): 261–74.

[27]   Easton, 'Worshipping a White God', p. 29.

[28]   J.T. Achen, 'From the Vicar' (2005), available at <http://www.marthoma.org.uk/html/vicar.html>, accessed 27 December 2005.

[29]   R.B. Williams (2000), 'South Asian Christians in Britain, Canada, and the United States', in H. Coward, J.R. Hinnells and R.B. Williams (eds), *The South Asian Religious Diaspora in Britain, Canada, and the United States* (Albany, NY, 2000), pp. 13–34. See p. 19.

A flavour of another St Thomas church, the Syro Malabar rite Catholics, can be found on the Internet at Clifton Diocese.[30] This conveys an impression of the celebration of Dukrana (St Thomas's Day), provides a brief account of Bristol's 'St Thomas Catholic' community, which was 'established in 2001 [as] the first full fledged congregation of the 50,000 strong Keralite Catholic immigrants in UK', and goes on to mention five other Syro Malabar congregations in the Clifton Diocese (in the south-west of England) alone.

State of Research

The scarcity of published research parallels the paucity of studies of Christian communities in South Asia itself, exceptions including Barton on Bangladesh and Webster on Punjab.[31]

Of the little research by British researchers that has taken place on the UK's South Asian Christians, the majority has focused upon Punjabis. Patricia Jeffery studied two extended families of Christians as part of a study of (otherwise) Muslim Pakistani families in Bristol, a sea port in the south-west of England,[32] I turned my attention to Punjabi Christians (from India) in Coventry, a city in the West Midlands of England,[33] and Barbara Easton's focus was Punjabi Christians (also of Indian background) in another West Midlands location, Wolverhampton.[34] Each of these studies has been small in scale (Jeffery's in parallel with study of other Pakistanis, mine in parallel with research into other Christian communities, and Easton's lasting only a few months). Lack of funding for studies of South Asian Christian communities in the UK is one factor in the paucity of research.

---

[30] Clifton Diocese, '"Dukrana" Festival Celebrated in Bristol' (2006), available at <http://www.cliftondiocese.com/Articles/415/>, accessed 20 June 2006.

[31] M. Barton, *Scripture as Empowerment for Liberation and Justice: The Experience of Christian and Muslim Women in Bangladesh* (Bristol, 1999); J.C.B. Webster, *The Christian Community and Change in Nineteenth Century North India* (Delhi, 1976); J.C.B. Webster, *The Dalit Christians: A History* (New Delhi, 1992).

[32] P. Jeffery, *Migrants and Refugees: Muslim and Christian Pakistani Families in Bristol* (London, 1976).

[33] Nesbitt, 'The Punjabi Christian Community in Coventry'; E. Nesbitt, 'The Transmission of Christian Tradition in an Ethnically Diverse Society', in R. Barot (ed.), *Religion and Ethnicity: Minorities and Social Change in the Metropolis* (Kampen, 1993). pp. 159–69; E. Nesbitt, 'Drawing on the Ethnic Diversity of Christian Tradition in Britain', *Multicultural Teaching*, 11/2 (1993): 9–11; E. Nesbitt, 'Punjabis in Britain: Cultural History and Cultural Choices', *South Asia Research*, 15/2 (1995): 221–40; E. Nesbitt, *Intercultural Education: Ethnographic and Religious Approaches* (Brighton, 2004).

[34] Easton, 'Worshipping a White God'.

Figure 1.1   Young South Asian Christians distributing Christian leaflets after a South Asian Christian convention. (Photo: Eleanor Nesbitt)

My ethnographic study of Punjabi Christians in Coventry was part of research documenting the religious nurture, both formal and informal, of children associated with 12 Christian denominations.[35] The fact that I was carrying out research in parallel in Christian families of a range of ethnic backgrounds,[36] and that I had also conducted fieldwork among Punjabis – including caste fellows – from other faith communities,[37] heightened my awareness of the multiple intersections between culture, ethnicity and religious tradition, and pointed up distinctive features.[38]

The American Raymond Brady Williams's, emphasis – by contrast with UK researchers' work – has been on South Indians, and he draws useful comparisons between the communities taking shape in the UK and North America. So, for example, the migration of Indian Christians to the USA and Canada was (unusually among South Asian migrations) spearheaded by women, because of the demand

---

[35]   The study was part of Ethnography and Religious Education Project No. R00232489, funded by the Economic and Social Research Council.

[36]   R. Jackson and E. Nesbitt, 'The Diversity of Experience in the Religious Upbringing of Children from Christian Families in Britain', *British Journal of Religious Education*, 15/1 (1992); Nesbitt, 'The Transmission of Christian Tradition'; Nesbitt, 'Drawing on the Ethnic Diversity of Christian Tradition'; Nesbitt, *Intercultural Education*.

[37]   Jackson and Nesbitt, *Hindu Children in Britain*; E. Nesbitt, 'Aspects of Sikh Tradition in Nottingham' (unpublished MPhil. thesis, University of Nottingham); Nesbitt, E., *My Dad's Hindu, My Mum's Side are Sikhs': Issues in Religious Identity* (Charlbury, UK, 1991).

[38]   Nesbitt, 'Punjabis in Britain'.

for nurses. In the UK, by contrast, doctors outnumber nurses among South Asian Christians,[39] and nurses are a smaller proportion of the Christian women in the UK as compared with North America.[40] Moreover, a higher percentage of the UK's South Asian Christians are the children and grandchildren of the first settlers, and currently migration to North America exceeds migration to the UK. A further difference is that South Asian Pentecostals are more numerous in North America than in the UK.[41]

The research to date highlights issues around identity and language, relationships with other groups, cultural continuities, the development of distinct organizations and networks and related processes of change, and it is to these issues that we now turn.

Identity

Identity is a crucial issue for South Asians of all communities in the UK, as evidenced by abundant studies.[42] But for Christians, there is a further twist as they face a widespread unawareness, in both the white majority and among other South Asians, of even the possibility of being both South Asian and Christian. This is particularly acute for Punjabi Christians, given the very much larger UK Punjabi communities of Sikhs, Hindus and Muslims. Barton contrasts the popular awareness of African and Caribbean Christians as, stereotypically, Pentecostal Christians with the fact that:

> To many British, 'Asian Christian' is a contradiction in terms. People generally believe that Asians could have any religion other than Christianity.[43]

Similarly, Easton reported that 'Informants spoke of the incomprehension of white people that they could be both Asian and Christian: "English people think you're trying to be white."'[44] Barton relates individual experiences of people assuming that Christians were Muslim or Hindu.[45] Only with difficulty would some accept that even a South Asian priest wearing a cross or a clerical collar was Christian. Barton locates her explanation of this incomprehension in Britain's colonial history and a persistent tendency to regard people from the East as 'other' and non-Christian. This classification is as prevalent among fellow South Asians as among the rest of UK society. Easton records:

---

[39] Williams, 'South Asian Christians in Britain, Canada, and the United States', p. 16.
[40] Ibid., p. 19.
[41] Ibid., p. 24.
[42] Among them Nesbitt, *'My Dad's Hindu, My Mum's Side are Sikhs'*.
[43] Barton, *Rejection, Resistance, Resurrection*.
[44] Easton, 'Worshipping a White God', p. 32.
[45] Barton, *Rejection, Resistance, Resurrection*, pp. 67–72.

There are also difficulties with other Asians who expect solidarity from people of the same heritage: 'Indians think you're letting them down ... The things people say, it's horrible. Like 'Oh, what are you worshipping a white God for?'[46]

A comment that Barton reports on the significance for Asian Christians of having their own church, and of its name being the 'Good News Asian Church', underlines Asian Christians' feeling of being regarded as non-Christian:

> If this church had an ordinary name, when we go in and out of the church the outsiders will think we are people of another faith community who have hired the place.[47]

Christians sometimes voice regret and frustration that local and central government grants are available for non-Christians for building community centres and other purposes, but not for South Asian Christian communities. The fact that South Asian Christians are neither perceived as a problem nor as needing premises, in view of the large number of church buildings that exist in the UK, can contribute to their feelings of marginalization and discrimination.

Language

Members of some (non-Christian) South Asian communities in the UK identify strongly with a family language, regardless of their own proficiency in it. This is the case with Sikhs *vis-à-vis* Punjabi, and many parents send children to language classes to acquire basic literacy. However, although my field work in Coventry disclosed the fact that children in Punjabi Christian families were using their mother tongue, Punjabi, in the home to a greater extent than their Greek or Ukrainian Christian counterparts were using their mother tongues, none the less the children were literate in neither Punjabi nor the related languages of Hindi and Urdu (which senior relatives used in worship), and none attended classes in any of these languages. To quote one parent:

> We don't see a need for Punjabi because we can read the Bible in English as well as Punjabi. We don't bother what language they do it in as long as they praise the Lord one way or the other.

Unlike, say, Greek Cypriot Christians or South Asian Hindus, Muslims and Sikhs, or St Thomas Christians of earlier generations, for South Asian Christians there is no link between the script of their sacred text and the script of their families' first language. This lessens motivation to set up classes to perpetuate their home language(s). At the same time, many value churches for their conservation of language (see below).

---

[46] Easton, 'Worshipping a White God', p. 32.
[47] Ibid., p. 67.

Cultural Continuities

Indeed, South Asian Christians have a greater linguistic, social and cultural affinity with non-Christian South Asians than with other Christians. For example, Keralite Christians share with fellow Malayalees in celebrating the festival of Onam. In the Punjabi Christian community that I studied, not only familiarity with Punjabi language and a home cuisine featuring Punjabi dishes, but also the dress of older women, the decor of living rooms (with religious pictures very much in evidence) and people's ready hospitality were more consistent with Punjabi families in general than with surrounding 'white' society.

Cultural norms (regardless of faith allegiance) include the dominant role of males, in particular of a father or an elder brother. Thus, if he has converted to Christianity, the whole family must follow suit. If a Christian father moves congregation, then the rest of the family must do so too.[48] Alternatively, if a senior male didn't approve of one member's conversion to Christianity, then the convert would keep it secret out of anxiety, fear or simply respect and love.[49] In one Coventry instance, a Gujarati Catholic avoided telling her father (who served as a priest in the Hindu temple) as she felt that he had suffered tragedies enough already.

The dominant influence extends to young people's education, choice of career and of marriage partner. Thus Punjabi Christians' assumptions about the duties inherent in particular relationships and the patterns of gift exchange surrounding marriage also conform broadly to practice in other Punjabi families, especially those of the same caste with whom they particularly socialized.

Easton reported that Punjabi Christians were acutely aware of caste-based differences in fellow Punjabis' turn of speech, and though preaching caste equality, recognized that caste membership was the accepted basis for eligibility as a marriage partner. This differs from assumptions in some Goan families that marriage is most likely to be with non-Goans.

Both Barton and Easton describe the strength of the family as a unit that worships together.[50] Families pray together at mealtimes, at bedtime, and in midweek prayer groups at home. The linguistic and musical medium of worship varies. My observation in Coventry was that much of the singing, prayer and Bible reading in the weekly prayer group was in Punjabi and Urdu, and that the melodies of devotional songs were South Asian, with accompaniment provided by the *tabla* (drums) and harmonium. Community members with memories of growing up in Punjab relished these, while those reared in the UK preferred English words and Western tunes.

Christian practices from the sub-continent included inviting a priest to bless the house by sprinkling holy water, and at the time of a death, paying last respects

---

[48]   Ibid.

[49]   Ibid., p. 38.

[50]   Barton, *Rejection, Resistance, Resurrection*, p. 64; Easton, 'Worshipping a White God', p. 41.

to the deceased in an open coffin prior to burial. Following death, a relative's uncovered coffin is kept in the house, amid wailing and praying. Before the cortege sets out the vicar is expected to come to the house to lead prayers. Men and women sit separately in the church, with men at the front and the women, in white, at the back.

In the UK all this is out of step with mainstream practice as English Christians use closed coffins and, frequently, opt for cremation.

Attitudes to Other Faiths

Despite the cultural distinctiveness of many South Asian Christians which connects strongly with patterns among non-Christians of the same ethnicity, Christians' attitudes to other faiths are often negative. Thus, consistent with the denunciations of the missionaries who converted them or their forebears, many condemn the 'idolatry' of Hindus. Compounding these negative views is awareness of anti-Christian events in their countries of origin, which include sporadic attacks on churches in India and Pakistan.[51] The expectation in UK schools, including Christian schools, that pupils will study other faiths and visit mosques, temples and gurdwaras is confusingly unwelcome to some South Asian Christian parents. In balance with this, Goans are 'down the line Vatican II types, happy to work with all faith groups, showing respect … and, for the most part, being reasonably uninterested in the theological questions related to them'.[52]

Relationship with Other Christian groups

Perhaps unsurprisingly, given their perception of the UK as a predominantly Christian country, South Asian Christians have tended not to view the possible impact of surrounding social mores with as much fear or hostility as some South Asian faith communities have done. This point was made clearly by Jeffery when reporting her study of Muslim and Christian Pakistanis in Bristol in the 1970s.[53]

In the case of South Asian Catholics (and so of most Goans), children share experience of both schooling and church attendance with Catholic peers from other ethnic communities.[54] But research among Coventry's Punjabi Christians

---

[51]   See L. Kingsley, 'Something Inside So Strong', *Teartimes* (Summer 2002): 4–9; W. Dalrymple, 'Cross to Bear: Can Christianity Survive in the Muslim World?', *Guardian* supplement, 30 October 2001, pp. 1–3.

[52]   Gavin D'Costa, personal communication, 10 June 2006.

[53]   Jeffery, *Migrants and Refugees*.

[54]   See, for example, D. Breen, 'The Responsive Catholic School: A Leap of Faith?' (unpublished MSc. dissertation, Faculty of Social Science, University of Leicester, 2005), on a Leicester primary school attended by pupils from Daman.

revealed that while schools and Sunday schools reinforced some aspects of young people's religious tradition, they overturned norms of the home, such as the expected ways of showing respect to elders and of spouse selection. Easton suggested that those Punjabi Christians who attended schools that had no faith basis felt a lack of affirmation of their Christian heritage, while those who attended an Anglican school discovered that their non-Asian friends couldn't sympathize with their families' different values and prohibitions.[55]

Figure 1.2   South Asian Christians looking at Christian literature in South Asian languages at a South Asian Christian convention. (Photo: Eleanor Nesbitt)

Like their Caribbean counterparts, and like the Goans before them, Punjabis and many South Indian Christians gravitated first to the congregations of mainstream British denominations with which they already identified. (Mar Thoma Christians tended to join Church of England congregations.) In some cases, as in one Catholic church in Cambridgeshire, pressure would subsequently build up to hold some services in the mother tongue. Williams suggests that there is an ecumenical strategy whereby Christians from several churches and geographical areas in India unite in new congregations. Thus families attend an established church on a regular basis, and. more infrequently (say, monthly) worship with an inter-denominational gathering of South Asian Christians.[56] Among South Asian Christians, shared culture and language, as Punjabis or Keralites for example, often takes precedence

55   Easton, 'Worshipping a White God', p. 36.
56   Williams, 'South Asian Christians in Britain, Canada, and the United States', p. 18.

over denominational divides. Easton observed that converts who had lost their families because of converting valued the family feel of Asian fellowships.[57]

Barton also identifies the concern of Asian Christians to 'reclaim their common heritage in a foreign land'[58] – music, instruments, language, food, integration of social events. One of the first South Asian churches was Birmingham's Good News Asian Church, 'which is claimed to be the first South Asian church in the world outside the Indian sub-continent'.[59] Similarly, Williams notes in relation to Keralite Christians that churches, are 'the only place outside the home where the native language of Malayalam … can be spoken and where many aspects of the accompanying identity can be enjoyed'.[60] Parents hope that their children will come to love the only partially understood services in Indian languages, much as they (or more likely previous generations) did services in Latin or in Syriac.[61] Where South Asian congregations are established, this is sometimes because of denominational distinctness from existing UK denominations (as with Syrian Malankara Christians), but in other instances it is because of cultural distinctness from the 'white' congregation and/or because of racism, whether explicit or implicit, including the unwelcoming attitude of some white clergy and congregations, and the importance of 'time-keeping' for at least one vicar.[62]

The sense of exclusion and prejudice that encourages congregations to form on ethnic rather than denominational lines is not only a recent phenomenon. Suspicion and hostility towards South Asian Christians has a long and persistent history in the UK. Gordon Weaver charts the harassment from 1876, including a grave miscarriage of justice, of the Reverend Shapurji Edalji and his family. The Reverend Edalji, a Parsi from Bombay, had converted to Christianity and been appointed vicar of a parish in South Staffordshire on the estate of the Earl of Lichfield, whose son stigmatized him as a 'Hindoo parson'.[63]

Contemporary South Asian Christian commentators draw attention to continuing experiences of racism and exclusion in the church: Barton offers a theological response,[64] and Woolrych records instances in a Quaker context.[65] Outside their congregations too South Asian Christians are at the receiving end of negative attitudes that 'people of colour' of all communities experience.

---

[57]   Easton, 'Worshipping a White God', p. 48.
[58]   Barton, *Rejection, Resistance, Resurrection*, p. 61.
[59]   Ibid., p. 63.
[60]   Williams, 'South Asian Christians in Britain, Canada, and the United States', p. 18.
[61]   Ibid., p. 27.
[62]   Barton, *Rejection, Resistance, Resurrection*, pp. 60–61.
[63]   G. Weaver, *Conan Doyle and the Parson's Son: The George Edalji Case* (London, 2006).
[64]   Barton, *Rejection, Resistance, Resurrection*.
[65]   Woolrych, *Communicating across Cultures*.

Change

As the summary of phases of Goan presence in the UK above suggests, and as the generational differences in Punjabis' preferred language and music illustrate, change is continuously underway. Easton noted the example of older Punjabi Christians exchanging the distinctive greeting 'Jai Masih' ('Victory to Christ'), whereas young people 'just say "hallo"'.[66] When new arrivals are already members of an existing UK denomination and are also comfortable with English (as has been the case for most Goans), the trajectory can be integration and assimilation in the UK congregation as well as in secular society.

One change is in some individuals' drift from church attendance. This is consistent with wider tendencies in the UK, and may also be one result of the lack of specific quality provision for the young in some congregations.[67]

Trends are not, however, unidirectionally towards Westernization and secularization. Easton reported a recent emphasis on Asianness, as indicated by the St John's Fellowship using a chapatti for afternoon communion.[68] Similarly, Raj Patel, a Gujarati Christian, urged Christians to resist pressure to deny their Indian culture,[69] and the AAC is developing Asian music for worship.[70]

Leadership is an area of concern. Priests who were trained in India are a welcome 'bit of India' for parents, whereas their children need someone who can understand and communicate with them.[71] This parallels the situation *vis-à-vis* Sikhs', Hindus' and Muslims' religious functionaries. South Asian Concern is working with theological colleges to develop training for Asian Christian religious leaders and offers support to those 'wanting to develop new forms of Church'.[72]

Virtual communities, connected via the Internet, are a recent and flourishing development, as the World Wide Web disseminates matrimonials, information and educational material, and encourages contact and outreach. Thus, for example, <http://groups.msn.com/ICONIndianChristianOrthodoxNetwork> is the Website for the Indian Orthodox Church (Malankara Orthodox Syrian Church, Kerala).

The fact that South Asian Christians belong to conspicuously transnational communities – the Goans retaining strong linkages with India, Portugal, East Africa and Canada, for example, and the South Indians with India and North America,[73]

---

[66] Easton, 'Worshipping a White God', p. 32.

[67] Ibid., p. 46.

[68] Ibid., p. 33.

[69] R. Patel, 'Why Do Christians Wear Ties?', in P. Grant and R. Patel (eds), *A Time to Speak: Perspectives on Black Christians in Britain* (Nottingham, 1990), pp. 87–93.

[70] Easton, 'Worshipping a White God', p. 32.

[71] Williams, 'South Asian Christians in Britain, Canada, and the United States', p. 30.

[72] South Asian Connection, 'Featured Articles' (2006), available at <http://www.southasianconnection.com/>, accessed 13 April 2006; Easton, 'Worshipping a White God', p. 49.

[73] Williams, 'South Asian Christians in Britain, Canada, and the United States', p. 14.

Germany and Switzerland – makes Internet linkages all the more welcome. One Website, 'South Asian Connection – Portal for South Asian Christians', provides the facility of 'online dating' and features 'articles', many highlighting conversion experiences.[74] Not least via the Web, the USA, with its stronger, growing Christian communities, is influencing Christians in the UK.[75]

Individual South Asian Christians' Contributions in the UK

Individual South Asian Christians are distinguishing themselves in diverse roles, including political leadership. In the arts, Caroline Jariwala's contribution as an artist of Christian faith and Gujarati Hindu heritage not only shines out in terms of achievement, but also engages compellingly, through its style and symbolism, with the heart of being a diasporic South Asian Christian. Unmistakably Indian rhythms of line and colour are informed by Jariwala's immersion in European art – Byzantine and Renaissance – as well as by a sub-continental female culture of domesticity, dance and devotion.[76]

In the political arena, at national level, Keith Vaz, MP for Leicester East, a Goan Catholic who came to the UK as a child from Aden, became in 1987 the first person of Indian origin for many years to sit in the House of Commons (three Zoroastrians had done so in the nineteenth century). In 1999, he became Minister for Europe.

At local level, the Punjabi James Shera, who served as Mayor of Rugby 1979–80, was the first Asian mayor in the UK, an achievement which particularly inspires his fellow Dalits in the UK. Another Punjabi, the East African businessman and philanthropist Ram Gidoomal, came to media prominence when he stood as London mayoral candidate in 2004 for the Christian People's Alliance.[77]

In 1995, Michael Nazir Ali, who had grown up in a largely Shi'a Muslim family in Karachi, Pakistan became, as Bishop of the Anglican Diocese of Rochester, the 'first ethnic minority diocesan bishop' and in 1999 'the first non-white Lord Spiritual', a 'Lord Spiritual' being the designation of bishops who are members of the House of Lords.[78]

Easton records that 'there are at least 9 South Asian Methodist ministers, all of whom were born outside Great Britain'.[79] In 2000, the Reverend Inderjit

---

[74]   South Asian Connection, 'Featured Articles'.

[75]   Williams, 'South Asian Christians in Britain, Canada, and the United States', p. 18.

[76]   See <http://www.carolinejariwala.com>.

[77]   M. White, 'Year of the Ram?', *Guardian Unlimited* (2004), available at <http://politics.guardian.co.uk/elections2004/story/0,14549,1235304,00.html>, accessed 12 April 2006.

[78]   BBC, 'UK Asian Bishop Joins Lords' (1999), available at <http://news.bbc.co.uk/1/hi/uk_politics/381823.stm>, accessed 22 May 2006.

[79]   Easton, 'Worshipping a White God', p. 28.

Bhogal, who is in his own words 'a minister in the Church, with roots in the Sikh faith',[80] was appointed President of the Methodist Conference. Bhogal was the first president to come from an ethnic minority, and in 2005 he received the award of an OBE for his work in inter-faith relations. Bhogal's upbringing was in a devout Kenyan Sikh family, and he has described himself as 'very much part of Sikh culture'.[81] He became a Methodist because of the welcome which a local Methodist congregation gave him when he 'was a stranger in their midst' after he came to Britain and experienced racism.

Conclusion

This chapter has drawn attention to both diversity and commonality. The diversity has been traced in terms of regional origins in South Asia and the associated traditions of language and culture, and in terms of history (particularly the history of Christian conversion in South Asia and the history of migration and settlement) as well as generational, educational and socio-economic diversity. The commonality inheres in being visibly South Asian in a country with a 'white' majority and substantial South Asian communities from other faiths. The UK's colonial past, its accommodation of minorities and at the same time certain persistent tendencies to marginalize and misunderstand contribute a shared frame and texture for many South Asian Christians' experience.

The UK's South Asian Christians are increasing in number and assurance, but are invisible to the general public and to many church leaders. Yet the church stands to be enriched by what South Asians could contribute spiritually, socially and practically.[82] Scholarship too will benefit from much-needed research. Fieldwork will disclose continuities and change, and both commonality and diversity. Empirical study will need to take into account factors that include denomination, ethnicity and the contribution of Britain's South Asians to Christianity in the UK. Until then, our understandings of diaspora and evangelism, and of the many interconnections between faith, identity, aspiration and achievement, will remain incomplete.

---

[80]   T. Holmes, 'Reverend Bhogal: A Follower of Jesus Christ with Roots in the Sikh Faith', *The Sikh Times* (2003), available at <http://www.sikhtimes.com/bios_010403a. html>, accessed 23 May 2006.

[81]   R. Gledhill, 'Sikh Chosen to Lead Methodist Church', *The Times*, 22 June 1999, p. 5.

[82]   H. Dodhia, 'What the Western Church Can Learn from People of Other Faiths – to Develop and Enrich its own Spirituality', in P. Grant and R. Patel (eds), *A Time to Speak: Perspectives on Black Christians in Britain* (Nottingham, 1990), pp. 79–85; Easton, 'Worshipping a White God', p. 33.

References

Abbas, Tahir, *British Islam* (Cambridge: Cambridge University Press, 2007).

Achen, J.T., 'From the Vicar' (2005), available at <http://www.marthoma.org.uk/html/vicar.html>, accessed 27 December 2005.

Alliance of Asian Christians, *Introducing: Alliance of Asian Christians* (Birmingham: AAC, 1999).

Bance, P., *The Duleep Singhs: The Photograph Album of Queen Victoria's Maharajah* (Stroud: Sutton Publishing, 2004).

Barton, M., *Scripture as Empowerment for Liberation and Justice: The Experience of Christian and Muslim Women in Bangladesh* (Bristol: Centre for Comparative Studies in Religion and Gender, Department of Theology and Religious Studies, University of Bristol, 1999).

Barton, M., *Rejection, Resistance, Resurrection: Speaking out on Racism in the Church* (London: Darton, Longman and Todd, 2005).

BBC, 'UK Asian Bishop Joins Lords' (1999), available at <http://news.bbc.co.uk/l/hi/uk_politics/381823.stm>, accessed 22 May 2006.

BBC, 'Where I Live: Gloucestershire' (2006), available at <http://www.bbc.co.uk/gloucestershire/untold_stories/asian/christian_community.shtml>, accessed 13 April 2006.

Breen, D., 'The Responsive Catholic School: A Leap of Faith?' (unpublished MSc. dissertation, Faculty of Social Science, University of Leicester, 2005).

Brierley, P., *UK Christian Handbook Religious Trends 1998/9 No. 1* (London: Christian Research and Carlisle: Paternoster Publishing, 1998/89).

Caleb, M., 'Christian Sunday Worship in a Punjabi Village', in J.C.B. Webster (ed.), *Popular Religion in the Punjab Today* (Batala, India: The Christian Institute of Sikh Studies, 1974), pp. 119–26.

Campbell, C., *The Maharajah's Box* (London: HarperCollins, 2000).

Chakrabarty, R.R., *Duleep Singh: The Maharajah of Punjab and the Raj* (Birmingham: D.S. Samra, 1988).

Clifton Diocese, '"Dukrana" Festival Celebrated in Bristol' (2006), available at <http://www.cliftondiocese.com/Articles/415/>, accessed 20 June 2006.

Dalrymple, W., 'Indian Journeys', BBC Television documentary, 17 April 2000.

Dalrymple, W., 'Cross to Bear: Can Christianity Survive in the Muslim World?', *Guardian* supplement, 30 October 2001, pp. 1–3.

De Souza Eremita, 'Church Worry as Goa's Catholic Population Declines' (Missio Hilfe für eine andere Welt, 2005), available at <http://www.missio-aachen.de/menschen-kulturen/nachrichten/Church_people_worry_>, accessed 22 May 2006.

Dodhia, H., 'What the Western Church Can Learn from People of Other Faiths – to Develop and Enrich its own Spirituality', in P. Grant and R. Patel (eds), *A Time to Speak: Perspectives on Black Christians in Britain* (Nottingham: Racial Justice and Black Theology Working Group, 1990), pp. 79–85.

East, BBC 2 Television programme, 30 August 1991.

Easton, B., 'Worshipping a White God: A Study of the Religious Experience of Young Asian Christians' (unpublished MA in Religious Education dissertation, Institute of Education, University of Warwick, 2000).

Gledhill, R., 'Sikh Chosen to Lead Methodist Church', *The Times*, 22 June 1999, p. 5.

Holmes, T., 'Reverend Bhogal: A Follower of Jesus Christ with Roots in the Sikh Faith', *The Sikh Times* (2003), available at <http://www.sikhtimes.com/bios_010403a.html>, accessed 23 May 2006.

Hooker, P., *His Other Sheep*, Grove Pastoral Care Series no. 37 (Nottingham: Grove Books, 1989).

Jackson, R. and E. Nesbitt, 'The Diversity of Experience in the Religious Upbringing of Children from Christian Families in Britain', *British Journal of Religious Education*, 15/1 (1992): 19–28.

Jackson, R., and E. Nesbitt, *Hindu Children in Britain* (Stoke on Trent: Trentham, 1993).

Jeffery, P., *Migrants and Refugees: Muslim and Christian Pakistani Families in Bristol* (London: Cambridge University Press, 1976).

Juergensmeyer, M., *Religion as Social Vision: The Movement against Untouchability in Twentieth-century Punjab* (Berkeley, CA: University of California Press, 1982).

Kingsley, L., 'Something Inside So Strong', *Teartimes* (Summer 2002): 4–9.

Mackenzie, C., 'Extrait Choisi: The Hindu Sources of a European Christian Artist' (no date), available at <http://www.voiesorient.be/Bulletin/carolineuk.htm>, accessed 23 May 2006.

Mukherjee, A., *Nirmal Babu's Bride* (New Delhi: Indialog, 2002).

Nesbitt, E., 'Aspects of Sikh Tradition in Nottingham' (unpublished MPhil. thesis, University of Nottingham, 1980).

Nesbitt, E., *'My Dad's Hindu, My Mum's Side are Sikhs': Issues in Religious Identity* (Charlbury, UK: National Foundation for Arts Education, 1991).

Nesbitt, E., 'Religion and Identity: The Valmiki Community in Coventry', *New Community*, 16/2 (1991): 261–74.

Nesbitt, E., 'The Punjabi Christian Community in Coventry: Its Development and Pointers to the Future' (unpublished paper presented at Punjab Research Group, Coventry University, 26 October 1991).

Nesbitt, E., 'Drawing on the Ethnic Diversity of Christian Tradition in Britain', *Multicultural Teaching*, 11/2 (1993): 9–11.

Nesbitt, E., 'The Transmission of Christian Tradition in an Ethnically Diverse Society', in R. Barot (ed.), *Religion and Ethnicity: Minorities and Social Change in the Metropolis* (Kampen: Kok Pharos, 1993), pp. 159–69.

Nesbitt, E., 'Punjabis in Britain: Cultural History and Cultural Choices', *South Asia Research*, 15/2 (1995): 221–40.

Nesbitt, E., *The Religious Lives of Sikh Children: A Coventry Based Study* (Leeds: Community Religions Project, Department of Theology and Religious Studies, University of Leeds, 2000).

Nesbitt, E., *Intercultural Education: Ethnographic and Religious Approaches* (Brighton: Sussex Academic Press, 2004).

Norton, T., 'Goan Migrants Swell Catholic Community', *The Tablet*, 6 October 2007: 40.

Patel, R., 'Why do Christians Wear Ties?', in P. Grant and R. Patel (eds), *A Time to Speak: Perspectives on Black Christians in Britain* (Nottingham: Nottingham Racial Justice and Black Theology Working Group, 1990), pp. 87–93.

South Asian Connection, 'Featured Articles' (2006), available at <http://www.southasianconnection.com/>, accessed 13 April 2006.

The Goan Community of London, 'The Goan Community of London' (no date), available at <http://www.portcities.org.uk/london/server/show/ConNarrative.50/chapterId/727/The-Goan-Community-of-London.html>, accessed 26 May 2006.

Weaver, G., *Conan Doyle and the Parson's Son: The George Edalji Case* (London: Vanguard, 2006).

Webster, J.C.B., *The Christian Community and Change in Nineteenth Century North India* (Delhi: Macmillan, 1976).

Webster, J.C.B., *The Dalit Christians: A History* (New Delhi: ISPCK, 1992).

White, M., 'Year of the Ram?', *Guardian Unlimited* (2004), available at <http://politics.guardian.co.uk/elections2004/story/0,14549,1235304,00.html>, accessed 12 April 2006.

Wikipedia, 'St Thomas Christians' available at <http://en.wikipedia.org/wiki/Saint_Thomas_Christians>, accessed 22 May 2006.

Wikipedia, 'Syrian Malabar Nasrani', available at <http://en.wikipedia.org/wiki/Syrian_Malabar_Nasrani>, accessed 22 May 2006.

Williams, R.B., 'South Asian Christians in Britain, Canada, and the United States', in H. Coward, J.R. Hinnells and R.B. Williams (eds), *The South Asian Religious Diaspora in Britain, Canada, and the United States* (Albany, NY: State University of New York Press, 2000), pp. 13–34.

Woolrych, L., *Communicating across Cultures: A Report by Joseph Rowntree Fellow 1992/93* (York: Joseph Rowntree Trust, 1998).

Chapter 2

Religion as an Arena for the Expression of Identity: Roman Catholic Pondicherrians in France[1]

Brigitte Sébastia

Since the Second Vatican Council, the episcopate has embarked upon some reconsideration and upon the publication of texts to improve the integration of Catholic communities into a culture which, though their own, is dominated by a non-Christian religion, and the integration of Catholic migrants into the culture of their adopted country. As applied to Indian Catholics, these works led to the inculturation of the church in India with a liturgy integrating Indian (Hindu) customs, as well as to the creation of a chaplaincy in Paris to welcome and to help French Pondicherrians who chose to live in France. However, the study of the religious activities developed by Pondicherrians in France presents an important gap between the aim of these works and the results, which latter feature a strong ethnicization of the chaplaincy, proliferation of festivals, and a hierarchization of the community which promotes competition and break-up. This has been facilitated by the appointment of a Tamil priest to the chaplaincy and by the devotion of Pondicherrians to Arokkiya Mata of Velankanni, the Virgin of the Tamils *par excellence*.

Pondicherrians form the largest community of Indians residing in France. They began emigrating to France in 1956, the date of the treaty of the *de facto* transfer of the French trading posts to the Indian government, and came in increasing numbers after the ratification of the treaty in 1962,[2] and after the withdrawal of

---

[1]   This chapter is part of the anthropological research I undertook in 1999 from observations and interviews collected from 1996 onwards, and more intensively during 1998–99. This study received the financial support of Mission du patrimoine ethnologique of the Direction Régionale des Affaires Culturelles of Île de France, and was published as Brigitte Sébastia, *Les Pondichériens de l'Ile de France. Etude des pratiques sociales et religieuses* (Toulouse, 1999).

[2]   The treaty of transfer of territories of Pondicherry, Karaikal, Yanaon and Mahe was signed on 28 May 1956. Chandernagor, the fifth territory, had been returned in 1947 and included in Bengal State. Regarding the history of the French in India, see Pierre Bourdat, *Eighteenth-century Pondicherry. Pondichéry XVIIIème* (Pondicherry, 1995); Ajit K. Neogy *Decolonisation of French India: Liberal Movement and Indo-French Relations 1947–1954*

American troops from Vietnam in 1975.[3] They came as French citizens, either having opted, as residents of Pondicherry territories, for French nationality at the time of the *de facto* transfer, or having acquired citizenship automatically if they were living outside the territory of the trading posts.[4] Nowadays, the immigration of Pondicherrians continues, with young French nationals who come to France to study or work,[5] and also through marriage, which is a way for Indian citizens to acquire French nationality. The number of these immigrants in metropolitan areas is estimated as 45,000–55,000; it is difficult to be precise about numbers when the people concerned are all French citizens. They live mainly in Île de France, the urban area composed of Paris and of its large suburbs, whereas many career soldiers, active and retired, inhabit garrison towns.

The Pondicherrians established in France are mostly natives of the Pondicherry and Karaikal territories, two areas enclosed within the State of Tamil Nadu, and thus speak Tamil; they define themselves as both Pondicherrian and Tamil. Regarding religion, they are mostly Roman Catholics, due to a variety of circumstances, such as the significant presence of missionaries in Pondicherry during the colonial period, the abandoning of Hinduism by the families of *renonçants* in the nineteenth century, or the conversion of one partner in mixed marriages.

The study presented here deals with Pondicherrians established in Île de France who are Tamil and Catholic. The relevance of research on this community became clear to me in 1996, when I was carrying out a study on the Catholic shrine of Velankanni, a pilgrim centre very famous for its Virgin, named Arokkiya Mata ('Our Lady of Good Health') or Velankanni Mata. During that period, I heard about two annual festivals in honour of Velankanni Mata organized by the Pondicherrian communities in Paris and in Pontoise, to the north of Paris. These festivals gave me the opportunity to study the role this Virgin plays for Pondicherrians living in France. By taking part in these festivals, I realized from their number, from the recurrence of attempts to organize a new one, from the cultural features in their content, as well as the criticisms invoked, what it is like to be interested

---

(Pondicherry, 1997); Gabriel Piesse, *Pondichéry de 1954 à 1963: de la République française à la République indienne, histoire d'une transition* (Nantes, 1999); A. Ramachandran (ed.), *Pondicherry through the Ages* (Pondicherry, 1997), and Jacques Weber, *Pondichéry et les comptoirs de l'Inde après Duplex. La démocratie au pays des castes* (Paris, 1996).

[3]   These Pondicherrians are those who had stayed in what had been Indochina after the departure of the French authorities.

[4]   Natives who were in the metropolis or in a French territory at this time (soldiers, administrative agents, students) were granted French nationality, but had the option of refusing it.

[5]   According to the estimate by the French Consulate in Pondicherry of French Pondicherrians presented by W.F.S. Miles, *Imperial Burdens: Countercolonialism in Former French India* (Boulder, CO, 1995), p. 20.

in religious activities organized by a community in an immigration situation, and I was able to comprehend its needs and difficulties.[6]

The cultural rites included in certain of the masses that are organized by Pondicherrians conform entirely to the recommendation of the episcopate during the Second Vatican Council to recognize the cultural diversity of Christians within the Catholic community. To this purpose, the constitution of *Sacrosanctum Concilium*, published on 4 December 1963, invites the clergy of each country to adapt the liturgy to the norms defined by the constitution of the Sacred Liturgy and to use the vernacular language instead of Latin. The constitution *Gaudium and spes*, published on 7 December 1965, recognizes the importance of the culture of societies and supports its expression. The decree *Ad Gentes divinitus* promotes the development of the local clergy in the newly Christianized countries by encouraging them to spread the Christian message and to help erase social and economic inequalities. These constitutions and decrees have implications in two contexts: internal and external. In the internal context, the clergy must improve the integration of newly converted communities into their society through the use of customs and cultural concepts shared by Indians, implicitly Hindus, in order to avoid their being stigmatized as foreigners in their own country, and must diffuse Christianity within the culture. In the external context, they have to facilitate the integration of migrant communities in their chosen countries by helping them to express their cultural richness.

If the cultural rites used in the liturgy of festivals of Pondicherrians in France correspond to the will of the episcopate, nevertheless, it is noticeable that they are rarely performed in masses celebrated in India. In India, the majority of parishioners and priests are hostile to what are called 'inculturation rites',[7] and this attitude

---

[6]   Concerning Indians overseas, there exist some works specializing in their religious activities which are interesting to compare with this present study: Jean Benoist, *Hindouismes créoles. Mascareignes, Antilles* (Paris, 1998); R. Burghart, *Hinduism in Great Britain: The Perpetuation of Religion in an Alien Cultural Milieu* (London, 1987); Harold Coward, John R. Hinnells and Raymond Brady Williams, *The South Asian Religious Diaspora in Britain, Canada, and the United States* (Albany, NY, 2000); John Y. Fenton, *Transplanting Religious Traditions: Asian Indians in America* (New York, 1988); R.I.M. Lee, 'Taipucam in Malaysia: Ecstasy and Identity in a Tamil Hindu Festival', *Contributions to Indian Sociology*, 23/2 (1989): 317–37; Aparna Rayaprol, *Negotiating Identities: Women in the Indian Diaspora* (Delhi, 1997), and earlier, Hugh Tinker, *The Banyan Tree: Overseas Emigrants from India, Pakistan, and Bangladesh* (Oxford, 1977).

[7]   The term 'inculturation' is defined as an acculturation in a double direction: (1) adaptation of the evangelical message by taking the culture of the country concerned into account; (2) acclimatization of the cultural identity of the country confronted with the message of the Christ in order to enrich the conception of the Word of this culture. According to Catherine Clémentin-Ojha, 'Indianisation et enracinement: les enjeux de l'"inculturation" de l'Eglise en Inde', *Bulletin de l'EFEO*, 80/1 (1993): 107–33, p. 110, the neologism 'inculturation' was used by theologists in the 1960s. The first pontifical document to mention the term, in 1977, defines it as a process of adjustment of the Christian faith to

is also shared by many of the Pondicherrians who participate in the religious activities of their community in France. This chapter will aid comprehension of the role of the religious realm in the situation of immigration and show how it enables cultural identity to be expressed.

The Foundation of the Tamil Chaplaincy: A Very Indian Institution

The religious activities of the Catholic Pondicherrians in Île de France are closely supervised by the ecclesial institution, which, according to episcopal texts, has been in favour of immigrant communities and supported the creation of an Indian chaplaincy in 1981.

The chaplaincies, under the direction of the Roman Catholic Church, have been created to come to the assistance of the immigrant Catholic communities. The migrant, like any human being:

> has the right to freedom of movement and of residence within the confines of his own State. When there are just reasons in favour of it, he must be permitted to emigrate to other countries and take up residence there. The fact that he is a citizen of a particular State does not deprive him of membership in the human family, nor of citizenship in that universal society, the common, world-wide fellowship of men. (*Pacem in Terris*, art. 24, 1963)

Whether the immigrant has chosen to flee his country for economical, ideological or political reasons, it is the duty of the Christian community to protect him from rejection by offering him every aid in communicating in his own language and in finding comfort from closeness to a priest who shares his culture. In furtherance of this aim, Pie II published in 1952 a text on the foundation of the ethnic chaplaincies, *Exsul familia*,[8] in which he stipulated the new jurisdiction

---

the culture, and of the adaptation of the Christian message to various socio-cultural areas. Father Lucien Legrand of MEP in 'Inculturation. Quelques points de repère bibliques', *Bulletin de documentation des Missions Etrangères*, 279 (1993): 133–41, p. 133, states that this word has belonged to the official vocabulary of the ecclesiastical documents since the Fifth Synod of Bishops, 1977. It was used at the beginning of the 1960s by P.J. Masson to replace the terms 'adaptation' or 'accommodation', which were obviously too intrinsic to the culture. Lastly, Father Rossignol of MEP thinks that this word was employed for the first time during a missiological week at Leuwen in 1959, and was then used during the Synod of Bishops in 1974 and at the 32nd Congregation General of the Society of Jesus (1974–75) (personal communication).

[8]   This Constitution was published in *Acta Apostilicae* (September 1952, p. 30), and was following by a number of proposals presented during and after the Second Vatican Council. It is mentioned *Pacem in terris* (1963), published by John XXIII, or *Pastoralis migratorum cura* (1969), in which Paul VI insisted on the need to take the spiritual and cultural heritage of migrants into account so that pastoral work may be carried out effectively,

of the Consistorial Congregation regarding Migrants. This Congregation must pay attention to providing the migrant communities with priests of the same linguistic origin, called 'missionaries to migrants'. These priests are appointed by their diocese, and the congregation must facilitate their immigration and their installation in the host country and oversee the running of their ministry.

Until 1981, members of Tamil communities (Indians and Sri Lankans) in France, could consult a Tamil student-priest and attend a Tamil mass celebrated each month in the crypt of the Chapel in MEP (Mission Etrangères de Paris, 'Foreign Mission of Paris'). To prevent this mass from being the sole religious activity of these Tamils, and to maintain them in their parishes, an ex-missionary of MEP in Tamil Nadu created an Indian chaplaincy. He developed monthly masses in the Tamil language in various parishes around Paris where Tamil families were established (Sarcelles, Gonesse, Gretz). He then organized three annual masses in the Tamil language: one in December at the Chapel of the Miraculous Medal, Paris, one in January to celebrate the *Ponkal*,[9] and the last in June at the Basilica of the Sacred Heart of Montmartre, Paris. At the time of his retirement in 1985, he pleaded for the appointment of a Tamil priest to the function of missionary to migrants.

The French father claimed that, except for the refusal of inculturation of the liturgy he tried to introduce, he never encountered any difficulty during his ministry to the Tamils. This was not, however, the case for the priests who replaced him, and as soon as a priest of the Pondicherry diocese was appointed to run the chaplaincy (a four-year appointment), the Pondicherrians found a context favourable for the expression of prestige, hierarchy and precedence. Among the Tamil priests who managed the Indian chaplaincy, two personages distinguished themselves by their inclination towards handling the hierarchy models and Indianizing the Catholic rites.

The first missionary to the Tamils (1985–89) belonged to the Vellalar, a 'good caste'[10] of landowners. Seizing this opportunity, some families of 'good caste' claimed and obtained a privileged position within the chaplaincy, from where they

---

or more recently, 'Au service de la catholicité de l'Eglise. Les aumôneries ethniques dans la pastorale des Migrants', a necessity insistently reiterated by Jean Paul II (*Documents Episcopat*, 1987).

[9]   *Ponkal* is a Tamil festival falling on the first day of the Tamil month of *tai*, and celebrating the harvest of the new rice. On this occasion, families prepare a *ponkal* – new rice cooked with milk and palm sugar (*vellam*). The preparation, which is cooked on the doorstep, is supposed to bring prosperity. This celebration and others such as *Tipavali*, Indian Republic Day and *Sarasvati puca*, were added to the Catholic calendar during the All India Catholic Bishops Conference in 1972. Their social dimension explains why they have been introduced.

[10]   I define by 'good castes' the castes of higher status such as *vellalar*, *mutaliyar*, *naitu* and *retiyar*, to which Pondicherrians mainly belong. These castes, belonging to the brahmanical category of *shudra*, are opposed to those of Untouchables.

put pressure on the priest to give up the charge of Sri Lankans,[11] and the 'Tamil chaplaincy' thus became the chaplaincy of Tamil Pondicherrians exclusively. In this new configuration, an event of great impact occurred: during a monthly mass at Sarcelles, a Pondicherrian woman complained to the Missionary to Migrants about her parish priest, who refused to install the statue of Arokkiya Mata that she had brought from Velankanni in thanksgiving for the cure of her husband after a heart attack. The Tamil priest suggested to her that the statue be installed in the chaplaincy and receive the devotion of Pondicherrians. The family accepted, and was then completely dispossessed of its statue by the dominant families led by this chaplain. According to Indian tradition, every deity installed must be honoured with an annual festival commemorating the founding day. This statue accordingly gave occasion for the organization of festivities in which the dominant families monopolized the marks of precedence, such as the actual organization of the festival, which favoured privileged bonds with the chaplain, decoration of the statue and its canopy and of the church, procession of the statue, and the offering of foods at the end of the ceremony, that are normally the prerogatives of the family responsible for the cult. This festival, instituted in May, the month of Mary, is celebrated each year in the gardens of the MEP.

While the hierarchy in India depends on caste, in the French context, the Pondicherrians at the head of the chaplaincy, besides belonging to 'good castes', shared a high socio-economic profile and military rank. Only one family distinguished itself from this by its Untouchable status, but the military rank of the household and its socio-economic situation compensated for its low status, and later even allowed it to take over the direction of the Pondicherrian Community of Paris when it was formed by a group of Pondicherrians.[12] In 1989, no priest was appointed to replace the previous one, and the chaplaincy was run by a few Tamil student-priests. Their lack of interest in the ministry to Pondicherrians favoured a laicization of the chaplaincy which was desired by the dominant families who used the institution to organize religious festivities with the aim of promoting Tamil identity. A priest of MEP intervened to restore order and asked for the appointment of a new missionary to migrants. Some of the dominant families chose to leave the chaplaincy, but were quickly replaced by others in search of prestige.

The second missionary to Tamil migrants (1992–97) also belonged to a 'good caste'. His management of the chaplaincy was completely different from that of his

---

[11] In fact, the Pondicherrians did not agree with the priest who used a part of the chaplaincy to store foodstuffs for the benefit of Sri Lankan refugees and spent too much time on them. The Sri Lankans received their first chaplain in 1995, attached to the parish of Saint-Joseph-of-Nations situated in the XIth arrondissement of Paris. The pilgrimage of Tamils to Lourdes experienced a similar fracture, so that since 1995 there have been two pilgrimages: Pondicherrians go in July, and Sri Lankans in August.

[12] I use an upper-case initial to distinguish a Community of Pondicherrians, a group of Pondicherrians who organize Tamil religious activities in their parish, from the community of Pondicherrians, that is, the ensemble of all Pondicherrians.

predecessor due to the difficulty he had in imposing his authority on it. Incapable of controlling the dominant families at the head of the chaplaincy, he turned to some Pondicherrian families established in Pontoise when he became aware of their wish to develop religious activities within their parish. He helped them to form a choir to accompany the monthly Tamil mass, and then, at their request, he interceded with the diocese for permission to install a statue of Velankanni Mata in the Church of Notre Dame de Pontoise. A festival was inaugurated, organized by the family that had brought the statue from India and their friends, when it was installed in October 1993. This new festival encouraged requests from Pondicherrians scattered around Paris to develop Tamil masses and celebrations and to install statues of Arokkiya Mata in churches; a fragmentation within the Pondicherrians was created which led to more competition, so that six communities were created in Paris, Pontoise, Sarcelles, Mantes-la-Jolie, Grigny and Trappes. The existence of these six communities is never presented as a breaking up of Pondicherrians, but rather as a means of offering the mass in Tamil to Pondicherrians unable to travel to Paris. The second missionary to Tamil migrants had, however always favoured the Community of Pontoise due to his involvement in its formation and to its interest in legitimizing his authority. He had especially close ties with the person responsible for bringing the statue from India. Although this man was an Untouchable and had held a low military rank before leaving the army to work as clerk in the French administration, his propensity for developing religious activities in his parish had attracted the priest, who wanted both to compete with the Pondicherrian Community of Paris and to promote innovations by using the annual festival of Velankanni Mata as a model for the celebrations organized by all the communities.

Religious Festivals of Pondicherrians in France: Indianization of the Liturgy

In 1999, as my study came to an end, Pondicherrians living in Île de France could attend five monthly Tamil masses at Sarcelles, Paris, Pontoise, Grigny and Mantes-la-Jolie,[13] six festivals in honour of Arokkiya Mata at Paris, Pontoise, Mantes-la-Jolie, Trappes, Antony and Lucé near Chartres, four annual celebrations at Sacred-Hearth Basilica of Montmartre, at Our Lady of the Miraculous Medal, *Ponkal* organized by the Pondicherrian Community of Paris and *uravu vila*[14] ('Feast of

---

[13]   Since, there have been some modifications: the monthly mass in Mantes-la-Jolie does not exist any more, a weekly mass is organized at St Bernadette's Chapel (Avenue de la Porte de Vincennes, Paris), which has been allotted to the Tamil chaplaincy from 1 September 2005, and a monthly Adoration of the Holy Sacrament is celebrated at Sarcelles. Concerning the families involved in religious activities, the list presented on the Website run by the Tamil Chaplaincy shows too little change compared with 1999.

[14]   The 'Feast of Friendship' was created to gather all the Pondicherrian Communities together in order to curb the breaking up of the community. Pondicherrian Communities take

Friendship') and one official pilgrimage to Lourdes. Except for monthly Tamil masses, all the celebrations are punctuated with inculturation features, that is to say, with cultural gestures and attitudes selected for their relevance to Indian culture, and are implicitly in the Hindu tradition. Their performance reinforces the communal atmosphere of these celebrations, in which scarcely any non Pondicherrians participate. To examine this subject, it is necessary to define the worship of Arokkiya Mata of Velankanni, as well as the cultural features used in celebrations with regard to the inculturation of the liturgy elaborated by the Indian episcopate.

Arokkiya Mata of Velankanni, the Virgin of the Tamils

It is noticed that festivals of Arokkiya Mata of Velankanni are of prime importance for Pondicherrians, but that there are fewer of them than the desire for them would suggest. This is because the clergy of some of the parishes where a statue has been installed, such as Saint-Denis Basilica, Nanterre or Sannois, have not agreed to an annual celebration,[15] or because the parish priest refuses the installation of a statue, and thus does away with any possibility of organizing a celebration. This was the case at Grigny, where the priest insisted that if he accepted one statue, he would be obliged to welcome the statues of all other communities belonging to his parish (there are 64) if they asked him to do so. The interest in the organization of such festivals is a reflection of the prestige and gratitude which anyone who takes the initiative in diffusing the cult of Velankanni Mata in France enjoys, due to the great devotion of Pondicherrians for her.

   Velankanni Mata is considered as the 'Virgin of Tamil Nadu': it was at the small village of Velankanni, on the shore of the Bay of Bengal, that she chose to appear three times, dressed in a sari worn in the Tamil style, to perform her miracles. Her worship, initiated by the Portuguese at the beginning of the seventeenth century, was developed over the centuries, and enjoys increasing success today, as may be measured by the hundred of thousands of pilgrims of all castes and creeds, and from every state in India, who attend her ten-day festival from 29 August to

---

it in turns to organize the festival; this involves renting a room, arranging the meal and organizing the religious office, while all the Communities come together to produce the spectacle.

[15]   According to my inventory, in July 1999 there were ten statues installed in churches around Paris, excluding the one in the chaplaincy. They are, in order of installation: Les Bâconnets, Antony; Tamil Chaplaincy, Paris; Saint-Jean-Baptiste, Mantes-la-Jolie; Notre-Dame, Pontoise; Saint-Georges, Trappes; Saint-Martin , Orly; Notre-Dame de la Paix, Corbeil-Essonne (photography); Saint-Paul-Saint-Pierre, Sannois; Saint Denis Basilica, Saint-Denis; Notre-Dame des Cités, Viry-Châtillon; Sainte-Geneviève Cathedral, Nanterre.

8 September.[16] She is the Virgin of the Tamils, but she is also the Virgin of Catholic Indians, and it was because of this identity that she was installed in an oratorio of the cathedral in Washington, DC on the occasion of the fiftieth anniversary of Indian Independence, 15 August 1997. Tamils have a deep veneration for this Marian figure, and in the form of statues, chromos, calendars and photographs, her representation is omnipresent in Catholic houses, and often in Hindu families.

Pondicherrians in France have maintained their great faith in Velankanni Mata, and they communicate it to their children through domestic prayers. In the continuity of tradition, the women assure the function of guardian of the wellbeing of the family by reciting a few prayers every evening in front of their domestic altar. Velankanni Mata is always at the centre of these prayers, especially when there are disturbances in family life, such as health problems, failures at school, cultural value differences, education, relationship and employment problems, or problems concerning the arranged marriage of children, and so on. Women constitute the category most weakened by the condition of being immigrants. Tending to speak little or no French, they stay in their apartments all day long, and are often completely alone on weekdays. This situation does not apply only to women who arrived in the 1960s, but is unceasingly reactivated by new wives arriving all the time from Tamil Nadu and Pondicherry. They are often preferred to Pondicherrian girls living in France for reasons such as preferential marriage,[17] dowry (French nationality is very much valued), caste and traditional education: a choice based on 'cultural imagination' that considers that these young women will be better wives and daughters-in-law and will not have the faults of girls educated in Western countries. In such marriages, as in India, it is not rare for women to be mistreated by their husband or their in-laws, due to quarrels, unpaid dowry, absence of a male descendant, and so on. They cannot count on the help of their own family as they could in India. The first birth is likely, by the same token, to be difficult for them because they must do without the traditional support of their maternal family.[18] These problems arising from living in France encourage religious activities in which it is possible to develop relationships within the community; they give women the opportunity to go out and to play a role in the organization of the celebrations;[19] at festivals, the participants immerse themselves

---

[16] Brigitte Sébastia, *Māriyamman–Mariyamman: Catholic Practices and Image of Virgin in Velankanni (Tamil Nadu)*, Pondy Papers in Social Sciences (Pondicherry, 2002).

[17] Dravidian kinship privileges uncle–maternal niece alliances, and more commonly now, cross-cousin alliances, especially ego–MBD (ego–mother's brother's daughter).

[18] According to the tradition, after the rituals for the seventh month of pregnancy, the future mother goes to her parents' house, where she stays until several months after the delivery to restore her health; the length of time spent in the maternal family depends on caste tradition.

[19] In contrast to India, there are the women organizers of Communities in France who dress the statue of Velankanni Mata and take charge of the decoration of the church. The study by Rayaprol, *Negotiating Identities*, shows that, in the USA, Indian women are

48   *South Asian Christian Diaspora*

in an Indian atmosphere and take the opportunity to make contacts towards the marriage of their children, especially of girls.[20] Thus is promoted the multiplication of statues of Velankanni Mata installed in parishes by way of thanks for favours such as cures, the finding of, or success in, work, marriage, family wellbeing, or simply for the protection of the family and of the community. Native to their own country, Velankanni Mata is certainly the deity best equipped to help them, because she knows all about the cultural context of Tamil women, a homology which is reinforced by the immigration situation she also shares:

> One feels close her like somebody of our family. While we have problems, we can go to the church and speak to her. We speak to her in Tamil and she understands our problems because she knows them. Only her can help us. It is for this reason we have installed her in the church, because she can help the other Pondicherrians families which live here. (Family which has installed a statue in Notre-Dame de la Paix at Corbeil-Essonne)

Rites of Inculturation: Discrepancies and Controversies

A comparison of the liturgical content of celebrations organized by Pondicherrians in France presents some interesting variations that reveal that rites of inculturation are used to mark otherness; this was, as I noticed during the celebrations in which I participated over three years, the policy adopted by the Pondicherrian Community of Pontoise. In order to distinguish itself from other Pondicherrian communities, the organizers saw to it that each celebration presented an innovation; in 1998, an inculturation feature that had been used experimentally in liturgical and catechist centres in India was added.

The liturgical model used in festivals organized by Pondicherrians in France is composed of: a coloured drawing on the floor, called a *kolam*,[21] if the parish

---

centrally involved in religious activities with the aim of developing relationships within the community and of socializing their children through identity awareness.

[20] The marriage of girls is an enormous problem: because of the preference for spouses from India, the number of Pondicherrian girls of marriageable age is increasing. This results in mixed marriages with French people that parents must accept from force of circumstance. Compared to her brothers, the Pondicherrian girl who lives in France is less subjected to an arranged marriage imposed by her parents, and her marriage is often the consequence of a hard-won compromise between her and her parents.

[21] A *kolam* is a more or less elaborate design made with rice powder or coloured chalk powder. In the morning, and sometimes in the evening too, the women wash the ground in front of their houses and draw a *kolam*. This custom is used for all auspicious occasions and festivities, religious and social. In France, where it is not always possible to draw on the ground, a carpet with a geometrical design evoking a *kolam* may be used, as in front of the statue of the Virgin of Velankanni installed in the Church of Saint-Pierre-Saint-Paul at Sannois.

priest allows it, a lamp (*kuttuvilakku*)[22] placed in the centre of the *kolam* and lit at the beginning of the mass, a rite called *arati* performed at the beginning of the mass and at the celebration of the Eucharist, a procession of offerings before the Eucharist, an offering of sweets or a more substantial meal (*annatanam*),[23] and in the case of festivals in honour of Velankanni Mata, a procession (*ter vila*), most often after the mass.

In the general way, the Pondicherrian families who organize the festivals, at Paris, at Pontoise or in different churches when the parish priest invites them to celebrate the mass according to the custom of their country, justify the Indianization of the liturgy by its ability to make the richness of Indian culture attractive, as it did to the Pondicherrians of Corbeil-Essonne, who explained:

> This is the parish priest who asked us to present the mass like we celebrate it in India. So we have discussed and we have decided to sing some Tamil songs. Before the mass, we draw a *kolam* to receive the *kuttuvillakku*. When the mass begins, we light the lamp, then, three young girls of our community make the *arati* at Eucharist that we accompany in singing. The parishioners and the priest have been very glad of this manifestation. Many people have found it very beautiful.

These comments are in tune with the episcopal movement of valorization of the culture of migrants. The use of certain rites such as *arati*, is, however, controversial among Catholic Tamils in both India and France.

In South India, except in Catholic centres such as convents or seminaries, ashrams and centres specializing in inculturation, such as in Tindivanam (training of catechists), or the National Biblical Catechetical Liturgical Centre of Bangalore (NBCLC), *arati* is very rarely performed,[24] even if it was defined during the Catholic Bishops' Conference of India (CBCI) of 1966. It belongs to the 12 points of inculturation approved by the majority of the bishops of India and submitted to the Episcopal Commission of the Liturgy of Rome. These proposals were accepted on 25 April 1969, in the text *Consilium ad exsequendam constitutionem de sacra*

---

[22]   The *kuttuvilakku* is a large lamp whose upper part is a receptacle for oil that feeds five cotton wicks. Its function is to place a ceremony, whether religious or social, under good auspices. The Catholics have adopted this lamp by replacing a Hindu symbol such as swan, peacock or phallic form, with a cross.

[23]   The offering of food, which belongs to the thanksgiving, is made to thank a divinity for favours or to support a request or vows. Here, however, as in religious festivals, it is made as a mark of precedence.

[24]   In India, although I attended many masses on various occasions (marriage, ordination, calendar feast and so on), I observed the practice of *arati* only once, in a mass on 15 August at Nellitope (a satellite town of Pondicherry) celebrating the Independence of India conjointly with the Assumption of the Virgin. The *arati* was presented at the Eucharist by six small girls dressed and placed so that they embodied the three colours of the Indian national flag (green, white, saffron).

liturgia. The use and the definition of the rite of *arati* are stipulated in items 10 and 12 of the text:[25]

  10.   – The preparatory rite of the Mass may include:
        a. the preparation of gifts
        b. the welcome of the celebrant in an Indian way, e.g. with a single *arati*, washing of hands, etc.
        c. the lighting of the lamp
        d. the greeting of peace among the faithful in sign of mutual reconciliation. ...
  12.   – In the Offertory rite, and at the conclusion of the Anaphora the Indian form of worship may be integrated, that is, double or triple *arati* of flowers, and/or incense, and/or light.

Although the content of the masses organized by Pondicherrians in Île de France corresponds entirely to the formulation in the text on the inculturation of the liturgy, it does not conform to reality, since such masses are not performed in India. If one compares the practices of *arati* authorized by the Episcopal Commission of Liturgy with the way it is performed in the worship (*puca*) of the Hindu divine images, and with how it is used in social functions, it may be noticed that these practices are inspired by both social and religious models. In the context of inculturation, *arati* is performed by young girls to welcome the priest, by the priest to welcome the faithful, and by young girls to welcome the Christ (Eucharist). In the Hindu context, it is performed by the priest to honour the image of the divinity, to protect it from the evil eye and to nourish it, and in the social context, by auspicious women to honour guests, persons of renown, newlyweds, pubescent adolescents, future mothers and so on, and to protect them from the evil eye. The two *arati* of the inculturation appear as original models, closer to the social than the Hindu one, so as to avoid confusion. Nevertheless, Catholic Tamils in India reject the use of *arati* in their masses even though they perform it during all auspicious social functions. This contradiction is certainly borne out by the clear distinction between social and religious realms, which, in turn, is due to a long history of rejection of cultural practices in the mass. Arguments such as the

---

[25]   The text is presented in D.S. Amalorpavadass, *Towards Indigenisation* (Bangalore, 1971), pp. 29–30. The other points of the text concern the posture of the priest and the faithful: sitting on the ground, removal of shoes, chasuble in the form of tunic and stole; gestures: *anjali hasta* (joined hands placed above the face) instead of genuflection, and in place of the kiss of peace, *pancanga* (a position of obedience expressed with five components of the body: arm, knees, head, voice, glance) as a part of the penitential rite, touching the objects with the hands and then bringing the hands to the eye to replace the kissing of objects, and in terms of liturgical objects and substances, more use of incense, an incense bowl in place of a censer, use of a tray instead of the corporal, and the use of oil lamps instead of candles.

following are current: 'If we have become Christian, it is not to practise the same thing that we did when we were Hindu.' In France, it is common to hear criticisms of those Pondicherrian organizers who use Indian rituals in festivals in order to gain power and prestige. Such criticisms were particularly sharp on two occasions: the mass organized at Pontoise in 1998, and the pilgrimage to Lourdes in 1999.

As regards the mass at Pontoise, the debate was over a third performance of the rite of *arati*. This rite, experimented with by the Catechetical Centre of Tintivanan, is performed by the priest to honour the open Bible. Implicitly, it honours the Evangelist who wrote the text chosen for the celebration, and thus it is conceptually close to the *arati* used in *puca*. This rite was performed in Paris on May 1998 at the Velankanni festival mass by a guest priest from Tindivanan in an effort to promote inculturation. The innovation received a chilly welcome from the faithful, but the Community of Pontoise seized the opportunity to integrate this rite into the Velankanni Festival Mass in October 1998. Their alacrity in adopting the rite confirmed the will of this Community to exert their supremacy over the other Pondicherrian Communities, and especially to outdo that of Paris, and to serve as model to all the other Communities.

As regards the official Tamil pilgrimage to Lourdes, the debate concerned the redundancy of cultural gestures used in the celebrations and the appropriateness of the dance performed during the international mass that was celebrated in the huge underground Basilica. The official Tamil pilgrimage to Lourdes was founded in 1989 by the Episcopal Delegate of Migrants of the diocese of Tarbes-Lourdes, who manages it with the help of a young Pondicherrian woman from southern France who was its instigator. For three days, the Pondicherrians celebrate Tamil masses in the prestigious places of the shrine, such as the Grotto and the Basilica, and are principals in one procession, the Marian Procession or Corpus Dei, and in an international mass. Of these events, the international mass is the one in which Indian culture is the most visible: in addition to the rite of *arati* at the time of the serving of the Eucharist, there is a performance of *bharati natam* by a dancer. The Church has become more permissive regarding bodily movements used to express devotion, and now tolerates those that are anchored in social tradition as long as they have no role in any non-Christian religion. The *bharati natam* is now considered as the Indian dance *par excellence*, but it is not forgotten that it was once, and in some parts of India still is, practised by *devadasi*, temple dancers and prostitutes of the priests. That explains the disapproval expressed by Pondicherrians who were present at these ceremonies and were very critical of the attitude of organizers, accusing them of exalting the Tamil identity at all the celebrations, and of using religion to express their domination and supremacy over the community. It often happens that Pondicherrians do not renew their participation in the festival. In spite of their great devotion for Our Lady of Lourdes[26] and the attraction pilgrimage has

---

[26]   Our Lady of Lourdes was promoted in India by the priests of the MEP – a missionary of the diocese of Mysore, a relative of father Peyramale, the priest of Lourdes at the time of Bernadette, imported the first statue – and by French Jesuits, who used to

for them, no more than 250 take part in this annual event. As for the organizers of the Pondicherrian Communities, they are attracted by this pilgrimage because it offers them an opportunity to gain prestige and recognition.[27] In the past, it was the representatives of the Community of Paris who dominated the pilgrimage, and by 1999 it was the Community of Pontoise, and it was difficult to ignore the will of two families, one from Paris and one from Evry-Grigny, to compete with the organizers of Pontoise. The Delegate of Migrants of Tarbes-Lourdes and the young Pondicherrian woman must make considerable use of diplomacy in keeping control of this pilgrimage and maintaining cohesion within the Pondicherrian community.

Conclusion

While the works on inculturation are not applied in India, those on the valorization of the culture of migrants are diverted from their objectives by Pondicherrians. The chaplaincy, created to respond to the spiritual and moral needs of the Tamil community, is frequented only by a small minority of Pondicherrians. The Sri Lankans were evicted by Pondicherrian representatives, and the greater part of the Pondicherrian community prefers to keep away from it in order to avoid the discriminatory attitudes of the organizers. Some Marian festivals (Paris, Pontoise) attract large numbers of Pondicherrians, but their attitudes of avoidance and of distance show that they participate in devotion to the Virgin, and not in order to meet their compatriots. In France, the inculturation features meet with pronounced disapproval, and Pondicherrian opponents of them, belonging to every caste, insist that the church not be used to glorify Tamil identity. They consider that their religious practices must be modelled on those in use in France, respecting as they do the values of equality and fraternity inherent to the Church as well as to the ideology of the French Republic, whereas, to them, Indianization brings in the pernicious values of the Hindu system. So, the members of a 'good caste' who have made the French cultural model their own do not take part in the festivals organized by their community, and prefer to join in the activities of their own parish. The same choice is made by Untouchables, who, benefiting from undeniable advantages in France, do not wish to suffer from caste discrimination.

---

organize processions to eradicate cholera epidemics. In Pondicherrry Territory, the Church of Villenur is an important centre of pilgrimage for this Virgin.

[27]   When I attended this pilgrimage in 1999, only the three Communities of Paris, Pontoise and of Evry-Grigny were present. It should be noted that the Community of Paris was very scantily represented owing to the fact that the person in charge of it, severely criticized for his hegemony, does not come to Lourdes any more. At that time, it was the banner of the Community of Paris which floated in the sky of Lourdes; today, it is that of Pontoise.

It should be stressed that a large part of the community belongs to the lower castes. For Catholic Untouchables, affirming a Christian identity means the rejection of everything that symbolizes Hinduism. Although their behaviours and their habits indicate a strong interiorization of Hindu customs, they condemn the hierarchical model that stigmatizes them and the Hindu rites that were defined in the past as 'superstitions'. It is a manner of priding themselves on belonging to a more advanced, equalitarian and fraternal religion. They have little interest in works on inculturation, which they find too intellectual or too abstract, and moreover, these works are too often inspired by erudite Brahmanical literature or Hindu spiritual movements,[28] since they emanate from a minority of, often higher-caste, priests who are more concerned with integrating the Church into the Hindu landscape than with responding to the needs of the Catholic community. Still perceived as a religion of Western origin, Indian Catholicism must build an 'authentically Indian' identity. Inculturation does not, however, meet with much more enthusiasm from the higher castes, who justify their resistance by the importance of preserving a Catholic identity which reflects the civilizing values specific to the Occident. On this level it may be noticed that, while the promoters of inculturation define themselves as 'modernists' in opposition to others defined as 'traditionalists', the denomination is implicitly reversed in the comments of the opponents. Untouchables describe inculturation features as reminiscent of superstitious gestures, and their use as a return to Hindu 'archaism'.

In allowing the migrants to use their mother tongue within the Catholic realm and by insisting on the importance of maintaining the original cultures, the policy of the Church is in contrast with the ideology of the French Republic, which considers that these cultures tend to accentuate the phenomenon of 'ghettoization'. As far as the Pondicherrians are concerned, the ideology of the church allows the valorization of their Tamil identity, whereas the republican policy, as it was applied in the French territories in India,[29] is to impose the French cultural model. However, the development of a community based on religion has undeniably been of help to the migrants, and more precisely to Pondicherrians, who must face many difficulties arising out of the great cultural gap between their country of origin and France. This development coincides with an awakening of identity due to several factors, notably children not knowing the Tamil language and culture, and the confrontation with Sri Lankans. While Pondicherrians have been considered to

---

[28] For example, see D.S. Amalorpavadass, *Towards Indigenation in the Liturgy*, Mission Theology for Our Times Series no. 6 (Bangalore, no date); E.J. Daly SJ, 'Inculturated Catechisms in India Today', *Word & Worship*, XXVI/1 (1993): 26–31; Wayne Robert Teasdale, *Toward a Christian Vedanta: The Encounter of Hinduism and Christianity According to Bede Griffiths* (Bangalore, 1987); J.A. van Leeuwen and O.F.M. Gerwing, *Fully Indian, Authentically Christian* (Bangalore, 1990), and Felix Wilfred, *Sunset in the East? Asian Challenges and Christians Involvement* (Madras 1991).

[29] See Jacques Weber, *Pondichéry et les comptoirs de l'Inde après Duplex. La démocratie au pays des castes* (Paris, 1996).

be well integrated into French society thanks to their employment in the French administration, their long-standing links with the French as colonizers and their ability to speak French, the arrival of large numbers of Sri Lankans has involved an increase in the visibility of Pondicherrians. They are seen as assimilated to Sri Lankans, and are confronted by increased racist abuse from society. Moreover, they must undergo criticisms from Sri Lankans for their 'corrupted' way of speaking Tamil, their lack of economic dynamism, and their lack of interest in the Tamil culture and language and their inability to transmit it to their children. It is true that today, the use of bilinguism in foreign families is more accepted by school teachers, while just a few decades ago it was considered as an obstacle to learning French. Most of the Pondicherrians born in France before the 1990s speak little or no Tamil, and do not read or write it. This ignorance of the language is considered as a handicap to maintaining bonds with the family and the country. So some Pondicherrians justify the use of the Tamil language and Tamil cultural features in Community festivals as a means of interesting the children in their culture of origin, thereby giving these religious activities an additional function: that of socializing the children through identity awareness.

References

Primary Sources

Ad Gentes Divinitus, 7 December 1965, Decree on the Church's missionary activity, Paul VI.
Documents Episcopat, 6 March 1987, 'Au service de la catholicité de l'Eglise. Les aumôneries ethniques dans la Pastorale des Migrants', pp. 1–12.
Exul Familia Nazarethana, 1 August 1952, Apostolic Constitution, Acta Apostilicae, Pius XII.
Gaudium and Spes, 7 December 1965, Pastoral constitution on the Church in the modern world, Paul VI.
Pacem in Terris, 11 April 1963, Encyclical on Establishing Universal Peace in Truth, Justice, Charity, and Liberty, John XXIII.
Pastoralis migratorum cura, 15 August 1969, Motu proprio, Paul VI.
Sacrosanctum Concilium, 4 December 1963, Constitution on the Sacred Liturgy, Paul VI.

Secondary Sources

Amalorpavadass, D.S., *Towards Indigenation in the Liturgy*, Mission Theology for Our Times Series no. 6 (Bangalore: National Biblical Catechetical and Liturgical Centre, no date).
Amalorpavadass, D.S., *Towards Indigenisation* (Bangalore: National Biblical Catechetical and Liturgical Centre, 1971).

Benoist, Jean, *Hindouismes créoles. Mascareignes, Antilles* (Paris: C.T.H.S, 1998).

Bourdat, Pierre, *Eighteenth-century Pondicherry. Pondichéry XVIIIème* (Pondicherry: Musée de Pondichéry, 1995).

Burghart, R., *Hinduism in Great Britain: The Perpetuation of Religion in an Alien Cultural Milieu* (London: Tavistock, 1987).

Clementin-Ojha, Catherine, 'Indianisation et enracinement: les enjeux de l'"inculturation" de l'Eglise en Inde', *Bulletin de l'EFEO*, 80/1 (1993): 107–33.

Coward, Harold, John R. Hinnells and Raymond Brady Williams, *The South Asian Religious Diaspora in Britain, Canada, and the United States* (Albany, NY: State University of New York Press, 2000).

Daly SJ, E.J., 'Inculturated Catechisms in India Today', *Word & Worship*, XXVI/1 (1993): 26–31.

Fenton, John, Y., *Transplanting Religious Traditions: Asian Indians in America* (New York: Praeger, 1988).

Lee, R.I.M., 'Taipucam in Malaysia: Ecstasy and Identity in a Tamil Hindu Festival', *Contributions to Indian Sociology*, 23/2 (1989): 317–37.

Legrand, Lucien, 'Inculturation. Quelques points de repère bibliques', *Bulletin de documentation des Missions Etrangères*, 279 (1993): 133–41.

Miles, Williams F.S., *Imperial Burdens: Countercolonialism in Former French India* (Boulder, CO: Lynne Rienner, 1995).

Neogy, Ajit K., *Decolonisation of French India: Liberal Movement and Indo-French Relations 1947–1954* (Pondicherry: Institut Français de Pondichéry, 1997).

Piesse, Gabriel, *Pondichéry de 1954 à 1963: de la République française à la République indienne, histoire d'une transition* (Nantes: Université de Nantes, 1999).

Ramachandran, A. (ed.), *Pondicherry through the Ages* (Pondicherry: Pondicherry University, 1997).

Rayaprol, Aparna, *Negotiating Identities: Women in the Indian Diaspora* (Delhi: Oxford University Press, 1997).

Sébastia, Brigitte, *Les Pondichériens de l'Ile de France. Etude des pratiques sociales et religieuses* (Toulouse: Mémoire de DEA, EHESS, Centre d'Anthropologie sociale et ethnologie, 1999).

Sébastia, Brigitte, *Māriyamman–Mariyamman: Catholic Practices and Image of Virgin in Velankanni (Tamil Nadu)*, Pondy Papers in Social Sciences (Pondicherry: French Institute of Pondicherry, 2002).

Teasdale, Wayne Robert, *Toward a Christian Vedanta: The Encounter of Hinduism and Christianity According to Bede Griffiths* (Bangalore: Asian Trading Corporation, 1987).

Tinker, Hugh, *The Banyan Tree: Overseas Emigrants from India, Pakistan, and Bangladesh* (Oxford: Oxford University Press, 1977).

Van Leeuwen, J.A. and O.F.M. Gerwing, *Fully Indian, Authentically Christian* (Bangalore: National Biblical Catechetical and Liturgical Centre, 1990).

Weber, Jacques, *Pondichéry et les comptoirs de l'Inde après Duplex. La démocratie au pays des castes* (Paris: Denoël, 'Destins croisés', 1996).
Wilfred, Felix, *Sunset in the East? Asian Challenges and Christians Involvement* (Madras: St Paul's Seminary, Tiruchirapalli, 1991).

Chapter 3

The Seventieth Anniversary of 'John Matthew': On 'Indian' Christians in Germany

Urmila Goel

In this chapter, the seventieth anniversary of one male migrant from Kerala is taken as a framework to provide some insights into the lives and experiences of 'Indian' Christians in Germany. Christians from Kerala form the largest part of 'Indian' Christians in Germany, as in the 1960s and 1970s young female nurses were recruited there by Catholic institutions. Since then, a 'Malayalee community' has developed in Germany, and the anniversary was one of many meeting points of them.

The chapter uses the tools of social and cultural anthropology to draw a picture of 'Indian' Christians in Germany. Theoretically, it is based on theories of racism and othering. Besides the history of migration to Germany, it describes different strategies of the migrants to deal with experiences of racism and othering there. In doing so, it illustrates not only the perspective of the migrants and their children, but also that of the 'white' Germans, with the help of participant observation at the anniversary. The chapter models from the empirical material a picture which is arbitrary, biased and at the same time typical. It is a tool to gain more insights into the lives of 'Indian' Christians in Germany.

A Church Service in the Community Centre

A summer day in 2006: in the community centre of a small West German town, a mobile altar is set up below the medals and trophies of the local *Schützenverein*.[1] Nuns in their full habit busy themselves in preparing everything for the service. The young priest talks over the details of the service with the daughter of the man whose life it will honour. She knows the community centre well – her parents celebrated their silver wedding here, and she her wedding party. The hall is

---

[1] The *Schützenverein* is a typical association for most of the more rural parts of Germany. Most members of a parish will be active in it. It serves in urban discourses as a symbol of 'Germanness'.

decorated for the occasion of the seventieth anniversary of her father. At long tables, a hundred or so guests will be seated in a few minutes.

The priest begins the service in German. He explains that it will be held according to the Syro-Malabar rites, and describes these a little. He is from India, or more precisely from Kerala, just like the nuns, the man who is celebrating and most of his guests. The priest has been in Germany for a few years. His parishioners are migrants from Kerala, who belong to the Syro-Malabar denomination. There is also a priest for the Orthodox denomination located somewhere else in Germany and several priests from India working for the ('white') Roman Catholic Church. On Sundays and the major Syro-Malabar festivals like Easter and *Onnam* (the harvest festival), the priest offers Syro-Malabar services in Malayalam. These services are well attended: the migrants from Kerala come and bring their children along. Their religion and its performance plays an important part in their lives.

This seventieth anniversary service has been prepared by the priest together with the family of the one to be honoured. While it mainly follows the Syro-Malabar rites, the latter have been careful to introduce German songs and prayers, since among the congregation there are also 'white' Germans and others unfamiliar with Malayalam. Most of those present participate actively in the service, joining in the songs and the prayers. The participation of the 'Indians' in both the German and the Malayalam parts is, however, greater; some 'white' Germans do not seem so comfortable with the unfamiliar rites. The daughter and the son are joined by a 'white' friend in the intercession. I am surprised at the big attendance by 'Indians' and 'white' Germans alike at the communion.

Attending the Celebration as a Participant Observer

During the service, I follow the others in what they are doing. For me, it does not matter whether the service is in Malayalam or in German: I do not know the rites in either. I live in a secular 'white' German environment, and am surprised both by the religiosity of the 'Malayalees', the migrants from Kerala, and the local 'white' Germans. There are otherwise hardly occasions where I meet so many practising Christians. In my field work on migrants from India in Germany and their children, I have already met and interviewed many Christians, but this is the first time I have participated as an observer at one of their services.

My research interests cover the experiences of othering in Germany and their consequences, the establishment and functions of own ethnicized spaces, in particular of the 'second generation', and the history of migration from India to Germany in general. Currently, I am working on the research project 'The Virtual

Second Generation',[2] which analyses how 'Indians of the second generation' use an ethnically defined Internet space to negotiate their ethnic identities.[3] Theoretically, I refer to constructivist approaches of social identities[4] and theories of racism and othering.[5] I question essentialist notions of social identities and communities.[6] A term like 'India' is anything but unambiguous: it refers to an idea of something which is linked to the Republic of India but does not necessarily mean the same. 'Indians' are those who are believed to come from and belong to India. 'White' are those who, in the racist structuring of the modern world, possess 'white' privileges.[7] 'Christians' are those who are believed to be members of a Christian denomination.

I am part of my field of observation, in so far as I am marked as an 'Indian' in the German context because my father migrated from India to Germany. Although he is neither from Kerala nor a Christian, from childhood on I had contact with 'Indian' Christians. They lived in the neighbourhood, they were active together with my father in the Indo-German Society, I met them at seminars and made friends among them. Since 1997, I have also repeatedly done field work among them and have written about them.[8] This seventieth anniversary I attend both as a friend and a researcher.

---

[2]   See Urmila Goel, 'Fatima and theinder.net – A refuge in virtual space', in Angelika Fitz, Merle Kröger, Alexandra Schneider and Dorothee Wenner (eds), *Import Export – Cultural Transfer – India, Germany* (Berlin, 2005), pp. 201–7, as well as Kathleen Heft and Urmila Goel. *Räume der zweiten Generation – Dokumentation eines Workshops* (Frankfurt and der Oder, 2006), available at <http://www.urmila.de/UDG/Biblio/Raeume_der_zweiten_Generation.pdf>.

[3]   More information on my research can be found on my Website, <http://www.urmila.de>.

[4]   See Richard Jenkins, *Social Identity* (London, 1996), and Richard Jenkins, *Rethinking Ethnicity: Arguments and Explorations* (London, 1997).

[5]   Avtar Brah, *Cartographies of Diaspora: Contesting Identities* (London, 1996); Maureen Maisha Eggers, Grada Kilomba, Peggy Piesche and Susan Arndt (eds), *Mythen, Masken, Subjekte – Kritische Weißseinsforschung in Deutschland* (Münster, 2005); Paul Mecheril, *Prekäre Verhältnisse – Über natio-ehtno-kulturelle (Mehrfach-) Zugehörigkeit* (Münster, 2003).

[6]   Fredrik Barth, *Ethnic Groups and Boundaries* (Boston, MA, 1969); Gerd Baumann, *Contesting Culture: Discourses of Identity in Multi-ethnic London* (Cambridge, 1996); Anthony Cohen, *The Symbolic Construction of Community* (London, 1985); Roger Brubaker, *Ethnicity without Groups* (Cambridge, MA, 2004). Compare also Urmila Goel, 'Indians in Germany – The imagination of a community', *UNEAC Asia Papers* no. 20 (2007), available at <http://www.urmila.de/UDG/Forschung/texte/community.html>, accessed 20 July 2008.

[7]   Eggers et al. (eds), *Mythen, Masken, Subjekte.*

[8]   Urmila Goel, *The Malayali Community in Germany: An Analysis of the Magazine Wartha* (MA dissertation, London: SOAS, 1998), available at <http://www.urmila.de/DesisinD/Geschichte/malayali/wartha/warthanindex.html>; Urmila Goel, 'Von

The celebration I describe has taken place, but the representation I make here is my modelling of it.[9] It is neither representative of the 'Indian' Christians in Germany nor is it a unique case. I use it to illustrate aspects of the life of people thus categorized. Writing an ethnography, I use the tools of social and cultural anthropology to approach the topic of 'Indian' Christians in Germany. The one whose birthday is celebrated – let's call him John Matthew – is both unique and typical of the others who have migrated from Kerala to Germany. Like the celebration, I model his life without intending my model to represent his life. I anonymize him as much as possible. Those who discover the 'real' John behind this modelled John should be aware of my distortions of his life, his actions and the celebration.

Taking John's anniversary as the framework for this chapter, I do introduce a gender bias into the analysis. The main migration from Kerala to Germany was female. To be true to this particular migration history, I would thus have to focus on the nurses, their reasons to migrate, their experiences in Germany. John is doubly untypical, as not only is he a male migrant, but he is also one of the few who came on his own. Most others came to Germany as the husbands of nurses who were settled there already. It was by chance that John's anniversary not only took place just at the time I had planned to write this chapter, but that it also offered me such a suitable framework for it, as it illustrates not only the role of religion, but also the interaction with other 'Malayalees' and 'white' Germans. Such a framework could also have been provided by the anniversary of one of the nurses, though it would probably not have been the seventieth, as they are younger. If it had, for example, been the birthday of John's wife, Mercy, that probably would have been very similar, in particular the service could well have taken place as well. The difference, however, is that John has a different position in the 'Malayalee community' than Mercy. He is one of the spokespersons. As in 'white' German society, there are among the 'Malayalees' many more men in such positions than women. There are also female social workers, presidents of associations and journalists, but the men – in my outside perspective – dominate in these functions. Men's voices seem to be heard most; they also speak for the women, just like in this chapter. This is a shortcoming I am aware of, and hope to keep it as small as possible.

Freiheitskämpfern zu Computer-Indern – Südasiaten in Deutschland', *Südasien*, 22/1 (2002): 70–73; Urmila Goel, 'Indische Engel in Deutschland', *Südasien* 22/2 (2002): 61–3; Urmila Goel, 'Ausgrenzung und Zugehörigkeit – Zur Rolle von Staatsbürgerschaft und Einbürgerung', in Christiane Brosius and Urmila Goel (eds), *masala.de – Menschen aus Südasien in Deutschland* (Heidelberg, 2006), pp. 123–60.
9   Mecheril, *Prekäre Verhältnisse*, pp. 32–56.

The Life of John Matthew and the 'Malayalees' in Germany

John's children organized much of his seventieth anniversary. They asked his friends and relatives to contribute short texts on their friendship with John. Out of these and his *curriculum vitae*, they have made an album documenting his life in Germany, which they present to him at the celebration. His daughter – whom I will call Asha – gives a short speech in which she sketches major events in his life and welcomes people related to these such as his and Mercy's witnesses to marriage, his secretary, colleagues and long-standing friends. The local 'white' parish priest, in whose congregation the family is active, is also present, but needs to leave soon after as he has to attend the local parish fair.

John migrated to West Germany in 1966. He is originally from Kerala, studied and worked in Mumbai, and came from there to the West. Like other migrants from South Asia to both Germanies in this period, he came on his own, was well educated, and wanted to know more about the world and improve his standard of living.[10] In contrast to the migrants from more urban and middle-class backgrounds, who came from well-off families, one motivation of John's migration was furthermore to support his family in Kerala financially. Many rural families in Kerala depend on the remittances of migrants to finance the education and marriages of younger siblings. Thus there has been a long history of inter-Indian and international migration among 'Malayalees'.[11] This migration is not predominantly male; many young women go abroad or to other parts of India to be able to support their families. Thus, when in the 1960s the Catholic Church recruited nurses and trainee nurses in Kerala to help meet a shortage of health staff in West Germany, they found many women and their families willing to take the opportunity. At the beginning of my research, this willingness came as a surprise to me. I have experienced much of India as a patriarchal society in which the movement of women is controlled and restricted. That families in such a system agree to an international migration of their teenage daughters seemed a contradiction to me. The explanations I received in my interviews were that on the one hand there had already been a long tradition of female migration, and on the other the Catholic Church as recruiter was seen as a guarantee for the wellbeing of the daughters.

So far, there has been little systematic research on migrants from India to Germany. Reliable statistics about them other than the number of Indian citizens (43,566 in 2003), and an estimate by the Indian Embassy of the number of PIO (Person of Indian Origin) card holders (around 17,500) does not exist. Desai

---

[10]   Compare Urmila Goel, 'Indische Engel in Deutschland 2002', Urmila Goel, 'Ausgrenzung und Zugehörigkeit – Zur Rolle von Staatsbürgerschaft und Einbürgerung', and Urmila Goel, 'Germany', in Brij V. Lal (ed.), *The Encyclopaedia of the Indian Diaspora* (Singapore, 2006), pp. 358–60.

[11]   Compare Prema Kurien, *Kaleidoscopic Ethnicity: International Migration and the Reconstruction of Community Identities in India* (New Brunswick, NJ, 2002).

and Punnamparambil were the first to publish on the topic, but they hardly meet academic standards.[12] The majority of publications have been journalistic rather than academic, or students' theses of varying quality, such as my own early texts.[13] On the migration of several thousands of 'Malayalee' nurses to West Germany, there is even less literature available, and the statistics are even more unreliable. Punnamparambil offers some information,[14] Goel gives a short overview of the migration history,[15] and Fischer and Lakhotia discuss the life of 'Indian' nuns in Germany.[16] In addition to these, there are several magazines for 'Malayalees' published in Germany, such as *Meine Welt*, *Ente Lokam*, *Wartha* and *Rasmi*. All four are edited by migrants from Kerala, the first three by current or former social workers employed by Catholic institutions. The latter are also the publishers of these three magazines. Except *Meine Welt*, all the magazines are written in Malayalam. I have been part of the editorial team of *Meine Welt*, have analysed *Wartha*,[17] have conducted interviews with several social workers, nurses, their husbands and children, as well as attended seminars and festivals as participant observer. This chapter is founded on the observations I have thus made.

When John came to West Germany in 1966, several 'Malayalee' nurses, some of them nuns, lived there already. They had been recruited to work in Catholic hospitals and homes for the elderly. They were sent by their families or convents to send remittances back and return after some years. Some were directly recruited by the church and migrated in small groups, others followed friends or relatives to West Germany. Most of them thus had contact with other 'Malayalees' when they arrived, and the Catholic institutions provided them with some support and ethnic as well as religious infrastructure. This was necessary as when they came, most of the nurses had little knowledge of Germany and German, felt alien in the strange environment, and some were faced with exploitative working conditions. The racism they faced was not so much direct and obviously violent but rather institutional, subtle and exoticizing. So, for example, the nurses were portrayed as ever-smiling 'Indian angels' who were naturally kind and caring, thus reproducing 'white' German stereotypes about 'Asian' women. Most of their names were changed in their pronunciation to fit German articulation. The full

---

[12]   Elisabeth Desai, *Hindus in Deutschland. Documentation 1993 Hindus in Europe/Germany* (Moers, 1993); Jose Punnamparambil, 'Die indische Gemeinschaft in Deutschland', in Berliner Institut für Vergleichende Sozialforschung (ed.), *Handbuch ethnischer Minderheiten in Deutschland* (Berlin, 1995).

[13]   A bibliography can be found at <http://www.urmila.de/DesisinD/Forschung/forschungstart.html>.

[14]   Punnamparambil, 'Die indische Gemeinschaft in Deutschland'.

[15]   Goel, 'Indische Engel in Deutschland'.

[16]   Anjali Fischer and Anita Lakhotia, '"Wo der liebe Gott mich haben will, gehe ich hin" – Indische Ordensschwestern in Deutschland', in Christiane Brosius and Urmila Goel (eds), *masala.de – Menschen aus Südasien in Deutschland* (Heidelberg, 2006), pp. 189–207.

[17]   Goel, *The Malayali Community in Germany*.

force of institutional racism hit when in the late 1970s, unemployment rates in West Germany had risen and there were enough 'white' nurses who wanted to work in the health sector. The authorities, especially in the federal states where conservative parties formed the government, refused to extend the work and residence permits of the 'Indian' nurses. The social workers employed by Caritas or the dioceses supported the nurses in this case as they had done before when there were problems with their employers or in the families. Several memorandums against the refusal of further permits to stay were formulated, and these gained some media coverage but no political success. Only nurses resident in the more liberal states like North Rhine-Westphalia and those married to German citizens could stay. The others had to return to India or migrate further to Canada, the Middle East or elsewhere. Thus a concentration of 'Malayalee' nurses in North Rhine-Westphalia developed. The disregard for the effects of the policies on the individual migrants was clearly illustrated when, twenty years later, there was again a shortage of nurses and some of those who were sent away in the 1970s were re-recruited, this time, however, under the condition that their families were not allowed to join them.

Back in the 1960s, John was one of the few 'Malayalee' men who had come on their own. He had contact with other South Asian migrants, and also with nurses. One of them, Mercy, he fell in love with and married. She had come to Germany through a priest in 1968. They married in Germany, thus depriving their respective families of a big celebration in Kerala. More than twenty-five years later, their daughter Asha tried to make up for this by marrying her 'white' German partner according to all 'Malayalee Christian traditions' in John's home town. For the 'community' and friends in Germany, they organized in the same community centre a wedding party afterwards. Asha was one of the first of the 'second generation' to get married, and she was still breaking a taboo by not marrying a suitable boy from the same 'community'. In the 1960s and 1970s, the taboo was even greater, and only few of the nurses married 'white' Germans or other 'Indians' living in West Germany. Those who took this step risked being othered by the other 'Malayalees'. Thus it seems that in the 1970s, most nurses had an arranged marriage in Kerala.

By this time, they were attractive spouses on the marriage market, as they were settled abroad with a good income. Their husbands were accordingly mainly graduates. Through the marriage, they gained the right of residence as spouses in West Germany. For the first few years, however, they were not eligible for a work permit. They were thus forced to stay at home while their wives earned the money, and were more familiar than them with the country of residence and its language. Few of the men used this forced pause from employment to improve their qualifications; most looked after the household and the children who were soon born. This forced change in gender roles was experienced by many as a degradation. In extreme cases, it led to alcoholism and domestic violence. A refuge from the enforced social isolation, and also something the nurses longed for, was to found a number of sports, religious and cultural associations. Both the nurses and their husbands participated in these associations, creating a space of their own where they were the norm and could exchange experiences without much need of explanation.[18] Here they could remember their 'home' Kerala and feel at home. Thus the 'Malayalee' infrastructure in West Germany was developed further, mostly with men as spokespersons. The nurses also engaged themselves in 'white' German congregations, went to local services, took their families along, and worked there as volunteers. Once the children were old enough, Malayalam schools and dance classes were installed to preserve the 'Indian culture' among them. They were taken along to the 'Indian' masses and introduced to 'Indian Christianity'. Many, however, experienced this as an ordeal, as they understood little of the Malayalam and the rites. When the husbands were finally eligible for a work permit, they had been out of work for several years, and since their Indian qualifications were not recognized in West Germany, they had to enter the labour market in the less qualified sector. In many cases, they joined the same hospitals as their wives, but mostly in less qualified positions. The nurses in the mean time progressed in their careers as far as the health system with its social hierarchies and inherent racist structures would allow them.

John did not experience the degradation in the economic field as much as the husbands who joined their wives. He was able to work until his retirement in positions related to his Indian qualifications. Once he tried to re-emigrate to India with his family, but after working a year in Northern India, he decided to go back to West Germany. Other families resettled in India, sometimes one spouse stayed in West Germany to earn and the other went back. Yet others migrated further to Canada or the Middle East. Back in Germany, John, like most of the other migrants, was engaged in voluntary work for the 'community'. His motto in this was (like that of many others as well as the Catholic institutions): 'integration into German society and preservation of my own culture'.

An Academic Intervention: Information, Irony and Assimilation

In his effort to both improve integration into the 'white' German society and preserve the 'Indian culture', John is active in the 'community', acts as an adviser to other 'Malayalees', writes articles, gives presentations and networks a great deal. In the course of this, he heard about the work of the psychologist and researcher in educational science Paul Mecheril, and grew interested in it. John's special wish for his seventieth anniversary was that Mecheril would give a presentation.

Paul Mecheril's parents are, like John, migrants from Kerala. Being born in the 1960s, he is one of the oldest members of the 'second generation', to use this form of labelling for the children of the migrants. He was thus also one of the first to enter a professional career, and is by now a senior university researcher. His research interests are in particular the analysis of concepts of 'national' belongingness, the situation of the 'second generation', inter-cultural processes in education as well

---

[18]   Compare Goel, 'Fatima and theinder.net'.

as methodological questions in the analysis of social differences.[19] His research is highly complex, and not the usual fare at a seventieth anniversary. Mecheril thus articulates the impossibility of his task at the beginning of his presentation.

When I now summarize his speech, I will describe his main points, refer occasionally to his published work and illustrate his arguments with my own empirical material. Thus, like the whole celebration, Mecheril's presentation will also be modelled in the following, and thus reinterpreted for the purpose of this chapter. The fact that Mecheril was the guest speaker at this occasion was a lucky coincidence for me, as much of my analytical work is based on his theories.

As Mecheril does not know John personally, he approaches him through one of his texts and starts the speech with an analysis of an excerpt. In this, John describes himself as 'I am a Third World man', and then goes on to assert, 'Otherwise I am a totally developed man'. Mecheril interprets this as an account of a 'black' academic who comes to Germany, is no longer recognized as an academic, and instead is reduced to being 'black' in the eye of the 'white' Germans. In analysing the text, Mecheril discovers three strategies to deal with this degradation: firstly, provide information to the 'white' Germans; secondly, use irony to deal with the degradation, and thirdly, assimilate as much as possible.

The attempt to provide information assumes that the experiences of othering and racism are founded in a lack of knowledge on the side of 'white' German society. This strategy presumes that discrimination will diminish with reduced ignorance. John, like many others, has pursued it all his migrant life. Many of the associations which have been formed aim at the provision of 'correct' information to 'white' German society as well. But John not only pursues this path, in his text he also uses irony to deal with the degradation faced. He describes, for example, how his front garden is even tidier than that of his 'white' neighbours and still he is considered an 'underdeveloped' man. Mecheril argues that irony is a perfect tool for those who are considered migrants. It allows them to bring together inconsistencies and ambivalences in their daily lives, to deal with the paradox of their lives which is created through ascription and discrimination.[20] In my field research, especially when analysing the Internet portal <http://www.theinder. net>,[21] I have also come across several instances of irony used to cope with and express experiences of othering. Mecheril adds that there are also other means to

---

[19]   Important publications are Paul Mecheril and Thomas Teo (eds), *Andere Deutsche. Zur Lebenssituation von Menschen multiethnischer und multikultureller Herkunft* (Berlin, 1994), and Paul Mecheril and Thomas Teo (eds), *Psychologie und Rassismus* (Hamburg, 1997), as well as Paul Mecheril, *Deutsche Geschichten* (Münster, 1996), Paul Mecheril, *Prekäre Verhältnisse*, and Paul Mecheril, *Einführung in die Migrationspädagogik* (Weinheim, 2004).

[20]   Compare ibid., pp. 127–32.

[21]   Goel, 'Fatima and theinder.net'.

deal with the inconsistencies,[22] and in the extreme cases these can be alcoholism and aggression. As was discussed above, several 'Malayalee' men have taken this path when they could not cope in a more productive way with their lives in Germany. Mecheril then focuses in his analysis on the tendency of self-assimilation, on the attempt to become more 'German' than the 'white' Germans. Part of this is to keep the front garden even tidier than the neighbours, another is to teach the children to be everything but 'uncultivated', to behave differently than a 'foreigner' or 'guest worker' – that is, not to fulfil the stereotypes of 'white' Germans. To this strategy, one could also add the tacit acceptance of the 'Germanization' of 'Indian' names which many nurses were given, or the generally displayed pressure on the 'second generation' to perform well in education. However, this process conflicts, as Mecheril illustrates, with the aim of conserving 'Indian culture', which is one of John's aims as it is of other 'Malayalees'. How can one self-assimilate and conserve one's own culture at the same time? And how are members of the 'second generation' supposed to do so?

Underlying these strategies is the prevalent belief that 'Everyone is the architect of his or her own fortune', as Mecheril argues. It is the belief that one can oneself counter the experiences of racism and othering, that these are results of ignorance, and not of power asymmetries. Mecheril, however, despite the festive occasion, questions this belief. He argues that there are structural differences in the German society, such as those due to racism, which restrict the scope of the individual's agency.[23] He argues that accordingly, self-assimilation cannot be successful. However much the 'Malayalees' try to blend in, they will never be accepted as 'Germans', they will always stay the other. Mecheril thus finishes his presentation by quoting another text of John's in which the latter maintains: 'My world is the world between Germany and India.' Mecheril follows this idea, and suggests that this space in between should be inhabited and developed. He argues that the unquestioned belongingness to one 'national' context has been lost in the course of migration, and that one has to deal with this.[24]

The Neighbours Take the Stage

After this unlikely presentation at a birthday gathering, the programme resumes 'normality'. Not only do the 'Malayalee' family and friends of John present something, but also his 'white' neighbours. A group of 11 takes the stage, and honour with music and rhymes their long-standing friendship with John. He was

---

[22]   See Paul Mecheril, 'Die Lebenssituation Anderer Deutscher. Eine Annäherung in dreizehn thematischen Schritten', in Paul Mecheril and Thomas Teo (eds), *Andere Deutsche. Zur Lebenssituation von Menschen multiethnischer und multikultureller Herkunft* (Berlin, 1994), pp. 57–94.

[23]   Mecheril, *Prekäre Verhältnisse*.

[24]   Ibid.

one of the first 'Malayalees' not only to build a big representative house in Kerala, but also to buy one in West Germany, thus documenting his decision to settle down – a step few other 'Malayalees' managed to take so early. Until the 1990s, most believed in the 'myth of return', used their savings to build houses in Kerala, and lived in flats in Germany. John, in contrast, has been living in his own house since 1982. The neighbours and John's family got to know each other through their children, and have celebrated many parties together. The neighbours even travelled to Kerala in order to attend the marriage of John's daughter Asha several years back. She married her 'white' German partner in a church in Kerala, organizing a joint service between a Catholic and a Protestant priest. Already at this occasion the neighbours from Germany had given a presentation in honour of the occasion. At John's anniversary, they tell the story of their friendship, as musical background they use a Gospel song, and also in their story they repeatedly refer to their common religion. While they are performing, I remember that they have also participated actively in the service before. Christianity seems to be one of the common reference points of John's family and the neighbourhood. Even if the language, food and rites are different, the religion to some extent makes the 'Malayalees' less 'alien' than other migrants. This distinguishes the experiences of the 'Malayalee' migrants from those of others perceived to follow a different religion. Nijhawan, for example, shows how Sikhs face marginalization and racism in Germany on the basis of their religious affiliation.[25]

When Asha announces the neighbours' presentation, she mentions their irritation with Mecheril's speech. They have told her that if everything he had said was true, then this was really bad. But they are sure that in their neighbourhood such problems have never existed, and describe it as an oasis. John later in the programme will say that one should discuss what Mecheril has said; one should not talk about it as true or false, but rather as a description of reality. He adds that the neighbourhood is very special, that for twenty-four years they have had a great life together. This denial of the existence of racism and othering by the 'white' neighbours as well as the attempts to appease their irritation by the migrants is typical for the German context. Racism as a structuring element of the society is generally denied.[26] There is a general belief that German society is homogenously 'white' and that 'migrants' are 'foreigners' or 'strangers', who are different. Those who are constructed as the other are demanded to 'integrate' and to adapt to the imagined German norms. 'White' Germans, on the other hand, are not considered to have a part in the construction of the 'strangers'. In cases where the 'strange' is connoted with 'positive' ascriptions, such as caring nurses, exotic India or nice neighbours, the inherent racist structures of constructing the other and the

---

[25] Michael Nijhawan, 'Bin Laden in der U-Bahn und andere Verkennungen: Beobachtungen in der Sikh Diaspora', in Christiane Brosius and Urmila Goel (eds), *masala. de – Menschen aus Südasien in Deutschland* (Heidelberg, 2006), pp. 98–122.

[26] Eggers et al. (eds), *Mythen, Masken, Subjekte*.

declaration of 'white' Germans as the norm are even less recognizable for the majority of 'white' German society.[27]

While it was apparent to me that there exists a long-standing friendship between the neighbours and John's family, not only their denial of racism irritated me. When they spoke of him, they never used his given name, John, but rather spoke of Jon, a 'Germanized' version of John which links better to their local dialect. It did not seem to disturb them that everybody else at the anniversary called him 'John'; for them he is 'Jon', like his daughter has always been 'Asa' rather than Asha. She told me that her parents had never objected to this 'wrong' pronunciation of their names. This might be understood as an attempt at self-assimilation, of blending in, of accepting the rules of the 'host' society. On the part of the 'white' Germans, this renaming, which many nurses also experienced in hospitals, can be understood as a disregard for the migrants and their children. Even their names have to be adapted to 'white' German norms; 'white' Germans cannot be expected to learn the 'Indian' pronunciation of these names. While John never complained, Asha at some stage started to assert her name in the 'Indian' pronunciation. She told her neighbours and friends that her name is actually Asha, and not 'Asa'. Some have accepted that, others were unable to change the pronunciation they had got used to, and not all understood her motivation.

The Performance of the 'Second Generation'

As Mecheril has argued, the attempt to self-assimilate in order to be accepted as German and to preserve the 'Indian culture' in order to stay 'Indian' necessarily leads to conflicts. Migrants struggle with this dual task and its impossibility. They experience daily that they are not accepted as equals by the 'white' German society, at the same time as they fear losing their 'Indian culture and values'. Being not able to succeed themselves, they pin their hopes on their children. The 'second generation' is given the task of both achieving a high social and economic status in German society while at the same time remaining 'Indian'. In all the associations and magazines, at all events a special attention is placed on the 'second generation'. In magazines like *Wartha*, there are always several success stories about members of the 'second generation'. In these, the achievement of something (no matter what) outstanding takes centre stage. Thus not only successes in 'Indian' dancing and singing are honoured, but also achievements in academics, politics, German entertainment and even being chosen as a model for a charity poster depicting a starving child.[28] The two members of the German Parliament, Sebastian Edathy and Josef Winkler, who both have a parent from Kerala are claimed as part of the 'community' even if they have never really participated in it and their parents

---

[27] And are also denied by many migrants; compare Goel, 'Ausgrenzung und Zugehörigkeit'.

[28] Goel, *The Malayali Community in Germany*.

lived isolated from other 'Malayalees'. In the case of the anniversary, this status of pride in the 'second generation' seems to be transferred to Paul Mecheril. In the breaks, several 'Malayalees' approach him and ask him whether he remembers them, claiming him to be one of them.

As usual at gatherings of 'Indians' in Germany, the 'second' and in this case also the 'third generation' are given the stage. There are two professional dancers of the 'second generation' who perform adaptations of Bollywood choreographies. A ten-year-old girl sings very professionally in Hindi, and Asha's five-year old son sings a German birthday song. It is Asha's function to announce these contributions, and she takes on the role of entertainer, small-talking with the performers. She tells the dancer, 'I knew you already when you were so small,' and adds that this is exactly the same thing she was always told. Then she goes on to ask whether the dancers are dancing voluntarily or whether there was parental pressure to take up dance lessons. Asha thus refers to the fact that a high proportion of the 'second generation' has been pressured to study dance or some other 'Indian' form of arts, and the question remains open whether the children really wanted to perform or were forced to do so. The dancer answers vaguely that she 'dances more or less voluntarily'. Similarly, Asha asks the young singer whether she knows Malayalam, whether she can read and write it. This is also one of the symbols of preserving 'Indianness' among the 'Malayalees'. Other symbols would be going to 'Indian' mass and marrying an 'Indian' spouse. Asha, in guiding the programme, takes the wishes and worries of the migrants seriously, and at the same time shows their ambivalences, making her contributions slightly more ironic.

In fact, the 'second generation' at this celebration (as at most other events) performs according to their parents' wishes, contributing to the imagination of being able to 'integrate' successfully and conserve 'Indianness' at the same time. The members of the 'second generation' also perform on their own terms, according to their own needs and interests. Asha and her brother have prepared much of the celebration, they guide through the programme and shape it. They have organized the programme, and their voices are heard most of the time. It is not only on this occasion that the 'second generation' is doing this. For several years they have no longer just accompanied their parents to events, they have organized them themselves and created their own spaces such as parties, seminars, youth groups and Internet portals.[29] Here, they develop what Mecheril has called the 'space in between'. The way they do it, the strategies they follow in it, are as diverse as they are themselves. Many of them see, like their parents, the need to provide the 'correct' information to the 'white' Germans, other pursue paths of self-assimilation, yet others emphasize difference, many want to preserve 'Indianness',

---

[29]   Urmila Goel, 'Indische Wurzeln – Deutsche Heimat', *Festschrift zum 50-jährigen Bestehen der Deutsch-Indischen Gesellschaft 1953–2003* (Stuttgart, 2003), pp. 83–6; Goel, 'Fatima and theinder.net'; Heft and Goel, *Räume der zweiten Generation*.

and irony is often used. But even if the strategies are similar to those of the parents, the contents are different, shaped to fit the needs of the 'second generation'.[30]

The paths they pursue are influenced through the framework provided by 'white' German society and their 'Indian' parents. They have to react to experiences of racism and othering, have to deal with the given structures. At the same time, they have to deal with the 'values' and norms taught by their parents. Among these, for most the Christian religion plays a major role. For them, from their German perspective, India and Kerala are synonymous. They use the terms interchangeably. 'Kerala' furthermore, is defined for them through Christianity; many have no idea that in this Indian state, people follow many different religions. There seems to be hardly any interaction in Germany with the few Hindu and Muslim 'Malayalees'. Most members of the 'second generation' go to 'Indian' masses regularly in Germany. Many are active in either the 'Indian' or the 'white' German parishes as altar servers and volunteers (see special issue of *Meine Welt*, 22/2, 2005, esp. pp. 3–9). Being Christians links them on the one hand to the ideal-type German, and on the other it distinguishes them, as their rites and teachings differ from those of 'white' German Christians.

Celebrating Together

During the programme, John repeatedly wants to speak, but Asha always asks him to wait till later. His speech is then the last part of the programme, the climax. He very emotionally thanks all the contributors, his family and the guests, and then takes them along on a journey back to his arrival in West Germany in 1966. He sings a love song for his wife, and asks his son to recite his favourite poem. At the end of his speech, he then does something he has done hundreds of times before: he starts singing a Malayalam song, and asks the others to join in. For those unfamiliar with the song, the text has been distributed with a German translation. Most of the 'Malayalees' and also several other guests join in the refrain; the song gets ever faster, the singers are in high spirits and clap along.

John and his friends have often sat together and sung this song. They share several decades of friendship. The 'Malayalees' in Germany have gone to church together, played sports together, played in theatres, met at seminars like the annual *Kerala Mela* and have celebrated together in private. They have developed their own ethnic and religious infrastructure in order to have their own spaces, where they are the norm, where they do not feel alien. Their sense of 'community' is great, even if most live predominantly in a 'white' German environment. The anniversary gathering could have been larger, if there had not been on the same evening a wedding and a silver wedding celebration to which many of the guests had also been invited. So some have not come at all, others leave earlier or come later. Some guests have travelled from far away, others have busied themselves

---

[30]   Goel, 'Fatima and theinder.net'.

in the days before helping John's wife Mercy to prepare the buffet. The 'Indian' food has to be home cooked and plentiful. The migrants and the 'white' guests relish it. Several of the 'second generation' prefer the 'non-Indian' food which is also available. After the program has ended, close friends stay on to talk, sing and laugh together. It is their space they have created here.

Impressions from the Seventieth Anniversary

The seventieth anniversary of John Matthew is a singular event. By the coincidence of its taking place just at the moment I needed to write this chapter, I have taken it as a framework. I could also have taken another celebration, the meeting of some association or an interview with a nurse. All these would have been as singular as the anniversary, and at the same time they would have been as typical. Instead of taking a member of the Syro-Malabar denomination, I might have taken one of the Orthodox or of yet another of the numerous 'Indian' Christian denominations present in Germany. Although the 'Malayalees' form the largest homogenous group in terms of origin, language and religion among 'Indian' migrants in Germany, they are anything but homogenous. While their origin in Kerala, the language Malayalam, the Christian religion and the occupation as nurses unites them, otherwise they are very diverse, with many splits and opposing factions. Taking another event as a framework might have provided for the analysis a different gathering, different rites and to some extent different people. Most certainly there would not have been a presentation by Mecheril, but there could very well have been participation by one of the members of the German Parliament. If I had taken a different approach and focused on an interview with a nurse, I could have focused more on the individual experiences of a female migrant. But in all approaches I would have come across experiences of othering and racism in Germany, even if most of the time they would have been narrated primarily implicitly. In this respect, John's anniversary, in its singularity, is typical.

To bring this chapter to a close, I want to refer back to Mecheril's analysis. As strategies to cope with the othering experienced in the course of migration, he identified: firstly, the attempt to provide information about the migrants to the 'white' Germans in order to cure misconceptions; secondly, to use irony in dealing with the prevalent ambivalences, and thirdly, to attempt to become more German than the 'white' Germans. He furthermore argued that the first and the third strategies, which are founded on the belief that the individual can counter the processes of othering, are bound to fail. German society, like most others, is structured on the basis of social differences constructed by ideologies such as racism and heteronormativity. These cannot be changed individually. 'Black' migrants will always stay the 'other' no matter how much they inform about their ascribed 'culture' and 'background', no matter how much they attempt to blend in. Female nurses will be confronted with gender stereotypes inter-linked with racist beliefs. Thus, even though they were the primary migrants who succeeded in the German society, they will be considered as victims of the system and their husbands rather than as agents in their own right. Members of the 'second generation' will have to deal with the double othering experienced through the 'German' society and their parents.[31] They will have to deal with the norms of the heteronormative society, reacting to expectations by 'white' Germans and their parents about their sexual relationships,[32] to name just a few consequences of the structuring of societies on the basis of social differences.

One refuge from these experiences is the one suggested by Mecheril – to inhabit and shape a space in between, a space which does not require unambiguous 'national' belongingness, which takes account of ambivalences and inconsistencies. Even if this might not have been done consciously, one can identify several own spaces which have been created by the migrants and their children. In these spaces, they can escape from othering for some time; here they are the norm; here they can exchange experiences with others having similar experiences to them.[33] These own spaces can be temporary events like this anniversary or parties, or permanent ones such as associations or Internet portals. The strategies negotiated in these spaces will be as diverse as the people are. Christianity is one important part in the self-definition. The experiences of othering and racism are the results of their categorizations as 'blacks' in Germany.

References

Barth, Fredrik, *Ethnic Groups and Boundaries* (Boston, MA: Little, Brown, 1969).

Baumann, Gerd, *Contesting Culture: Discourses of Identity in Multi-ethnic London* (Cambridge: Cambridge University Press, 1996).

Brah, Avtar, *Cartographies of Diaspora: Contesting Identities* (London: Routledge, 1996).

Brosius, Christiane and Urmila Goel (eds), *masala.de – Menschen aus Südasien in Deutschland* (Heidelberg: Draupadi Verlag, 2006).

Brubaker, Roger, *Ethnicity without Groups* (Cambridge, MA: Harvard University Press, 2004).

Cohen, Anthony, *The Symbolic Construction of Community.* (London: Routledge,1985).

Desai, Elisabeth, *Hindus in Deutschland. Documentation 1993: Hindus in Europe/ Germany* (Moers: edition aragon, 1993).

---

[31]   Mecheril, *Prekäre Verhältnisse*; Goel, 'Fatima and theinder.net'.

[32]   Goel, Urmila, '"Kinder statt Inder" – Normen, Grenzen und das Indernet', in Thomas Geisen and Christiane Riegel (eds), *Jugend, Zugehörigkeit und Migration* (Wiesbaden, 2007), pp. 163–81.

[33]   Goel, 'Fatima and theinder.net'; Heft and Goel, *Räume der zweiten Generation*.

Eggers, Maureen Maisha, Grada Kilomba, Peggy Piesche and Susan Arndt (eds), *Mythen, Masken, Subjekte – Kritische Weißseinsforschung in Deutschland* (Münster: Unrast, 2005).

Fischer, Anjali and Anita Lakhotia, '"Wo der liebe Gott mich haben will, gehe ich hin" – Indische Ordensschwestern in Deutschland', in Christiane Brosius and Urmila Goel (eds), *masala.de – Menschen aus Südasien in Deutschland* (Heidelberg: Draupadi Verlag, 2006), pp. 189–207.

Goel, Urmila, *The Malayali Community in Germany: An Analysis of the Magazine* Wartha (MA dissertation, London: SOAS, 1998), available at <http://www.urmila.de/DesisinD/Geschichte/malayali/wartha/warthanindex.html>.

Goel, Urmila, 'Von Freiheitskämpfern zu Computer-Indern – Südasiaten in Deutschland', *Südasien*, 22/1 (2002): 70–73.

Goel, Urmila, 'Indische Engel in Deutschland', *Südasien*, 22/2 (2002): 61–3.

Goel, Urmila, 'Indische Wurzeln – Deutsche Heimat', *Festschrift zum 50-jährigen Bestehen der Deutsch-Indischen Gesellschaft 1953–2003* (Stuttgart: DIG, 2003), pp. 83–6.

Goel, Urmila, 'Fatima and theinder.net – A refuge in virtual space', in Angelika Fitz, Merle Kröger, Alexandra Schneider and Dorothee Wenner (eds), *Import Export – Cultural Transfer – India, Germany* (Berlin: Parhas Verlag, 2005), pp. 201–7.

Goel, Urmila, 'Ausgrenzung und Zugehörigkeit – Zur Rolle von Staatsbürgerschaft und Einbürgerung', in Christiane Brosius and Urmila Goel (eds), *masala.de – Menschen aus Südasien in Deutschland* (Heidelberg: Draupadi Verlag, 2006), pp. 123–60.

Goel, Urmila, 'Germany', in Brij V. Lal (ed.), *The Encyclopaedia of the Indian Diaspora* (Singapore: Editions Didier Millet, 2006), pp. 358–60.

Goel, Urmila, 'Indians in Germany – The imagination of a community', *UNEAC Asia Papers* no. 20 (2007), available at <http://www.urmila.de/UDG/Forschung/texte/community.html>, accessed 20 July 2008.

Goel, Urmila, '"Kinder statt Inder" – Normen, Grenzen und das Indernet', in Thomas Geisen and Christiane Riegel (eds), *Jugend, Zugehörigkeit und Migration* (Wiesbaden: VS Verlag, 2007), pp. 163–81.

Heft, Kathleen and Urmila Goel, *Räume der zweiten Generation – Dokumentation eines Workshops* (2006), available at <http://www.urmila.de/UDG/Biblio/Raeume_der_zweiten_Generation.pdf>, accessed 20 July 2008.

Jenkins, Richard, *Social Identity* (London: Routledge, 1996).

Jenkins, Richard, *Rethinking Ethnicity: Arguments and Explorations* (London: Sage, 1997).

Kurien, Prema, *Kaleidoscopic Ethnicity: International Migration and the Reconstruction of Community Identities in India* (New Brunswick, NJ: Rutgers University Press, 2002).

Mecheril, Paul, 'Die Lebenssituation Anderer Deutscher. Eine Annäherung in dreizehn thematischen Schritten', in Paul Mecheril and Thomas Teo (eds),

Andere Deutsche. Zur Lebenssituation von Menschen multiethnischer und multikultureller Herkunft (Berlin: Dietz, 1994), pp. 57–94.

Mecheril, Paul, *Deutsche Geschichten* (Münster: Waxmann, 1996).

Mecheril, Paul, *Prekäre Verhältnisse – Über natio-ehtno-kulturelle (Mehrfach-) Zugehörigkeit* (Münster: Waxmann, 2003).

Mecheril, Paul, *Einführung in die Migrationspädagogik* (Weinheim: Beltz Verlag, 2004).

Mecheril, Paul and Thomas Teo (eds), *Andere Deutsche. Zur Lebenssituation von Menschen multiethnischer und multikultureller Herkunft* (Berlin: Dietz, 1994).

Mecheril, Paul and Thomas Teo (eds), *Psychologie und Rassismus* (Hamburg: Rororo, 1997).

Nijhawan, Michael, 'Bin Laden in der U-Bahn und andere Verkennungen: Beobachtungen in der Sikh Diaspora', in Christiane Brosius and Urmila Goel (eds), *masala.de – Menschen aus Südasien in Deutschland* (Heidelberg: Draupadi Verlag, 2006), pp. 98–22.

Punnamparambil, Jose, 'Die indische Gemeinschaft in Deutschland', in Berliner Institut für Vergleichende Sozialforschung (ed.), *Handbuch ethnischer Minderheiten in Deutschland* (Berlin: BVIS, 1995).

Chapter 4

Seeking the Blessing of the *Consolatrix Afflictorum*: The Annual Pilgrimage of Sri Lankan Tamils to the Madonna in Kevelaer (Germany)

Brigitte Luchesi

Since 1987, Tamil refugees from Sri Lanka have been meeting in Kevelaer once a year. Kevelaer, a town in the western part of Germany near the Dutch border, is an important Marian pilgrimage site, deriving its fame from the miraculous picture of the Madonna, known as *Consolatrix Afflictorum* ('Comforter of the Afflicted'). The annual visit of Tamils, popularly referred to as 'the Tamil pilgrimage', will be described here. The focus will be on aspects distinguishing this event from pilgrimages of other groups, and on the importance given to it by the participants themselves. Special attention is paid to the fact that not only Roman Catholics take part in the *Tamilenwallfahrt* ('Tamil Pilgrimage'), but a significant number of Hindus as well.

Prelude

Saturday 12 August 2006, 8.05 a.m., Düsseldorf main station. The regional train to Kleve, close to the Dutch border, is about to depart. A group of dark-skinned people hurry along the platform glancing doubtfully at the sign boards. The conductor, whistle in hand, calls out: 'Kleve', and 'Yes, Kevelaer.' Out of breath, the people jump on – several men and women, two of them with prams, and a number of boys and girls – and spread out on the seats, calling to each other in a language unfamiliar to the average German passenger. All of them are well dressed, especially the females. The women wear elegant saris, finished off with shining golden ornaments around their necks and wrists and in their ears; their long, dark, shining hair is either braided and adorned with colourful hairclips and flowers or freely flows down their backs. Some of the girls are in their Sunday best: frilly dresses with petticoats. Boys and men wear freshly pressed trousers, combined with matching shirts and jackets. At the next stop, more festively dressed dark-skinned passengers enter, and this is repeated at each of the stops during the one-hour train ride. The air is filled with the sounds of the foreign language; only occasionally do the young ones exchange a sentence or two in German before switching again to the language of the adults. At Kevelaer, the compartment suddenly empties, and the people spill out onto the narrow platform and immediately move towards the town centre.

By now, fellow passengers will have realized that these are Tamils on their way to their annual gathering at the shrine of the Kevelaer Madonna, and that it is the day of the so-called *Tamilenwallfahrt*. Following them through the narrow streets of the town, one can see other groups of Tamils appearing from side lanes or waiting at certain points. The moment one reaches the main street which directly leads to the city's central square with the important pilgrimage buildings, one is totally surrounded by Tamils. They are all heading for this square, where a long line has already formed, winding up towards a small building in its centre, the so-called Gnadenkapelle ('Chapel of Mercy'). This chapel houses the miraculous picture of Mary which brought fame to Kevelaer. Men, women and children are patiently waiting for their turn to step in the front of this picture, which – protected by a double sheet of glass – can be looked at from a very close distance. Many just fold their hands, gazing intently at the small copperplate print, some kiss the outer glass sheet, and others touch it with both hands, which they then bring to their breast or forehead. Children are lifted up to be at eye level with the picture, and they are often touched by their mother with the hand she has brought into contact with the glass.

Coming close to the renowned picture – in direct sight of the depicted Madonna – and offering short individual prayers are among the most important acts for many of this day's visitors. I will return to the various events below, after some general information on Sri Lankan people in Germany.

Tamils in Germany

The Tamil visitors to Kevelaer are Tamils from Sri Lanka. They belong to the approximately 60,000 Sri Lankan Tamils living in Germany at present.[1] Most of them came as refugees from the early 1980s onwards, fleeing the escalating civil war in their homeland. In the beginning it was mainly young men, but in the course of time their wives and children as well as older family members were able to join them.

The asylum seekers were distributed all over Germany by the German authorities in order to prevent clustering in certain areas and cities. Nevertheless, most probably because local jurisdiction was less rigid than in other German states, about 45 per cent of all immigrants are concentrated in North Rhine-Westphalia,

---

[1]   Martin Baumann, 'Von Sri Lanka in die Bundesrepublik: Flucht, Aufnahme und kulturelle Rekonstruktionen', in Martin Baumann, Brigitte Luchesi and Annette Wilke (eds), *Tempel und Tamilen in zweiter Heimat. Hindus aus Sri Lanka im deutschsprachigen und skandinavischen Raum* (Würzburg: Ergon Press, 2003), pp. 41–73, see p. 42.

one of the westernmost German states. The majority of the Tamil immigrants living in Germany are estimated to be Hindus – about four-fifths, or 46,000–48,000. The remaining roughly 12,000 persons are said to be Christians. According to Martin Baumann,[2] 15.8 per cent of the Tamils have declared themselves to be Catholics, and 4.1 per cent Protestants of various denominations. This means that not more than 9,500 are Catholics; this number comes as a surprise to many Germans, who still think that the majority of Tamils are Christians – a mistaken view which also seems to have been prevalent in other European countries.[3]

One of the most characteristic features of the *Hindu* Tamil immigrants in Germany is the way they have coped with the fact that there were virtually no public religious institutions for Hindus in their host country when they arrived. In the beginning, they had to be content with private domestic shrines. Within a very short time, however, they created opportunities to practise their faith outside their homes, too. They set up prayer halls and temples in converted basements and industrial sites, and even started to construct new buildings. By 2002, 25 prayer halls and temples (*alayam*) run by Tamils from Sri Lanka could be found, a quite astonishing fact if one looks at the comparatively few religious institutions of other Hindu groups in Germany.[4] The establishment of these temples has also brought about the celebration of yearly temple festivals and other major religious events, which in turn have called for special festival activities in the South Asian tradition. The most important ones are public processions, which since the early 1990s have been increasingly organized by a number of temples. The first to do so was the Sri Kamadchi Ampal Temple in Hamm-Uentrop in North Rhine-Westphalia; it is still the favoured place for those Tamils who wish to fulfil special vows or perform ascetic practices on the auspicious occasion of the annual festival.[5]

---

[2]   Ibid., p. 61, fn. 25. See also Martin Baumann and Kurt Salentin, 'Migrant Religiousness and Social Incorporation: Tamil Hindus from Sri Lanka in Germany', *Journal of Contemporary Religion*, 21/3 (October 2006): 307.

[3]   For Norway, see Knut A. Jacobsen, 'Settling in Cold Climate: The Tamil Hindus in Norway', in Martin Baumann, Brigitte Luchesi and Annette Wilke (eds), *Tempel und Tamilen in zweiter Heimat. Hindus aus Sri Lanka im deutschsprachigen und skandinavischen Raum* (Würzburg: Ergon Press, 2003), pp. 363–77.

[4]   Other Hindus with South Asian origins are those from India and Afghanistan; their estimated number lies between 30,000 and 40,000 (<http://www.remid.de/remid_info_zahlen.htm#hindu>). The immigration history of the Afghan Hindus resembles that of the Tamils: they mainly came as refugees fleeing the civil war in their homeland in the 1980s; they have opened four temples so far. A first permanent place of worship founded by Indian Hindus is in the process of emerging in Berlin; the ground-breaking ceremony for the planned Ganesha Hindu Temple took place on 4 November 2007.

[5]   In 1993, when the temple was still in the city of Hamm, 200–300 Tamil devotees accompanied the splendidly decorated image of the main goddess. The number of participants grew steadily; in 1996, more than 3000 persons were counted, and after the temple moved to an industrial area on the outskirts of the city, up to 10,000 visitors have been reported. Since 2002, the main day of the yearly temple festival has seen 12,000–15,000, visitors with a peak

The situation faced by the *Christian* Tamils when they reached Germany was different. There was no difficulty in finding a parish and a church offering regular Christian services. Difficulties, however, arose with regard to the language used in the services and in pastoral care. The majority of the Tamils knew little or no German, so communication with their German brethren was reduced to a minimum. They felt lost. A first step taken by the church to help ease their difficult lives was the establishment of Katholische Seelsorge für Tamilen ('Catholic Offices for the Pastoral Care of Tamils'). Their main task was to provide services by Tamil-speaking priests. A first headquarters was set up in Osnabrück in the west German state of North Rhine-Westphalia. Father Dr Francis Jeya Segaram, the first and at that time only Catholic Tamil priest in Germany, organized special services for Tamils.[6] This he did not only in Osnabrück, but also in other German cities which he routinely visited.[7] Dr Jeya Segaram has since returned to Sri Lanka, but his work was taken over by Father Bernard Regno, stationed in Essen.

Another important step was the idea of a common visit to the Marian shrine in Kevelaer. It was devised by Tamil members of the Essen diocese in the densely inhabited Ruhr area, and realized for the first time in August 1987, when 50 persons made the journey. It was repeated year after year with steadily increasing numbers of participants, who mostly came from North Rhine-Westphalia. Gradually, people from other parts of Germany joined in, as well as visitors from neighbouring countries, especially from the Netherlands. In 2002, the newspapers reported a gathering of 15,000 Tamil visitors, and this figure has regularly appeared in the press since then.[8]

The annual event which became popularly known as the *Tamilenwallfahrt* is organized by Father Bernard Regno from Essen. He is actively helped by Mr Thuraisingham Camillus, deacon (*Pfarrhelfer*) of the Tamil parish in Essen, who came to Germany in 1985 and is one of the initiators of the pilgrimage. Remembering the early years, he told a journalist from the regional newspaper: 'In the beginning we were only 50 pilgrims. We had a priest from Osnabrück who by the second year no longer wanted to participate. He felt that for such a small number of people it wasn't worth the effort.'[9] Asked why Kevelaer was chosen instead of other places

---

number of 20,000 in 2007 (cf. Brigitte Luchesi, 'Parading Hindu Gods in Public: New Festival Traditions of Tamil Hindus in Germany', in: Knut A. Jacobsen (ed.), *South Asian Religions on Display: Religious Processions in South Asia and the Diaspora* (London, 2008), pp. 178–90.

[6]   Compare Martin Baumann, 'Tamilische Tempelfeste und Wallfahrten in Deutschland', *Spirita*, 2 (1998): 23–5.

[7]   One of the places where he introduced services in Tamil once a month was Bremen. They are still held in the chapel of the Catholic St Joseph's Hospital.

[8]   For example, <http://www.offizialatsbezirk-oldenburg.de/index.php?myELEMENT =144496>. It resembles remarkably the figure given for the Hindu temple festival in Hamm in recent years. See note 5 above.

[9]   'Anfangs waren wir nur 50 Pilger. Wir hatten einen Pfarrer aus Osnabrück, der wollte schon im zweiten Jahr nicht mehr mitkommen. Das lohne sich ja nicht für so wenige Pilger', *Rheinische Post*, 8 August 2005.

of pilgrimage, he answered: 'This has to do with the image of the Mother of God. The Madonna in Kevelaer looks very much like the one in Mudhu [*sic*], our place of pilgrimage in Sri Lanka. When I realised this I took it as a sign. I told myself that this could not be a coincidence. And the way the Tamil pilgrimage to Kevelaer has developed indeed confirms that we chose the right place.'[10]

The Pilgrimage Site of Kevelaer

Kevelaer is a small city; in 2006 it had 28,000 inhabitants. It calls itself the largest pilgrimage town in north-west Europe.[11] Among Marian shrines in Germany, it is commonly given second place after Altötting in Bavaria. Its reputation as a pilgrimage site is based on events that took place in the seventeenth century, at the time of the Thirty Years War, when Kevelaer was an inconspicuous place. The following summary is based on the accounts as given in the religious pamphlets printed with ecclesiastical approbation in various languages[12] and in several pilgrimage guides.[13]

Around Christmas time 1641, a pious peddler by the name of Hendrick Busman travelled from Weeze to Geldern. As usual, he stopped at the crucifix placed at a crossroads near Kevelaer to pray, when he heard a voice telling him: 'Build a small chapel for me at this spot.' He heard the same voice giving the same order on two more occasions, and although he was a poor man, he obeyed and built a wayside shrine. The events were dealt with by the Venlo Synod in February 1647, where Busman was compelled to make a statement under oath. It is handed down to us: 'About a month before the Feast of Pentecost, my wife, Mechel Schrouse, had a vision during the night, and in the bright light she saw the chapel and the picture of the Blessed Mother of Our Lord as she had seen it shortly before in the hands of two soldiers.'[14] What Mechel had seen was a small copperplate print depicting Our Lady of Luxembourg which the soldiers had brought from Luxembourg, where,

---

[10] 'Das hat mit der Muttergottes-Abbildung zu tun. Die Madonna in Kevelaer hat fast die gleichen Züge wie in Mudhu, unserem Wallfahrtsort in Sri Lanka. Als ich das bemerkt habe, war es für mich wie ein Zeichen. Ich habe mir gesagt: Das kann kein Zufall sein. Und die Entwicklung der Tamilen-Wallfahrt bestätigt ja auch, dass wir mit Kevelaer richtig liegen' (ibid.).

[11] Official Website of the city: <http://www.kevelaer.de>.

[12] These small pamphlets with the picture of the Madonna on the front page followed by three pages of information are available in nearly all European languages as well as in some Asian languages, including Tamil. They can be purchased in the Basilica.

[13] For instance, *Kevelaer. Stätte der Besinnung. Wegweiser und Information* (2003); useful information can also be found at the Websites <http://www.kevelaer.de> and <http://de.wikipedia.org/wiki/kevelaer>, and in Robert Pötz, *Die Wallfahrt nach Kevelaer. Ein Wallfahrtsort und seine Geschichte* (Duisburg, 1986) and *Kevelaer. 350 Jahre Wallfahrt ohne Grenzen* (Kevelaer, 1992).

[14] See the pamphlet mentioned in note 12 above, English version.

since the epidemic of 1723, the Madonna was venerated as *Consolatrix Afflictorum*, 'Comforter of the Afflicted'. The print shows the Mother of Christ in royal pose, holding her infant son on her right arm. She is clad in precious clothes and a wide cape, a so-called 'protecting cloak' (*Schutzmantel*), and wears a crown on her head. In her hands she holds a sceptre and imperial orb. In the background on the left, the city of Luxembourg can be seen; on the right, a church or chapel towards which rows of people with standard-bearers in front are moving. A Latin inscription on a banner above the picture reads, 'Consolatrix Afflictorum ora pro nobis' ('Comforter of the Afflicted pray for us'), another text at the bottom, 'Vera Effigies Matris Iesu Consolatricis afflictorum in agro suburbano Luxemburgi Miraculis et Hominum Visitatione celebris, Anno 1640' ('True copy of the image of the Mother of Jesus, Comforter of the Afflicted, as it is well known through the many miracles and venerated by many in the neighbourhood of the city of Luxembourg. Anno 1640'). This devotional picture had been offered for sale to Busman's wife, but she had not bought it because its price seemed too high to her. After the miraculous night event, which was confirmed by the town's watchman who had witnessed the peculiar bright light in Busman's house, Hendrick Busman sent his wife to purchase the picture. It was placed in the new wayside shrine by the parish priest of Kevelaer on 1 June 1642. According to the protocol of the Venlo Synod, from the day of inauguration onwards, 'large groups of people from Geldern and other towns came to the little chapel. Many miraculous happenings took place which have all been recorded faithfully.'[15] The number of devoted visitors increased in spite of the Thirty Years War (which lasted up to 1648). By the time of the Venlo Synod in 1647, eight miracles had been recorded which were all acknowledged by the Synod. After only two days of hearings, Kevelaer was officially declared a pilgrimage site.

The appropriate development and architectural construction of the new place of pilgrimage was undertaken without delay. As early as 1643, work on the erection of the first church connected with the pilgrimage activities started, which is today's Kerzenkapelle ('Chapel of the Candles'). The name refers to the innumerable candles of different sizes which were and still are offered by individual believers as well as whole groups of pilgrims outside and inside the building. Four years later, in 1747, a monastery was constructed[16] which survived the centuries and nowadays houses the central pilgrimage bureau. In 1654, the simple wayside shrine erected by Busman was replaced by a hexagonal chapel, known as the Gnadenkapelle ('Chapel of Grace'), which is the one still *in situ*. A large opening in the northern wall makes it possible to catch a first glimpse of the miraculous original print from a distance, while a narrow ambulatory inside the building allows a close view (see Figure 4.1).

---

[15] Ibid.

[16] It was originally erected for the Oratorian Fathers called from Scherpenheuvel in Belgium by the Bishop of Roermond to take care of the growing number of pilgrims. Scherpenheuvel, another famous Marian pilgrimage site, is said to have originated *c.* 1500. See Pötz, *Die Wallfahrt nach Kevelaer*, p. 14.

Figure 4.1   Tamil visitors waiting in line to enter the Chapel of Grace and see
the miraculous image. (Photo: B. Luchesi)

The nineteenth century saw the erection of more pilgrimage-related buildings:
first of all the construction of the huge Basilica of the Blessed Virgin in which
services for large numbers of pilgrims can be celebrated. Another important place
near the central square is the Forum Pax Christi, started in 1948 with a chapel and an
open audience hall in front of it. The whole site was roofed over in 1999, and now
offers room for large gatherings regardless of the prevailing weather conditions.

The Annual 'Tamil Pilgrimage'

This section will concentrate on the movements and activities of the Tamil visitors on the day determined for the Tamil Pilgrimage, which is usually the second Saturday in August.[17] The term may evoke the picture of groups walking towards Kevelaer from quite a distance, or at least entering the inner part of the city together. The Tamil devotees, however, do not set out from their homes on foot or approach the sacred centre in groups led by a pilgrimage guide while singing devotional songs, as many pilgrimage groups from neighbouring towns and villages traditionally did and still do.[18] A characteristic feature of such groups is a huge decorated candle which is then ceremonially placed in the Chapel of the Candles. As these candles are usually adorned with the date of the pilgrimage and the name of the home town of the group in question, they provide immediate information about the donors. No such candles announcing a defined group of pilgrims are used by the Tamils. They approach the centre in small individual groups, mostly formed by family members, from wherever they have reached Kevelaer, be it one of the various parking lots on the outskirts of the town or the train station. Their meeting point is the central square around the Chapel of Grace itself (see Figure 4.2).

Figure 4.2   Tamil visitors lighting candles near the Chapel of the Candles.
               (Photo: B. Luchesi)

---

[17]   The following description is mainly based on participant observation on 12 August 2006, but also draws on observations of the same event in 2005, 2001 and 1999.

[18]   Another form of group pilgrimage has become quite popular – undertaking the pilgrimage on bicycles or motorbikes.

Figure 4.3   Tamil visitors waiting in line to enter the Chapel of Grace. To the
              right, persons can be seen lighting candles near the Chapel of the
              Candles. (Photo: B. Luchesi)

Here, most of the Tamils immediately line up to enter the Chapel of Grace (see
Figure 4.3). It is obvious that they will not content themselves with seeing the
miraculous image from a distance, but wish to come as close to it as possible. As
already described, in many cases the contact is not limited to a purely visual one,
but is intensified by touching the glass sheet in front of the picture with their hands
or forehead. Both forms of contact are acts of devotion which can be found all over
the Indian sub-continent and Sri Lanka.[19] That many Tamils decide to perform
them right at the beginning of the day's programme in Kevelaer seems to be an
indication of the importance they still have for them in Europe, too.

Having stood in front of the picture for a short time, people move on and enter
the narrow interior of the chapel itself, where they may pause to pray quietly. Many
also use the opportunity offered here to purchase a bundle of small consecrated
candles to take home. They may light one or two candles immediately and place
them on the supports provided on the outer wall of the Chapel of the Candles,
facing the main square. Far more common, however, is the custom of purchasing
much larger candles at the shops catering for the needs of pilgrims. Several dealers
have started erecting special stalls in front of their regular shops on the day of
the Tamil Pilgrimage, displaying plain candles in various sizes (see Figure 4.4).

---

[19]   These acts can be observed among Hindus, Buddhists and Christians. The overall
importance of the visual perception of the sacred in the Hindu context is excellently described
by Diana Eck in *Darśan: Seeing the Divine Image in India* (Chambersburg, PA, 1985).

Figure 4.4   Candles are chosen according to the height of the children who are
               going to offer them. (Photo: B. Luchesi)

'The Tamil Pilgrimage is especially important for the traders selling candles,'
commented the manager of the Kevelaer Pilgrimage Office.[20] Compared with other
pilgrims, Tamils buy and place an immense number of candles. The innumerable
flames generate such a heat that damage to the church walls is feared, and the
candles burning have to be extinguished before new ones can be lit.[21] Not only is
the number of candles offered remarkable, but also the high percentage of huge
specimens. This is due to a custom which seems peculiar to Tamil visitors. They
like to choose the length of a candle according to the height of the child in whose

---

[20]   See <http://www.wz-newsline.de/index.php?redid=124066>, accessed 14 August
2006.
[21]   At least this is the explanation I was given as to why church employees repeatedly
appear and extinguish row after row of candles with a water hose. They are disposed of in
huge containers.

name they are going to offer it. As this is done not only for infant sons and daughters but also for older ones, candles of one metre in length and more are in high demand. These candles are specifically produced for the Tamil clients.[22]

Another main event of the day is the High Mass in the Basilica at 10 a.m., which, as usual, starts with a welcoming address to the pilgrims, among which the Tamils are explicitly mentioned. Immediately after the mass, the Tamil pilgrims line up again to defile past the reverse side of the high altar, where a depiction of the risen Christ can be seen. Many kneel before it and touch the feet of the picture before moving on. Other queues form in front of the visitors' books, where people can enter their names and note what seems pressing to them: thanks and wishes. Crowds also form around the tables, where small lights can be lit, including those in front of St Anthony.

No facilities are provided for lighting lights or candles inside the Chapel of the Candles. Many pilgrims use a visit to this church for a quiet rest, silent prayers and the contemplation of the statue of Mary above the altar. They may also look at the multitude of old and new candles and the innumerable pilgrimage signs covering the walls. For those who would like to write thanks or wishes here, a wooden box is installed into which pieces of paper can be slotted.

The special pilgrimage service for the Christian Tamil pilgrims takes place in the large Forum Pax Christi and is normally scheduled for 10.45 a.m. But many visitors come earlier to make sure that they have a seat; they spend the time studying the programme printed in Tamil and sold for 1 euro at the entrance, or watching the group decorating a small statue of the Madonna which has been put up on a pedestal in front of the auditorium.[23] This statue is said to depict the Madonna worshipped in Madhu in Sri Lanka. It will become another focus of veneration at the end of the service. People will again line up patiently until they are close enough to touch it. Shortly before the start of the service, young persons and children gather outside the Forum. Those among them who have recently taken their first communion are dressed in their festive communion outfit: frilly white dresses in the case of the girls, and black suits combined with white shirts in the case of the boys. They and a group of young people from Essen then lead the ceremonial entry of the assembled clergy consisting of Dr Regno from Essen and several German priests as well as various priests from neighbouring countries, all of them in full regalia. While the young communicants take theirs seats in the first row, the priests assemble around the altar. Welcoming words in German and English by a German speaker mark the beginning of an elaborate service in the Tamil language. The assembled laymen, filling the Forum up to the last seat with

---

[22]   Information from a shop assistant, 12 August 2006. She added that the previous extraordinarily hot July days had caused some nervousness among the candle makers: the wax didn't harden and they feared they might not be able to meet the demands of the Tamil customers.

[23]   This is usually done by a group of young Tamils from Essen guided by Mr Camillus.

hundreds standing in the aisles, take an active interest, and most join in the singing with skill and dedication. They are accompanied by an orchestra consisting of young Tamils with various musical instruments. At the end, a group of helpers with collection bags swarms out and collects money.[24]

By the time the mass has ended, lunch hour is near. Children are getting restless, so mothers start looking for a place where they can unpack the luncheon boxes they have brought along. The benches of the main square and the stone steps in front of the Basilica are soon filled with eating and chatting people. In former years, the entire sacred square was turned into a sort of huge picnic spot. Nowadays, most of the hungry visitors move towards the parking lot behind the Basilica, where a temporary market is installed. Food stalls sell vegetarian food and soft drinks, but also meat dishes, in both cases prepared according to the taste of South Asians. Apart from food for immediate consumption, all sorts of other goods are available: clothes, cooking utensils, fresh and tinned vegetables, various spices, Tamil videos and CDs, cosmetics, children's toys and the like. The various goods are to the taste and liking of South Asians; most of the traders are themselves of Sri Lankan or Indian origin.

Here at the latest, non-Tamil observers become aware that the large crowd which has meanwhile filled the city centre does not consist entirely of Catholic visitors. Or why do posters showing the Hindu goddess Lakshmi or the elephant-headed Ganesha find interested customers? For whom are the different brands of incense or the various items usually used in Hindu pujas? Obviously, some of the visitors are Hindus. Another clue is provided by the sheer number of participants. According to the estimates given by police and organizers and quoted in the newspapers, 15,000 persons have joined the Tamil pilgrimage during the last five years. But, as mentioned above, the overall number of Catholic Tamils in Germany is 9,500. It seems unrealistic to assume that all of them take part in the yearly pilgrimage. It is equally improbable that the remaining 5000–6000 are Catholic guests from other countries, although the number of visitors from France, Switzerland, Belgium, Luxembourg, the Netherlands and Denmark has increased year by year – even some pilgrims from England have been reported. The fact is that a very significant percentage of the assembled Tamils in Kevelaer are Hindus. The estimates vary, some speak of about 40 per cent, others even about 60 per cent and more.[25] It is difficult to establish exact figures, as the activities and behaviour of the Hindus do not noticeably differ from those of the other visitors. Many of them have come to worship the Madonna in the same way as their Christian brethren: by praying to her, thanking her or asking her favour, by seeing the miraculous picture, touching it, offering flowers, and above all, lighting lights and candles. This interesting fact will be taken up below.

---

[24]   The money is collected for various purposes. In 2005, the collection was intended for the tsunami victims in Sri Lanka.

[25]   For the figure of 70 per cent, see <http://www.wz-newsline.de/sro.php?redid=124066>, accessed 14 August 2006); for 40 per cent, see <http://www.offizialatsbezirk-oldenburg.de/index.php?my ELEMENT=14496>, accessed 10 August 2002).

The Importance of the Kevelaer Pilgrimage for Catholic Tamils

The yearly pilgrimage to Kevelaer has become an institution among Roman Catholic Tamils of Sri Lankan origin living in Germany. The steady growth of participants since 1987 and the consistently high figures of visitors during the past five years are proof of the importance the pilgrimage has gained in their religious life. In looking for possible explanations for this development, four points may be put forward.

Firstly, Kevelaer is an acknowledged site of Marian worship. The Madonna, being central to Catholic theology and devotional practice, is venerated by Catholics of all kinds and origins. Tamil Catholics, too, are known to have been devotees of the Mother of Christ for centuries. A number of churches consecrated to Mary and several Marian pilgrimage sites in Sri Lanka as well as in the Tamil-speaking areas of southern India attest to the high esteem in which she is held by many South Asians.[26] It seems a matter of course that a comparable place of worship would be looked for in the European diaspora.

Secondly, Kevelaer is not the only Marian pilgrimage site in Central Europe. Why was it chosen? First of all, it is situated within Germany, meaning that Tamil refugees with a limited residence permit face no difficulties visiting it. Another advantage is its comparatively easy accessibility for all those living in North Rhine-Westphalia, which is, as mentioned above, the residential district of a large percentage of Tamil immigrants in Germany. Unlike Altötting in Bavaria, the principal German Marian pilgrimage site in the south, it can be reached from many points in this area within an hour or two, which is an easy task for inhabitants of the Rhine–Ruhr area, accustomed to frequent commuting between places. It seems that this purely logistical aspect was not irrelevant for the decision.

Thirdly, the Kevelaer Madonna is explicitly known as the *Consolatrix Afflictorum*, the 'Comforter of the Afflicted'. In this capacity, she meets the needs of many Sri Lankan refugees who have experienced anxiety and many hardships in their homeland and a great deal of uncertainty as immigrants in the West: 'Many thousands come to the Mother of God, to get rid of their sorrows and distress,' explained Professor S.J. Emmanuel,[27] the former General Curate of the Jaffna diocese, who now lives in exile in Germany and works with Tamils who, like himself, had left their country because of immediate danger to their lives.

But the Madonna in Kevelaer is not only approached as a comforter, but also as a concerned mother and helping force in very concrete matters. She is obviously

---

[26] For Talawila, Kudagama and Madhu in Sri Lanka, see R.L. Stirrat, 'Shrines, Pilgrimage and Miraculous Powers in Roman Catholic Sri Lanka', in W.J. Sheils (ed.), *The Church and Healing* (Oxford, 1982), pp. 385–413. For Velankanni and Villiyanur in Tamil Nadu, see Matthias Frenz, *Gottes-Mutter-Göttin. Marienverehrung im Spannungsfeld religiöser Traditionen in Südindien* (Würzburg, 2004).

[27] <http://www.kirchensite.de/popup_print.php?myELEMENT=97554, accessed 6 November 2006.

understood as having manifold powers. Several Tamils have told me that after having appealed to her, she has helped their children to succeed in school or the head of the household to get a better job. Other wishes often put forward are: to pass an exam, to find a good husband or to get a German passport. The belief in the power of the Kevelaer Madonna may be due to the stories traditionally connected with her. The stories of wishes that came true encourage others to approach the Madonna. Vivid testimonies of this process are the entries in the intercession books which comprise requests as well as thanks.

Apart from these individual wishes, there are collective ones: in 2005, thoughts and wishes went out to the survivors of the tsunami catastrophe in Sri Lanka. The most prominent request, however, is the one for peace in their homeland[28] and for the safety and welfare of the people back home. There is hardly a Tamil who has no relatives, friends and neighbours in Sri Lanka.

Fourthly, Mr Camillus, Deacon in Essen, who was quoted above, explicitly pointed to the similarity of the Kevelaer Madonna to the one in Madhu. Madhu is a place situated halfway between Mannar and Vavuniya in the north-western Tamil part of Sri Lanka controlled by the *Liberation Tigers of Tamil Eelam*. Before the outbreak of the civil war, it was visited annually by at least one million pilgrims from the whole island, among them Hindus and quite a number of Buddhists.[29] Since then, access to the forest shrine has become difficult, the only exception being offered around 15 August (Assumption of the Blessed Virgin), when restrictions are somewhat loosened.[30] According to the official Website of the Mannar diocese, there are even bus services at this time connecting Madhu with all major Sri Lankan cities.[31]

For Tamil Christians, Madhu is 'The centre of Mannar devotion in the island'.[32] Its history reaches back to the sixteenth century, to a church in Manati which housed a statue of 'Our Lady of Good Health'. This statue was brought to the present site in the seventeenth century. Several miraculous events were connected with the finding of the new place, where the Madonna soon became renowned again for her healing capacities. Her special domain is said to have been helping

---

[28]   In 2003, when the peace talks brought the first positive results, the headline of the Internet site of the Münster diocese read: 'Tamil pilgrimage to Kevelaer: Prayer for peace was answered'; <http://www.kirchensite.de/index.php?myELEMENT=96272>, accessed 8 July 2003. Now that the promising moments of those months have vanished, hopes have made way for renewed anxiety and depression.

[29]   <http://libref.kaywa.ch/2000511>, 'Religionen in Sri Lanka'.

[30]   In 2002, 400,000 Tamil and Sinhala devotees from all parts of Sri Lanka were said to have attended the feast and prayed for peace; <http://www.tamilnet.com/art.html?catid= 13&artid=7279>.

[31]   Whether they were functioning in 2006 is not known to me. News about Madhu provided by the UN refugee agency concentrated on another topic: on the families having sought refuge in the church compound of Madhu. At least 500 families were counted; <http://www.unhcr.de/unhcr.php/cat/18/aid/1413>, accessed 7 November 2006.

[32]   Website of the Mannar diocese: <http://www.mannardiocese.org/madhushrine>.

in cases of snake bites. In 1872 the construction of the present church began, and in 1924 the statue of the Madonna was solemnly and officially crowned by a papal legate.

This statue is of the Luxembourg Madonna type.[33] The Madonna is shown with the infant Jesus on her right arm; both, mother and child, are crowned. Mary is clad in splendid bejewelled garments; in her right hand she carries a sceptre. Her overall appearance strongly resembles the Madonna depicted on the small copperplate print in Kevelaer. She receives ornaments in grateful recognition of her help, like the Madonna in Kevelaer. The likeness of the two Madonnas is not restricted to their outer appearances. In both cases, Mary is understood as a mother with protective motherly attitudes towards her devotees, and in both cases she is said to have miraculous healing powers. Most probably many Tamil visitors come to Kevelaer with the stories about the miraculous Madhu Madonna in mind, which can easily be combined with those about the Kevelaer one. A number of objects to be seen in the Kevelaer churches underline their credibility, above all the tablets donated by grateful devotees. They speak of convalescence from fatal illnesses and other serious ailments. Physical evidence, like crutches, points to the total recovery of formerly handicapped persons.

The Madhu Madonna not only played a decisive role in choosing Kevelaer as the site for the Tamil Pilgrimage, she is also represented by a true portrait of the original statue during the Tamil service in the Forum Pax Christi. Displaying Mary in this form in Kevelaer means having moved the place where Our Lady of Madhu can be met from northern Sri Lanka into the German diaspora. Like the statue in Madhu, she can be looked at by devotees, who may feel that their gaze is returned. She can also be touched. Most importantly, however, her presence in Kevelaer may give Tamil immigrants the feeling of a spiritual home away from home.

The 'Tamil Pilgrimage': A Common Event for Christians and Hindus

As pointed out above, the Madonna of Kevelaer attracts not only many Tamil Christians, but a large number of Tamil Hindus as well. This may surprise those unfamiliar with South Asian religions, but not scholars of this particular field. They are well aware of the fact that Mary is considered a divine female by many Hindus. Hindus worship a large number of goddesses; for the so-called *shaktas* ('goddess worshippers'), the supreme deity is female. The great goddesses Parvati, Durga, Lakshmi, even the fearsome Kali and the frightening Sitala, are referred to as *Ma*, *Mata*, *Amma* or *Tai*, all meaning 'Mother', and the various village goddesses of the south, too, are understood as life-giving, life-protecting and nourishing deities. To include Mary seems unproblematic: the Mother of God becomes the Divine Mother, as Annette Wilke has pointed out (1996, p. 280). Many Hindus in South Asia, but also in Germany, own statues of the Madonna, especially of the Lourdes

---

[33]   See photos on the Mannar diocese Website, ibid.

Madonna. They are kept in their house shrine, where Mary is venerated together with other gods and goddesses of the Hindu pantheon. Marian places in South India attract Hindus from near and far, an outstanding example being the Marian shrine in the fishing village of Velankanni on the east coast of South India (Tamil Nadu).[34] Stirrat has met Hindu visitors at the Marian pilgrimage sites of Talawila, Madhu and Kudagama in Sri Lanka.[35]

Several scholars have noted that in Europe, too, Hindus of South Asian origin can be observed visiting Marian shrines. Christopher McDowell was one of the first to describe the attraction of the Black Madonna at Einsiedeln in Switzerland for Hindu immigrants, especially for Tamil asylum seekers. He mentions the custom of writing wishes and/or promises on pieces of paper and leaving them near the Madonna. Passport photos of young men can also be found. In his view, Einsiedeln had become a Mariyamman shrine – a shrine of the dark South Asian village goddess of this name:

> The Black Madonna as Mariyamman, or another of the dark goddesses, had deep resonance for certain Hindu Tamils in Switzerland. Research suggested that the young men who left their photographs on the grotto wall belonged to the recent *asylum-seeking* population. For them, village goddesses were the repository of female power and a focus of stability and hope. Dark goddesses are deeply rooted in rural farming societies, and to pay devotion to them is to return to the life-giving soil, to the order of the village left behind: an order so many desperately wished to rediscover.[36]

McDowell's view that Einsiedeln had become a place of worship for predominantly single Tamil men and especially low-caste Hindus is contested by Damaris Lüthi, who holds that Hindus of all castes and classes visit Einsiedeln and the Madonna in Mariastein near Basle.[37] She also reports that half of the Hindus she interviewed regularly visit Catholic churches, and that many of her informants pointed out

---

[34]   See Paul Younger's vivid description of Velankanni Mata's main festival, which is attended by Christians and Hindus, in Paul Younger, 'Healing Mother Velankanni: Hindu Patterns of Worship at a Christian Shrine', in *Playing Host to Deity* (Oxford, 2002). He calls attention to certain Hindu patterns of worship at this Christian shrine: the offering of hair, the taking of a cleansing bath in the sea, the giving of food and animal offerings, presenting flower garlands to be touched to the feet of the image before being returned, falling into a trance, and buying 'holy oil'. See also Matthias Frenz's description of Velankanni in *Gottes-Mutter-Göttin*.

[35]   Stirrat, 'Shrines, Pilgrimage and Miraculous Powers in Roman Catholic Sri Lanka'; R.L. Stirrat, *Power and Religiosity in a Post-colonial Setting: Sinhala Catholics in Contemporary Sri Lanka* (Cambridge, 1992).

[36]   Christopher McDowell, *A Tamil Asylum Diaspora: Sri Lankan Migration, Settlement and Politics in Switzerland* (Oxford,1996), pp. 235–6.

[37]   Damaris Lüthi, 'Heimatliche Konventionen im Exil bewahren: Hinduistische und christliche Religiosität tamilischer Flüchtlinge in Bern', in Baumann, Luchesi and Wilke (eds), *Tempel und Tamilen in zweiter Heimat*, pp. 295–322, see p. 302.

that they used to do so in Sri Lanka, too. According to Lüthi, Marian worship by Hindus is no phenomenon brought about by exile. Nor is the practice of leaving written messages restricted to the worship of Black Madonnas. Annette Wilke has studied intercession books of the Catholic St Joseph's Church in Könitz near Basle which include many requests by Christian and Hindu Tamils.[38] One of her interesting conclusions is that there is only one difference discernible between them: the form of address. Christians use *mata* ('Mother'), whereas Hindus prefer *taye*, a Tamil word meaning 'divine mother' which is reserved for goddesses.

Another Madonna deeply respected by many Hindu Tamils is the Madonna of Lourdes.[39] Lourdes in France has become a quite popular destination for bus trips of whole groups of Hindus. Priests and members of the Bremen Hindu temple, for instance, made the journey in 2003, and they plan to repeat it. The interest in Lourdes should not be taken as a new phenomenon brought about in the diaspora. Kudagama in Sri Lanka has already been referred to; its famous shrine is one of 'Our Lady of Lourdes'. The same holds true for Villiyanur in Tamil Nadu. According to Frenz, most Catholic churches in South India have a chapel consecrated to the Lourdes Madonna.[40] It seems only logical that in Europe, devoted Tamils of both creeds should use the chance to visit the place where the Madonna is said to have originally appeared, provided they are allowed to travel to France and can afford it.[41]

The fact that the Madonna is held in high esteem by Hindu Tamils not only points to the possible rank of the Mother of Christ in the Hindu pantheon, but also challenges assumptions of one-dimensional religious adherence, of principally ascribing only one religious creed to a given person. Martin Baumann and Kurt Salentin have recently published the results of a quantitative statistical study undertaken among Sri Lankan Tamil Hindus in Germany to explore their religiousness and social incorporation into the host society. One of the important findings is that 8.1 per cent of the 874 persons they questioned consider themselves to be both Hindu and Roman Catholic. Asked to indicate their feelings as Hindu, Catholic, Protestant or other, a remarkable number of respondents described themselves as having a dual, sometimes even a treble 'membership': 'While most other mixed categories can be taken together, because they are small in number, one combination, namely Hinduism with Catholicism, stands out because of its

---

[38]   Annette Wilke, 'Mythos in Bewegung. Die Grosse Göttin in Symbolsystem, Kultus und Alltag', *Zeitschrift für Missionswissenschaft und Religionswissenschaft*, 4 (1996): 266–81.

[39]   I first learned about Hindus visiting Lourdes in 1998 at the Hindu temple festival in Hamm-Uentrop. A woman was performing ascetic practices which she had vowed to do to achieve the recovery of her sick husband. She also planned to travel to Lourdes to repeat her request there because of the great power of 'The Lourdes', as she called her.

[40]   Matthias Frenz, *Gottes-Mutter-Göttin*, p. 55.

[41]   A group journey by bus is comparatively inexpensive: a flyer distributed in Kevelaer in 2006 offered a five-day trip from and to Stuttgart for 100 euros per person.

size ... This means that almost one in three Catholics is Catholic only, while one in nine Hindus is also a Catholic.'[42] There are different degrees of 'religious overlap', as the authors call this phenomenon. Although further research into the complicated matter is required to make full use of this finding, it already provides an apt additional explanation for the large number of people the Tamil Pilgrimage attracts. Obviously, the annual event in Kevelaer, originally founded by Tamil Catholics, has also proved to be meaningful for all those Hindus who feel an affinity with Catholicism. They do not insist on religious boundaries or understand the Kevelaer event as a matter confined to their Catholic compatriots, but on the contrary, as one which has great importance for themselves.

One of the causes of religious overlap may be that there are often close family relationships between persons describing themselves as first and foremost Catholics and those who call themselves firstly Hindus. They know each other's religious beliefs and practices from their own immediate experience with their relatives: 'Back home we always celebrated our festivals together,' I was told by a member of the Hindu temple in Bremen. 'Some of our relatives are Christians. We take part in their festivals, and they come to take part in ours. Here in Germany we do the same.' The Kevelaer pilgrimage no doubt has become such an occasion to be celebrated together.[43]

Conclusion

Catholic and Hindu Tamil pilgrims of Sri Lankan origin visit Kevelaer to pay respect to and worship the Madonna in one of her best-known pilgrimage sites in Germany. They may ask for her help and protection, or wish to thank her. The Catholic devotees have a rare opportunity to take part in an elaborate mass specifically organized for them. They find themselves surrounded by thousands of compatriots who all are celebrating 'the largest Marian pilgrimage outside their native country' ('größte Marienwallfahrt außerhalb der Heimat'), as the Tamil priest Professor Emmanuel has put it.

Having concentrated on the religious aspects, I have somewhat neglected another important aspect – the fact that the Kevelaer pilgrimage has also developed into a large Tamil 'family meeting' or get-together of relatives, former neighbours and friends who are now dispersed over the whole of Germany and other parts of Europe. People look forward to getting in touch for a few hours, to seeing the growing children, to exchanging news and to speaking their language or even local dialect. And there is the prospect that a Middle European

---

[42] Martin Baumann and Kurt Salentin, 'Migrant Religiousness and Social Incorporation: Tamil Hindus from Sri Lanka in Germany', *Journal of Contemporary Religion*, 21/3 (October 2006): 297–323, quote on p. 307.

[43] I have no information on whether this holds equally true for the annual temple festival in Hamm.

city's central area will be completely filled with one's own people.[44] For once, other pilgrims and Western visitors are in the minority. The event takes on the characteristics of what in German is called a *Heimattreffen* – a meeting of persons with a shared ethnic and cultural background who try to preserve their traditions in alien surroundings.

It is in this context that the market should be mentioned again. The food stalls and various stands are no matters of secondary importance. The food is South Asian food, and most of the vendors offer goods which Tamil customers are fond of and which are not – or only with difficulty – available in other places. People visibly enjoy looking for things and exploring the goods on offer, pushing through the narrow passages between the stalls. The market does not include merry-go-rounds and other such things characteristic of full-blown fairs. But there are a number of stands selling toys, knickknacks and souvenirs typical of holiday spots. The whole atmosphere of the marketplace behind the cathedral is marked by a playful and relaxed note, a 'ludic component'[45] which complements the solemn mood in the various holy places. Victor and Edith Turner have described it as a well-known element present in nearly all pilgrimage contexts.[46]

As noted, the Tamil Pilgrimage in Kevelaer has turned into a well-established institution. There is no indication that it will change much in the years to come. Interestingly, it has become the largest pilgrimage by one single group (*Einzelwallfahrt*) to Kevelaer in the yearly pilgrimage programme. The number of Tamils participating in the *Tamilenwallfahrt* exceed the number of all other 'large' pilgrimages, be it the famous one of the motorcyclists (with approximately 400 vehicles) or the traditional ones organized by various villages and towns normally comprising no more than 250 participants. Kevelaer seems to appreciate the commitment of the Tamils, in particular the Wallfahrtsleitung (Central Pilgrimage Organization) and the shopkeepers. The Tamils' interest in Kevelaer and the Madonna increases the reputation of the city, nationally as well as internationally. They are good customers and considerate citizens, as police and organizers emphasize. It is likely that this positive reception will encourage the Tamils to go on meeting in Kevelaer – to individually seek comfort and help, to jointly celebrate a religious festival in a markedly Tamil style, to meet relatives and friends, and to take part in an event suited to preserving their identity.

---

[44]   A special function of this large meeting should not be forgotten – to look for possible marriage partners.

[45]   Cf. Victor Turner and Edith Turner, *Image and Pilgrimage in Christian Culture: Anthropological Perspectives* (New York 1978), p. 37.

[46]   Ibid.

References

Baumann, Martin, 'Tamilische Tempelfeste und Wallfahrten in Deutschland', *Spirita*, 2 (1998): 23–5.

Baumann, Martin, *Migration, Religion, Integration. Buddhistische Vietnamesen und hinduistische Tamilen in Deutschland* (Marburg: diagonal, 2000).

Baumann, Martin, 'Von Sri Lanka in die Bundesrepublik: Flucht, Aufnahme und kulturelle Rekonstruktionen', in Martin Baumann, Brigitte Luchesi and Annette Wilke (eds), *Tempel und Tamilen in zweiter Heimat. Hindus aus Sri Lanka im deutschsprachigen und skandinavischen Raum* (Würzburg: Ergon Press, 2003), pp. 41–73.

Baumann, Martin and Kurt Salentin, 'Migrant Religiousness and Social Incorporation: Tamil Hindus from Sri Lanka in Germany', *Journal of Contemporary Religion*, 21/3 (October 2006): 297–323.

Baumann, Martin, Brigitte Luchesi and Annette Wilke (eds), *Tempel und Tamilen in zweiter Heimat. Hindus aus Sri Lanka im deutschsprachigen und skandinavischen Raum* (Würzburg: Ergon Press, 2003).

Eck, Diana, *Darśan: Seeing the Divine Image in India*, 2nd rev. and enlarged edn (Chambersburg, PA: Anima Books, 1985).

Frenz, Matthias, *Gottes-Mutter-Göttin. Marienverehrung im Spannungsfeld religiöser Traditionen in Südindien* (Würzburg: Ergon Press, 2004).

Jacobsen, Knut A., 'Settling in Cold Climate: The Tamil Hindus in Norway', in Martin Baumann, Brigitte Luchesi and Annete Wilke (eds), *Tempel und Tamilen in zweiter Heimat. Hindus aus Sri Lanka im deutschsprachigen und skandinavischen Raum* (Würzburg: Ergon Press, 2003), pp. 363–77.

Jacobsen, Knut A. (ed.), *South Asian Religions on Display: Religious Processions in South Asia and the Diaspora* (London: Routledge, 2008).

Luchesi, Brigitte, 'Wege aus der Unsichtbarkeit. Zur Etablierung hindu-tamilischer Religiosität im öffentlichen Raum der Bundesrepublik Deutschland', in Martin Baumann, Brigitte Luchesi and Annette Wilke (eds), *Tempel und Tamilen in zweiter Heimat. Hindus aus Sri Lanka im deutschsprachigen und skandinavischen Raum* (Würzburg: Ergon Press, 2003), pp. 99–124.

Luchesi, Brigitte, 'Tamil Hindu Places of Worship in Germany', in Knut A. Jacobsen and P. Pratap Kumar (eds), *South Asians in the Diaspora. Histories and Religious Traditions* (Leiden: Brill, 2004), pp. 116–33.

Luchesi, Brigitte, 'Parading Hindu Gods in Public: New Festival Traditions of Tamil Hindus in Germany', in Knut A. Jacobsen (ed.), *South Asian Religions on Display: Religious Processions in South Asia and the Diaspora* (London: Routledge, 2008), pp. 178–90.

Lüthi, Damaris, 'Heimatliche Konventionen im Exil bewahren: Hinduistische und christliche Religiosität tamilischer Flüchtlinge in Bern', in Martin Baumann, Brigitte Luchesi and Annette Wilke (eds), *Tempel und Tamilen in zweiter Heimat. Hindus aus Sri Lanka im deutschsprachigen und skandinavischen Raum* (Würzburg: Ergon Press, 2003), pp. 295–322.

McDowell, Christopher, *A Tamil Asylum Diaspora: Sri Lankan Migration, Settlement and Politics in Switzerland* (Providence, RI: Berghahn Books, 1996).

Pötz, Robert, *Die Wallfahrt nach Kevelaer. Ein Wallfahrtsort und seine Geschichte* (Duisburg: Mercator-Verlag, 1986).

Pötz, Robert, *Kevelaer. 350 Jahre Wallfahrt ohne Grenzen* (Kevelaer: Katalogband, 1992).

Stirrat, R.L., 'Shrines, Pilgrimage and Miraculous Powers in Roman Catholic Sri Lanka', in W.J. Sheils (ed.), *The Church and Healing* (Oxford: Basil Blackwell, 1982), pp. 385–413.

Stirrat, R.L., *Power and Religiosity in a Post-colonial Setting: Sinhala Catholics in Contemporary Sri Lanka* (Cambridge: Cambridge University Press, 1992).

Turner, Victor and Edith Turner, *Image and Pilgrimage in Christian Culture: Anthropological Perspectives* (New York: Columbia University Press, 1978).

Wilke, Annette, 'Mythos in Bewegung. Die Grosse Göttin in Symbolsystem, Kultus und Alltag', *Zeitschrift für Missionswissenschaft und Religionswissenschaft*, 4 (1996): 266–81.

Younger, Paul, 'Healing Mother Velankanni: Hindu Patterns of Worship at a Christian Shrine', in *Playing Host to Deity* (Oxford: Oxford University Press, 2002).

Chapter 5

Perpetuating Religious and Social Concepts in the Extended Motherland: Tamil Christians in Berne (Switzerland)

Damaris Lüthi

On a Sunday evening a fortnight before Christmas, in the bright, austere hall of the Spanish Mission in the Bernese suburb of Ostermundigen, the 7-year-old Shiva (name changed) faces a three-headed jury. Hesitantly he looks at the audience, consisting of rhetorically gifted Catholic Tamil children and their parents. He starts to speak, and with a clear voice he recites in Tamil – his other mother tongue apart from Swiss German – a religious poem on the theme 'Christmas'. Shiva is an entrant in the Tamil Christian poetry competition for children conducted by the Tamil Catholic parish of Berne. The best recitation of spoken Tamil, and hence command of the language and public speaking, is prized. Smartly dressed in dark trousers, a white shirt and waistcoat, Shiva looks like a small adult. The dress code prescribes that the outfit should 'neither be modern nor sexy, neither sleeveless, nor must it show too much of the chest, but it should preferably be quite traditional', explains Jacqulen Rose Francis, a Tamil and Sunday school teacher, and the co-organizer of the event. Now Shiva waves his arms to stress the contents of his presentation, then puts them behind his back. Other children in the competition, dressed up in suit-like outfits and frilly dresses, are observing him. The boy finishes his speech, and the audience applauds. The jury, consisting of the priest Peter Manohar and two Tamil teachers – from other Swiss cantons to avoid prejudice – bow over the evaluation sheets specifically developed for poetry competitions, and write down their verdicts. Under scrutiny are various aspects of the presentation, such as the modelling of the beginning and end, the pronunciation, the intonation, the use of the tongue in connection with specific sounds, the control over and comprehension of the text, the gestures as well as the attire. The favoured types of texts are song (*patal*) or poetry (*kavital*). Participants should be between 5 and 14 years old, and are divided into five two-year age groups. The youngest children are very happy to participate, which declines with age. Incidentally, there are more girls in the competition than boys, and they perform better.

For preparation, each member of the Sunday School received a Tamil text, written in Tamil script and different for each age group. The content of each, authored by Peter Manohar and Jacqulen Francis, who also writes children's books, is of an 'ethical-religious type', they explain. The first step is to learn the text by heart. The 5-year-olds have to struggle with three four-liners, while the 14-year-olds have to master a full 25 lines. The writing is partly in *Centamil*, pure Tamil, which means that all foreign words, including Sanskrit expressions, have been eliminated. This is considered a very elegant style. Tamil Catholic poetry competitions take place once or twice yearly, and similar events are organized in Lucerne and Geneva. The topic for the texts is changed each time. This time the topic is 'Christmas', last time it was 'The Last Supper'.

After almost five hours, the event reaches its end. The three best recitations of each age group are honoured with medals, and each of these achievements is publicly commentated on by the jury. For the first time this year, the prizes are not in the form of trophies, as these would be undeserved, explains Jaqulen Francis: 'Performance in the past years has diminished, and so we had to offer shorter texts which deserve only medals.'[1]

---

[1]   This chapter is based on data collected during the research project 'Social Change among Sri Lankan Tamil Refugees in Switzerland', supported by the Swiss National Science Foundation (2001–2003). The religiosity of the Tamils was only a peripheral theme of the research, and of interest mostly in connection with the social and cultural continuity and change of this group. My data on religious practices are therefore only fragmentary, and the information presented here is far from a representative documentation of Swiss Tamil Christian concepts and practices. As concerns the research methodology, the all-female research group, consisting of myself and two PhD students, Johanna Vögeli and Marie-Anne Fankhauser, worked with the well-established social anthropological method of participant observation, accompanying 90 persons and their families over a period of 18 months. Inspired by Pierre Bourdieu, *Entwurf einer Theorie der Praxis* (Frankfurt am Main: Suhrkamp, 1976 [1972]), the study focused on shared concepts and habits. Geographically, concentration was on the city and surroundings of Berne. The focus was on female representatives of Tamil society. The author was in regular contact with a group of 28 adults (21 women and 7 men), and in addition, had spontaneous conversations with spouses, children or parents, as well as single long conversations with an additional 6 persons. The majority of these informants belong to higher castes, mostly to the Vellalar, the dominant caste in many Tamil areas in Sri Lanka. The informants gave their caste origin as (high caste) Vellalar (21), (middle to low caste) Karaiyar (4), Brahmins (1), as well as (very low caste) Pallar (1). Two thirds of them are Hindus, one third are Christians (18 Hindus, 4 Catholics, 1 Church of South India, 3 belong to evangelical movements and 1 Hindu woman also attends services of the evangelical Philadelphia Mission Church). At the time of research, they were between 25 and 59 years old (average 39.2; only 2 informants were aged below 30). Almost all the married informants had two or three children. In addition, information collected by the co-researcher Johanna Vögeli on migrants with a similar social and religious profile was integrated into the evaluation. All names have been changed. Publications related to the research are Marie-Anne Fankhauser, 'Tamilische Jugendliche in der Schweiz', *Tsantsa*, 8 (2003): 173–6; Damaris Lüthi, 'Das mediale Fenster zur Heimat. Tamilinnen und Tamilen im Schweizer Exil und der indische Film', in Alexandra Schneider (ed.), *Bollywood. Das indische Kino und die Schweiz* (Zurich, 2002), pp. 154–60; Damaris Lüthi, 'Heimatliche Konventionen im Exil bewahren: hinduistische und christliche Religiosität tamilischer Flüchtlinge in Bern', in Martin Baumann, Brigitte Luchesi and Annette Wilke

Export of Cultural Values

Contests in the Tamil language, poetry and public speaking, by their practice of religious contents in a specific Tamil way – irrespective of whether they take place in a Christian or Hindu context – are one expression of the desire to maintain and preserve the culture brought to exile. For the refugee generation, this is still related to the much-awaited return to their own Tamil state. While structurally the first generation of Tamils, who fled to Switzerland in the 1980s, are quite well integrated[2] into Swiss society – in so far as is shown by their economic participation in the lowest, worst-paid sector of catering, nursing and cleaning, and their handling of the legal framework – in many respects they have preserved relative self-sufficiency, such as cultural and religious values and social organization.

So Christian religiosity practised by Tamil exiles in and around Berne is – as are the religious belief and practices of the Tamil Hindus – an integral part of everyday life, as well as a transnational extension of Sri Lankan Tamil traditions.

(eds), *Tempel und Tamilen in zweiter Heimat. Hindus aus Sri Lanka im deutschsprachigen und skandinavischen Raum* (Würzburg, 2003), pp. 295–322; Damaris Lüthi, *Umgang mit Gesundheit und Krankheit bei tamilischen Flüchtlingen im Raum Bern*, Arbeitsblatt Nr. 26 des Instituts für Ethnologie (Berne, 2004); Damaris Lüthi, *Soziale Beziehungen und Werte im Exil bewahren.Tamilische Flüchtlinge aus Sri Lanka im Raum Bern*, Arbeitsblatt Nr. 30 des Instituts für Ethnologie (Berne, 2005); Damaris Lüthi, 'Die kulturelle Identität bewahren', in Vera Markus (ed.), *In der Heimat ihrer Kinder. Tamilen in der Schweiz* (Zurich, 2005), pp. 18–27; Damaris Lüthi, 'Die "kulturelle Identität" bewahren. Tamilische Dichtkunst im Poesieverein', *Terra cognita, Schweizer Zeitschrift zu Integration und Migration*, 8 (2006): 76–7; Damaris Lüthi, Simone Büchi et al., 'Bedürfnisse und Erwartungen von tamilischen Frauen in der Schwangerenvorsorge eines Schweizer Universitätsspitals', *Pflege. Die wissenschaftliche Zeitschrift für Pflegeberufe*, 19 (2006): 295–302; Damaris Lüthi, 'Sri Lanka Tamilen in der Schweiz', in Klaus J. Bade, Pieter C. Emmer, Leo Lucassen and Jochen Oltmer (eds), *European Encyclopaedia of Migration* (Paderborn, 2007); Johanna Vögeli, '"Stärker als ihr denkt". Tamilische Frauen in der Schweiz', in Baumann, Luchesi and Wilke (eds), *Tempel und Tamilen in zweiter Heimat*, pp. 323–43; Johanna Vögeli, *Sumangali, die Glücksverheissende. Tamilisch-hinduistische Frauen in der Schweiz* (Berne, 2004); Johanna Vögeli, *Ohne Shakti ist Shiva nichts. Tamilische Geschlechterbeziehungen in der Schweiz*, Arbeitsblatt Nr. 27 des Instituts für Ethnologie (Berne, 2005).

2   I follow the terminology for 'assimilation', 'integration' and 'acculturation' used by Richard H. Thompson, 'Assimilation', in David Levinson and Melvin Ember (eds), *Encyclopedia of Cultural Anthropology*, vol. 1: (New York, 1996), pp. 112–15. Thompson defines 'assimilation' as synonymous with 'integration' as a 'process by which individuals of a foreign or minority culture enter the social positions of the standard or dominant culture in which they reside' (ibid., p. 112). Closely related is 'acculturation', used for the acquisition of language, habits and values of the standard or dominant culture. He distinguishes between acculturation as a cultural, and assimilation as a social process. I prefer to use the terms in a slightly different way, and see 'assimilation' as the result of both 'structural integration' – integration into, for example, legal, economical or educational structures – as well as 'acculturation', that is, 'cultural integration'.

Religiosity is an important aspect of the cultural, psychological, social and political identity of the exiles – irrespective of specific belief systems. Among Christians, this is manifest in attendance at sermons, in the celebration of religious festivals, in 'cultural' and political events with religious features, as well as in the plagiarism of Hindu attitudes towards childbirth, menstruation and death; it shows in the worship of Mary – in which the Hindus also join – in trips to pilgrimage sites, and in adherence to evangelical movements. Religiosity, moreover, manifests its importance in the specific support it provides when dealing with the problems of exile. Religiosity is hence one refuge for exported conventions of the Tamil homeland.

That for the Tamils religion – mostly theistic popular Hinduism,[3] and various forms of Christian belief, which according to Mosse's research in Tamil South India could probably be characterized as 'devotional bhakti'[4] – is not only very important in their home country, but is also central in the Swiss exile was noticeable from the beginning of their immigration in the early 1980s.[5] It manifested itself in the private worship of deities, church visiting, the popularity of devotional music, as well as the worship of Mother Mary. Today, religiosity also encompasses more public religious activities, such as attending Tamil temple *pujas* or church masses.

Apart from the predominantly Hindu Tamil population in Switzerland, there are 13 per cent Christian Tamils, the majority of Roman Catholic denomination.[6] The members of the *Karaiyar* fishing caste, who are the backbone of the dominant Tamil liberation movement, the LTTE (Liberation Tigers of Tamil Eelam), are in the majority Catholics.[7] A small percentage of refugees were already members of the Protestant Church at home, for example the CSI (Church of South India),[8] which

---

[3]   Christopher J. Fuller, *The Camphor Flame: Popular Hinduism and Indian Society* (Princeton, NJ, 1992), p. 5.

[4]   David Mosse, 'South Indian Christians, purity/impurity, and the caste system: Death ritual in a Tamil Roman Catholic community', *Journal of the Royal Anthropological Institute* (n.s.), 2 (1996): 461–83, see p. 473.

[5]   Barbara Messerli, *Maria wird zur Göttin. Hindu-TamilInnen verehren die christliche Madonna* (Berne, 1998), p. 27; Fides Vögeli, *Tamilische Frauen in der Schweiz. Was hilft ihnen in der Migration?* (Freiburg, 1996), p. 71; Hans-Rudolf Wicker, Geert Jan van Dok, Claudia Fischbacher, Damaris Lüthi, Mimi Marbach and Michèle Zufferey, *Tamilen in der Schweiz. Sozio-kulturelle Hintergründe, Flüchtlingssituation, Perspektiven* (Berne, 1984), pp. 13–14, see p. 46.

[6]   In all, 87 per cent of the Tamils who immigrated between 1983 and 1991 were Hindus, 10.5 per cent Roman Catholics, and 2.5 per cent Protestants, according to Christopher McDowell, *A Tamil Asylum Diaspora: Sri Lankan Migration, Settlement and Politics in Switzerland* (Oxford, 1996), p. 120. In Sri Lanka, there are one million Roman Catholics, among them 300,000 Tamils. See R.L. Stirrat, *Power and Religiosity in a Post-colonial Setting: Sinhala Catholics in Contemporary Sri Lanka* (Cambridge, 1992), p. 6.

[7]   McDowell, *A Tamil Asylum Diaspora*, p. 138.

[8]   See Lionel Caplan, 'Fundamentalism as Counter-culture: Protestants in Urban South India', in L. Caplan (ed.), *Studies in Religious Fundamentalism* (London, 1987), p. 159.

is present in both South India and Sri Lanka. In Switzerland, they visit Protestant churches, but these do not offer a Tamil sermon because the protestants want to refrain from missionary activities.[9] Instead, for example, the St John's Church in Berne conducts a monthly 'peace sermon' directed at all Christian foreigners. An impressive number of Tamils are members of evangelical movements such as the Philadelphia Missionary Church (PMC), the Pentecostals, the Christian Gnaden Gemeinde, the Salvation Army or the Jehovah's Witnesses. Apparently, many of the Tamil members of these sects were converted from Hinduism to Christianity in exile. Many of these evangelical movements are also present in Sri Lanka, as some informants explained, among them the Salvation Army, Adventists or Pentecostals, who spread the Word from the Tamil area of South India.[10]

Vani (36), a converted Hindu woman, has adopted her new Christian belief with dedication. Her timetable, apart from her duties as a housewife and mother of three little children, is filled with PMC activities: prayers on Saturdays, women's group on Tuesdays, Bible meeting on Wednesdays, and nightlong prayers once a month in the church. She converted while still in Sri Lanka, after the Hindu deities had failed when her husband was imprisoned. 'He was suspected to be a *puli* ['Tiger', member of the LTTE],' she explains:

> I was in love. When my husband was jailed, I prayed for seven days and performed the red and white flower oracle in the temple. 'White' means that the wish will come true, 'red' that not. When I had a white flower, I was convinced that my husband would soon be released from prison, and I at once travelled to Colombo to pick him up. But he did not come out.

Then, when she stayed with her husband's relatives in Vavuniya, she attended a service offered by the PMC: 'In my heart I prayed to Jesus to give me my husband back. Jesus answered that he would be released, and on the same day he got out!' In spite of all that, her husband did not show interest in Christianity, and adamantly refused to go to church. But after coming to Switzerland, he had some very bad experiences: he lost money gambling, and had health problems. He regularly fainted and was hospitalized, but no cause could be found. 'He used to lie on the sofa, sleep and drink a lot,' explained Vani. Then one day at the railway station in Berne, he was addressed by a man who invited him to his church. 'My husband wanted to die, went to his room and said: "If you are God, please help me." That was in 1994. Since then, he has not been in hospital any more; since then, he goes to church.'

Some informants argued that the new belief offers clear moral guidelines for orientation in an incomprehensible Swiss society. Many Hindus and Roman

---

[9] Information from Brigitte Morgenthaler Subramaniam, Fachstelle Migration der Reformierten Kirchen Bern-Jura, personal communication.

[10] Stirrat, *Power and Religiosity in a Post-colonial Setting*, p. 60; Caplan, 'Fundamentalism as Counter-culture', p. 168.

Catholics, however, are annoyed that Tamil members of evangelical communities often try to convert their own family and friends.

Centrality of Religious Practice

Catholic Tamil families in Berne go to mass on Sundays, preferably to the one performed in Tamil, which takes place twice monthly in the Holy Trinity Church. Their children attend Sunday School. Important events of the religious calendar are often opportunities for festivities. Central for Christians are Christmas, Easter and Pentecost, and cantonal associations conduct yearly festivals for saints: in May in Berne in honour of the holy Joseph, in June in Basle for the holy Antonius, and at the beginning of August in Mariastein for Mary. The Catholics celebrate the first communion, the Protestants the confirmation of their children.

Many of the evangelical movements offer services in Tamil. The PMC in its church in the centre of Berne offers several services in Tamil each weekend, and one Pentecostal sub-group conducts services with translation into Tamil every other Sunday at St Thomas's Church in Köniz near Berne.

The Christians also invite Hindus to some public festivities. For example, the Catholic 'celebration of light', Olivizha, in December is celebrated jointly by Christians and Hindus: they stage the Christmas tale as well as perform Bharata Natyam dances and music (see Figure 5.1). For Christmas, the Christians bake *motakam* and *vatai*s and give some to their Hindu friends, and at the Hindu *Tai Pongal* in January, receive snacks in return from the Hindus.

Figure 5.1   Girl reciting her poem on the theme 'Christmas', 2005. (Photo: Kaspar Grossenbacher)

As well as their religious significance, church visits and public festivities have a social meaning.[11] They offer the opportunity to meet compatriots who live in Switzerland geographically rather dispersed, they enable meeting potential marriage partners, or are an opportunity to dress up and demonstrate wealth.

Tamil Christian religiosity also manifests itself in private worship, though to a lesser extent than among Hindus. For Christmas, the Christians install a Christmas tree in the living-room of their flats and give gifts to their children, and so do many Hindu families. The Hindus explain that their children know about the festivity from school, and have certain expectations. 'We like to make them happy with this,' said Kala (43), mother of two girls and a very solid Hindu. 'After all, there is only one God, which manifests itself in various forms.' Some Catholics and members of evangelical movements conduct fasts before Easter. Incidentally, fasting (*viratam*) for Tamils does not necessarily indicate the reduction of food consumption, but means first of all renouncing meat and rice. Many Catholics at such times not only omit meat but – like the Hindus – also fish.

The vitality of Christian religious values manifests itself further in the fact that – as for the Hindus – religious wedding ceremonies conducted by a priest are considered proper, that is socially legal, marriage, rather than civil ceremonies. Religiosity also emerges in the political rhetoric and programs of the LTTE in the service of its national and transnational politics of liberation.[12] On *mavirar*, the 'Great Heroes Day', which is celebrated annually around 27 November, Christian and Hindu symbolism is drawn on too, though the whole event can hardly be called religious.[13] It is the national day of Tamil Eelam and the joint public memorial day for all those who lost their lives in the liberation struggle. Organized by the LTTE, the event is celebrated in a big way both in the Sri Lankan Tamil homeland as well as in the diaspora. In 2001 in Switzerland, it attracted more than 12,000 Tamils to the Forum Fribourg. As well as political speeches, Bharata Natyam dances and martial plays, in the huge hall there was a procession of artificial coffins, accompanied by penetrating political slogans. The deceased fighters-turned-Great Heroes were worshipped in a gallery with photos and decorated shrines, as well as through the installation of an artificial cemetery with tombstones (see Figure 5.2). Similarly, at the '*Mavirar* Cup', the annual national football tournament of Swiss Tamil clubs, an artificial tombstone is placed in the corner of the playing

---

[11]   See Martin Baumann, *Migration, Religion, Integration. Buddhistische Vietnamesen und hinduistische Tamilen in Deutschland* (Marburg, 2000), pp. 20, 144, and Parminder Bhachu, *Twice Migrants: East African Sikh Settlers in Britain* (London, 1985), pp. 40, 41.

[12]   See, for example, Peter Schalk, 'Beyond Hindu Festivals: The Celebration of Great Heroes' Day by the Liberation Tigers of Tamil Eelam (LTTE) in Europe', in Baumann, Luchesi and Wilke (eds), *Tempel und Tamilen in zweiter Heimat*, pp. 391–420.

[13]   See Michael Roberts, 'Filial devotion in Tamil culture and the Tiger cult of martyrdom', *Contributions to Indian Sociology* (n.s.), 30/2 (1996): 245–72; Arjun Appadurai, *Modernity at Large: Cultural Dimensions of Globalization* (Minneapolis, MN, 1996), pp. 15, 22, 147.

field – Christian and Hindu elements are here synthesized in the tombstone, which is moreover a Hindu *camati* (Sanskrit *samadhi*) or *natukal* ('planted stone'), referring to Tamil hero worship in the historical *Pallava* age. An artificial graveyard is apparently a substitute for the *tuyilum illam*s ('abode of rest') installed by the LTTE since the battle at Anaiyiravu in 1991 for both Christian and Hindu fallen heroes, for these to be close to the soil, where they change into seeds as the basis for new life.[14] A religious metaphor turns into a political symbol.

Figure 5.2   Artificial cemetery, *mavirar*, 2001, Fribourg. (Photo: Damaris Lüthi)

Worship of the Virgin Mary

While many Tamil Hindus visit churches as well as temples, Christians hardly ever visit temples. Yet there are many personal, religious and political contacts between Catholics, Protestants and Hindus. For example, Hindus and Christians, apart from the joint Christmas celebration, also celebrate a yearly refugee service (*mamanitar*) as well as *mavirar* together. Members of evangelical movements, however, try not to get involved with the others. They tend not to attend *mavirar*, for example, because of its martial character.

Both Tamil Christians and Hindus in Switzerland visit churches to worship the Virgin Mary, called Mata.[15] Almost half of the Hindus we asked explained that they regularly go to church. The Udayakumars, for example, visit the Murugan

---

[14]   Peter Schalk, 'The Revival of Martyr Cults among Īlavar', *Temenos*, 3 (1997): 181ff.

[15]   See Wicker et al., *Tamilen in der Schweiz*, p. 13; McDowell, *A Tamil Asylum Diaspora*, pp. 232ff.; Messerli, *Maria wird zur Göttin. Hindu-TamilInnen verehren die christliche Madonna*; Vögeli, *Tamilische Frauen in der Schweiz*, pp. 72ff.; Annette Wilke,

temple on Fridays, but on Tuesdays go to a church in Muri, where there is a statue of Mata, and which is close to their home. Many informants tell about pilgrimages to the 'Black Madonna' in the Benedictine monastery of Einsiedeln, as well as to the Madonna in the Catholic church of Mariastein near Basle. Both have been popular pilgrimage sites among Tamils since the 1980s. As some Hindu informants mentioned, the worship of Mata in the churches in the 1980s to a certain extent even served as a substitute before there were Hindu temples.[16] Some Hindus added that church visits were not new to them in exile, because they had already visited churches in Sri Lanka. Apparently, the worship of Virgin Mary has a long tradition in Sri Lanka and – for example, at the shrine of Our Lady of Lourdes in Kudagama – also attracts Hindus.[17] This confirms the information given by Messerli's informants that the worship of the Virgin is not a phenomenon caused by the exile situation, but that many Hindu refugees had already worshipped Mata back home.[18] Notably, among our informants the Mata worship was not a lower-caste habit, as claimed by McDowell, but was very popular among members of higher castes too.[19]

Religiosity upon Crises

In the fragile exile situation, religiosity and specific religious movements for some migrants become a refuge for feelings of anxiety. At times of crisis and when subjected to blows of fate such as infertility, illness, loneliness, alcoholism, domestic violence or financial debts, religiosity often becomes important for Swiss Tamils, even for persons who are normally rather inactive in that respect. Many Tamil Christians and Hindus in a precarious situation visit temples, go to church, worship specific deities such as Mata, or join a sect, to ask the deities for assistance and peace of mind – similar to common practice back home.[20] Many informants told stories of people who were very ill but recovered after praying to Jesus after they converted to Christianity. For many people, membership of an evangelical movement has a therapeutic effect. The PMC even provides its own healer, who has helped many devotees. During his visit to the Berne community in mid-2001, a whole series of male church members swore to recoveries: one person declared himself cured of cancer, another healed his stomach ulcer, another

---

'Mythos in Bewegung. Die Grosse Göttin in Symbolsystem, Kultus und Alltag', *Zeitschrift für Missionswissenschaft und Religionswissenschaft*, 80. Jahrgang, 1, 4 (1996): 265–283.

[16]   See Wicker et al., *Tamilen in der Schweiz.*

[17]   Stirrat, *Power and Religiosity in a Post-colonial Setting*, pp. 26–7, 153.

[18]   Messerli, *Maria wird zur Göttin*, pp. 12, 20.

[19]   McDowell, *A Tamil Asylum Diaspora*, p. 235.

[20]   See also Bryan Pfaffenberger, 'The Second Self in a Third World Immigrant Community', *Ethnos*, 60/1–2 (1995): 59–80, p. 69; Fuller, *The Camphor Flame*, p. 71, 224; Dennis B. McGilvray, *Symbolic Heat. Gender, Health and Worship among the Tamils of South India and Sri Lanka* (Ahmedabad and Boulder, CO, 1998), p. 61.

no longer suffered from migraine, and a total of seven went on stage and claimed that the healer had cured them of heavy alcoholism. A number of Tamil women informants stressed the positive effect that conversion to evangelical Christianity had on their men: that they had stopped beating them, that they did not waste money on consumer goods any longer, or that they had curbed heavy alcoholism.

For some people, a problem can also be the reason for a pilgrimage. For example, the 32-year-old Hindu Narayanan, who was diagnosed schizophrenic after long and lonely alcoholism, explained that he visited the church of Mariastein and there promised to Mata in writing that he would never again touch alcohol. Countless informants have made a pilgrimage to Lourdes, and some have visited the Luz-Mata in Paris, who is said to possess special *cakti* ('power'). During trips to relatives in South India, Christian as well as Hindu families visit the famous Velankanni ('Virgin Mary') church. Pilgrimages to holy sites are a frequent phenomenon in South Asia,[21] where many people make a 'contract' with a deity to fulfil an important wish and undertake a pilgrimage to express their vow.

Copying Hindu Im/purity Restrictions

Swiss Tamil Christians, mostly Catholics, to a certain extent observe im/purity restrictions followed by the Hindus[22] – generally, as my informants explained, in a dominant Hindu context, Christians tend to copy Hindus.[23] Only members of evangelical movements stressed that they did not follow any impurity restrictions.

As is well known, among Hindus menstruation, childbirth and death, as well as belonging to a low caste and pursuing a certain lifestyle, are considered to have a polluting (in Tamil, *tittu* or *totakku*) influence on the body.[24] An impure body is considered *pavam* ('sinful', 'poor'), and hence incompatible with the presence of deities, who can inflict misfortune. This excludes worshipping them in an impure

---

[21]   James Cartman, *Hinduism in Ceylon* (Colombo, Sri Lanka, 1957), pp. 113, 120–30; Fuller, *The Camphor Flame*, pp. 204ff.

[22]   Lüthi, 'Heimatliche Konventionen im Exil bewahren'; Lüthi, *Soziale Beziehungen und Werte im Exil bewahren.Tamilische Flüchtlinge aus Sri Lanka im Raum Bern*.

[23]   See also Damaris Lüthi, *Washing Off Sin: Cleanliness in Kottar, South India* (Berne, 1999), p. 176.

[24]   See, for example, Louis Dumont, *Homo hierarchicus. Le système des castes et ses implications* (Paris, 1966); John Henry Hutton, *Caste in India: Its Nature, Functions and Origins* (Cambridge, 1963 [1946]); Lüthi, *Washing Off Sin*; Charles Malamoud, 'Observations sur la notion de "reste" dans le brahmanisme', in *Cuire le monde. Rite et pensée dans l'Inde ancienne* (Paris, 1989); Michael Moffat, *An Untouchable Community in South India: Structure and Consensus* (Princeton, NJ, 1979); M.N. Srinivas, *Religion and Society among the Coorgs of South India* (London, 1952); H.N.C. Stevenson, 'Status Evaluation in the Hindu Caste System', *Journal of the Royal Anthropological Institute*, LXXXIV/1–2 (1954): 45–65.

state in the temple or at the house shrine.[25] However, the Christian God, according to my informants, is not angered by impurities, and therefore visiting churches in polluted states is possible.[26] All the same, some of our Christian informants said that they avoid church visits at such times, while Hindus said that in a polluted state, they sometimes choose a church instead of a temple, because this is allowed.

Like Hindus, Catholic women during their menstruation pay special attention to their personal hygiene, and after three days take a full shower or bath. Moreover, they also pay special attention to the first menstruation,[27] and Catholic girls stay at home in seclusion for several days. But there is no special bath – no ceremonial purification by a priest. Nor is the puberty ritual a precondition for a Christian marriage. Yet the social element, the presence of the *mama*s (MB) and *mami*s (MBW) during the final event, is as important as among Hindus. Similarly, the Protestants (CSI) give the first period special importance, and meet for prayers with the vicar. Relatives, including cross-relatives, as well as friends are invited, and the girl appears in a white dress and successively in saris of various colours. Sometimes the celebration is postponed for a few years and conducted at the same time as the religious confirmation.

After giving birth, Catholic women – though to a lesser extent than the Hindus – are considered impure, and do not leave the house with their newborn child for 31 days.[28] However, in contrast to Hindu habits, it is not considered polluting to eat food prepared by members of the birth house, nor is it necessary to have a shower before re-entering one's own house after a visit, and there is no priestly purification ritual. On the 31st day, everything is washed and the woman takes a full shower, including her head. The child is decorated with gold chains and rings, and the family goes to church for the first time after the birth. Church visits are allowed before, but as one informant explained, if the woman did not wait until the 31st day, people would complain about her. The child's *mama* (MB) plays a similar role as among the Hindus. He offers a full bed outfit for the newborn, and for the first time puts the child in its own bed after the family has prayed for it. There is no name-giving ritual at the end of the impurity period. Instead, Christians baptize the child, which normally takes place on the 40th day, but also sometimes only after two months or one year. Some tonsure their child upon baptism, 'as part of Tamil culture'.

---

[25]   Lüthi, *Washing Off Sin*, pp. 119, 124.

[26]   Ibid., p. 68; Mosse, 'South Indian Christians, purity/impurity, and the caste system', p. 476.

[27]   See also Lüthi, *Washing Off Sin*, p. 71; Kalpana Ram, *Mukkuvar Women. Gender, Hegemony and Capitalist Transformation in a South Indian Fishing Community* (London, 1991), p. 80; Deborah Winslow, 'Rituals of first Menstruation in Sri Lanka', *MAN*, 15/4 (1980): 603–25.

[28]   See also Lüthi, *Washing Off Sin*, pp. 74ff.; Bryan Pfaffenberger, *Caste in Tamil Culture: The Religious Foundations of Sudra Domination in Tamil Sri Lanka* (Syracuse, NY, 1982), pp. 196, 206.

Protestants handle birth similarly: they stay at home for 31 days, 'out of convention', as one informant explained. Thereafter, they clean everything, but there is no priestly purification. Baptism can take place on the 31st day or later. However, as I was told, the *mama* (MB) does not play a special role.

After a death, Catholics and Protestants follow similar restrictions and ceremonies to Hindus, again without priestly purification,[29] and church visits are allowed. Catholics do not attend auspicious events such as weddings, puberty celebrations or birthdays for some time, but the mourning period is shorter than among Hindus. The anniversary of a death is marked by a mass. Protestant informants observe similar ceremonies and restrictions, except that the family of the deceased does not need to avoid auspicious events, though many voluntarily follow that convention.

Caste Values

In keeping with the partial validity of im/purity values, caste values are also valid among Christians. However, as among Hindus, the term 'caste' and the various caste names are taboo in the official discourse of Christian exiles – analogous to practice at home and in other diasporas.[30] To avoid using the terms 'high-caste' or 'low-caste' or the caste names, people now often distinguish between 'good' and 'bad' castes. Christians share caste membership as well as many of the associated values and habits with Hindus. Thus Christian informants explained that they were members of specific castes, such as the high Vellalar caste (originally landlords; consisting of Hindus, Catholics, Protestants and members of evangelical movements), the middle- to lower-caste Karaiyar (originally fisher people; Hindus and Catholics) as well as the lower-caste Maravar (Hindus and Catholics). Most Catholic informants belonged to the Karaiyar caste. The background for the Karaiyar is that conversion to Catholicism during the Portuguese colonial occupation in the sixteenth century was an expression of autonomy *vis-à-vis* the dominant position of the Vellalar.[31] By the middle of the twentieth century, this caste was relatively well educated and occupied respectable, middle-range occupations apart from fishing.[32] The caste associates itself with the Kshatriya *varna*.[33] Among the Swiss Tamil diaspora, the

---

[29]   See also Lüthi, *Washing Off Sin*, pp. 84ff., 181ff.; Mosse, 'South Indian Christians, purity/impurity, and the caste system'; Pfaffenberger, *Caste in Tamil Culture*, p. 196).

[30]   See, for example, Baumann, *Migration, Religion, Integration*, p. 110; Øivind Fuglerud, *Life on the Outside: The Tamil Diaspora and Long-distance Nationalism* (London, 1999), p. 111.

[31]   Bryan Pfaffenberger, 'The Political Construction of Defensive Nationalism: The 1968 Temple Entry Crisis in Sri Lanka', in Chelvadurai Manogaran and Brian Pfaffenberger (eds), *The Sri Lankan Tamils: Ethnicity and Identity*, (San Francisco, CA and Oxford, 1994), pp. 143–68, see p. 146.

[32]   Cartman, *Hinduism in Ceylon*, p. 135.

[33]   Kenneth David, 'Hierarchy and Equivalence in Jaffna, North Sri Lanka: Normative Codes as Mediator', in Kenneth David (ed.), *The New Wind: Changing Identities in South*

Karaiyar are nowadays respected and considered a 'good caste', probably not least because many members of the dominant liberation movement LTTE, including its head, Prabhakaran, have this caste background.

Besides the partial following of im/purity restrictions related to physical states, Christians also believe that the purity of food has a certain influence on the cleanliness of the body, and thereby the family and caste, as it has for Hindus. This is based on the South Asian idea that food, due to its inner quality as well as the physical impurities of the person who is cooking it, can have a polluting effect on the body and mind of the higher-caste eater.[34] While vegetarian food is considered pure and is tolerated by the gods, meats are polluting. Food impurity restrictions are graded in line with caste affiliation. Thus, like the Hindu Vellalar of certain sub-castes, the Christian Vellalar eat lamb, chicken, fish and eggs, but avoid pork and beef. Yet the lower-caste Karaiyar, both Hindus and Catholics, eat crab as well as beef and pork in addition to these meats.

Similarly, for Christians, occupation has a status meaning comparable to that for Hindus. In the traditional caste order, each caste performed a hereditary occupation, whose degree of im/purity co-defined its status in the hierarchy.[35] Very unclean occupations – those dealing with street waste (Sweepers), uterine blood (Washermen), death and food refuse – had a strong and permanently polluting influence on the family and caste, and hence on its position in the social hierarchy. The awareness of these values is still present among the first generation of Swiss Tamils, irrespective of their religious affiliation. The often very impure occupations performed by most Tamils in the Swiss cleaning, catering and nursing sector are considered humiliating, yet accepted as unavoidable for the first generation of immigrants. Esther (Protestant Vellalar), who works as a kitchen help, explains that a Tamil friend came to see her in Switzerland, and then back in Sri Lanka told her parents: 'She is doing fine in Switzerland, and she is well off, but don't ask me what kind of work she does!' Julie (Catholic Karaiyar) stressed that she kept secret from her mother in Sri Lanka that she works as a cleaning woman, because she would be shocked: 'It would mean that I am the same as the Pallar and toilet

---

Asia (The Hague, 1977), pp. 179–226.

[34] See, for example, Dumont, *Homo hierarchicus,* pp. 63ff. and 168ff.; Hutton, *Caste in India*; Lüthi, *Washing Off Sin*, pp. 103ff.; Malamoud, 'Observations sur la notion de "reste" dans le brahmanisme', pp. 13, 17; Jonathan Parry, 'The end of the body', in Michel Feher (ed.), *Fragments of a History of the Human Body, Part Two* (New York, 1989), pp. 490–517, see p. 500.

[35] See, for example, Simon Charsley, '"Untouchable": What is in a name?', *Journal of the Royal Anthropological Institute* (n.s.), 2/1 (1996): 1–23; Dumont, *Homo hierarchicus*; Lüthi, *Washing Off Sin*; Michael Moffat, *An Untouchable Community in South India: Structure and Consensus* (Princeton, NJ, 1979), p. 89; Mosse, 'South Indian Christians, purity/impurity, and the caste system', p. 74; Parry, 'The end of the body', p. 88; Srinivas, *Religion and Society among the Coorgs of South India*, p. 28; M.N. Srinivas, *The Remembered Village* (Delhi, 1976), p. 179; Stevenson, 'Status Evaluation in the Hindu Caste System'.

cleaning Paraiyar [two of the lowest castes], who used to come to our house to clean,' she said.

Apparently, in the short term, these Swiss impure occupations do not have an effect on the imported caste status, nor do they have any equalizing impact on those Tamils with varying caste affiliations working in the same lower-level jobs. On the contrary, many people are indignant that they are not placed according to their social background, and find it unfair and upsetting that they should have to share the workplace with compatriots of lower caste status. Some higher-caste people find that it is much harder for them than for members of lower castes to perform degrading occupations. In mainly Tamil work teams with a head who belongs to a lower caste than some subordinates, it can lead to conflict. At the time of our research, this happened among the women of two cleaning teams in Bernese hospitals. In both cases, the subordinates explained to outsiders that their boss was a 'Paraiyar', and a Catholic Karaiyar as well as a Vellalar employee explained the problem they had with their boss with reference to her low-caste background.

As among Hindus, for the Christian Tamil diaspora the caste – the purity status of a couple – is still central for reproduction, and hence for marriage. For the Tamil exiles who arrange their marriages transnationally, the caste affiliation of the couple, even the membership of a certain caste segment, is still important.[36] Incidentally, this is the only subject on which our informants openly conceded that caste still played a role – in spite of the ban on caste and the strong support for inter-caste marriages by the LTTE.[37] The differentiation and separation of castes is therefore perpetuated by caste-endogamous marriages. A clear majority of our married informants had wedded a member of the same caste in an arranged marriage. Among them are 20 persons who even married cross-cousins.[38] The majority of the informants consider caste endogamy normal and meaningful, and criticize inter-caste marriage – which is used as a synonym for 'love marriage'

[36] See Johanna Vögeli, *Cuvicil Tirumanaceeval (Heiratsdienste in der Schweiz). Ethnographie über Heiratsstrategien und Verwandtschaft bei Tamilen und Tamilinnen im Kanton Bern* (Berne, 1998). Similarly, for Sri Lankan Tamils in other exile countries, see Fuglerud, *Life on the Outside*, pp. 99, 111; Pfaffenberger, 'The Second Self in a Third World Immigrant Community', p. 64, and Kurt Salentin, *Tamilische Flüchtlinge in der Bundesrepublik. Eine Bestandsaufnahme sozialer, ökonomischer und rechtlicher Aspekte der Integration* (Frankfurt am Main, 2002) pp. 161, 184; for other South Asian diasporas, see Roger Ballard, 'Migration and kinship: The differential effect of marriage rules on the processes of Punjabi migration to Britain', in Colin Clarke, Ceri Peach and Steven Vertovec (eds), *South Asians Overseas: Migration and Ethnicity* (Cambridge, 1990), p. 230; Bhachu, *Twice Migrants*, pp. 63, 168.

[37] Adele Balasingham, *The Will to Freedom: An Inside View of Tamil Resistance* (Mitcham, UK, 2001), p. 299; Dagmar Hellmann-Rajanayagam, 'The Tamil "Tigers" in northern Sri Lanka: Origins, factions, programmes', *Internationales Asienforum*, 17 (1986): 63–85.

[38] See Lüthi, *Soziale Beziehungen und Werte im Exil bewahren. Tamilische Flüchtlinge aus Sri Lanka im Raum Bern*, and Vögeli, *Cuvicil Tirumanaceeval (Heiratsdienste in der Schweiz)*, pp. 137ff.

– as unstable as well as incompatible with the different 'cultures' of the castes involved. Moreover, children of mixed couples are not accepted as members of their caste by the higher one of the two participating castes. Generally, inter-caste marriages are avoided because they harm the reputation of the families involved, and thereby obstruct marriage arrangements for younger siblings.

Summary

The religiosity and social values of the first-generation Christian Tamils in Berne, similar to the religiosity of Tamil Hindus,[39] seem closely related to conventions in the Tamil areas of Sri Lanka. The style of worship, the faith in miracles, the rules in connection with impurities or the contiguous importance of caste differentiation indicate the perpetuation of tradition. Many values and practices illustrate a strong Hindu influence, especially those related to im/purity concepts. Hindus conversely tend to pragmatically incorporate Christian deities into their belief system and practices of worship.

Hence, Christian faith among Tamil exiles is not an indication of integration, as is sometimes claimed,[40] but an extension of tradition. It is not always the type of religion which points to closeness or difference. The style of religious practices may be closer to traditions of the homeland and to other religions, such as Hinduism, than to habits of the new country.

In line with this, contests in Tamil-language poetry and public speaking, whether they take place in a Christian or Hindu context, by expressing religious ideas in a specific Tamil way, are one indication of the weight given to the maintenance of the immigrant 'culture' in view of the much-desired return to a Tamil Eelam. By preserving their language and other cultural elements, the refugee generation intends to prevent the second generation from becoming alienated from its Sri Lankan Tamil roots. However, in spite of these efforts, after puberty many second-generation Tamils tend to detach themselves from the traditional religious and social values of their parents.

Thus specific Tamil religiosity – be it Christian or Hindu – exported from the 'motherland' is perpetuated in exile as an extension of 'moral space'.[41] It constitutes an important aspect of joint 'cultural', psychic, social and political identity, exemplified in the tombstone–*camati*–*natukal* as a shared religious-political-historical symbol for all Tamils.

---

[39]   Lüthi, 'Heimatliche Konventionen im Exil bewahren'.

[40]   Baumann, *Migration, Religion, Integration*, pp. 17, 19, 176.

[41]   Pnina Werbner, *The Migration Process: Capital, Gifts and Offerings among British Pakistanis* (Oxford, 1990), p. 336; Hans-Rudolf Wicker, 'From Complex Culture to Cultural Complexity', in Pnina Werbner and Tariq Modood (eds), *Debating Cultural Hybridity: Multi-cultural Identities and the Politics of Anti-racism* (London, 1998), p. 210.

References

Appadurai, Arjun, *Modernity at Large: Cultural Dimensions of Globalization* (Minneapolis, MN: University of Minnesota Press, 1996).

Balasingham, Adele, *The Will to Freedom: An Inside View of Tamil Resistance* (Mitcham, UK: Fairmax Publishing, 2001).

Ballard, Roger, 'Migration and kinship: The differential effect of marriage rules on the processes of Punjabi migration to Britain', in Colin Clarke, Ceri Peach and Steven Vertovec (eds), *South Asians Overseas: Migration and Ethnicity* (Cambridge: Cambridge University Press, 1990), pp. 219–49.

Baumann, Martin, *Migration, Religion, Integration. Buddhistische Vietnamesen und hinduistische Tamilen in Deutschland* (Marburg: diagonal, 2000).

Bhachu, Parminder, *Twice Migrants: East African Sikh Settlers in Britain* (London: Tavistock, 1985).

Bourdieu, Pierre, *Entwurf einer Theorie der Praxis* (Frankfurt am Main: Suhrkamp, 1976 [1972]).

Caplan, Lionel, 'Fundamentalism as Counter-culture: Protestants in Urban South India', in L. Caplan (ed.), *Studies in Religious Fundamentalism* (London: Macmillan, 1987), pp. 156–76.

Cartman, James, *Hinduism in Ceylon* (Colombo, Sri Lanka: M.D. Gunasena, 1957).

Charsley, Simon, '"Untouchable": What is in a name?', *Journal of the Royal Anthropological Institute* (n.s.), 2/1 (1996): 1–23.

David, Kenneth. 'Hierarchy and Equivalence in Jaffna, North Sri Lanka: Normative Codes as Mediator', in Kenneth David (ed.), *The New Wind: Changing Identities in South Asia* (The Hague: Mouton, 1977), pp. 179–226.

Dumont, Louis, *Homo hierarchicus. Le système des castes et ses implications* (Paris: Editions Gallimard, 1966).

Fankhauser, Marie-Anne, 'Tamilische Jugendliche in der Schweiz', *Tsantsa*, 8 (2003): 173–6.

Fuglerud, Øivind, *Life on the Outside: The Tamil Diaspora and Long-distance Nationalism* (London: Pluto, 1999).

Fuller, Christopher J., *The Camphor Flame: Popular Hinduism and Indian Society* (Princeton, NJ: Princeton University Press, 1992).

Hellmann-Rajanayagam, Dagmar, 'The Tamil "Tigers" in northern Sri Lanka: Origins, factions, programmes', *Internationales Asienforum*, 17 (1986): 63–85.

Hutton, John Henry, *Caste in India: Its Nature, Functions and Origins* (Cambridge: Cambridge University Press, 1963 [1946]).

Lüthi, Damaris, *Washing Off Sin: Cleanliness in Kottar, South India* (PhD thesis, Berne University, 1999).

Lüthi, Damaris, 'Das mediale Fenster zur Heimat. Tamilinnen und Tamilen im Schweizer Exil und der indische Film', in Alexandra Schneider (ed.), *Bollywood. Das indische Kino und die Schweiz* (Zurich: Edition Museum für Gestaltung, 2002), pp. 154–60.

Lüthi, Damaris, 'Heimatliche Konventionen im Exil bewahren: hinduistische und christliche Religiosität tamilischer Flüchtlinge in Bern', in Martin Baumann, Brigitte Luchesi and Annette Wilke (eds), *Tempel und Tamilen in zweiter Heimat. Hindus aus Sri Lanka im deutschsprachigen und skandinavischen Raum* (Würzburg: Ergon Verlag, 2003), pp. 295–322.

Lüthi, Damaris, *Umgang mit Gesundheit und Krankheit bei tamilischen Flüchtlingen im Raum Bern*, Arbeitsblatt Nr. 26 des Instituts für Ethnologie (Berne: Institut für Ethnologie der Universität Bern, 2004).

Lüthi, Damaris, 'Die kulturelle Identität bewahren', in Vera Markus (ed.), *In der Heimat ihrer Kinder. Tamilen in der Schweiz* (Zurich: Offizin Verlag, 2005), pp. 18–27.

Lüthi, Damaris, *Soziale Beziehungen und Werte im Exil bewahren. Tamilische Flüchtlinge aus Sri Lanka im Raum Bern*, Arbeitsblatt Nr. 30 des Instituts für Ethnologie (Berne: Institut für Ethnologie der Universität Bern, 2005).

Lüthi, Damaris, 'Die "kulturelle Identität" bewahren. Tamilische Dichtkunst im Poesieverein', *Terra cognita, Schweizer Zeitschrift zu Integration und Migration*, 8 (2006): 76–7.

Lüthi, Damaris, 'Sri Lanka Tamilen in der Schweiz', in Klaus J. Bade, Pieter C. Emmer, Leo Lucassen and Jochen Oltmer (eds), *European Encyclopaedia of Migration* (Paderborn: Ferdinand Schöningh/Wilhelm Fink, 2007).

Lüthi, Damaris, Simone Büchi et al., 'Bedürfnisse und Erwartungen von tamilischen Frauen in der Schwangerenvorsorge eines Schweizer Universitätsspitals', *Pflege. Die wissenschaftliche Zeitschrift für Pflegeberufe*, 19 (2006): 295–302.

Malamoud, Charles, 'Observations sur la notion de "reste" dans le brahmanisme', in *Cuire le monde. Rite et pensée dans l'Inde ancienne* (Paris: Editions La Découverte, 1989).

McDowell, Christopher, *A Tamil Asylum Diaspora: Sri Lankan Migration, Settlement and Politics in Switzerland* (Oxford: Berghahn Books, 1996).

McGilvray, Dennis B., *Symbolic Heat. Gender, Health and Worship among the Tamils of South India and Sri Lanka* (Ahmedabad and Boulder, CO: Mapin Publishing and University of Colorado Museum, 1998).

Messerli, Barbara, *Maria wird zur Göttin. Hindu-TamilInnen verehren die christliche Madonna* (Berne: Lizentiatsarbeit, Religionswissenschaftliches Institut der Universität Bern, 1998).

Moffat, Michael, *An Untouchable Community in South India: Structure and Consensus* (Princeton, NJ: Princeton University Press, 1979).

Mosse, David, 'Idioms of subordination and styles of protest among Christian and Hindu Harijan castes in Tamil Nad', *Contributions to Indian Sociology* (n.s.), 28/1 (1994): 67–106.

Mosse, David, 'South Indian Christians, purity/impurity, and the caste system: death ritual in a Tamil Roman Catholic community', *Journal of the Royal Anthropological Institute* (n.s.), 2 (1996): 461–83.

Parry, Jonathan, 'The end of the body', in Michel Feher (ed.), *Fragments of a History of the Human Body, Part Two* (New York: Zone, 1989), pp. 490–517.

Pfaffenberger, Bryan, *Caste in Tamil Culture: The Religious Foundations of Sudra Domination in Tamil Sri Lanka* (Syracuse, NY: Syracuse University, 1982).

Pfaffenberger, Bryan, 'The Political Construction of Defensive Nationalism: The 1968 Temple Entry Crisis in Sri Lanka', in Chelvadurai Manogaran and Brian Pfaffenberger (eds), *The Sri Lankan Tamils: Ethnicity and Identity* (San Francisco, CA and Oxford: Westview Press, 1994), pp. 143–68.

Pfaffenberger, Bryan, 'The Second Self in a Third World Immigrant Community', *Ethnos*, 60/1–2 (1995): 59–80.

Ram, Kalpana, *Mukkuvar Women: Gender, Hegemony and Capitalist Transformation in a South Indian Fishing Community* (London: Zed Books, 1991).

Roberts, Michael, 'Filial devotion in Tamil culture and the Tiger cult of martyrdom', *Contributions to Indian Sociology* (n.s.), 30/2 (1996): 245–72.

Russo Chrysostom, Chitra, *Katpakam. Ein Treffpunkt für tamilische Frauen* (Zurich: Diplomarbeit, Schule für Soziale Arbeit Zürich, 1994).

Salentin, Kurt, *Tamilische Flüchtlinge in der Bundesrepublik. Eine Bestandsaufnahme sozialer, ökonomischer und rechtlicher Aspekte der Integration* (Frankfurt am Main: Verlag für Interkulturelle Kommunikation, 2002).

Schalk, Peter, 'The Revival of Martyr Cults among Īlavar', *Temenos*, 3 (1997): 151–90.

Schalk, Peter, 'Beyond Hindu Festivals: The Celebration of Great Heroes' Day by the Liberation Tigers of Tamil Eelam (LTTE) in Europe', in Martin Baumann, Brigitte Luchesi and Annette Wilke (eds), *Tempel und Tamilen in zweiter Heimat. Hindus aus Sri Lanka im deutschsprachigen und skandinavischen Raum* (Würzburg: Ergon Verlag, 2003), pp. 391–420.

Srinivas, M.N., *Religion and Society among the Coorgs of South India* (London: Clarendon Press, 1952).

Srinivas, M.N., *The Remembered Village* (Delhi: Oxford University Press, 1976).

Stevenson, H.N.C., 'Status Evaluation in the Hindu Caste System', *Journal of the Royal Anthropological Institute*, LXXXIV/1–2 (1954): 45–65.

Stirrat, R.L., *Power and Religiosity in a Post-colonial Setting: Sinhala Catholics in Contemporary Sri Lanka* (Cambridge: Cambridge University Press, 1992).

Thompson, Richard H., 'Assimilation', in David Levinson and Melvin Ember (eds), *Encyclopedia of Cultural Anthropology*, vol. 1 (New York: Henry Holt, 1996), pp. 112–15.

Vögeli, Fides, *Tamilische Frauen in der Schweiz. Was hilft ihnen in der Migration?* (Freiburg: Lizentiatsarbeit, Philosophische Fakultät der Universität Freiburg, 1996).

Vögeli, Johanna, *Cuvicil Tirumanaceeval (Heiratsdienste in der Schweiz). Ethnographie über Heiratsstrategien und Verwandtschaft bei Tamilen und Tamilinnen im Kanton Bern* (Berne: Lizentiatsarbeit, Institut für Ethnologie der Universität Bern, 1998).

Vögeli, Johanna, '"Stärker als ihr denkt". Tamilische Frauen in der Schweiz', in Martin Baumann, Brigitte Luchesi and Annette Wilke (eds), *Tempel und*

Tamilen in zweiter Heimat. Hindus aus Sri Lanka im deutschsprachigen und skandinavischen Raum (Würzburg: Ergon Verlag, 2003), pp. 323–43.

Vögeli, Johanna, *Sumangali, die Glücksverheissende. Tamilisch-hinduistische Frauen in der Schweiz* (Berne: Reformierte Kirchen Bern-Jura-Solothurn, Fachstelle Migration, 2004).

Vögeli, Johanna, *Ohne Shakti ist Shiva nichts. Tamilische Geschlechterbeziehungen in der Schweiz*, Arbeitsblatt Nr. 27 des Instituts für Ethnologie (Berne: Institut für Ethnologie der Universität Bern, 2005).

Werbner, Pnina, *The Migration Process: Capital, Gifts and Offerings among British Pakistanis* (Oxford: Berg, 1990).

Werbner, Pnina and Tariq Modood (eds), *Debating Cultural Hybridity: Multicultural Identities and the Politics of Anti-racism* (London: Zed Books, 1998).

Wicker, Hans-Rudolf, Geert Jan van Dok, Claudia Fischbacher, Damaris Lüthi, Mimi Marbach and Michèle Zufferey, *Tamilen in der Schweiz. Sozio-kulturelle Hintergründe, Flüchtlingssituation, Perspektiven* (Berne: Projektgruppe 'Tamilen' der Hilfswerke Brot für Brüder, Caritas Schweiz, Fastenopfer, HEKS, Helvetas und Swissaid, 1984).

Wicker, Hans-Rudolf, 'From Complex Culture to Cultural Complexity', in Pnina Werbner and Tariq Modood (eds), *Debating Cultural Hybridity: Multi-cultural Identities and the Politics of Anti-racism* (London: Zed Books, 1998), pp. 29–45.

Wilke, Annette, 'Mythos in Bewegung. Die Grosse Göttin in Symbolsystem, Kultus und Alltag', *Zeitschrift für Missionswissenschaft und Religionswissenschaft*, 80. Jahrgang 1, 4 (1996): 265–83.

Winslow, Deborah, 'Rituals of first Menstruation in Sri Lanka', *MAN*, 15/4 (1980): 603–25.

Chapter 6

Creating Sri Lankan Tamil Catholic Space in the South Asian Diaspora in Norway

Knut A. Jacobsen

The majority of the South Asian Christians settled in Norway are Roman Catholics from Sri Lanka. Most of them are Sri Lankan Tamils from the Tamil-dominated areas of northern Sri Lanka. Only a few of the Sri Lankans are Indian Tamils from Sri Lanka or Sinhalese Catholics.[1] A small number of Catholic Tamils from Tamil Nadu, India have also settled in Norway. In addition, there are also Tamils in Norway who are Baptists and Pentecostals, and there have been some conversions of Tamils settled in Norway from Roman Catholicism to Baptism and Pentecostalism. Only a few Hindus have converted to Roman Catholicism. For the Tamils from Sri Lanka living in Norway, Catholicism is primarily an inherited religious identity and tradition. There are weekly masses in Tamil in several Roman Catholic churches in Norway (St Paul's Church, Bergen, St Hallvard's Church, Oslo), and on these occasions all those present, with a few exceptions, are Tamils. The rituals are the most important reason for attending the church, and the Catholic Church in Norway has created space for the Tamils in the church for them to reproduce as much as possible of the ritual atmosphere of the Tamil Catholicism of Sri Lanka. Of great importance are the festivals organized for the celebration of St Anthony, an important saint in Sri Lanka, and for Our Lady of Madhu, the most important Catholic pilgrimage shrine in Sri Lanka.

---

[1] There are two different Tamil populations in Sri Lanka, The Sri Lankan Tamils (12.7 per cent of the population according to the 1981 Census) are descendants of several waves of immigrants from South India who settled in northern Sri Lanka in ancient times. The descendents of more recent immigrants from South India brought to Sri Lanka to work on British-owned plantations are distinguished as Indian Tamils (or People of Indian origin, PIO). According to the 1981 Census, Indian Tamils made up 5.3 per cent of the populations; see C.A. Gunawardena, *Encyclopedia of Sri Lanka*, 2nd rev. edn (Elgin, IL, 2005). Since they are now Sri Lankan citizens, there is an increased dissatisfaction with the designation 'Indian', 'Hill Tamils' being the preferred term for some; (V. Suryanarayan, 'Land of the displaced', *Frontline*, 18/12 (2003)). The Sri Lankan Tamils and the Indian Tamils in Sri Lanka have considered themselves two separate ethnic groups. The percentage of Christians among Indian Tamils is difficult to estimate, but probably less than the Sri Lankan Tamils, although there have been many conversions to Christianity. A third Tamil-speaking group is the Muslims, but they do often not consider themselves Tamils.

Roman Catholicism in Sri Lanka

Only around 7.5 per cent of the population of Sri Lanka is Christian. This is the same as the percentage of Muslims, and half that of Hindus. The majority, around 70 per cent of the population, are Buddhist. However, Sri Lanka is divided into two major ethnic groups, the Tamils and the Sinhalese, and a much higher percentage of the Sri Lankan Tamils are Christians (16.7 per cent) than the Sinhalese (6.5 per cent). The majority of the Sinhalese are Buddhists, while the majority of the Sri Lankan Tamils are Hindus. Of the Christian population in Sri Lanka, around 90 per cent belong to Roman Catholicism. The reason a much higher percentage of the Sri Lankan Tamils are Christians than the Sinhalese is that the Catholic missionaries who brought Roman Catholicism to Sri Lanka concentrated their mission in the north and on the coast, and these are the areas where the Tamils live. Christianity came to Sri Lanka under the Portuguese, the earliest colonial power in Sri Lanka, and the strongest presence of the Portuguese was in the northern and western areas. The Indian Tamils were brought to Sri Lanka in the nineteenth century by the British as indentured labour to work on tea plantations. A smaller percentage of those are Christians.

While it is true that Catholicism was brought to Sri Lanka from outside, it should be remembered that Buddhism and Hinduism also came from outside. Compared to Buddhism and Hinduism, the presence of Catholicism is more recent, though it has been practised in Sri Lanka for five hundred years. Catholicism is therefore considered as much a traditional religion of Sri Lanka as are Buddhism and Hinduism. Catholics in Sri Lanka do not consider their religion foreign. Like Buddhism and Hinduism in Sri Lanka, Catholicism in Sri Lanka is a tradition and identity people are born into, inherited from parents. Few convert to Roman Catholicism, although conversions do occur. In the Tamil diaspora, conversions from Hinduism to Roman Catholicism do also occur, but not in significant numbers.[2] Most Catholics respect the religion of their parents, have themselves maintained the tradition they inherited, and make an effort to transfer the religion to their own children.

Portugal was involved as a colonial power in Sri Lanka between 1505 and 1658, and its most notable legacy in Sri Lanka was the introduction of Roman Catholicism.[3] The Portuguese had not primarily been interested in ruling the island. Their interest was in religion and economy, that is, in converting people to Roman Catholicism and in the cinnamon trade. The Franciscans, the Jesuits, the Augustinians and the Dominicans carried out missionary work under the Portuguese. At the time of the Portuguese arrival, the island was divided into three kingdoms, two Sinhala kingdoms with centres in Kotte and Kandy, and the Tamil kingdom of Jaffna. The Portuguese were drawn into politics by conflicts in Kotte from 1521, when they were asked to help the weaker parties in a conflict in the

---

[2]   In Norway, several cases have been reported; interview with Iruthayanathan Pethurppillai, priest in St Magnus's Church, Lillestrøm, Norway, 12 January 2007.
[3]   K.M. De Silva, *A History of Sri Lanka* (London, 1981), p. 127.

kingdom. The whole kingdom of Kotte was brought under the rule of Dharmapala, who had allied himself with the Portuguese, and when Dharmapala died in 1597, his kingdom was given to the Portuguese. Jaffna was conquered by the Portuguese in 1619. From that time, the Portuguese became the main rulers of the island, but Kandy remained independent. The Portuguese rule did not last long. In 1658, the Dutch replaced the Portuguese, and in 1796 the Dutch capitulated to the British East India Company.[4] Under both the Dutch and the British, Protestant missionaries worked hard to win converts, but only Roman Catholicism managed to create a significant Christian presence in Sri Lanka.

Converts to Catholicism were numerically significant, especially along the coast north of Colombo and in the Jaffna area. The Portuguese missionaries entered the Tamil areas in the 1540s, and Tamils converted to Catholicism in great numbers, especially on the island of Mannar. However, the conversions caused a violent response from the Hindu ruler, and a large number of Catholic converts were killed.[5] This was brutally avenged by the Portuguese, and many Hindu temples were destroyed. Opposition to the Portuguese remained strong, partly because of hostility to the Roman Catholic religion,[6] but when the Portuguese managed to conquer Jaffna, part of their success was due to 'the presence of a pro-Portuguese Christian minority in Jaffna'.[7]

Given the violence involved and the short period of Portuguese rule, it is remarkable that Catholicism remained a permanent presence in Sri Lanka in the post-Portuguese period. The violence related to the spread of Catholicism did not mean that Catholicism disappeared once the Dutch dismantled Portugal as the foreign power and set itself up as ruler. One reason for this might be that Catholicism was no longer associated with a dominant colonial power in Sri Lanka. The Dutch Protestants perhaps had a greater hatred of the Catholics than of the Hindus, and Catholicism became a religion of the persecuted. Under Dutch rule, missionaries from Goa and the south-west coast of India came secretly to Sri Lanka and kept Catholicism alive.[8] When the British followed the Dutch as colonial rulers, this changed.[9] The British allowed Catholic missionaries. Because of the Dutch opposition to Catholicism and the fact that the British were not Catholics, the identity of the Catholics was partially freed from the stigma of being a religion of a colonial power.

The narrative of the sacred place of St Anthony, one of the most popular saints in Sri Lanka, at Kochchikade in Colombo, confirms this role of Catholicism.

---

[4]   See ibid., pp. 100–127.

[5]   Ibid., p. 101.

[6]   Ibid., p. 115.

[7]   Ibid., p. 117.

[8]   W.L.A. Don Peter, 'The Catholic Presence in Sri Lanka Through History, Belief, and Faith', in John Ross Carter (ed.), *Religiousness in Sri Lanka* (Colombo, Sri Lanka, 1979), pp. 243–72, 247.

[9]   Ibid.

The narrative is about persecution by the Dutch and the Catholic priest Father Anthony, being helped by the Sri Lankans, performing a miracle to help them. The short text about St Anthony of Kochchikade that is sold at this sacred place visited by both Catholics and Hindus tells about the persecution by the Dutch, who 'were determined that Portuguese influence be totally destroyed'.[10] Despite persecution, Catholics 'continued to practise their faith in secrecy', and soon after the Dutch had prohibited Catholicism, priests came in disguise from India. One of those was Father Anthony, who was stationed in Colombo. He disguised himself as a fisherman, but the Dutch obtained information about him, and in 1740 Dutch soldiers came to arrest him. At the same time, fishermen had found it increasingly difficult to dry their nets because of erosion of the beach. They saw the fleeing priest and surrounded him, hoping he could help them. They told him they would prevent the Dutch from harming him if he prayed to his God and helped them solve the problem with the eroding beach. The Dutch soldiers who had followed Anthony heard the request, and decided to wait and see what would happen when it became obvious that he could not help the fishermen. They thought the fishermen then would see the foolishness of Catholicism. Anthony took his cross and planted it in the sand at the place of the erosion and prayed. Tradition portrays a miracle: the waves receded while he prayed, and a sandbank formed. The fishermen then protected the priest, and the soldiers ran back to the Dutch governor. The narrative concludes that the governor saw the danger of arresting him, and gave him instead a plot of land. Anthony built a hut there, and the place was given the name Kochchikade, since Anthony was from Cochin. The statue of St Anthony in the church today is believed to be in the exact location where Anthony placed his cross.[11]

The story of Kochchikade unites Catholicism with the land of Sri Lanka. The planting of the cross that marks the beginning of the miracle symbolizes the transformation of the land to Catholic sacred space. The cross creates a sacred centre, and literally causes new land to arise from the sea to protect against the water. Water is a symbol of chaos. The cross, symbol of Christianity, defeats chaos, and a sacred centre is created. That the water recedes signifies victory over chaos. The planting of the cross marks a place where the sacred is accessible in a special powerful way. It is a Christian *tirtha*, and the Hindus of Sri Lanka recognize this church as a *tirtha*. The foundation myth is meant to show that Catholicism is inherent and not foreign to the land of Sri Lanka. The planting of the cross is also a public display of what is considered Catholic territory. Interestingly, the story portrays the Dutch as ultimately tolerant of the Catholics, in the way that they recognize the sacredness of the Catholic missionary. That both the Catholic St Anthony, and the Indian missionary Father Anthony have the same name might be a coincidence, but it is perhaps intended as a mark of continuity between Catholicism in Europe and in Sri Lanka.

---

[10]   *St Anthony of Padua: A Short History of the Saint's Life*, compiled by Manel Abhayaratna (Colombo, Sri Lanka, 2001), p. 24.

[11]   Ibid., pp. 25–6.

One distinguishing mark of Catholicism in Sri Lanka that sets it apart from other traditions of Catholicism is the worship of saints connected to the sacred places of Sri Lanka. R.L. Stirrat notes in his study of Sinhala Catholics in Sri Lanka that from the late nineteenth century, there has been a spread of public statues of saints throughout the Catholic belt. He interprets this as the laity's resistance to change. Statues of saints were introduced by the missionaries 'as a public display of what they considered Catholic territory'.[12] From the 1960s, there was a boom in construction of statues of the Virgin, St Anthony and other saints along the roads throughout Sri Lanka.[13] These statues construct a sacred geography, and integrate Catholicism with the landscape of Sri Lanka. The worship of the Virgin Mary and the saints is an important dimension of Roman Catholic ritual practice in Sri Lanka. Most villages with a large Catholic population have their own saint, but some saints are more popular than others. Places of pilgrimage have developed around these saints. Important Catholic sacred places in Sri Lanka, in addition to the shrine of St Anthony of Kochchikade, are the shrines of Our Lady of Madhu, St Jude of Indigolla and St Anne of Talawila. Large pilgrimage traffic and annual festivals with great attendances have grown up around these saints. Not only Catholics but also Hindus attend the festivals.[14] Also in the diaspora, a significant part of the religious practice of the Roman Catholic Tamils from Sri Lanka is, as we shall see, the worship of these saints.

The persecution of Roman Catholics under the Dutch makes Roman Catholic identity in Sri Lanka different from Roman Catholic identity in India, such as in Goa and Puducherry. In Goa as well as in Puducherry, Roman Catholicism was always associated with the rulers (the Portuguese and the French). In Sri Lanka, Catholicism was a religion of opposition during the rule of the Dutch and the British, and did not, as in Goa, become permanently identified with the religion of the rulers. Rather, it was preserved by the Sri Lankans even in the absence of foreign priests. The historian K.M. de Silva writes:

> It is to the credit of the Portuguese that conversions to Roman Catholicism stood the test of the harassment and persecution under the Dutch and indifference of the British. In sharp contrast, Calvinism, which the Dutch propagated with much the same zeal if not quite the same means as the Portuguese did Roman Catholicism, developed no strong roots among the people, and its influence evaporated with the collapse of Dutch power.[15]

The Portuguese had given the converts preferential treatment and exemption from certain taxes. Roman Catholicism appealed both to those at the top of society who aspired to leadership and to those at the bottom who wanted to get away

---

[12]   R.L. Stirrat, *Power and Religiousity in a Post-colonial Setting: Sinhala Catholics in Contemporary Sri Lanka* (Cambridge, 1992), p. 55.

[13]   Ibid.

[14]   Don Peter, 'The Catholic Presence in Sri Lanka Through History, Belief, and Faith'.

[15]   De Silva, *A History of Sri Lanka*, p. 128.

from the low status given them in the Buddhist or Hindu hierarchy. In the Jaffna area, 'being a Hindu was disadvantageous; no one could aspire to upward mobility without first becoming a Christian',[16] but groups associated with fishing, usually ranking low in the caste hierarchy, also converted. Nevertheless, many of those who had converted to Catholicism also kept their faith when there were no material gains from keeping it. That almost 90 per cent of the Christians in Sri Lanka today are Catholics is a clear indication of this.

In spite of the way Roman Catholicism was introduced in Sri Lanka, the Catholic identity is today integrated into the Tamil identity.[17] Among the Tamils, being Tamil means being either Hindu or Christian. The Roman Catholics in Sri Lanka consider themselves fortunate that Catholicism was brought by the Portuguese to Sri Lanka:

> Although Catholics represent a minority of the inhabitants of Sri Lanka, there remains among them an awareness of being singularly fortunate that they are able to profess the catholic faith, which they greatly value, and which has been handed down from generation to generation for centuries. Indeed they regard it as a blessing that the Portuguese were instrumental in opening the way for European missionaries to bring the catholic faith to Sri Lanka, although the contact which Sri Lanka had with Portugal as a colonial power was damaging to the country in many respects.[18]

The Sri Lankan Tamil Catholic Diaspora in Norway

Less than 60,000 South Asians live in Norway. More than half of them are Muslims with roots in Pakistan, a quarter are Hindus from India and Sri Lanka. Around 10 per cent are Sikhs, and only around 5–7 per cent are Christians, mostly Roman Catholics. These Christians are part of the larger Sri Lankan Tamil diaspora. The unity of the Tamil community transcends religion to some degree. The Sri Lankan Tamil diaspora is partly a product of the failed nation state of Sri Lanka and of

---

[16]   R.F. Young and S. Jebenesan, *The Bible Trembled: The Hindu–Christian Controversies of Nineteenth-century Ceylon*, Publications of the de Nobili Research Library, vol. XXII (Vienna, 1995), p. 43. The authors note that Jaffna was never as securely subjugated as Goa, which was like a self-contained city-state (p. 43).

[17]   After 1850, there was an increase of conflicts between religious groups in Sri Lanka, caused by Protestant missionaries. The attack by Catholics on Buddhist processions in Colombo in 1883, writes Stirrat, 'marked the beginning of a series of clashes between religiously defined groups involving all the major religions of the island'; Stirrat, *Power and Religiosity in a Post-colonial Setting*, p. 20. Stirrat's book is only about the Sinhala Catholics. Stirrat notes that 'except for some historical writings, very little work has been done on the Tamil Catholics in Sri Lanka' (ibid., p. 204, n. 1).

[18]   Don Peter, 'The Catholic Presence in Sri Lanka through History, Belief, and Faith', p. 244.

the politics of the Sinhala Buddhist nationalists that first came to power after the parliamentary election in 1956. Sinhala Buddhist nationalism defined Sri Lanka as a nation for the Sinhala-speaking Buddhist majority only. Although originally a criticism of Christianity and its missionary success under colonialism, Sinhala Buddhist nationalism became increasingly hostile towards the Tamil minority. Experiences of discrimination, persecution, and from 1983, a civil war, have produced a large Tamil diaspora. The largest city of Sri Lankan Tamils is no longer Jaffna, but Toronto in Canada.

The first Sri Lankan Tamil to arrive in Norway, Anthony Rajendram, was a Roman Catholic. He arrived in 1956. The next Tamils came in the late 1960s and early 1970s. In the late 1970s, only a few hundreds had arrived, and all of them belonged to the network of a single person, Antony Rajendram. His picture decorates the walls of the living rooms of many Tamils in Norway. He had travelled from Sri Lanka to Europe on a motorbike. His goal was to educate himself about fisheries in the UK. His motivation was to enable himself to help the fishermen in the Jaffna region. His purpose was not to settle in Europe, but to develop projects that could help the poorest group of fishermen in the Jaffna area, many of whom were Christians, and among whom consumption of alcohol had become a problem. Shortly after arriving in England, Rajendram met some Norwegian students who told him that Norway would be a better place for his fishing industry education. Rajendram then left for Norway. Here he educated himself in the various aspects of the fishing industry, such as fishing, fish processing and boatbuilding. In 1967, Rajendram and a few other Tamil youths who had joined him in Norway managed to involve a Norwegian youth organization that worked against alcohol consumption in collecting money for a fishery project in Sri Lanka. With additional money from the Norwegian government, the group bought land in Karainagar in Northern Sri Lanka and began boatbuilding. Soon thereafter, they also started processing, production and the sale of ice, and trawler fishing. Cey-Nor Development Foundation, as the organization came to be called, was established in 1971.[19] Cey-Nor established a fish net factory in 1975. To educate workers in the fishery activities, they were given training in the fish factories of northern and western Norway. In the early 1970s, the fishing industry in Norway lacked workers, and many of the Sri Lankan Tamils who came to Norway decided to stay. Many managed to get work permits for family and friends. Those who applied for jobs in the Cey-Nor projects in Sri Lanka were helped with job applications for work in Norway when there were no jobs available in the Cey-Nor project, and once a person had a job offer, he or she could get a visa.[20] From 1975, immigration to Norway was restricted, but not for education at the Folkehøyskoler, a private college system that offered one-year non-degree courses. These were small colleges spread around Norway. During the 1980s, the Tamils were by far the

---

[19]   *Report on the Mission* (1980).

[20]   Øivind Fuglerud, *Life on the Outside: The Tamil Diaspora and Long-distance Nationalism* (London, 1999).

largest group of foreign students in this school system.[21] In addition, after civil war broke out in Sri Lanka in 1983, a large number arrived as refugees and many also arrived through the universities. The Tamils were one of the largest groups of foreign students in Norwegian universities in the years around 1990.

Rajendram's activities had opened up channels for Sri Lankan Tamils to come to Norway, and he had made Norway known to the Tamils in Sri Lanka so that during the civil war Norway became a favoured choice for those seeking asylum. Tamils have settled everywhere in Norway, but from the early 1990s most Tamils have settled in Oslo, the capital of Norway.[22] Because of the tragedy of the civil war in Sri Lanka, many of those who came were thankful to Rajendram, who had helped bring them to Norway as if he had foreseen the tragedy.

In the first period of immigration of Tamils from Sri Lanka to Norway, the period from 1970 to 1983 when the civil war broke out, the majority of those arriving in Norway were Catholics. From its beginning, Sri Lankan Tamil immigration to Norway was, to a large degree, a Christian immigration. Most of those who came to Norway from Sri Lanka at that time were relatives or friends of Anthony Rajendram. He was a Catholic, and therefore most of his relatives and friends were Catholics. Immigration was through networks. Only 15 per cent of the Tamils in Sri Lanka are Catholics, but of the first 1000 Tamils to settle in Norway, the majority were Catholics.[23] Because so many of the Tamils who arrived early were Catholics, for a long time the perception in Norway was that the Tamils were mainly Christians (Jacobsen, 2005).[24]

Creating Tamil Catholic Space in Norway

Religious institutions and rituals are of utmost importance in the establishment of Tamil communities in the diaspora. Among the Sri Lankan Tamil Hindus, a well-known characteristic feature of the diaspora has been the establishment of a large number of temples worldwide. The temple festivals of the Sri Lankan Tamils are

---

[21]   In the school year 1986–87, 338 Tamils attended the Folkehøyskoler, 286 in 1985–86, and 167 in 1984–85; ibid., p. 56.

[22]   For further details, see Knut A. Jacobsen, 'Settling in Cold Climate: Tamil Hindus in Norway', in Martin Baumann, Brigitte Luchesi and Annette Wilke (eds), *Tempel und Tamilen in zweiter Heimat. Hindus aus Sri Lanka im deutschsprachigen und skandinavischen Raum* (Würzburg, 2003), pp. 363–77.

[23]   The dominance of the Catholics among the early Tamils in Bergen created a perception that the Tamil immigration was a Catholic immigration. When I gave a public lecture on the Sri Lankan Hindus in Bergen in April 2000, a person in the audience who had been associated with the Catholic Church in Bergen (St Paul's Church) in the 1980s and 1990s stood up and said that what I had told them was all wrong – the Tamils from Sri Lanka are all Christians, not Hindus!

[24]   Knut A. Jacobsen (ed.), *Verdensreligioner i Norge*, 2nd edn (Oslo, 2005).

often the largest Hindu festivals in the Hindu diaspora communities of a country. About this ritualization, Fred W. Clothey writes:

> Tamils settling outside their ancestral homes have used a variety of strategies by which they negotiate their identities and transmit their heritage in not always hospitable cities. One of these strategies is ritualization in its various forms. In fact, even the casual observer cannot but notice the proliferation of ritual events, especially in the temples of overseas South Indian Tamils ... these events are part of a larger strategy by which temples become cultural spaces and the venues for a pragmatic ritualism ... ritual expresses and purveys the essence of Hindu (or for that matter, Muslim or Christian) identity. Rituals also serve to maintain and restate historical identities at the same time that they are expected to ease transition into new situations.[25]

Although Clothey in his book on the Tamil diaspora does not elaborate on the Tamil Christian diaspora, the statement is also valid for the Roman Catholic Tamils from Sri Lanka. One way the Tamil Hindus deal with the diaspora situation is with proliferation of temples. Many researchers have noted this.[26] What, then, about the Catholics? Catholic Tamils in diaspora usually do not establish separate Tamil Catholic churches. They instead join the Catholic churches already established in the new countries. They then have to create and establish a Tamil ritual space within these churches. The Catholic Church is also interested in attracting them to the church, and it adds features of Tamil Catholicism to the church rituals.

In the diaspora, much work and energy goes into preserving the cultural heritage. This is particularly true for the religious traditions of the diaspora group, and these traditions often attain new functions in the diaspora. An important function of religion in the diaspora is to help preserve features of the culture of the place of origin, such as language, aesthetic traditions and normative social traditions. Religions often function as preservers of traditions inherited from the past, especially because their rituals are repetitive and their norms considered eternal or transcendent. Tamil Catholicism in Norway is no exception.

In Norway, the Catholic Tamils came to a country in which Christianity was the dominant religion. However, Norway is a Lutheran country and Catholicism is a minority religion. The Catholic Tamils created Tamil space within this minority church. The leadership of the church allowed them or encouraged them to form separate communities within the church. In these separate communities within the church, the Roman Catholic Tamils used ritualization, as Clothey describes for the Tamil Hindus, to maintain and re-state identities and to ease the transition to permanent settlement in Norway. The Tamil ritual events of the Roman Catholic

---

[25]   Fred W. Clothey, *Ritualizing on the Boundaries: Continuity and Innovation in the Tamil Diaspora* (Columbia, SC, 2006), pp. 13–14.

[26]   Baumann, Luchesi and Wilke (eds), *Tempel und Tamilen in zweiter Heimat*; Jacobsen, *Verdensreligioner i Norge*; Knut A. Jacobsen and P. Pratap Kumar (eds), *South Asians in the Diaspora: Histories and Religious Traditions* (Leiden, 2004).

churches in Norway have become important expressions of Sri Lankan Tamil identity. In the same way as the Tamil Hindus organized separate temples, the Tamil Catholics organized separate sacred spaces and times within the Catholic churches. The purpose of this chapter is not to compare the Tamil Hindus and Tamil Catholics in Norway, but it should be noted that there are several parallels in the development of the ritualization of the Catholic and Hindu Tamils, such as the use of Tamil language, the organization of Tamil church/temple committees, the bringing in of Tamil priests from abroad, the incorporation of Tamil food in the rituals, and the institutionalization of processions.[27]

The Catholic Church has played a significant role in the ritualization and organization of the traditions of the Tamil immigrants in Norway. For those arriving in the 1970s and 1980s, the Catholic Church became an important organizational arena. The Catholic Church made contact with the Tamils because it wanted to involve the Tamils in the church. The initiative was from the church, not from the Tamils. The Catholic priest in Bergen took the initiative and visited Tamil Catholics in their homes and convinced them that they would be welcome in the church. When Rajendram took the initiative to organize the first Tamil language classes for children in Bergen, this was done through the Catholic Church. The school started in 1987, and was one of the first immigrant Tamil language schools in Europe. In the 1970s and 1980s, the Catholic Church in Norway was a small church, and basically a Norwegian one. The Tamils joined a church with mostly Norwegian members. Because of large-scale immigration from Catholic countries, most recently from Poland, today the situation is very different. The Tamils were the first group of immigrants arriving from non-European countries of which a large percentage belonged to Catholicism. However, the Chileans and Vietnamese followed soon after. In 2008, the Catholic Church in Norway has become an immigrant church with only 10 per cent of its members being non-immigrants. But in the 1970s it was perceived as a Norwegian church, and not a church with which it would be natural for Sri Lankan Tamils to seek contact. The first Catholic Tamils who arrived in Norway did not regularly go to mass in the church. They did not strongly identify with the Norwegian Catholic Church. Gradually, Tamil space was created in the church to allow for rituals that the Tamils recognized as authentic Tamil catholic rituals.

In western Norway in 2007, around 900 Tamils were registered members of the Catholic Church. The Hindu temple in Bergen, which organizes many of the Hindus living in western Norway, the majority of whom are Tamils, has around

---

[27]   See Knut A. Jacobsen, 'Procession, public space and sacred space in the South Asian diasporas in Norway', in Knut A. Jacobsen (ed.), *South Asian Religions on Display: Religious Processions in South Asia and in the Diaspora* (London, 2008), pp. 191–204, and Knut A. Jacobsen, 'Establishing Tamil Ritual Space: A Comparative Analysis of the Ritualization of the Traditions of the Tamil Hindus and the Tamil Roman Catholics in Norway', (forthcoming).

800 members.[28] In Oslo and eastern Norway, the number of Tamil Catholics is around the same, but the number of Tamil Hindus is much larger.

Attendance of the Catholic Church among the Tamils in Norway has been and continues to be dependent on the presence of Tamil priests to lead the mass in Tamil. Tamils attend the church in great numbers mainly when there is a Tamil priest. In Bergen, during periods without Tamil priests, fewer Tamils came to church. In those years there was a Tamil mass every first Sunday of the month, and mostly a Tamil priest from Oslo or Tønsberg (Arulanandam, currently – 2008 – living in Porsgrunn) would attend. Every Monday there was mass for the Tamils, and on some occasions the attendance was good, but the Tamil priest always drew a larger crowd.[29] Attendance in the masses of the Catholic Church had become quite low when the current Tamil priest, Jagath Premanath Gunapala, arrived in Bergen in 2004. The reason for the lack of attendance was that many of the Tamils did not want to attend a non-Tamil mass as individuals. They would attend when the rituals were recognizably Tamil and as part of a celebration of a Tamil Roman Catholic identity. When Gunapala arrived, Bergen had been without a Tamil priest for eight years, and the Tamils had stopped attending the church. Gunapala therefore visited each family and organized a Tamil church group, and he instituted the celebration of two Tamil Catholic festivals, the festival of St Anthony, 13 June, and the festival of Our Lady of Madhu, 15 August, the day of the ascension of Mary.

Celebration of Our Lady of Madhu and of saints who are popular in Sri Lanka have been important in the institutionalization of the Sri Lankan Tamil Catholic tradition in Norway. St Anthony and Our Lady of Madhu were celebrated in Bergen when the previous Tamil priest, Iruthayanathan Pethuruppillai, was in office there (1987–96). When he moved to St Olav's Church in Oslo in 1998, he also introduced the worship of them in Oslo. In the period after Pethuruppillai, Bergen was without a Tamil priest. When asked why they go to church, Tamils in Norway emphasize Tamil culture and the rituals. They emphasize that these rituals should be as similar as possible to the way they are performed in Sri Lanka. They emphasize that the importance of the church is not that it brings Tamils together – the Tamils have other non-religious organizations for this – but that it is an arena for Roman Catholic rituals. The rituals when performed should be as similar as possible to the rituals in Sri Lanka. The majority of the Tamils started to attend the Catholic Church when the Tamil cultural way of practising Catholicism was introduced.

The situation for the Tamil Catholics in Oslo is similar to Bergen. Most Tamils attend mass when there is a Tamil mass. The Tamil Catholic priests arrange special ritual events for the Tamils in order to attract them to the church. When the priest Pethuruppilai arrived in 1998, he started the Tamil celebration of the festival of Our

---

[28] Jacobsen (ed.), *Verdensreligioner i Norge*, p. 94. Hindus do not register to the same degree in temple organizations as the Catholics do in their church, since Hindus can worship perfectly well at home, but the number is nevertheless significant.

[29] Thanks to Michel Becker for this information.

Lady of Madhu (15 August) and the celebration of one the saints who is popular in Sri Lanka, St Anthony. When Pethuruppilai was at St Olav's Catholic Church in Oslo, he placed the image of St Anthony in the church room every Tuesday to make the image available to Tamil Christians for the whole day. He did this in order to show that the church accepted the Tamil form of Catholicism. This was Pethuruppilai's way of creating a larger Tamil Catholic space in the church. However, three years ago, after a conflict that caused a majority of the Tamils to stop visiting the church, Pethuruppilai was transferred to St Magnus's Church in Lillestrøm. The new Tamil priest, Clement Inpanathan Amirthanathan, had a different view of the worship of St Anthony. Amirthanathan realized, he says, that many Tamils in Norway considered St Anthony to be a god, and that he was prayed to as Hindus pray to Hindu gods. 'They worshipped St Anthony instead of Jesus,' he explained.[30] The worship of St Anthony in this church was stopped. After consulting with the Tamils in Oslo, an annual feast and procession to Our Lady of Madhu was organized. This procession is arranged in a centre owned by the Catholic Church at Mariaholm in Spydberg, on the weekend closest to 15 August. The centre is surrounded by natural beauty. For the last three years, from 2006, Tamil Catholics have celebrated Our Lady of Madhu with a procession of her statue (see Figure 6.1). This procession ritual has become the largest celebration of Tamil Catholicism in Norway. Two Tamil priests are brought in from Rome for the occasion to assist in this annual festival.[31]

In Bergen, in connection with the festival, the Tamil priest takes the statue of Madhu Mary to each and every Tamil Catholic family in the city. He thinks of this as a substitute for the procession that in Sri Lanka would pass through the houses or neighbourhoods of all the Catholics in the village.[32] Since the Tamil population is not concentrated in one area of the city, it does not make sense to have a procession in the city, and the priest instead drives with the statue and performs the ritual in the living room of every family. On the last day, the statue is carried around inside the church as a substitute for the village. But only the priest and selected members of the church leadership walk in the procession inside the church. To the question of why an outside procession is not organized, the priest answered that it is too cold and too rainy in Bergen and that the point would be to visit the areas where the Catholic Tamils live, and that would be impossible.[33]

---

[30]   Interview with Inpanathan Amirthanathan, 9 February 2007.

[31]   Robrecht Boudens, *Catholic Missionaries in a British Colony: Successes and Failures in Ceylon 1796–1893* (Immensee, 1979) notes that in building the church at the pilgrimage place of Our Lady of Madhu (the cornerstone was laid in 1872), the emphasis was on providing 'a deep religious experience' and that 'it should not be so much an occasion to implore favors, but it should be primarily an opportunity for conversion' (ibid., p. 159). He concludes that 'for many of the faithful, the pilgrimage meant an interior renewal' (ibid.). This probably sums up the purpose of the Madhu festival of Mariaholm in Norway: a confirmation of religious identity and a possibility of making new converts among the Tamil Hindus who participate.

[32]   Interview with Jagath Premanath Gunapala, February 2006.

[33]   Ibid.

Figure 6.1   Procession of Our Lady of Madhu in Mariaholm, Norway, August
2006. (Photo: Tamilsk katolske råd, Oslo)

When Catholicism was spread in Sri Lanka five hundred years ago, the missionaries deliberately stressed devotion and emotion over strict adherence to norms.[34] They used fervent devotion to patron figures such as Francis Xavier: 'Fervent devotion to the patron figures was therefore characterized by processions and fairs, plays and dances, feasts and fasts, *pujas* and *tirthams*; and attachment was to such symbols as images, statues, bells, pictures and crosses'.[35] Festivals and processions preserve and build traditions without people having to understand the details of their meaning. Today, large public rituals such as processions and festivals are important for maintaining and building religious identity in multi-religious societies. In the Tamil Catholic diaspora, procession rituals involve a large number of Tamil Catholics in order to confirm their Catholic identity.

Participation in festivals has to do with the wish to preserve the traditions of the past and transfer them to the next generation. The perpetuation of tradition is tied to the public celebration of large-scale rituals. The great public festivals in which a large percentage of the members of the group participate gives identity to the group. These rituals become the main vehicles to preserve and express religious identity.

---

[34]   Charles R.A. Hoole, *Modern Sannyasins: Protestant Missionary Contributions to Ceylon Tamil Culture* (Berne, 1995), p. 174.

[35]   Ibid., p. 175.

The Catholic Church in Norway has members from many countries of the world. The church organizes separate masses for several of the different immigrant groups, among them the Tamils. Although the Roman Catholic mass is universal and more or less the same in all countries, language is unique for each culture. Tamils who attend the mass want the mass to have a recognizable Tamil dimension. Although most understand Norwegian, they nevertheless prefer the mass to be in Tamil. Allowing for other languages than Latin was a consequence of the Second Vatican Council. It meant that the mass could be more easily assimilated into Tamil culture. This is one reason for there being five Tamil priests working in the Catholic Church in Norway. Some of them do not work only with Tamils, but they nevertheless have special responsibilities for them, and visit churches in the areas where Tamils have settled. Pethuruppilai organizes the celebration of St Anthony in St Magnus's Church in Lillestrøm. Even though Pethuruppilai came to Norway to take care of the Tamil Catholics, he now performs other duties in the church, and he is priest not only for the Tamils. The rituals of the Catholic Church are universal. Pethuruppilai is a Tamil priest in the Catholic Church in Lillestrøm, but he performs the mass and sacraments for Vietnamese Catholics, Catholics from the Philippines, Poland, France, Spain and so on. He is a priest for the whole Catholic community. It is a global community, with members from a large number of countries. Other Tamil priests in Norway serve as priests only for Tamils.

Tamil Catholic religious practice in the diaspora is concerned with preservation of religious identity – that is, being Catholic the Tamil way. Both the language used and the rituals performed signify Tamilness. It has been of utmost importance for Catholic Tamils to have Tamil priests in Norway. But the priest in Oslo also encourages the families to go to one mass in Norwegian every month, because the priests realize that the second-generation Tamils in Norway will not want to identify themselves only with Tamil Catholicism to the same degree. Too much emphasis on Catholicism as an ethnic religion might mean losing the next generation, who might feel their Norwegian identity is more important than the Tamil one. It is also significant that many Tamils in Norway eat Norwegian Christmas food at Christmas and Norwegian traditional food at the New Year celebration, while on the festivals of St Anthony and Our Lady of Madhu, Tamil food is a significant element. Tamil Catholicism is thus clearly distinguished from Norwegian Catholicism. Tamils give gifts for New Year, not for Christmas, which also distinguishes their form of Catholicism from traditional Norwegian Catholic practice.

For the Tamils, taking care of the Catholic tradition in Norway is a way to honour the parents who raised their children in Sri Lanka in that tradition. The Tamils say that since their parents found it wise to raise their children within this faith, they feel obligated to do the same with their children. Maintaining the Catholic practice is a way for them to honour their parents and also to transfer the tradition they received from their parents to their own children. In this way, both the family and Tamil culture are honoured. As one informant said: 'My parents gave me a religion I am fond of. They gave me a culture I am fond of. If I forget this, I forget my parents, and the parents made me who I am.'[36]

The Tamil Catholics of Norway attend church for rituals, and these are the same rituals as in Sri Lanka. But the Tamils who have been on pilgrimage to Rome or other centres of the Roman Catholic faith recognize that the same mass, except for the language, is also used there, and this gives a feeling of belonging to a global church. But by celebrating Our Lady of Madhu and St Anthony, Norwegian space is claimed as Tamil Catholic space. The Catholic Church in Norway has a policy of multi-culturalism. Each ethnic group, if it is big enough, is given separate space and time in the church. The church has created Tamil Catholic sacred time as well as Tamil Catholic sacred space. One is reminded of the story, already mentioned, of Anthony at Kochchikade and the creation of Catholic space, and the erection of statues of Catholic saints in Sri Lanka. This was, writes Stirrat, 'a deliberate effort to reaffirm Catholic identity and mark off what was considered to be Catholic space'.[37] The statues of Our Lady of Madhu and St Anthony made available in the church or moved around in processions are about establishing Tamil Catholic space and time within the Catholic Church in Norway. Tamil masses in the Catholic Church, celebrations of St Anthony and Our Lady of Madhu and the rituals surrounding them affirm Tamil identity, and are examples of Tamils' ritualization in the diaspora as a strategy to negotiate identity and transfer the tradition.

References

Baumann, Martin, Brigitte Luchesi and Annette Wilke (eds), *Tempel und Tamilen in zweiter Heimat. Hindus aus Sri Lanka im deutschsprachigen und skandinavischen Raum* (Würzburg: Ergon Verlag, 2003).

Benny, M. Aguiar, 'India and Sri Lanka', in Adrian Hastings (ed.), *Modern Catholicism* (London: SPCK, 1991), pp. 377–86.

Boudens, Robrecht, *Catholic Missionaries in a British Colony: Successes and Failures in Ceylon 1796–1893* (Immensee: Nouvelle Revue de science missionaire, 1979).

Clothey, Fred W., *Ritualizing on the Boundaries: Continuity and Innovation in the Tamil Diaspora* (Columbia, SC: South Carolina Press, 2006).

De Silva, K.M., *A History of Sri Lanka* (London: Oxford University Press, 1981)

Don Peter, W.L.A., 'The Catholic Presence in Sri Lanka through History, Belief, and Faith', in John Ross Carter (ed.), *Religiousness in Sri Lanka* (Colombo, Sri Lanka: Marga Institute, 1979), pp. 243–72.

Fuglerud, Øivind, *Life on the Outside: The Tamil Diaspora and Long-distance Nationalism* (London: Pluto Press, 1999).

---

[36]   Interview with Eugene Sebastian, 29 January 2007.

[37]   Stirrat, *Power and Religiosity in a Post-colonial Setting*, p. 55.

Gunawardena, C.A., *Encyclopedia of Sri Lanka*, 2nd rev. edn (Elgin, IL: New Dawn Press, 2005).

Hoole, Charles R.A., *Modern Sannyasins: Protestant Missionary Contributions to Ceylon Tamil Culture* (Berne: Peter Lang, 1995).

Jacobsen, Knut A., 'En verdensreligion i diaspora: Sri Lanka tamilenes hinduisme i Bergen', in Lisbeth Mikaelsson (ed.), *Religionsbyen Bergen* (Bergen: Eide, 2000), pp. 159–74.

Jacobsen, Knut A., 'Settling in Cold Climate: Tamil Hindus in Norway', in Martin Baumann, Brigitte Luchesi and Annette Wilke (eds), *Tempel und Tamilen in zweiter Heimat. Hindus aus Sri Lanka im deutschsprachigen und skandinavischen Raum* (Würzburg: Ergon Verlag, 2003), pp. 363–77.

Jacobsen, Knut A., 'Establishing Ritual Space in the Hindu Diaspora in Norway', in Knut A. Jacobsen and P. Pratap Kumar (eds), *South Asians in the Diaspora: Histories and Religious Traditions* (Leiden: Brill, 2004), pp. 134–48.

Jacobsen, Knut A. (ed.), *Verdensreligioner i Norge*, 2nd edn (Oslo: Universitetsforlaget, 2005).

Jacobsen, Knut A., 'Procession, public space and sacred space in the South Asian diasporas in Norway', in Knut A. Jacobsen (ed.), *South Asian Religions on Display: Religious Processions in South Asia and in the Diaspora* (London: Routledge, 2008), pp. 191–204.

Jacobsen, Knut A. (ed.), *South Asian Religions on Display: Religious Processions in South Asia and in the Diaspora* (London: Routledge, 2008).

Jacobsen, Knut A., 'Establishing Tamil Ritual Space: A Comparative Analysis of the Ritualization of the Traditions of the Tamil Hindus and the Tamil Roman Catholics in Norway', (forthcoming).

Jacobsen, Knut A. and Pratap Kumar (eds), *South Asians in Diaspora: Histories and Religious Traditions* (Leiden: Brill, 2004).

Report on the Mission to Evaluate the Activities in Sri Lanka of Ceynor Development Foundation LTD (Sri Lanka) and Norges Godtemplar Ungdomsforbund (Norway), Appointed by NORAD (Oslo: NORAD, 1980).

St Anthony of Padua: A Short History of the Saint's Life, compiled by Manel Abhayaratna (Colombo, Sri Lanka: Colombo Catholic Press, 2001).

Stirrat, R.L. 'Shrines, Pilgrimage and Miraculous Powers in Roman Catholic Sri Lanka', in W.J. Sheils (ed.), *The Church and Healing* (Oxford: Basil Backwell, 1982), pp. 385–413.

Stirrat, R.L., *Power and Religiosity in a Post-colonial Setting: Sinhala Catholics in Contemporary Sri Lanka* (Cambridge: Cambridge University Press, 1992).

Stirrat, R.L., 'Place and person in Sinhala Catholic pilgrimage', in John Eade and Michael J. Sallnow (eds), *Contesting the Sacred* (Urbana, IL: University of Illinois Press, 2000), pp. 122–36.

Suryanarayan, V., 'Land of the displaced', *Frontline*, 18/12 (2001).

Young, R.F. and S. Jebenesan, *The Bible Trembled: The Hindu–Christian Controversies of Nineteenth-century Ceylon*, Publications of the de Nobili Research Library, vol. XXII (Vienna, 1995).

Chapter 7

Goans and Damanians in Portugal: An Overview of a Singular Diaspora

Helena Maria Mauricio C. Sant'ana

The Process of Christianization as a Form of Assimilation

Economic interests combined with the propagation of the Gospel were the forces that drove the Portuguese to colonize the coastal territories of Konkan and Gujarat in the course of the fifteenth century. Taking advantage of Hindu discontent with the Muslim Bhamanid invaders, Afonso Albuquerque found allies among the Hindu *rajas*, who preferred a Portuguese alliance to the unwanted Muslim yoke. In this way, Portugal entered India by way of its involvement with the Hindu military elite, helping to destroy Muslim ascendancy. Almost five centuries of cultural contact have produced a particular identity that typifies the Christian inhabitants of Goa and Daman: this characteristic is expressed in the diaspora which is to be found in Portugal.

Over the centuries, Portuguese political influence, based on the missionary work of the religious orders that established themselves there, was a decisive factor in the profound assimilation of Catholic values. Thomaz argues that Christianization was a slow process which was initially restricted to supporters of the Portuguese authorities.[1] 'In Goa, as to a certain extent everywhere, the first Christians were … the wives of the married men …'.[2] It is usually assumed that the lowest stratum of the population was converted on account of the essence of the Christian message, which presented itself as more universal and inclusive, as committed to social reconciliation, and as a message unmarked by the antagonisms that occurred with Hinduism and Islam.

The changes in religious identity influenced the society and culture. When the Goans became Catholic, they started other professional careers under the influence of the Portuguese administration (public servants) and developed other social and even cultural environments (house building, food habits, literature, music, way of life, beliefs). Those changes did not, however, alter the system of castes (especially in Goa), whose endogamy was maintained:

---

[1]   Luís Filipe Thomaz, *De Ceuta a Timor* (Lisbon, 1994).

[2]   Ibid., p. 250. 'The married men' was a term used to describe the Portuguese who married local women and settled in the country. These mixed marriages were encouraged by Afonso de Albuquerque in order to build a sociological bridge between the new masters and the local population.

Two of the main restrictive caste practices relate to food and marriage. Christian Goans failed to observe the first but retained the second. They were converted to meat, including beef, transgressed with alcohol and rid themselves of prejudices, accepting food prepared by people of a lower caste.[3]

In Daman, the social situation underwent greater change, since Christianization managed to abolish the caste system and create a more equal society at the level of the Christian group, albeit a society that was spatially divided on the basis of religion.[4] Even today, the small group of converts represents only 6 per cent of the total population of the area,[5] and, perhaps for this reason, is given the epithet *fanga* ('foreign').

Conversion to Christianity produced a politically and ethnically different identity from other Indians. Although forced, in the first instance, to adopt Portuguese names and simulate Christian symbols and rites, many possessed a dual culture: a public and politically correct Christian dimension, and another, a Hindu dimension, which was only to be seen within their own home. Conversion to Catholicism operated as a way of demarcating social status. Being a Christian implied the ability to participate in local political structures, upward social and economic mobility, and the maintenance of status, especially among Goan Brahmins.

In a political effort to win allies in a place where the influence and strength of Portuguese troops was so small, Afonso de Albuquerque established a policy of marriage, encouraging matrimony between military personnel of the lesser Portuguese nobility and young Goans of local high status. These marriages produced so-called lineages of *descendants*, who were distinguished from Hindu Goans that converted later to Catholicism. However, in Porta's opinion:

> racial mixing did not become common in Goa. The native population's rejection of the mixed marriages desired by Albuquerque, the result of Hinduism's strong convictions on endogamy, seems to have prevailed. Precisely because of the failure to mix the blood, another kind of mixing, cultural or spiritual as they also called it, has been so intensely encouraged.[6]

The Christianization of these populations can be succinctly characterized thus: forced conversion,[7] which most of the population were driven to accept, and strategic conversion, adopted by the group with the highest status, with the specific purpose of maintaining their social status.

---

[3]   Catarina Portas and Inês Gonçalves, *Goa, História de um encontro* (Coimbra, 2001), p. 218.

[4]   Still today in Daman, the population is distributed spatially on the basis of religion.

[5]   Thomaz, *De Ceuta a Timor*.

[6]   Portas and Gonçalves, *Goa, História de um encontro*, p. 53.

[7]   Teotónio Souza, 'Is There One Goan Identity, Several or None?', *Lusotupie* (Paris, 2000).

The arrival of the Jesuits in 1542 spurred on the evangelization process. However, not going against local customs, they allowed the new converts to keep the caste system, winning the sympathy of the highest castes, whose hierarchy remained intact despite the change in religious faith. To penetrate further into the territory, the Jesuits adapted certain features of Hinduism, creating an illusion of pseudo-syncretism: the organization of Christian worship with a structure similar to the Hindu and the production of Christian texts in the form of *Puranas* (recounting the life of Christ or stories of the saints). At the beginning, the two religious creeds lived together without conflict. The arrival of the Inquisition, however, brought a complete change in official policy and in the attitude towards Hindus. First of all, in alliance with political interests, the church proceeded to impose high taxes on Hindu temples, to the point of their destruction. The intolerance reached its extreme in the seventeenth century. The main goal of Portuguese policy was the total assimilation of the population, a strategy based on the colonizing power's consciousness of its weakness: in forced Christianization and these methods of assimilation, it found a way of increasing the Portuguese population and the numbers of those supporting the Portuguese Crown. Conversion to the Catholic religion brought with it a change in individual identity: altered eating habits,[8] Western dress, imported models of house construction, modified ideas on the space inside the home and, above all, the adoption of a fundamental element of identity: the language.

The Language Question

Konkani, the vernacular language, had its repository in the Hindu temples, where the priests were its principal keepers and disseminators. In the first phase of Portuguese occupation, in 1510, the Jesuits considered the local language a factor of value. Mastery of the language was a tremendous instrument of power, and so, in complicity with the religious order, the Portuguese Crown compelled the Catholic priests to learn Konkani or risk having their jurisdiction withdrawn. During this phase, they compiled grammars, dictionaries and catechisms, and translated Hindu religious texts, gaining awareness of the huge source of knowledge of that civilization.[9] Years later, after the first conversions and the training of new members of the order, local priests began to be appointed, but they did not show the same interest in maintaining knowledge of the local language. When the Inquisition was set up in Portugal, the first measures to suppress the Konkani language appeared, in 1664. All native-born people were compelled to learn Portuguese within three years, on pain of not being able to marry or maintain a trading establishment.[10]

---

[8]   With the introduction of other foods in day-to-day life, the Hindus of Goa and Daman, whose diet included fish, mutton and chicken, began to eat pork and beef (a taboo in Hinduism). However, this dietary innovation initially occurred among converts belonging to the higher castes.

[9]   Jorge de Abreu Noronha, 'A língua concani', *Goa*, II série, no. 1 (1996).

[10]   Because commercial documentation had to be written solely in Portuguese.

The elimination of Konkani had a basic goal: to limit the means of communication of the most educated people, focusing on the Brahmins, with the rest of the population. But the linguistic separation of the highest castes from the population had a perverse effect: their subordination to Portuguese interests.[11] In their turn, the descendants of the Portuguese, who were interested in filling the top governmental and local army positions, supported the Inquisition's activities and encouraged the destruction of literary texts written in Konkani, under the illusion that this would destroy the bases on which the local culture rested. By the time of independence, Konkani had become 'the servants' language':

> We didn't learn Konkani. We went to Portuguese schools and Konkani was spoken in the villages. It was said that Portuguese was the language of civilization and Konkani was for the people. We only learnt it with the servants. (interview with a Goan)[12]

However, the rule of suppressing the local language was not the same for all Portuguese possessions in Asia. Daman and Diu were subject to a different evangelization policy, since they were, above all, trading posts in nature, a fact that allowed them to retain the teaching of Gujarati in schools.

Goa and Daman, which lie almost 700 kilometres apart, represent two distinct linguistic areas. Daman Portuguese, known as 'the language of Badrapor',[13] is spoken light-heartedly by the diaspora: it creates a feeling of closeness. It is a typical creole, produced by suppressing the final syllable of a word, as in *nóss ling* (*nossa língua* – 'our language').

> We speak Portuguese correctly. The Damanians who live here cannot be distinguished by their pronunciation, though some are embarrassed to speak the Portuguese of Daman … we speak better than the Goans. (interview with a Damanian)

The original linguistic differences are responsible for the different accents that distinguish Damanians from Goans, whose intonation has a musical element that resembles the sonority of the Konkani language. On 20 August 1987, the Goan Legislative Assembly recognized Konkani as the official language of the state

---

[11]   In 1787, certain Brahmins who understood their subordinate role in Portuguese political power conceived a movement that became known as the *Pintos* plot – a more or less fictitious plot created in an attempt to eliminate all and any cultural resistance that existed, not to the Portuguese presence, but to Portuguese cultural domination.

[12]   For this chapter, we carried out 15 interviews with association leaders and other Goans and Damanians. The quotations provided throughout the chapter exclusively reflect the opinions of the interviewees.

[13]   According to António Colimão, *Boletim informativo da Associação Fraternidade Damão e Diu*, no. 32 (2004), it is supposed that this is a corruption of the expression *gente das bandas de Tarapor* ('people of the bands of Tarapor'), Portuguese who fled to that region during the Maratha persecutions.

of Goa, a date that began to be commemorated by the diaspora in the United Kingdom in 1999 and in Portugal in 2001.

A Diaspora in Two Movements: Part I

The concept of a diaspora was first used to explain the forced emigration of large groups of a population. After the 1980s, the idea began to be used as an analytical term to designate a certain system of migration, of complex international contacts and flows.[14] The concept of a diaspora as a social construction implies the maintenance of ties between migrating populations coming from the same territory and the preservation of an identity and cultural specificity. The migration of Christian Indians to Portugal, though conceptually understood as a diaspora, also involves particular characteristics of their history, development and forms of integration. Although migratory movement in the Indian territories conquered by the Portuguese is a phenomenon that pre-dates the Portuguese period, reflecting the importance of the trading network that connected this coastal region with the Middle East and the East African coast, it was to assume a highly specific direction and character as a result of the process of Christianization/assimilation. Migration increased during the sixteenth century, especially on account of the Inquisition's persecution of the non-Christianized population. In this period, many Hindu families moved to places close to Goa and Daman,[15] keeping contact with their native villages, above all because they needed to worship the family's patron goddess.

The Goan diaspora began to assume greater proportions during the French Revolution. Portugal allowed its British ally to station its navy in Goa to protect the coast against French attacks on possessions in India. This gave Goans, especially those of lower socio-economic status, the opportunity to migrate to the neighbouring territories in British India. British ethnocentricity led them to prefer their services, on account of their eating habits, close to those of Europeans, and their Western dress. From 1870, the construction of the railway made communications easier between British and Portuguese India, and migration to British India accelerated. Countless Goan Christians, educated in Portuguese schools, became auxiliaries in the British administration. Those without high qualifications sought employment as traders or workers in hotels, British trading houses, insurance companies, banks and shipping companies. Those who were educated in parish schools obtained employment as musicians in bands and orchestras. Westerners (the British and other nationalities) preferred to employ Goans, since, in contrast to Hindus, they were not restricted by dietary taboos: they were often contracted as cooks. The fact of knowing Portuguese and English, being Christian and having contact

---

[14]   Jorge Macaísta Malheiros, *Imigrantes na região de Lisboa: os anos da mudança* (Lisbon, 1996); Jorge Macaísta Malheiros, 'Circulação migratória e estratégias de inserção local das comunidades católica goesa e ismaelita', *Lusotopie* (Paris, 2000).

[15]   State of Maharashtra and Karnataka or, in the case of Daman, Gujarat.

with Western eating habits and customs gave Indian Christians an advantageous position where emigration was involved.

The development of the Goan diaspora during the nineteenth century was directly associated with the severe economic crisis prevailing in the territory. Portuguese India was suffering from very serious problems in its administration. The worsening of the population's economic conditions and living standards, whose origin went back at least two centuries, caused poverty, unemployment, a lack of support, and alcoholism.[16] During the Provincial Council meeting of 1917, a report was given on the grievous situation: the mass exodus of the disadvantaged, mostly Hindus, who moved to British India every year.[17]

From 1869, with the abolition of slavery, workers from poorer castes began to be recruited for the plantations of Mauritius, Guyana and Natal. However, extended social and political relationships in the metropolis encouraged many Goans of the Chardo caste to work in Mozambique. Since the British colonies to the west of Mozambique had no seaports and goods had to pass through the territory to reach the coast, dozens of forwarding agents sprang up in the province. In these firms and railway companies, it became a common practice to employ Goans, who had a good grounding in the English language. As the caste system was maintained, it was not uncommon for the same occupation to remain in the hands of a family that carried out administrative functions in the same company for two or three generations.

In the mean time, another kind of migration to Portugal developed, a more highly qualified migration. Goan Christians, who generally belonged to the intellectual and land-owning elite (*bhatcars*), emigrated to continue their studies and start a professional career, not for economic reasons. Since the Indian Christians of Goa never freed themselves from the caste system, a situation of which the Portuguese government was not unaware,[18] those who in reality emigrated to Portugal were Brahmins and, later, some Chardos.

Among Goan Catholics, a small educated minority had developed, which had gradually become a class of prosperous, Catholic, mixed-race landowners that came to be referred to as Indo-Portuguese. It was this minority that would play an extremely important role as the intermediaries between the colonists and the colonized, discharging legal and administrative duties in Portuguese India and, later, the African colonies. In the Portuguese imagination, from the end of the seventeenth century, Goa became the repository of Latin civilization in Asia, as

---

[16] The report by the Governor, João Moura, in 1902 refers to the territory of Diu as 'very poor' and Daman as afflicted with economic problems. A constant criticism of the governors of India, moreover, was the uniform legislation for all the territories of Portuguese India: this led to the subjection of the very small territories, which were not in a position to compete.

[17] During the 7th Provincial Congress of Portuguese India in 1927.

[18] They adopted a slightly different hierarchical structure from the traditional one, composed of Brahmins, Chardos and Sudras, with some considering a last group, the Gaurés.

well as 'the Court' – as it was called at the time – and intellectual and academic metropolis of the Portuguese possessions in the East.[19]

The Importance of Education as a Migratory Strategy: A Qualified Migration

Until 1962, Indian Christians who were born in Goa or Daman and moved to Lisbon could not be considered immigrants, as they did so within the same national territory. They were, however, migrants within the framework of a particular kind of diaspora: immigration carried out within a cultural context, on the basis of a language and religion, which were identity references for most Goan and Damanian migrants living in Lisbon. These migrants were a socio-economic elite that multiplied outside of Goa, in Portugal and Africa, and maintained family links with their place of origin.

During the nineteenth century, the closeness of the Goan elite to Portuguese political power caused a population movement towards the metropolis that may be subdivided into two forms of migration:

1. the temporary migration of young students who came to finish their studies in Portuguese universities and returned to India or were posted to Africa (Mozambique and Angola) as part of the colonial administration;
2. permanent migration, to a lesser degree, in cases in which young men established a lasting relationship with the metropolis, marrying Portuguese women or remaining to exercise an occupation in Portugal.

Costa describes Goa as an Indian colony that pioneered education, under the direction of religious orders, mainly the Jesuits, in the private schools.[20] This order carried out activities of enormous educational and cultural importance in the Indian colonies, and its suppression led to the decline of education in Daman. However, in driving education forward in eighteenth-century Portugal, Pombal[21] also influenced primary and secondary education in Goa, which then started to be provided by the native-born. From 1831, the Portuguese government encouraged education in India and offered scholarships for boys to study medicine and surgery in Portugal, on condition that they taught in the school of medicine and surgery in Goa. Between 1833 and 1857, of a total of 100 students from all the Overseas Provinces, 48 came from Goa, and of these students, only 7 did not live up to initial expectations.[22] In spite of the incentive, the dispatch of the scholars did not have a positive effect on

---

[19]   P.J. Peregrino Costa, *A expansão do Goês pelo Mundo* (Goa, 1956), p. 20.

[20]   Ibid.

[21]   Sebastião José de Carvalho e Mello, known as the Marquês de Pombal, was Prime Minister of the Kingdom of Portugal during the reign of Dom José I (1750–77). A charismatic figure, he represented 'enlightened despotism' in Portugal. He was responsible for far-reaching administrative, economic and social reforms that modernized the country.

[22]   They did not finish the course or they followed other, parallel, careers.

the contingent of degree-holders practising in Goa. In most cases, the young people chose to remain in Portugal or went abroad, to the point that, in 1856, the Governor of India referred to the matter in the following terms:

> The State of India has drawn no benefit … from the young people who have gone to study in Europe at public expense, since, after graduation, they have refused to return to their country ….[23]

From 1841, various institutes of higher education emerged, and the number of trade schools and occupational schools for arts and crafts expanded greatly. But this was short-lived, due to 'the excessively literary and speculative *tendencies* of the Goans and, consequently, the teaching methods adopted, which were not very practical and, above all, bookish'.[24] However, it was this literary tendency, already in the eighteenth century, that led to the rise of an intellectual elite that would produce important names in literature, history, medicine, higher education, the judiciary and theology. Throughout the last three centuries, hundreds of Goans have discharged duties of major social, political and military importance in Portugal.[25]

From the eighteenth century, Mozambique became a second pole of attraction for Christian Goans. The administration of the Province of Mozambique depended on Goa until 1752, when the Marquis of Pombal separated it from the State of India by the Royal Charter of 9 May 1752. The Indian Christians who migrated there went to discharge duties in the public administration, the legal profession and judiciary, engineering and medicine. The courses in medicine at the Goa medical school were intended for the practice of the profession in Goa and the African colonies, since to practise medicine in Portugal, a student needed to attend

---

[23]   Costa, *A expansão do Goês pelo Mundo*, p. 23.

[24]   Ibid., p. 19.

[25]   Occupying top posts in the administrative and government services in the metropolis. Examples are: José Paulo Lobo de Saligão, who became the civil governor of Portalegre; civil engineers and economists; veterinary surgeons, lawyers and judges (Luís da Cunha Gonçalves, who wrote the *Treatise on Civil Law*); heads of hospital services, with prestigious careers in medical research and tropical medicine; army and navy officers; teachers in various branches of higher education; writers such as António João de Frias, Rodolfo Dalgado, Eduardo Gelásio Dalgado, Adeodato Barreto, Gama Pinto and Froilano de Melo, and primary and secondary education teachers. Other Goans made their mark in the world of politics, in particular during the Liberal Struggles: Bernardo Peres da Silva, the first colonial member of the Portuguese Parliament to become a defender of Liberalism, Bernardo Francisco da Costa, member of the Cortes (Parliament) for India and President of Almada City Council, and Raimundo Rodrigues, a professor at the University of Coimbra, member of the Cortes for Coimbra and president of Coimbra City Council. After the establishment of the republic: Alberto Xavier, who became *chef de cabinet* of the Minister of Justice and President of the Council, and later Director General of the Treasury, and Caetano Gonçalves, a Republican who was a notable parliamentarian and the member for Benguela at the Constituent Assembly of the Republic.

Portuguese universities for two more years.[26] In the words of a Damanian living in Portugal:

> The Goans always took care to educate their children. Even very simple people. They had gold and they used it. Their concern was education. And it wasn't only the high castes that educated their children; the lowest castes also sought to give their children a schooling. (interview with a Damanian)

However, those who migrated to Mozambique did not put their children into the schools in the province. The official statistics of that country show that high school attendance by Indians, whether Christian or Hindu, was minimal. Goan emigrants preferred to send their children to Goa, where the quality of education, combined with the maintenance of ties with the ancestral line and the roots of their identity, offered them a passport to success in their careers.

In Daman, the situation was very different. It was not easy to obtain an education. In this more remote territory, there was only one secondary school in Moti Daman, another in Nani Daman, a Gujarati school maintained by the Portuguese government, and a private school of Franciscan nuns. Once the period of education was over, young people had few alternatives. Families rarely sent boys to the seminary, where they could learn English, whereas girls, who were educated to carry out instrumental roles, gave up their studies. Although Daman was only about 170 kilometres from Mumbai and transport was always plentiful, families did not dare to allow their children to go very far from the territory. This resulted in an ethno-linguistic community that was distinguished by its educational level, which was reflected in the more limited quantity and quality of duties assigned to Damanians during the colonial period and in their more limited ability to migrate.

The Fall of an Empire

Indian independence in 1947 triggered the nationalist movement that led to the decolonization of Portuguese India and a new migratory process. In 1950, Nehru tried to talk with the Portuguese government, with the aim of the territory being integrated into the Indian Union. Salazar gave short shrift to any attempt at negotiation, and in response, caused alterations to be made to the Colonial Act,[27]

---

[26]   Susana Sardo, *A música e a reconstrução da identidade: um estudo etnomusicológico de 'grupo de Danças e Cantares da Casa de Goa'* (cyclostyled) (Lisbon, 1994).

[27]   In 1933, the Prime Minister, Oliveira Salazar, reformulated the Constitution of the Republic and published the Colonial Act, a measure that represented a step backwards in relation to earlier legislation. During the Liberal Monarchy of 1821, the Constitution considered the territories under Portuguese administration as provinces. Every province could elect at least one member of the Cortes, with the Province of Portuguese India reaching the point of returning six members of parliament. Between 1820 and 1920, all citizens of the Asian colony had guarantees of liberty enshrined in the Civil Code, regardless of whether

with a view to justifying the existence of the colonies. Altering the Constitution, the Salazar government changed the term 'colonies' to 'provinces', legitimizing those territories as integral parts of Portugal. The Portuguese government supposed that this manoeuvre would secure the country from the independence fever that had been raging since the end of the Second World War. The Indian Union replied by putting an embargo on supplies, barring transit by foreigners and Goans between Portuguese territories and the Union, and cancelling emigrant remittances:

> This may be around a few dozen million escudos per year, which in the international balance of the Indian Union represent nothing at all and can easily be made good in the State of India's accounts. But in tiny Goa they represent an average income for many families. (Salazar, 1954)

In the words of Peregrino da Costa, emigrants were the greatest source of wealth in those territories:

> around 100,000 Goans who are dispersed around that vast Hindustan as far as Karachi and Calcutta and, with the meagre savings that they remit here, contribute to the economic balance of Goa.[28]

In effect, the economic crisis had already been being felt since the 1930s, causing seasonal and permanent migrations. In a report presented to the IX Provincial Congress, a civil servant complained about the shortage of hands, the product of an emigration taken as 'a necessary evil'.[29] But if, on the one hand, that brought advantages for the whole territory, on the other hand, the emigrant who returned home without success was condemned to unemployment. In effect, emigration in those territories increased at the start of the 1950s as a result of the economic blockade. The inability to continue remitting funds to Goa made it more practical to move families outside the territory than leave them there without the income on which they depended to survive.

In June 1953, Nehru closed the diplomatic mission in Lisbon, while members of the Satyagraha Sabha invaded the enclaves of Dadra and Nagar Aveli. In reply, Portugal appealed to the International Court of Justice in the Hague, in an attempt to obtain recognition of the centuries-old right of transit between Daman, Dadra and Nagar Aveli, but in the following year the enclaves were formally annexed by India. From the 1950s, integrationist policies were winning supporters

---

they were Hindu or Christian. After the rise to power of Salazar in 1928, with the passage of the new Constitution in 1933, into which the Colonial Act was merged, citizens of the Province of Goa saw all earlier liberties and prerogatives abrogated. The political power of Salazar associated the church with the imperial designs of the state.

[28]   Costa, *A expansão do Goês pelo Mundo*, p. 115.

[29]   Alvaro Dionisio Viegas, *A nossa crise: memória apresentada ao 9º congresso provincial da Índia portuguesa* (Nova Goa, 1931).

around the world, and the Indian nationalist movement had repercussions in the Portuguese Indian territories, with the greatest impact in Goa. Even before Indian independence, on 18 July 1946, Ram Manohar Lohia, one of the founders of the socialist movement in India,[30] organized a rally in Goa: this was the impulse that awoke nationalist consciousness.

Although the Portuguese government systematically declared that the Indo-Portuguese were loyal to Portugal, a nationalist movement formed in Goa, among whose particularly notable figures were Julião Menezes, founder of the Gomantak Praja Mandal and editor of the weekly publication *Gomantak*, and Tristão Bragança da Cunha, leader of the Goan Congress Committee. Many Goans argued for autonomy in a confederation of republics, in which the territories would be autonomous, though part of a Portuguese federation.

Portugal made several attempts to mobilize the international community, in particular British intervention. But in the political circumstances of the time, it was of no interest to the UK to act against its old colony, with which it wanted to develop trading relations. Although the International Court in the Hague recognized the right of transit for the enclaves of Dadra and Nagar Aveli on 12 April 1961, international opinion had changed radically. In the face of the total failure of diplomatic intervention, Salazar's policy consisted of revealing the fallaciousness of the Satyagraha movement[31] to the eyes of international public opinion by cutting the number of troops in Portuguese India. However, during a Lock Sabha meeting, Nehru put forward the possibility of using violence in the case of Goa. On 17 December 1961, with 50,000 men, the Indian Army invaded Goa, which had merely 3500 military personnel to mount the Portuguese defence.

Some Goan communities in East Africa and Nairobi showed their solidarity with the Portuguese government, but the occupation of Goa led to various demonstrations against the regime. Between March and June 1962, an academic crisis developed on a national scale. It was the beginning of the movements that politicized the student youth, spilling over into other sectors and culminating in the Portuguese revolution of 1974.

From 1961, Goans with sympathies for the Portuguese regime preferred to migrate to Lisbon, embarking on the ship *India* that Salazar sent to pick up the refugees from the Indian Union invasion. In each immigrant family, there were numerous questions and fears among those who had never been to Portugal:

Some of the people said at the time: What country will be waiting for us? Where are we going? What are we going to find? It was a great adventure! (Damanian)

My father was an adventurous type. A fighter. He got hold of all his children (10) and we came. Within a week, we left the government facilities and went to work. Even my brother aged 14. Later we studied ... we made our way in life. (Damanian)

---

[30] A founding member of the Congress Socialist Party in 1934.
[31] A non-violent resistance movement.

Among the Indian Christian population, a complete social reorientation took place at that moment: it had consequences for the social structure, and included family ties. In the words of the Goan Bernardo Colaço, currently Deputy Attorney General of the Public Prosecution Service:

> In the time of Portuguese government, the limited number (about 400,000 people)[32] and a certain rigidity with regard to the distinction or separation among the classes into which Goan society was structured (the castes) meant that there was a great closeness in family relationships, expressed in family visits, events and celebrations. Well, from 1961, the rise in the population, the economic boom and emigration meant that these relationships weakened and became more tenuous, if they didn't even break down in many cases.

Even today, there are no precise figures that can tell the total number of immigrants from Portuguese India, but José Dias has put forward an estimate: 'About 3000 Goans or more ... emigrated from Goa, Daman and Diu after 18 December 1961 within the context of the decolonization movement.'[33] A proportion of those Indian Christians took up residence in Portugal, occupying posts in the administration or practising a profession; others were employed in the African colonies as senior civil servants, returning to Portugal after the 1974 revolution.

A Diaspora in Two Movements: Part II

After the independence of Portuguese India, the migrations of Goans and Damanians to Portugal diminished. There were a large number of Indian Christians in the African colonies, and the social composition was no longer based on the elite intermediary class in the Portuguese administration, but included a heterogeneous group of individuals employed in various occupations involving crafts and services. Social difference and, in the Goan case, distinctions in caste were apparent in daily life and in the diaspora associations in Portuguese territories: they were based on origin, place of birth and family. In Mozambique, most of all, the Goan community was large and well integrated, but built on a fairly rigid hierarchical social system resembling the type of sociability existing in India:

> Those of Brahmin origin constituted the high society, the high-class. The Chardos were the middle class and the Sudras the workers; in Mozambique that was still more or less the way in the clubs, the associations ... but in Portugal none of this is any longer apparent. (Goan)

The independence of the African colonies after the revolution in 1974 triggered the process of decolonization. This caused the exodus of thousands of Asian

---

[32]   That is, of Christians.

[33]   José Manuel Graça Dias, *Boletim informativo da Casa de Goa*, no. 4 (1997), p. 4.

Christians, Hindus, Muslims and Portuguese,[34] who, as a result of the climate of social instability, chose to settle in Portugal. Many of these migrants experienced various migrations and re-adaptations throughout their lives in a migratory trajectory that covered three continents:

> My sister has already had to move four times: from Nagar Aveli to Damão, from Damão to Portugal, then to Mozambique and from Mozambique she came back to Portugal. Do you know what she says now? I'll never move again in my life! (interview with a Damanian)

However, if in the first phase of migration almost all the Indian Christians who moved to the metropolis belonged to the upper echelons of the Portuguese public service, in the second phase more heterogeneous Indian Christians arrived, including some who did not speak Portuguese. However, history only mentions those who were successful, since generally speaking:

> Society tends to show its models and hide its defects ... there are other Goans (*not only*) who go unnoticed because they are ordinary citizens, and still others who perhaps live in some difficulty.[35]

For some, migration represented a continuation of life's tasks and habits, while for others, without networks of contacts, integration was painful, with a loss of status and quality of life:

> I worked for a British railway company in Mozambique. After 25 April, I also lived in Rhodesia for two years but the desire to come to Portugal was so great that here we are. Here in Portugal, there were so many changes ... we had three little children ... I even worked as a brick carrier.

The movement of the *retornados* ('returnees') did not only bring to Portugal those who had opted for Portuguese nationality after independence in India. Thousands of Indian Christians had settled in Mozambique[36] a few generations earlier, and knew neither India nor Portugal. The Goans and Damanians living[37] in Mozambique were jokingly nicknamed *Canecos*, a form of discrimination used by the Mozambique Portuguese to disparage the Indo-Portuguese group. In comparison with the first-generation Indian Christians, many of whom had

---

[34]   According to Pena Pires's estimates, in the years 1974–75 Portugal received 'around half a million Portuguese who were repatriated from the ex-colonies in Africa'. See Rui Pena Pires, *Migrações e Integração* (Oeiras, 2003), p. 132. The numbers include other ethnic and religious groups.

[35]   Valentino Viegas, 'Os Goeses em Portugal', *Goa*, no. 8 (1994): 189.

[36]   In Angola, the Indian Christian community was very small.

[37]   People belonging to the second and third generation.

settled in Portugal in the 1960s, the Mozambique *Canecos* had a different social framework, which was maintained in Portugal.

The Nationality Issue

The continuing decolonization process produced Decree Law No. 308 – A/75, whereby the lawmakers withdrew nationality from those born or domiciled in the African ex-colonies. However, a special situation was taken into consideration for those born in the former state of India. In this way, it was sought to resolve ambiguous aspects of the status of those territories and the question of the nationality of those born there before they became independent.[38] In effect, no law on the nationality of people born in the former state of India was revoked from 1959.[39] Since Goa, Daman and Diu became independent in 1961 and the effects of the recognition of Indian sovereignty relate to 1975, all individuals born in the Indian territories before the annexation by the Indian Union have always remained Portuguese citizens. As the flow of immigration from Portuguese India, and even from the African colonies, was considered inter-regional migration, it did not show up in the 'statistics on the entry of foreigners to the national territory'.[40] In these circumstances, it became statistically impossible to calculate the exact number of individuals from those territories who arrived in Portugal. Even so, in 1992, Malheiros put forward an estimate of around 11,000 Indian Christians (that is, Goans, Damanians and Diuans) who arrived in Portugal during the period of African decolonization.[41] During the integration process, they were spread throughout the Portuguese territory, revealing sociabilities close to the rest of the population – the result of a long process of racial mixing and a high level of integration.

Why Invisible?

In contrast to other Indians, Catholic Indians have not grouped together in residential zones or mounted co-ethnic or family businesses as an economic or

---

[38]   In 1962, after the territories had become independent, Law No. 2112 of 7 February was still passed. It continued to apply Portuguese legislation on nationality to the inhabitants of the state of India, while Portuguese sovereignty was not exercised.

[39]   After the integration of Goa, Daman and Diu in 1961, diplomatic relations between Portugal and India were cut off. The difference between them was only resolved in 1975, when Decree Law No. 206/75 of 17 April ratified the treaty recognizing Indian sovereignty over the territories. According to the Portuguese Constitution of 1933, which was still in effect in 1962, the territories of the state of India formed an integral part of Portuguese territory. Furthermore, Law No. 2098 of 29 July 1959, which considered all individuals born in Portuguese territory as Portuguese, was similarly not revoked. The situation endured until 1975, in the hope that the territories would be regained.

[40]   Maria do Céu Esteves (ed.), *Portugal, País de Imigração* (Lisbon, 1991), p. 20.

[41]   Malheiros, *Imigrantes na região de Lisboa*.

social integration strategy. The importance of sociability in a universe of Christian origin reflects a different world view. Although they feel they have a heritage with a twin identity, they do not recognize themselves as an ethnic group. Being Goan is, above all, an inherited attribute.[42] Being Goans or Damanians in Portugal does not correspond to the assumption of being an ethnic minority. On certain occasions, debate has arisen among the members of the associations, but conclusions have never been reached on the existence of ethnicity, and not all of them agree on their inclusion in a community:

> Community? We're not a community! We're spread throughout the country. I, for one, have been here over 30 years and I don't live my life with other Goans. All my friends are Portuguese. (interview with a Goan)

This example is an illustration of those who, like Machado, consider that a community exists when 'in an ethnically different minority population, the ethnicity is sufficiently strong' (2001, p. 4).

Most Indian Christians do not see themselves as an ethnic group. They have never established themselves as a cultural or ethnic minority or even developed community-building strategies, which are common among Diu and Gujarati Hindus.[43] According to Sardo, Goans 'are culturally identified with the society that has received them, as was so even at the moment that preceded migration'.[44] The same opinion is held by some of the Goans and Damanians who live in Portugal.[45] Goans 'have a culture of their own, which is a peculiar symbiosis between the culture of Goa, that of Continental Portugal and Indian culture'.[46] Yet the question is not quite so linear. In Portugal, there are at least four types of Indian Christians, who are distinguished by their place of birth and their generational position:

1. first-generation Indian Christians, who were born in Goa or Daman and came to Portugal directly;
2. Indian Christians in India, who migrated to Mozambique and later to Portugal;
3. those of the second generation who were born in Portugal;
4. those of the second generation who were born in Mozambique.

---

[42] Sardo, *A música e a reconstrução da identidade*, p. 58.

[43] The identity strategies used, for example, by non-Christian Asians (Hindus, Muslims and Ismailis) seeks to preserve their cultures by reinventing them in daily life, on the basis of dietary practices, language, religious observances and marital and family ties, or in festivals, demonstrating an 'us' different from 'them'.

[44] Sardo, *A música e a reconstrução da identidade*, p. 64.

[45] Viegas, 'Os Goeses em Portugal'; Jorge de Abreu Noronha, 'A identidade de Goa e o Goês na Diáspora', *Goa*, II série, no. 5 (2000).

[46] Viegas, 'Os Goeses em Portugal': 17.

To a certain extent, the phenomenon reflects the project of Portuguese colonization, in particular in Goa and Daman, which over roughly five hundred years (1510–1961) produced peculiarities in relationships, of a colonialist nature. For example, those born in Mozambique are classified as belonging to the category of those who 'do not understand two words of Konkani' and as never having visited Goa. Among themselves, whether they remained in Portugal or went to Africa, first-generation Christian Indians cultivated an identity that is not to be seen in the second generations.

In a relationship that is almost the opposite of that of other Indian groups, such as the Hindus, Christian Indians share similar cultural products with the Portuguese, 'because they are also the result of their political and social history. In this way, the ambiguity of an ethnic demarcation is also circumvented'.[47] How, then, is the process of self-identification carried out? How does it feel to be Goan or Damanian in Portugal? The question is interpreted differently depending on the generation:

> Goans – I mean the first generation and not the second, since the latter have no difficulty in fitting into the Portuguese population, body and soul – have never felt restrictions on their integration into society or met any kind of hostility from those around or the environment. They just continue the kind of life they had in Goa. It was different, without doubt, but the consciousness and feeling of the living together were the same. (interview with a Goan)

Without marking differences between Damanians and Goans, the common core of the Indian Christian tradition is religious identification with the Christian universe, the use of Portuguese first names and surnames, and communication in Portuguese – since, undoubtedly, language has 'the ability to produce imagined communities, effectively constructing particular forms of solidarity'.[48] Thus these populations see themselves in imagined communities[49] – imagined because, in an essentialist sense, the community is an invented product and therefore does not exist.[50] From the instrumental aspect, however, it functions as a wide network, to a greater or lesser extent, of kinship and friendships, in which favours and complicities of various kinds are exchanged: political, economic and social. They may be communities of dreams, common memories or a connection, sometimes already tenuous, with a key to identity:

> I am a Portuguese of Goan origin. Will this be my identifying mark? I don't exactly think so. I'm a Portuguese of Goan origin, I'm Portuguese like any other Portuguese and why? Because if you talk of a Goan sentiment, i.e. feeling Goan, you only feel

---

[47]   Sardo, *A música e a reconstrução da identidade*, p. 67.

[48]   Benedict Anderson, *Comunidades Imaginadas* (Lisbon, 1991), p. 176.

[49]   See the concept developed in ibid., *passim*.

[50]   In the opinion expressed by Ernest Gellner, *Thought and Change* (London, 1964).

Goan in the specific case that you were born in Goa or have ancestors connected with Goa by birth and cultivate this connection or are proud of it, without any antagonism, contradiction or distinction with regard to the society in which you are integrated. I mean, anyone who cultivates this connection and is proud of it, wherever they are. (interview with a Goan)

If the first generation of Indian Christians can speak their mother tongue (Konkani or Gujarati), the second generation can rarely keep up a conversation in their parents' language:

At home I never spoke Konkani with my parents. Always Portuguese. As my wife is Portuguese, my children won't speak Konkani, either. Anyway, I have only visited India once and I don't have any contact or relationship with it. (interview with a Goan)

However, if there is no ethnic demarcation, there are attempts to maintain the people's cultural identity, even in a heterogeneous group, not only in relation to origin, but also social status and class.[51]

The Associations and Inter-community Differences

First-generation Goans belong to the Christian social elite and are the main people responsible for founding some of the associations promoting Goan identity. They are a social group of mainly intellectual and scientific professionals who occupy top positions in Portuguese society.[52] The first association was founded in Portugal in 1987 under the name 'Goa House'. It was the idea of a small group of Brahmins, most of whom came from Salcete and the Pangim region, places where the population remained closer to Portugal. The association's first statutes had a discriminatory character from the point of generation,[53] and more subtly, social status, a fact that caused dissension and criticism which, in a veiled fashion, persists:

There was that policy of castes. Those in command didn't want the people. And the people are always with us, aren't they? For us, in India, workers can't mix with other occupations ... (interview)

The association, whose media power is directly related to its members' social status, created a group of dancers and singers, Ekvat,[54] that seeks to capture the second generations by collecting and performing the folklore of Goa. The group is made up of young people aged 15–28 and has a sub-group, formed later, for children of 8–14. The *mandó* and *dulpadas* are reinterpreted according to the approach

---

[51]   Especially the Hindus of Diu, Goa and Gujarat, Indian Muslims, Ismailis of Indian descent and Sikhs.

[52]   The thesis of Sardo, *A música e a reconstrução da identidade*, should be consulted.

[53]   They limited the society to those who were born in Goa.

[54]   Meaning 'cultural roots'.

of the migrant culture, in which syncretism and contextual reinterpretations predominate. In an endeavour to motivate members and, in this case, attract the second generations, the association holds a weekly get-together, 'Five O'clock Tea' and cultural meetings such as 'Balcony Conversations', which brings together important figures of the Goan intelligentsia.[55] The quarterly periodical *Goa* is a source of historical information, articles of opinion, ethnographic information, cookery, photography, the presentation of books on India and Goa, and announcements of social gatherings and cultural evenings. Like the provincial associations that exist among the emigrant Portuguese, another Goan association, the group of dancers and singers called 'Surya', transposed a repertory of music and dance from Goa in the conviction that the purpose of these cultural events is to convey an image of Goa that results from the group leaders' experience and lives in Goa, which are recognized as valid by the other members.[56]

The generation that was born in India but lived in Mozambique or Angola represents the largest group in ARCIP (the Indo-Portuguese Recreational and Cultural Association), which was founded in 1999 and brings together people of lesser socio-economic status and other castes, principally Chardos.[57] Originally, a circle (*tertúlia*) of Goan friends from Mozambique who met weekly in a well-known cafe in Lisbon started to publish a monthly newsletter, *A Voz da Tertúlia*, or *Tertúlia Oriental*. In 1999, they founded a quarterly publication, *A Voz do Oriente*, that was suspended in 2006 in favour of *Ecos do Oriente*. The new publication seeks to be exempt from 'narrow-mindedness and caste clubism', and has the purpose of promoting cohesion in the collective identity of the Catholic communities from Goa, Daman and Diu:[58]

> It is not too much to have various associations. And, as we are based in Odivelas, it doesn't suit us very well to come to Alcantara, to that place.

There is also a small association in Coimbra called the 'Cultural Association of the Friends of Goa, Daman and Diu', which curiously includes all the 'communities' of Portuguese India.

Both the Goan and Damanian communities claim unrivalled Portugueseness, but in reality, the two communities almost do not recognize each other. Although the associations have all-inclusive names, that does not mean that the people really socialize among themselves:

---

[55]   In 2006, there were 600 families registered as 'Goa House' associates, though only a small number participate in the cultural and recreational activities organized.

[56]   Sardo, *A música e a reconstrução da identidade*, p. 142.

[57]   In the mean time, the existing associations contain people from all groups and generations. However, there is (or there was when these groups were formed) a tendency for individuals from the different strata and 'communities' to be collected together.

[58]   ARCIP currently has 210 associate families, mainly from Mozambique.

The Damanians are different from the Goans because they enter the Portuguese way of life better. The Damanians are more Portuguese than the Goans. (Damanian)

The Damanian community, which is as scattered as the Goan, has an association called the 'Daman and Diu Fraternity', which was set up by a priest in 1983:

One day I decided to send some invitations ... very simple ones .... As Damanians are tied to the Christian faith, they came to mass and all brought their own food. I expected a hundred or so but in the end about 800 people turned up.

The association that founded the Goa, Daman and Diu choral group resurrected Indo-Portuguese songs that had been forgotten in the day-to-day life of Daman. The group became known and began to perform at various celebrations throughout the country:

We sing lots of things. Not just from Daman, but also Macau, Malaca, Goa, Ceylon, Timor ....

To re-create an image of Daman, they retrieved the traditional dress. Older women managed to rediscover a form of dress that had been lost, the *anak-sarak*, which was prepared with fabric brought from Diu and is worn during performances:

My nurse used to wear this costume on a Sunday. It is no longer worn today but we have retrieved it and wear it for performances .... (Damanian priest)

In Daman, a small social milieu, all families maintained the ties through which they socialized with each other and were acquainted with each other. In Portugal, they also recognize each other, but it is difficult to get all the people together, since they are scattered geographically. They are less well-off than the Goans, and have greater difficulty with the costs of travelling. They always ensure, however, that they are present at religious festivals such as that of our Lady of the Candles, or of the Purification, which is politically connected in Daman with the entry of Agostinho de Bragança into the city, a date that is still officially celebrated in Daman today. Like the Goans, they celebrate the main local patron saints, the saints of the people, and the major annual religious festivals (Christmas and Easter), maintaining a special veneration for the symbolism of St Francis Xavier on account of his enormous influence on the Catholic community in India.

They gather together in the parish hall or around a church in the capital, under the leadership of the charismatic figure of Father Colimão. They meet to socialize, recall the past, see friends and family again, and taste traditional cooking, with certain special dishes for festive occasions being prepared. The great specialty of Damanian cuisine is the 'Damanian spit', which is usually prepared as a barbecue in the open air. Since people do not possess these conditions at home, they flock to these gastronomic gatherings. Another item on the menu is the Damanian *sarapatel*, which is different in taste and preparation from the Goan form and is also highly appreciated during the gatherings:

> The first generation ... those who were born there are today ... I won't say old, but tired, and so everything is done with greater moderation. As for the young people, they want other things ....

However, though the associations play an important role in strengthening identity, they do not represent the Indian Christian population in Portugal. Above all, they bring together groups of old friends and family members who meet for cultural evenings, afternoon teas, celebration dinners and family parties, leaving out most of those who would technically be part of the communities in question. Many do not even know the associations exist, and others consider them elitist[59] and the 'representatives of a sectarian stratum'.

In Portugal, where integration is fairly high, neither Damanian nor Goans have plans to return, although they permanently maintain the family networks. Some still possess family houses and property that they regularly visit, others maintain close ties with family members who never migrated, keeping contact by telephone and e-mail. They generally try to get to know the extended family scattered over four continents:

> We go on holiday, but more than two months are difficult to take. You know, we're very used to the lifestyle we have in Portugal. In India, it's very different .... (Damanian)

The second generations – those born in Africa and those born in Portugal – display regular characteristics, which portends an accelerated loss of the traits of identity maintained by their parents. It is common for them to mix with the rest of the population by way of marriage, abandoning caste endogamy, knowledge of the language, values, dietary habits and any individualizing or identifying element:

> All of them, or almost all of them, marry people from here. We, the older ones, are not going to lose our individuality and identity for a few years yet ... but the younger ones .... (interview with a Goan)

However, Goan and Damanian identity in Portugal is distinct from the identity of those who remained in India. It is a question of a reinvented identity, since only a minority of the population of both the territories emigrated to Portugal, minorities that identified completely with Portuguese values and habits. Considering themselves different with respect to their culture of origin, both Goans and Damanians are part of an invisible, scattered group that is integrated to the point of assimilation and has put down roots in the local society, which, for historical and cultural reasons, they feel to be their own.

---

[59] A situation that occurs among the Goans.

Perhaps the reason for the invisibility of this population is summarized in the words of Viegas:

Almost all Goans[60] resident in Portugal are Portuguese. Portugal is their adopted country but we are not Portuguese by adoption. We were born and grew up Portuguese. We are Portuguese in the fullness of the term, like or better than any other Portuguese.[61]

References

Anderson, Benedict, *Comunidades Imaginadas* (Lisbon: Ed.70, 1991).

Colaço, António Bernardo, *Questionar a relação: Goa/ Portugal* (cyclostyled) (Lisbon: Sociedade de Geografia de Lisboa, 1996).

Colimão, António, *Boletim informativo da Associação Fraternidade Damão e Diu*, no. 32 (2004).

Costa, P.J. Peregrino, *A expansão do Goês pelo Mundo* (Goa: Repartição central de estatística e informação, 1956).

D'ano, Plínio, 'Goês de Moçambique: Monhé?', *Goa*, II série, no. 2 (1996).

Dias, José Manuel Graça, *Boletim informativo da Casa de Goa*, no. 4 (1997).

Esteves, Maria do Céu (ed.), *Portugal, País de Imigração* (Lisbon: IED, 1991).

Gellner, Ernest, *Thought and Change* (London: Weidenfeld and Nicholson, 1964).

Gracias, Fátima, 'Quality of life in colonial Goa: Its hygienic expression (19th–20th centuries)', in Teótonio Souza (ed.), *Essays in Goan History* (Delhi: Concept Publishing, 1989).

Léonard, Yves, 'O Império Colonial Salazarista', in Francisco Bethencourt and Kirti Chaudhuri (eds), *Historia da Expansão Portuguesa*, vol. IV (Navarra: Circulo de Leitores, 1999).

Machado, Fernando Luis, *Contrastes e Continuidades* (Oeiras: Celta, 2002).

Malheiros, Jorge Macaísta, *Imigrantes na região de Lisboa: os anos da mudança* (Lisbon, Colibri, 1996).

Malheiros, Jorge Macaísta, 'Circulação migratória e estratégias de inserção local das comunidades católica goesa e ismaelita', *Lusotopie* (Paris: Khartala, 2000).

Mendes, Sushila Sawant, 'Dr. Lohia and Goa's freedom struggle', in Teotónio Souza (ed.), *Essays in Goan History* (Delhi, Concept Publishing, 1989), pp. 173–84.

Moura, João Herculano Rodrigues, *Relatório sobre administração e serviços do Governo do Distrito de Diu* (Nova Goa: Imprensa Nacional, 1902).

Noronha, Jorge de Abreu, 'A língua Concani', *Goa*, II série, no. 1 (1996).

---

[60]   When the author refers to 'Goans', he is generally indicating all Indian Catholics who have settled in Portugal.

[61]   Viegas, 'A identidade de Goa', p. 11.

Noronha, Jorge de Abreu, 'A identidade de Goa e o Goês na Diáspora', *Goa*, II série, no. 5 (2000).

Pires, Rui Pena, *Migrações e Integração* (Oeiras: Celta, 2003).

Pissurlencar, P., 'Os primeiros Goeses em Portugal', *Boletim Vasco da Gama*, 31 (1936): 1–20.

Portas, Catarina and Inês Gonçalves, *Goa, História de um encontro* (Coimbra: Almedina 2001).

Salazar, António Oliveira, 'Goa e a União Indiana, Goa e o mundo, Goa e o cristianismo na Ásia, Goa e nós próprios, Goa e o futuro', *Comunicação à Assembleia Nacional* (Lisbon, 1954).

Sardo, Susana, *A música e a reconstrução da identidade: um estudo etnomusicológico de 'grupo de Danças e Cantares da Casa de Goa'* (cyclostyled) (Lisbon: UNL, 1994).

Souza, Bento Graciano, *Goan Society in Transition* (Bombay: Popular Prakashan, 1975).

Souza, Teotónio, 'Some contrasting visions of luso-tropicalism in Índia', *Lusotopie* (Paris: Khartala, 1997).

Souza, Teotónio, 'Is There One Goan Identity, Several or None?', *Lusotupie* (Paris: Khartala, 2000).

Thomaz, Luís Filipe, *O Cristianismo e a tradição pagã da Índia Portuguesa* (Lisbon: JIU, 1965).

Thomaz, Luís Filipe, *De Ceuta a Timor* (Lisbon: Difel, 1994).

Viegas, Alvaro Dionisio, *A nossa crise: memória apresentada ao 9° congresso provincial da Índia portuguesa* (Nova Goa: Tip Bragrança, 1931).

Viegas, Valentino, 'Os Goeses em Portugal', *Goa*, no. 8 (1994).

Viegas, Valentino, 'A identidade de Goa', *Goa*, II série, no. 4 (1997).

Chapter 8
Surinamese East Indian Christians in the Netherlands

Freek L. Bakker

The migration of East Indians[1] from Suriname to the Netherlands – a group normally referred to as the Hindustanis – peaked around the mid-1970s. It was closely associated with the independence of Suriname from the Netherlands on 25 November 1975. Several ethnic groups, including the East Indians, Creoles and Javanese, concerned about their future in Suriname, used their Dutch passports to settle on the shores of the North Sea. This chapter analyses developments in the East Indian Christian community since their arrival in the Netherlands in order to provide greater understanding and perception of their situation in their new context. It initially provides an outline of the beginnings of the East Indian Christianity in Suriname itself. It needs to be emphasized that the present chapter will merely present some insights into what occurred within the East Indian Christian community, as time was too short to conduct sufficient research to write a fully-fledged analysis. Yet these insights may be of significance in identifying modalities for the future and sustainability of Christianity within this community.

Suriname

The first East Indians arrived in Suriname in 1873 to work as contract labourers on plantations in the Dutch colony. The Surinamese plantation owners had learnt that British planters in the neighbouring countries (including British Guyana and Trinidad) had successfully contracted workers on indenture from British India to

---

[1] The term 'East Indians' refers to Indian migrants from the previously colonized regions in the Caribbean, to distinguish them from the indigenous Indians, the latter being often called Amerindians or Indigenous. In Suriname, the immigrants from India are called Hindustanis. The term 'Hindustani' is purely ethnic, and merely refers to people having their roots in India; it does not mean that these people are Hindus. So Hindustanis can be Hindus, Muslims, Christians or even atheists. In the Netherlands, the term 'Hindustani' refers to the Indians who had immigrated from Suriname or to persons whose parents or grandparents may have come from Suriname. Indians, who have come directly from India are called Indiërs ('Indians'). This chapter confines itself to the Indians from Suriname, and uses the terms 'East Indians' and 'Hindustanis' as synonyms.

meet the labour needs of their plantations. The Dutch planters therefore requested the Dutch government to negotiate with the British government to recruit workers for the plantations in Suriname, as the former slaves were unwilling to work on the plantations after the abolition of slavery in 1863. From that period until 1917, some 34,304 Hindustani immigrants were transported to Suriname, out of which 22,681 decided to remain in the country.[2] The vast majority of the East Indians were Hindus, with nearly 20 per cent being Muslim,[3] and some individuals being Christians.[4] However, the first baptism of a Hindustani – a migrant contract labourer who had been working in the British colonies – had already taken place as early as 1870.[5] She became a member of the Evangelische Broedergemeente (EBG, 'Congregation of Evangelical Brethren'), the church founded by the Moravian brethren in Suriname. In 1873, two other East Indians were baptized in the EBG.[6] Two Christians of Indian origin led the Hindustani Christians of the EBG during the early period of immigration, but time and time again they asked for a European missionary to assist them. In 1901, Rev. Julius Theodoor Wenzel (1873–1920) arrived from Europe for this purpose. In the mean time, the number of East Indian EBG members rose to 70.[7] Under the guidance of Wenzel, the Moravians founded a Christian school for Hindustani children in Paramaribo in 1905.

The first East Indian Roman Catholics were baptized in 1872. A number of them had come into contact with the Roman Catholic Church on the French islands in the Caribbean. During the first thirty years, they were guided by some fathers working among the Creoles and by some laypeople. In 1904, the Roman Catholics also started missionary work among the East Indians in Suriname. This task was entrusted to Father L. Luykx (d. 1912). He started his work with great enthusiasm,[8] which, however, also caused much irritation within the EBG.[9] Not surprisingly, the missionary activities of both churches were resisted by the

---

[2]   C.J.M. de Klerk, *De immigratie der hindostanen in Suriname,* 2nd edn, vol. 2 (The Hague, 1998), p. 73; Stan Verschuuren, *Suriname: Geschiedenis in hoofdlijnen* (The Hague, 1994), p. 61.

[3]   C.J.M. de Klerk, *Cultus en ritueel van het orthodoxe hindoeïsme in Suriname,* 2nd edn, vol. 1 (The Hague, 1998), p. 11.

[4]   Jan M.W. Schalkwijk, *Hindoestaanse zending 1901–2001* (Paramaribo, 2001), p. 16

[5]   She had come from the British colonies in the West Indies. British Indian contract labourers had been present there since 1838; ibid., p. 15.

[6]   Ibid., p. 15.

[7]   J.T. Wenzel, *Schetsen van den zendingsarbeid der Evangelische Broedergemeente onder de Britsch-Indiërs in Suriname* (Zeist, 1908), p. 3. Schalkwijk, *Hindoestaanse zending 1901–2001,* pp. 16–20.

[8]   De Klerk, *De immigratie der hindostanen in Suriname,* vol. 2, pp. 216–18; J.G. Vernooij, *De Rooms-Katholieke Gemeente in Suriname* (Paramaribo, 1998), p. 90.

[9]   De Klerk, *De immigratie der hindostanen in Suriname,* vol. 2, p. 218; H.G. Steinberg, *Ons Suriname: De zending der Evangelische Broedergemeente in Nederlandsch Guyana* (The Hague, 1933), p. 292.

Hindus.[10] The Protestants and the Roman Catholics regarded each other as rivals, and although their relations improved in the 1970s,[11] many, particularly among the Protestants, continued to hold this view.

Both the EBG and the Roman Catholic Church used similar strategies for their mission work in Suriname. They established separate churches and schools for the East Indian Christians, as many East Indians resisted joining the Creole churches. This was because the East Indians felt that, as minorities in the Creole churches, they would have little space for their own Hindustani language and culture. In addition, there was strong pressure from the side of the East Indian Hindus to return to the heritage of their ancestors. Both the Moravian brethren and the Roman Catholics founded a number of boarding schools and children's homes, where orphans and other children entrusted to them were given good school training and education, However, these facilities were provided in an environment which segregated and isolated the East Indian children from their cultural backgrounds. Of course, this training also included a thorough introduction into their own variety of Christianity.[12]

Discussions on disintegrating the separate ethnic departments within the church were initiated within the Surinamese Roman Catholic Church at the end of the 1950s. In spite of the major objections put forward by the fathers working among the East Indian Catholics, these separate ethnic departments were gradually abolished in 1968. In the EBG, however, the separate department for Hindustanis continued to exist.[13]

In the mean time, a number of Pentecostal and Evangelical[14] congregations were founded in the country, some of them being led by East Indian ministers. These congregations attracted a small number of East Indians. In the 1990s, some Hindustani congregations were founded, the most well-known being the Shekinah congregation.[15] This gives the impression that, from then on, the ethnic differences between Creoles and Hindustanis were emphasized. Although this may be true, it would be justified to conclude that the rift between Hindustanis and other population groups was smaller in Pentecostal and Evangelical congregations because, unlike the ethnic departments of the Moravians and the Catholics, the

---

[10]   Ibid.

[11]   Vernooij, *De Rooms-Katholieke Gemeente in Suriname*, pp. 94–6.

[12]   For the details, see: De Klerk, *De immigratie der hindostanen in Suriname*, vol. 2, pp. 217–20; Vernooij, *De Rooms-Katholieke Gemeente in Suriname*, pp. 90–92; Schalkwijk, *Hindoestaanse zending 1901–2001*, pp. 20–42.

[13]   Vernooij, *De Rooms-Katholieke Gemeente in Suriname*, pp. 121–2, 129–32; Schalkwijk, *Hindoestaanse zending 1901–2001*, pp. 33–40.

[14]   These Evangelical congregations mostly identify themselves as Volle Evangeliegemeenten ('Full Gospel Congregations').

[15]   Ariane Liebe, '"Eén in de Heer": Bekering en convergentie van creolen en hindostanen in de Surinaams evangelisch charismatische beweging' (unpublished master's thesis, Utrecht University, 2004), pp. 48–55. See also: Schalkwijk, *Hindoestaanse zending 1901–2001*, p. 40.

Hindustani-dominated congregations of the Pentecostals and the Evangelicals always included a large number of Creoles and Javanese.[16]

It is very difficult to obtain accurate figures of East Indian Christians in Suriname. The census of 1964 indicates that there were 4021 Hindustani Roman Catholics and 1008 Hindustani Moravian Protestants, whereas the census of 1972 put the figure at about 4494 Hindustani Roman Catholics.[17] Jan M.W. Schalkwijk (1923–2002) estimated the number of East Indian Moravian Protestants in 1975 to be approximately 1250.[18] The number of Pentecostal and Evangelical Christians was probably very small at the time.

The Netherlands

As previously noted, there was a major flux of migration of Surinamese East Indians to the Netherlands in the mid-1970s. This, however, did not mean that there were no Hindustanis in this country prior to this period. It was very common in the 1950s for Surinamese adolescents to pursue a study programme for higher education at one of the colleges and universities in the Netherlands. Most of them, however, returned to the West Indies. In the 1970s, the Surinamese came to settle in the Netherlands. These migrants were no longer only students, but now originated from all layers of the population.

The Moravian Protestants

As early as in 1958, a Hindustani Conference, which included a large gathering of many prominent East Indian Moravian Protestants, was held in Suriname. During this conference, it was decided to request European missionaries who were on leave in the Netherlands to visit the East Indian Moravians in the country. In 1972, a national-level Hindoestaanse Christelijke Werkgroep ('Hindustani Christian Working Committee') consisting of five (later six) persons was set up in the Netherlands. In co-operation with the Central Board of the Dutch EBG, the committee appointed W.F. Soekram Heera to become part-time missionary for the East Indians living in the Netherlands. A missionary, following the traditions of the EBG, had the responsibility for pastoral care among the faithful of his own denomination as well as for missionary work. Until his departure for Suriname in 1979, Heera visited many East Indians. Some other Hindustani Christians assisted him, among them the former Surinamese politician and minister W.E. Juglal, who at that time lived in the Netherlands. Over time, many home meetings were organized, and every year there were important collective Christmas celebrations.

---

[16]   Liebe, '"Eén in de Heer"', pp. 110–12.

[17]   Vernooij, *De Rooms-Katholieke Gemeente in Suriname*, p. 153.

[18]   Schalkwijk, *Hindoestaanse zending 1901–2001*, p. 36.

In addition, a journal was issued, *Masiehie Awaaz* ('The Christian Voice').[19]After 1979, Heera was succeeded by a European minister.[20]

There is some disagreement about the number of East Indians Moravians in the Netherlands today. Schalkwijk estimates the number to be in the order of 300 addresses and 1000 members,[21] whereas the present General Secretary of the working group, Vidjaj Shantiprekash, calculates it to be approximately about 750 addresses.[22] Shantiprekash suggests that the figures of Schalkwijk refer to an earlier date. It is clear, however, that not all people living at the addresses mentioned by Shantiprekash are members of the EBG. Taking on board these different issues, he therefore put the number of East Indian members of the EBG at around 2000 (see Figure 8.1 for a photo of their church in The Hague).

Until the mid-1980s, the Dutch EBG, dominated by Creoles, resisted the establishment of a separate working group for the Hindustani Moravians. So the work of this branch of the EBG was – and still is – financed by the Zeister Zendingsgenootschap (ZZG, 'Zeist Mission Society'). The East Indians explained that this structure was helpful for missionary work among Hindu and Muslim East Indians, as the chance that their hearts would be touched was greater if they heard the message of the Gospel from their Christian fellow Hindustanis, who knew their language and culture and understood the problems they had with Christianity. Later, particularly after the intervention of the German headquarters of the Moravian brethren, the approach of the Hindustanis was better appreciated, and subsequently the Dutch EBG even created national-level working committees for the Javanese, the Chinese and the Marrons. The working group for the Javanese was closely attached to working group for the Hindustanis in a so-called Asian working group. Interestingly, the Chinese were left out of this working group. The activities of the working group for the East Indians expanded over time. Services are currently organized every Sunday, although this takes place in a different town each week. In this way, monthly services are held in The Hague, Amsterdam, Rotterdam, Zeist, Eindhoven and Groningen. Zoetermeer is also a centre of activities. These services are usually visited by 15–35. In 2006, 130 persons attended the yearly Christmas celebration, which always takes place in The Hague.[23]

---

[19]　Ibid., pp. 43–4.

[20]　They were the Rev. Jan M.W. Schalkwijk (1979–88), the Rev. Arie van der Deyl (1988–98), the Rev. Harold Lenz (1998–99) and the Rev. L. Johannes Jensen (2001–2007); ibid., pp. 44–5, and personal information of the present author. The East Indian ministers the Rev. Johannes Rambaran and the Rev. Fred Lachman assisted during the period when they were studying in the Netherlands (1979–83).

[21]　Schalkwijk, *Hindoestaanse zending 1901–2001*, p. 46.

[22]　Interview with J.S. (Mitra) Rambaran, 7 February 2007; interview with Vidjaj Shantiprekash and Ernst Lachman, 2 March 2007; personal communication by the Rev. L. Johannes Jensen.

[23]　Personal communication by the Rev. L. Johannes Jensen, 14 March 2007.

Figure 8.1   The church of the Moravian Protestants in The Hague. (Photo: Freek
              L. Bakker)

The services of the working group follow the common liturgy of the Moravian
brethren. What makes these services special are that a number of songs are sung in
Sarnámi, the Hindi dialect originating from Indian languages in Suriname, as well
as the fact that the Bible passages are read in Sarnámi. Since many of the services
are also meant for the Javanese, certain songs are also sung in Javanese. These
songs include ancient Moravian songs translated into Hindi[24] as well as songs
composed in Indian *bhajan* style.[25] The great majority of these *bhajan*-style songs
were derived from *Sacred Songs and Solos*, a songbook containing some 1200
songs compiled by Ira David Sankie[26] which was brought across by Christians who
had come directly from India. *Bhajan*s are traditionally songs of devotion to God,
composed according to particular melodies and rhythms and sung in the Hindu
temples. Naturally, the contents of these songs have been changed so that they are
now genuine Christian *bhajan*s. The Surinamese EBG composed a songbook of
these Christian *bhajan*s entitled *Giet Poestak Masie Mandlie Kie* ('Songbook of

---

[24]   Some of the translations were carried out by the Rev. Peter Martin Legêne (personal
communication by the Rev. L. Johannes Jensen, 14 March 2007).

[25]   Schalkwijk, *Hindoestaanse zending 1901–2001*, pp. 41–2; interview with Vidjaj
Shantiprekash and Ernst Lachman, 2 March 2007.

[26]   Personal communication by the Rev. L. Johannes Jensen, 14 March 2007.

the Christian Congregation') in 1965. The East Indian Christians also make use of CDs and DVDs containing East Indian Christian music. The New Testament readings are often derived from the Sarnámi translation made in 1997 by the Summer Institute for Linguistics. The use of Sarnámi, however, is not undisputed, as a number of East Indians prefer the use of Standard Hindi.[27] The priests in the Hindu temples in the Netherlands also prefer to speak Standard Hindi in their official addresses. So the use of Sarnámi affects the esteem for their own religion, as it gives the impression that Christianity is something meant for lower people. Minister L. Johannes Jensen, however, is of the opinion that the great majority of the East Indian Christians do not understand Modern Standard Hindi.[28]

What is significant is that the services of the working group have a certain Hindustani flavour which is virtually absent in the common services of the Dutch EBG. There the language is Dutch, and often also Sranan, the language of the Creoles in Suriname.

In the 1980s, contacts were made with the Roman Catholic Hindustanis. There were even some ecumenical services, but after the appointment of Rev. Arie van der Deyl (b. 1932) in 1988, these ecumenical contacts ended.[29] A small group of predominantly Moravians continued these ecumenical activities in the still existing Vriendenkring ('Circle of Friends'), which meets monthly. They publish a small monthly magazine called *Masihie Sanghatan* ('Christian Companions'), and they sometimes participate in the services of other churches.[30] At present, however, the period of ecumenism appears to have ended.

Since the 1970s, East Indian Moravians' attitude towards the heritage of their Indian ancestors has changed. A large proportion of the first generation had become acquainted with Christianity in their youth, when they were educated in one of the boarding schools of the Moravian Church in Suriname. These institutes were managed and guided by European missionaries, so these East Indians had the impression that becoming Christian also meant that they had to, at the same

---

[27] Themselves, they prefer to say *Shuddh Hindi* ('Pure Hindi'). Interview with J.S. (Mitra) Rambaran, 7 February 2007; interview with Vidjaj Shantiprekash and Ernst Lachman, 2 March 2007.

[28] Interview on 22 February 2007. This view was confirmed by the East Indian Haridat Rambaran on 7 March 2007, who emphasizes that the great majority of East Indian Hindus do not understand Modern Standard Hindi either. Modern Standard Hindi, also known as Khariboli Hindi, is the official language used by the government of India. It consists of the variety of Hindi spoken in Delhi and its surroundings. This variety differs widely from Sarnámi, as Sarnámi developed from the varieties of the Hindi language spoken in the eastern part of the state of Uttar Pradesh. So it is no surprise that many Surinamese Hindistanis have great difficulties understanding Modern Standard Hindi. Cf. Michael C. Shapiro, *A Primer of Modern Standard Hindi* (Delhi, 1989), pp. 3–5; Dick Plukker, Moti Marhé and Narain Mathura, *Hindi voor starters*, Part A (The Hague, 2001), pp. 14–16.

[29] Interview with Vidjaj Shantiprekash and Ernst Lachman, 2 March 2007.

[30] *Masihie Sanghatam* (November 2006). One of the most prominent members of the Vriendenkring is the widow of Rev. Johannes Rambaran.

time, adopt a European lifestyle. Furthermore, it was understood that it was good to reject everything which was related to Indian culture, as this culture was largely stamped by Hinduism. So to be a Christian meant that one used a spoon and a fork at dinner. It also meant that one ate meat, including beef and pork. These habits widened the rift between the Hindustani Christians and their fellow Hindustanis, because the Hindus abstained from beef and the Muslims abstained from pork. The East Indian community, on their part, despised the Christians among them because of these customs. Moreover, these new habits proved to be an extra obstacle for non-Christian Hindustanis considering becoming Christians themselves. Yet, in spite of the contempt felt within the East Indian community, there continued to exist mutual respect between the Christians and their Hindu or Muslim relatives within the families.[31]

In the 1970s, the attitude of the East Indian Christians altered. Rev. Johannes Rambaran (d. 1983), who was later followed by other EBG ministers including Jan Schalkwijk, proposed making a distinction between Indianness and Hinduism, or between culture and religion. At the time, he was a minister in Suriname. Rambaran, for example, used to visit the marriage ceremonies of bridal couples consisting of a Hindu and a Christian partner, and even entered the *maro* (the marriage canopy) to introduce some Christian elements into these marriage ceremonies. Furthermore, Rambaran used to emphasize the unity of the Hindustani community, and advocated a dialogue between East Indians of different religious backgrounds. Later, this policy of distinguishing between religious elements and cultural elements was also followed in the Netherlands, and nowadays it has become the common attitude among the Dutch East Indian Moravians.[32]

At the same time, the vast majority of East Indian Moravians will never place an image of a Hindu deity in their room. For them, this practice is still closely associated with the Hindu religion, which is not theirs. In other words, only those elements that have no religious connotations are acceptable. A few practices, such as the Christian *bhajan*s, are accepted, however, but only if they have changed into genuine Christian ones.

Unsurprisingly, the attitude of the Moravians towards inter-religious dialogue was very cautious. Some individual ministers were willing to participate in these discussions in the 1980s.[33] However, as far as I know, only the Vriendenkring is really active in the field of inter-religious dialogue. For many years it participated in an inter-religious dialogue group in The Hague, and in December 2006 it was also prepared to visit a Christmas celebration of a Hindu association.[34] The influence

---

[31]   Interview with Dr Jozef P. Siwpersad, 1 December 2003.

[32]   Interview with J.S. (Mitra) Rambaran, 7 February 2007.

[33]   The Rev. Jaap Legène and the Rev. Johannes Rambaran, until their untimely death in the first half of the 1980s.

[34]   *Masihie Sanghatam* (November 2006), p. 7. For details of the Hindu–Christian dialogue in the Netherlands, see: Freek L. Bakker, 'The Hindu–Christian Dialogue in Europe: The Case of the Netherlands', *Dharma Deepika*, 10/2 (2006), pp. 23–37.

of the Evangelicals in the EBG is large, so many Moravians reject dialogue and prefer mission.

The position of the East Indian Moravians in the Netherlands is very problematic. First and foremost, they are strongly influenced by the secularization tendencies that dominate contemporary Dutch society, whereby the mainstream Christian churches throughout the country have witnessed a decline in membership. The diaspora situation also affects the situation of the East Indian Christians. In addition, they have to deal with strong competition from the Pentecostal and Evangelical churches, as several Hindustani Moravians have left their own church to join one of these congregations. A subsequent section will deal with this phenomenon. Overall, however, the EBG appears to have succeeded in keeping a small community of East Indian Moravians alive.

The Roman Catholics

The Dutch Roman Catholic Church followed the policy prescribed by the Surinamese Roman Catholic Church.[35] Unlike the Moravian Protestants, it did not create a special branch for East Indian Catholics, but established special branches for Surinamese Catholics, the so-called 'Surinamese communities of faith'. These communities functioned as parishes, but without the official status of a parish. They were established in Amsterdam, Rotterdam, The Hague, Utrecht and Tilburg. While all of them include a small number of Hindustanis, the community of The Hague included quite a substantial number of East Indian Catholics in the first decades of its existence.

The Hague community was founded in 1974. The first priest was the Redemptorist Father Henk Kluiters CSsR, who served the community till 1984. As the Roman Catholic missionary work in Suriname was entrusted to the Redemptorists in 1865,[36] it was only natural that this order felt the responsibility to provide support for the construction and guidance of Surinamese communities in the Netherlands as well. The Hague community organizes one Eucharist celebration every month, and during the first decade more than half of the visitors were East Indians. When Kluiters's successor, Father Wim van Pinxteren, took over the leadership in 1984, at least half of the 150 visitors of the special masses were Hindustanis. Today, however, the number of East Indians attending the special Eucharist celebrations for Surinamese in The Hague has diminished to less than 10 in an attendance of 75, the remainder including Creoles, Javanese

---

[35]   The information of this paragraph is derived from telephone interviews with the Roman Catholic East Indians Dien Sardjoe and his daughter, Florence Sardjoe, with Father Ben Vocking of the Surinamese community of faith in Rotterdam, and with Fathers Wim van Pinxteren and Jan Mul, who both functioned as priests in The Hague's Surinamese community of faith.

[36]   Vernooij, *De Rooms-Katholieke Gemeente in Suriname*, pp. 55–6.

and Chinese.[37] According to the present priest, Father Jan Mul, many Hindustani Catholics attend mass in their own environment, and do not feel the need to come to separate masses for Surinamese.

Once a year, the Roman Catholic Church in The Hague organizes a so-called 'international Eucharist celebration', with the participation of some 15 communities of faith of different ethnic backgrounds (such as the Indonesians, Portuguese, Antilleans, and so on). The boards of the five Surinamese communities in the Netherlands also meet twice a year.

A small number of Catholics was involved in the inter-religious dialogue with Hindus and Muslims. It is known that a prominent Catholic family even had made a house available to a pastor in The Hague who wished to have a place for all kinds of meetings, including inter-religious ones.[38]

It is useful to reflect further on the decline of East Indian Catholics in the Surinamese community of faith in The Hague. One agrees with the statement by Father Jan Mul that a number of East Indian Catholics attend the masses in their own environment all over the country. The differences between the masses in their own neighbourhoods and those in the Surinamese communities do not appear significant enough to warrant them attending special Surinamese celebrations. Another reason could be that the Surinamese celebrations are dominated by the culture of the Creoles. In Dutch Surinamese Catholic circles, the following sweeping statement goes round: 'The Creoles sing, the Hindustanis are silent.' Of course, this attitude is closely linked to the common attitude of Africans and Indians towards religious ceremonies in their own settings. None the less, this expression can also be a sign that the Creoles receive greater opportunities to express themselves in the Surinamese masses. This irritated a large proportion of the Hindustani Catholics belonging to the Hague congregation. During the first years of the existence of this congregation, many of its East Indian members flatly refused to sing songs composed in Sranan.[39] The role of the priest, including his personal stature, are also important in these instances. Father Kluiters had many contacts among Hindustani Catholics, more than his successors. In addition, the influence of secularization tendencies has been significant. As noted previously, Christians on the whole in the Netherlands have less inclination to attend church services. None the less, the conclusion seems justified that the Moravians are better able to retain their East Indian members than the Roman Catholics.

---

[37]   The Eucharist celebrations are in the Heilig Hart ('Sacred Heart') Church, Teniersstraat 19.

[38]   This meeting house was called 'De pleisterplaats', and was for many years run by the Rev. Jan Buikema, minister of the Protestant Church in the Netherlands. Information from Dien Sardjoe, 13 February 2007, and from the Rev. Jan Buikema, 6 March 2007.

[39]   Personal communication by Joop G. Vernooij, 11 March 2007.

Other Hindustani Christians

It was previously noted that the Pentecostal and Evangelical Christian congregations were able to attract many Hindustani Christians from the mainstream churches, and in particular from the EBG. Of particular importance in this process was the role of the special Christian congregation in The Hague called the Johan Maasbach Wereldzending ('Johan Maasbach World Mission'). This organization was founded in 1952 by Johan Maasbach (1918–1997), and has many similarities to the Pentecostal and Evangelical congregations, but strongly focused on its founder, particularly before his death in 1997. His children took over, and today there are 11 'Maasbach' congregations all over the country, but concentrated in the western part of the Netherlands.[40]

Other Pentecostal and Evangelical congregations also attracted the East Indians, in particular the Hindustani ones guided by Hindustani pastors, such as De Verheven Deur ('The Lofty Door'), Harvest Ministries, Kalykhan and Hoop voor Hindoestanen ('Hope for Hindustanis') in The Hague.[41] A small group of Hindustanis joined a Baptist church. Mohan Paltoe, who lived in Rotterdam, founded his own charismatic community, Jiwan Jyoti ('Light for the Soul').[42] What makes this group very special, in particular in the context of Pentecostal and Evangelical Christianity, is that they organize so-called Jisoe Kathas (Jesus *kathas*). A *katha* is a Hindu ceremony in which a priest reads and subsequently explains a part of the holy scriptures, concluding with a *puja*. A *puja* is a ritual in which all kinds of things, but in particular food, are offered to a deity, after which the food is divided among the people present. In the Jisoe Katha, only the first part is adopted, but instead of reading and clarifying the Hindu scriptures, it is the Bible text which is melodiously read and explained. Thus, by organizing Jisoe Kathas, to which they invite their family and friends, the members of Jiwan Jyoti preach the message of Jesus Christ among their fellow Hindustanis.[43]

Most Hindustani Pentecostal and Evangelical Christians return to the pattern adopted by the first generation of East Indian Moravians in Suriname. They integrate a Western lifestyle into their Christian way of living. Furthermore, they often follow the leaders of their congregations in labelling other religions like Hinduism and Islam as worship of the devil(s). In time, a number of the Hindustanis did not feel at home in these strongly Western-oriented congregations, which at the same time often vehemently rejected elements belonging to the culture of their

---

[40]   Website of the Stichting Johan Maasbach Wereldzending, <http://www.maasbach. com/Home.htm>, accessed 5 March 2007.

[41]   Personal communication by Joop G. Vernooij, 11 March 2007; Website of Harvest Ministries, <http://www.harvestministries.nl/index.php?id=6&lng=nl>, accessed 11 March 2007.

[42]   Schalkwijk, *Hindoestaanse zending 1901–2001*, p. 46. Interview with J.S. (Mitra) Rambaran, 7 February 2007.

[43]   Interview with J.S. (Mitra) Rambaran, 7 February 2007.

ancestors. Therefore, many of them have left these congregations after a couple of years, although there are some who have remained loyal.

This situation underscores the specialty of Jiwan Jyoti, which in fact follows a way similar to the one adopted by the EBG since the 1970s.

In addition, there exists a small Reformed Hindustani congregation in Rotterdam.[44] It holds bi-monthly services on Sunday afternoons in the Reformed Church of Rotterdam. Other activities of this group include courses on the relationship between Hinduism and Christianity, which are probably attended by a majority of its church members.[45] The congregation, in effect only a segment of the Reformed congregation, accounts for some ten East Indians and a small number of faithful of Pakistani origin. A proportion of the ten East Indians belong to the EBG.[46]

A Hindustani Christian with many contacts in Protestant East Indian circles, including those of the Pentecostals and the Evangelicals, estimates the number of East Indians in these circles at around 100, another at 300. These Christians, however, probably attend the meetings of their own congregations more regularly than the East Indians belonging to the EBG and the Roman Catholic Church.[47]

Conclusion

On the basis of this analysis, there appear to be around 2500 East Indian Christians in the Netherlands, the majority of them belonging to the Evangelische Broedergemeente. The number of East Indian Roman Catholics has declined more than that of the EBG. On the other hand, the Pentecostal and Evangelical congregations, including those of 'Maasbach' have attracted 100–300 members, of which a fair number have, however, subsequently left these congregations. It needs to be emphasized that these figures, apart from the numbers of EBG members and the figures of the Rotterdam Reformed Church, are somewhat tentative and based on the personal impressions and estimates of the people consulted.

Two distinct attitudes exist within Protestant circles with regard to the culture of their East Indian ancestors. Some of the Christians see the Christian lifestyle as something which is completely Western, and reject any element belonging to the culture of India. Another faction, which predominantly consists of Moravians, the people belonging to Jiwan Jyoti, and probably also many Catholics, makes

---

44   Schalkwijk, *Hindoestaanse zending 1901–2001*, p. 46.

45   Website of Evangelie en hindoes, <http://www.evangelie-hindoes.nl/>, accessed 5 March 2007. The minister organizing these activities is the Rev. A.S. van der Lugt.

46   E-mail from their former minister, the Rev. A.S. van der Lugt, 6 March 2007; Website of the Susmacraar – Missionaire Arbeid Rijnmond, <http://www.maronline.nl/phpws/index.php?module=pagemaster&PAGE_user_op=view_page&PAGE_id=13&MMN_position=19:19>, accessed 6 March 2007. The Rev. Van der Lugt moved to Delft in 2006.

47   Interview with Vidjaj Shantiprekash and Ernst Lachman, 2 March 2007; personal communication from J.S. (Mitra) Rambaran, 6 March 2007.

a distinction between Indianness and Hinduism. They like Indian music, films and clothes, and feel challenged to give their Christian faith a genuine Indian flavour and form. It seems that the last group forms the majority of all East Indian Christians in the Netherlands. Overall, however, and in spite of this somewhat cautious openness to Indianness, the great majority of Moravians, Pentecostals and Evangelicals view inter-religious dialogue as a step too far.

Finally, the power of secularization tendencies is strong, and many East Indian Christians are under great pressure to abandon their Christian faith completely. At the same time, it seems that the EBG is more successful in retaining its East Indian members than other Christian groups and churches. This suggests that the future of East Indian Christianity lies in a form of Christianity which does not deny the possibility of introducing elements of Indian culture into its liturgy and daily life. But it also underscores the importance of a separate structure for Hindustani Christians in the EBG.

References

Bakker, Freek L., 'The Hindu–Christian Dialogue in Europe: The Case of the Netherlands', *Dharma Deepika*, 10/2 (2006): 23–37.

De Klerk, C.J.M., *Cultus en ritueel van het orthodoxe hindoeïsme in Suriname*, 2nd edn, vol. 1 (The Hague: Amrit, 1998).

De Klerk, C.J.M., *De immigratie der hindostanen in Suriname*, 2nd edn, vol. 2 (The Hague: Amrit, 1998).

Liebe, Ariane, '"Eén in de Heer": Bekering en convergentie van creolen en hindostanen in de Surinaams evangelisch charismatische beweging' (Utrecht: unpublished master's thesis, Utrecht University, 2004).

Plukker, Dick, Moti Marhé and Narain Mathura, *Hindi voor starters*, Part A (The Hague: Haags Centrum voor Onderwijsbegeleiding, 2001).

Schalkwijk, Jan M.W., *Hindoestaanse zending 1901–2001* (Paramaribo: Theologisch Seminarie der EBGS, 2001).

Shapiro, Michael C., *A Primer of Modern Standard Hindi* (Delhi: Motilal Banarsidass 1989).

Steinberg, H.G., *Ons Suriname: De zending der Evangelische Broedergemeente in Nederlandsch Guyana* (The Hague: Algemeene boekhandel voor inwendige en uitwendige zending, 1933).

Vernooij, J.G., *De Rooms-Katholieke Gemeente in Suriname* (Paramaribo: Leo Victor, 1998).

Verschuuren, Stan, *Suriname: Geschiedenis in hoofdlijnen* (The Hague: SDU Uitgeverij, 1994).

Wenzel, J.T., *Schetsen van den zendingsarbeid der Evangelische Broedergemeente onder de Britsch-Indiërs in Suriname* (Zeist: Zendingsgenootschap der Broedergemeente, 1908).

PART TWO
North America

Chapter 9

The Culture of Asian Indian Catholicism in North America

Elizabeth Cameron Galbraith

This chapter is concerned with the Syro-Malabar and the Syro-Malankara Catholic Churches, both of which originate from the state of Kerala on the south-west coast of India. A brief overview of the origins of these two churches and their relationship to each other will help inform our understanding of their North American immigrant experience.

When the Portuguese missionaries reached a port in India named Cochin on the Malabar coast (now part of the state of Kerala) and established themselves there at the beginning of the sixteenth century, they were delighted to discover Christians already practising there. Among those Indian Christians, the tradition was that the apostle St Thomas had first brought Christianity to India in 52 CE, and that they had been practising Christianity ever since. They were even (and still are) referred to as the St Thomas Christians. Although the first-century origin of the Christian church in India is still a matter of scholarly debate,[1] there is evidence to suggest that Christian immigrants from Persia or Mesopotamia travelled to India in the fourth century and afterwards, and it is the case that the Christians in India eventually came to receive not only their bishops, but also their theology and liturgy from Mesopotamia.[2] The liturgy practised was the East Syrian, or Chaldean, using the Syriac language (the branch of Aramaic assumed to have been spoken by Jesus and the apostles), which explains why the St Thomas Christians of India also came to be known as the Syrian Christians.[3]

The delight on the part of the Portuguese was short-lived, as they soon came to suspect the Indian Christians of having adopted Nestorian heresies from Mesopotamia.[4] In an attempt to separate the St Thomas Christians from their

---

[1]   See I. Gilman and H.J. Klimkeit, *Christians in Asia before 1500* (Ann Arbor, MI, 1999), for a detailed account of the scholarly debate over the origins of Christianity in India.

[2]   Stephen Neill, *A History of Christianity in India: The Beginnings to AD 1707* (Cambridge, 1984), pp. 43–5; Gilman and Klimkeit, *Christians in Asia*, pp. 180–81.

[3]   Placid Podipara, 'Hindu in Culture, Christian in Religion, Oriental in Worship', in George Menachery (ed.), *The St. Thomas Christian Encyclopedia of India*, vol. II (Trichur, India, 1973), p. 107.

[4]   According to Nestorius, from whom the heresy takes its name, there were two separate Persons in the Incarnate Christ, the one divine and the other human. This

purportedly heretical patriarchs in the Middle East and from traditional Indian practices also considered suspect, the Portuguese convened the Synod of Diamper in 1599, at which they passed decrees calculated to bring Indian faith and cultural practices into conformity with Rome. The result of the Synod was that the East Syrian liturgy of the St Thomas Christians, though not entirely replaced, was Latinized,[5] with the resulting hybrid liturgy[6] becoming known as the Syro-Malabar rite,[7] a rite practised to this day by those Indian Christians who accepted the modifications required by the Portuguese at the end of the sixteenth century. To distinguish themselves from those Indians first converted by the Portuguese in the sixteenth and following centuries and who practised the Western (or Latin) rite (hence known as Latin Christians), the St Thomas Christians who accepted the Syro-Malabar rite became known as Syro-Malabar Christians.

However, not all of the St Thomas Christians were content with the changes to their liturgy and practices imposed by the Portuguese, and approximately fifty years after the Synod of Diamper, the discontents staged a historical rebellion, which precipitated what became known as the Coonan Cross Oath of 1653, renouncing their allegiance to the Portuguese. As a result, the Keralan Christian community became divided for the first time in its history, with the small breakaway group eventually leaving the Catholic Church entirely and joining the Syrian Orthodox Church.

Over two centuries later, in 1930, under the leadership of their Archbishop, Mar Ivanios, a small group of Indian Christians from within the Syrian Orthodox Church reunited with the Catholic Church. In doing so, they adopted neither the Latin nor the Syro-Malabar rite, but instead were able to maintain their own variant of the West Syrian Antiochean rite adopted upon entry into the Syrian Orthodox Church in the seventeenth century, and became known as the Syro-Malankara Christians. As a consequence, in Kerala today there are three distinct Catholic churches: the Syro-Malabar, the Latin Catholic and the Syro-Malankara Churches, the latter of which is the smallest of the three. The focus of this chapter is not, however, the status of such churches in India, but rather the Syro-Malabar and the Syro-Malankaran diaspora experience in North America.

The earliest groups of Indian immigrants came to North America between 1899 and 1920, but it was landmark changes in immigration law in the United States in 1965 that led to a large increase in Indian immigration. One might expect Canada's case to be radically different, given its long association with the Indian

---

interpretation of Christ's person is opposed to the accepted Christian doctrine that the incarnate Christ was a single Person, at once God and man. Nestorianism was declared a heresy at the Council of Ephesus in 431 CE.

[5]   Neill, *A History of Christianity in India*, pp. 214–16.

[6]   M. Vattakuzhy, 'The Three Rites in Malabar', in Menachery (ed.), *The St. Thomas Christian Encyclopedia Of India*, vol. II, p. 53.

[7]   A particular church's rite or liturgical tradition comprises the essential expression of that church's identity and cultural heritage through its forms of worship and traditions.

sub-continent through the British Empire and in the Commonwealth, both of which provided a context for immigration. Surprisingly, however, the story is little different there, with the first large wave of Indian immigrants arriving in the early 1970s. In the early waves of immigration, the state of Kerala provided a disproportionate percentage of the Christian immigrants coming from India to North America.[8]

Immigrant Catholics, like other Indian immigrants, are aware of the great opportunities that life in North America provides. They are able to achieve a high standard of living, together with a wealth of educational and other opportunities for their children. On first impressions, as Indian Christians, they also seem to be at an advantage compared with non-Christian immigrant Indians. For instance, Hindus who immigrate to North America are leaving a country where their religion is the native religion and where they are the religious majority, to live in a country for which Hinduism is a foreign religion and in which they are for the first time a religious minority. For Indian Christians, the case is different. Although not the native religion of North America any more than it is of India, Christianity has deep cultural roots in American soil, and is by far the majority religion there. Indian Christians find themselves leaving a country where Christians are a tiny minority (just over 2 per cent of the Indian population is Christian) to make a new home in a country where they are for the first time a religious, if not an ethnic majority. This does indeed bring a degree of acceptance, not to mention privileges not necessarily extended to other immigrant communities. And yet, for many Indian Catholics, and particularly for Syro-Malabar and Syro-Malankaran Catholics, the feeling of minority status even in a supposedly 'Christian land' has prevailed, and they have faced problems with regard to the preservation of their religious identity quite different from Hindus.

As noted by Williams in his *Religions of Immigrants from India and Pakistan*, a Catholicos of the St Thomas Christians of South India on an official visit to Rome in 1983 greeted the late Pope John Paul II:

> We bring you greetings from a small Church, the fruit of the preaching and martyrdom[9] of the Apostle St. Thomas – a Church as ancient as any, as faithful to the Tradition as any, and as proud of its heritage and autonomy as any. In a sense this is a meeting between the apostle St. Thomas and the apostles St. Peter and St. Paul in the persons of their successors.[10]

One of the first hurdles faced by Indian Christians abroad was a lack of awareness among Christians in North America about the long heritage of Christianity in India. Even more significant, however, was and is the distinction between Eastern, and Western Catholic Churches. For many in the West, such a distinction

---

[8]   Raymond Brady Williams, *Religions of Immigrants from India and Pakistan: New Threads in the American Tapestry* (Cambridge, 1988), p. 104.

[9]   St Thomas is thought to have been martyred on the eastern coast of India in 72 CE.

[10]   Quoted in Williams, *Religions of Immigrants*, p. 102.

will mean little, but Eastern Catholics are well aware of the difference. The fact that the Western world for the most part considers Roman Catholicism *the* Catholicism suggests that, at least in the West, there is a tendency to think of the Roman Catholic Church as the Universal Church. To much, if not most of the Western world, Roman Catholicism *is* Catholicism, when in fact the Roman Catholic Church, though by far the largest, is only one of 22 Catholic churches in the world,[11] the majority of which are Eastern. The lack of knowledge about and appreciation for such diversity in Catholicism in the West is the first indicator of the hurdles that Syro-Malabar and Syro-Malankaran Catholic immigrants in North America faced in diaspora. The size and dominance of the Roman Catholic Church among those churches that make up the communion of Catholic churches, makes it especially difficult for small churches like the Syro-Malankara Church to retain their distinctiveness.

But what exactly are the differences between Eastern and Western Catholic churches? In his groundbreaking 1985 study, *Keralites in America: A Community Reference Book*, K.P. Andrews noted:

> It is a fact that many Keralite Catholics of the Syro-Malabar rite used to attend church regularly – even on a daily basis – and receive communion every Sunday before they came to America. Now many of them go to church very irregularly … the real reasons for the fall in church attendance are several: one, many men do not like to become a contributing member of a Latin Catholic Church in America unless their children attend church schools; two, they do not feel at home in the worship language and rituals of American churches; three, they do not like to exchange their Syrian rite and Syrian priests for the dominant Latin rite and white priests … Most Kerala Catholics in America attend religious services several times a year at Latin Catholic churches. They are, however, reluctant participants at best.[12]

One of the keys to such religious alienation lies in the fact that, as noted above, both the Syro-Malabar and the Syro-Malankara Churches follow their own distinct rites. To many North Americans, in fact to most Western Catholics in general, the notion of different rites will also be unfamiliar, but there are in fact seven different rites[13] in the Catholic communion of churches, the Roman Catholic, or Latin rite, being just one of them. Only the Latin Indian Christians, namely those first converted by the Portuguese, follow the Latin rite performed in Western Catholic churches.

---

[11]   Albanian, Armenian, Belorussian, Bulgarian, Chaldean, Coptic, Ethopian, Greek, Hungarian, Italio-Albanian, Krizevei, Maronite, Melkite, Romanian, Russian, Ruthenian, Slovak, Syrian, Syro-Malabar, Syro-Malankara and Ukranian.

[12]   K.P. Andrews (ed.), *Keralites in America: The Community Reference Book* (Glen Oaks, NY, 1983), pp. 110–11.

[13]   Alexandrian, Armenian, Byzantine, Latin, Maronite, East Syrian (Chaldean) and West Syrian (Antiochian).

A rite comprises the essential expression of a church's identity and cultural heritage through its traditions and liturgy. According to Vatican Council II's *Constitution on the Sacred Liturgy*, it is through liturgy that 'the faithful are enabled to express in their lives and manifest to others the mystery of Christ and the real nature of the true Church'.[14] It is in the worship service in particular that the distinctive nature of a particular church's liturgy, and hence of its rite becomes apparent.

The first time I attended an Eastern rite service, and a Syro-Malankara Mass in particular,[15] I was struck by my own sense of dislocation. As one who had always marvelled at the fact that it was possible to enter a Roman Catholic mass just about anywhere in the world, in any foreign language, and still be able to follow the main order and ritual of the service, I suddenly found myself adrift. The service, referred to as Qurbana, is typically longer than a Roman Catholic mass, ranging from approximately one-and-a-half to three hours. The men and women of the congregation sit separately, on left and right-hand sides of the aisle facing the altar, and they stand for much of the service. The women also traditionally wear head veils. The liturgy followed is that of St James, thought to have been practised by the brother of Christ in Jerusalem, and arguably the earliest Christian liturgy. Prayers of great beauty and solemnity characterize this liturgy, as do chants set to solemn music. Although the vernacular has replaced the traditional language of the liturgy in most Indian churches,[16] some chants are occasionally still recited in Syriac. The sanctuary of the church is separated by a veil, representing the veil in the temple of Jerusalem, which is only opened during the mass between the Creed and the Eucharist. Like Eastern liturgies as a whole, considerable emphasis is placed upon the mystery and glory of the resurrection, as a result of which no crucifixes are found on the altar of the church. Everyone at the mass, including the clergy, faces the east, symbolically awaiting the second coming of Christ.

As mysterious and beautiful as the first Syro-Malankara service I attended felt, it was not particularly familiar to me, and I suspect that this unfamiliarity, only in reverse, must be what Syro-Malabar and Syro-Malankara Christians who find themselves in Latin rite services must also feel. Some of the responses I have received from Syro-Malankara Catholics confirm this impression. One priest mentioned that Syro-Malankara Christians, when they cannot attend a Syro-Malankara service, would rather go to an Orthodox service, with which they feel their services have more in common, than to the Roman Catholic mass! The prayers and chants of the liturgy of St James are important to many, as is the subtle but significant difference in emphasis between the Passion of Christ as central to Roman Catholic services

---

[14]   A. Flannery (ed.), *Vatican Council II: Constitutions, Decrees, Declarations* (Northport, NY, 1996), *Sacrosanctum Concilium* 2.

[15]   For a detailed study of the Syro-Malabar liturgy, as well as current debates about its reform, see F. Kanichikattil's *To Restore or to Reform? A Critical Study on Current Liturgical Renewal in the Syro-Malabar Church in India* (Bangalore, 1992).

[16]   Malayalam is the language spoken by Kerala Christians.

and the glory of the resurrection. As one person put it: 'If the service were to end with the passion then there would be no greater meaning in the incarnation of the Lord.' Although the Passion is commemorated, it is the fulfilment of the resurrection that comes as the climax of the Syro-Malankara service.

The more the priests and congregants talked about their worship services, the more it became clear to me that liturgy is crucial to the religious identity of these Syro-Malankara Catholics. Looking for a comparison, one Syro-Malankaran Catholic maintained that 'whereas for Protestants the Bible is the centre of their faith, for Syro-Malankarans it is liturgy'. In another attempt to help me understand the significance of the liturgy, another Indian Catholic suggested: 'It is in the blood: the prayers, the hymns, it is heard and taken to heart.' Liturgy is for these Catholics the very expression of their faith. Like other Eastern Catholics, and presumably like Roman Catholics too, Syro-Malabar and Syro-Malankaran Catholics see their rite not just as an essential part of their identity, but *as* their identity. When asked what makes their Catholic tradition unique, time and again the answer given is their rite, without which they would be, according to an old phrase, 'like salt without its savour'.

In recent church history, support for the retention of distinct rites within the Catholic communion of churches has come from the highest quarters. According to the Vatican Council II *Decree On the Catholic Eastern Churches*:

> All members of the eastern churches should be firmly convinced that they can and ought always preserve their own legitimate rites and ways of life, and that changes are to be introduced only to forward their own organic development. They themselves are to carry out all these prescriptions with the greatest fidelity. They are to aim always at a more perfect knowledge and practice of their rites, and if they have fallen away due to circumstances of times or persons, they are to strive to return to their ancestral traditions.[17]

Concerted efforts have been made to ensure that immigrant Indian Catholics communities in North America are able to maintain their own rites. One way in which this has been assured is by providing priests trained according to the appropriate rite to minister to the various communities and appropriate worship services. On 25 August 1985, a Syro-Malabar Catholic ministry was founded in Chicago when Bishop Pallickaparampil of Kerala joined Joseph Cardinal Bernadine in establishing a priest from Kerala. In the same year, St Thomas the Apostle Mission Parish (which includes Syro-Malabar, Syro-Malankara and Latin Malayalee Catholics) in the Archdiocese of Toronto was erected for the Indian Catholics there, and permission was given for priests from India, trained according to the appropriate rite, to minister to these small communities. The first Syro-Malankara priest to serve the Toronto mission was Father Peter Kochery in 1986,

---

[17]   Austin Flannery (ed.), *Vatican Council II, Orientalium: Constitutions, Decrees, Declarations* (Northport, NY, 1996), *Ecclesiarum* 6.

who took the lead in forming prayer meetings and the occasional celebration of the Syro-Malankara mass. Over time, the occasional celebrations became monthly events. Support from the Western Catholic Church, in addition to the passion for and loyalty to their own liturgical and cultural traditions on the part of the Indian Christians themselves, led to the permanent appointment of an Indian priest for the community in 1997. Now the community celebrates mass weekly.[18] Similar arrangements have been made in other North American Syro-Malankara missions.

Since 1997, there have also been major steps in the direction of the establishment of parishes for Indian Catholics on the part of the Roman Catholic hierarchies. On 1 July 2001, Bishop Jacob Angadiath was ordained bishop for the Syro-Malabar community in the United States, the first eparchy for the Syro-Malabar Catholics outside India. The seat of Bishop Angadiath, who serves 70,000 Malabar Catholics throughout the United States, is in Chicago. He was also appointed the permanent Apostolic Visitor to Canada. The establishment of this new diocese, together with eight parishes throughout the United States, not only enables the Syro-Malabar Catholics to practise their own rite, it is also a mark of recognition on the part of the Western Catholic Church of the Syro-Malabar community's contribution to the Catholic communion of churches.

The incredibly small size of the Syro-Malankara communities in North America explains to some extent why they do not yet have their own eparchies (dioceses), and as a result still function under the jurisdiction of the local Roman Catholic bishop. Consisting of approximately 500–600 families, there are currently 11 Syro-Malankara Catholic missions in the US (including five in the New York Metropolitan area: Staten Island, New Jersey, Queens, New Rochelle, Long Island, and one each in Philadelphia, Detroit, Chicago, Dallas, Washington, DC and Houston), and one, that of Toronto, in Canada. Significant, however, has been the support provided for these communities by their local archdioceses. The Chicago archdiocese, for instance, made a gift of a closed Roman Catholic church[19] in Evanston, Illinois to its small Syro-Malankaran Catholic community in 1995. Although at present this small Syro-Malankaran community is far from being able to meet the material and financial needs of a diocese, they are responsible for the financial upkeep of the church and the Indian priest who has been assigned to them, and they appear to relish the opportunity to worship according to their own rite and to maintain relative self-sufficiency. Moreover, even given the small size of the communities, the signs have also proven hopeful for a move towards more independence for the Syro-Malankara communities in North America.

Bishop Isaac Mar Cleemis,[20] ordained a bishop on 15 August 2001, was appointed by Pope John Paul II to minister to Syro-Malankara Catholics in North America and Europe. He is thus the first bishop specifically consecrated for

---

[18]   Today, there are approximately 800 Catholic families from Kerala (1400 Kerala Christians if you count non-Catholics) living in greater Toronto.

[19]   Ascension of Our Lord Parish Church in Evanston, Illinois.

[20]   Bishop Mar Cleemis earned a doctorate in Ecumenism at Rome.

the North American and European Syro-Malankara missions. Syro-Malankara immigrant communities view this move as a vital step on the route to the establishment of dioceses – that is, parishes that will eventually be under the authority of a bishop from their own rite rather than, as is presently the case, under the jurisdiction of the local Western or Roman (Latin rite) Catholic bishop. This move was also seen as a sign of the late Pope's desire to encourage their Eastern Catholic identity and connection with their own hierarchy.

In an interview at the Evanston church shortly after his ordination, Bishop Mar Cleemis expressed the hope of the Syro-Malankara Catholics that they will soon be fortunate enough to receive their own permanent bishop (and hence dioceses) in North America, and that this will make the retention and celebration of their Syro-Malankaran heritage and Eastern rite a viable legacy for future generations. As another individual commented optimistically: 'If Rome does establish a diocese, the Malankarites will come.' Support for the authentic rites and church hierarchy of such immigrant communities will prove vital to their survival in the West, and will better enrich the diversity within unity that characterizes authentic Catholicism.

Unfortunately, even given the great strides made to ensure the retention of Eastern rites outlined above, the attempt on the part of Indian Catholic clergy to serve the growing numbers of communities that exist somewhere in between traditional Indian and American culture brings with it specific problems that may prove difficult to prepare for and overcome. Many of the priests who serve the Syro-Malankara communities are in the US for short-term appointments or are trying to combine their ministry with theological training. For the few priests who are not also there to study, life in an immigrant community can be vastly different to the life of a priest in India. One Syro-Malankaran priest felt that whereas the role of the priest was often central to the social as well as the religious life of a typical parish in India, in North America the priest's role was primarily that of religious functionary. The 'busy' nature of American life, which can lead to the compartmentalizing of religion (that is, religion as one distinctive aspect of a person's life among many others, such as work, hobbies, and so on) means that communicants have less time to spend 'socially' with their priests and at church functions. I gained the distinct sense from this interviewee that the life of a Syro-Malankaran priest in North America can be a decidedly lonely one. Time does seem to be a major constraint for communicants in North America, in ways that it is not in India, and as a result there does not tend to be so much community-oriented religious life. The priest lamented the loss of real religious community in North America, and feared that as a result, uniquely Syro-Malankara traditions might survive no more than a couple more decades. He also worried that American prosperity might hinder professions to the priesthood, as he already detected a lack of encouragement toward the 'religious life' on the part of parents and little interest in it among children. This fear is of course already well realized in Western Catholic churches. Whereas poverty is the overriding concern in India, communities in the US are blessed with relative prosperity, health and education. Ironically, however, prosperity itself poses challenges. The privilege of good health, opportunities for education and high standards of living, attractive to many, may in fact come at the cost of vocations to the priesthood and religious community.

Although priests sent from India have thus far ministered to the diaspora communities, the experience of the priest mentioned above also raises the question of whether this practice will prove as effective with future generations of immigrants. Presumably, priestly vocations from within the immigrant community and culture would be ideal. At this time, however, vocations to the priesthood from within the immigrant communities are very small, and given the lacunae of Eastern rite training opportunities in the West, inevitably favour the Latin rather than the Syro-Malabar and Syro-Malankara rites.[21] Although returning to India for training would be an option, the linguistic and cultural hurdles that would be encountered by young adults born and raised in North America make this option unlikely to succeed. The current situation will continue to pose problems for representation on the part of Indian Catholicism in the North American priesthood and in North American society in general unless genuine steps are taken to counter the lack of knowledge of and instruction in Syro-Malabar and Malankara sacramental and liturgical traditions in theological formation programmes in seminaries and in academia in the West.

In addition to a culturally adept and appropriately trained clergy, the maintenance of Indian Catholic communities in diaspora will also continue to depend heavily upon the lay community. The communities I have visited in and around New York, in Evanston, Illinois and in Toronto, have been exemplary in their efforts to maintain their distinct religious traditions. Families meet regularly for religious services (often travelling long distances in order to do so) and social activities; they also arrange community-wide and even nationwide conventions every several years. Religion also provides an ideal pretext for maintaining cultural and ethnic ties, with the Malabar and Malankara communities practically substituting for family ties from the homeland. There seems little doubt that the adult members of the lay communities will continue to do all they can to maintain their Syro-Malabar and Syro-Malankara identities. Since the survival and flourishing of minority churches in a majority society depends upon the vibrancy of its lay community, providing support, such as more provisions for Syro-Malabar and Syro-Malankara services in mission areas, for these lay communities will continue to be essential.

Even assuming such support, however, and their own unquestionable allegiance to what are sometimes referred to as 'home traditions', some parents also fear that the younger generations will not remain as attached to their Indian Catholic roots, and that attrition to the Latin or to no church at all will become an increasing threat to their immigrant communities in the future. That this may occur despite their own commendable efforts to nourish in their children a love of their Indian religious and cultural traditions is a common concern among Indian Catholic parents, one echoed even in contemporary literature. In her recent novel

[21] Raymond Brady Williams, *Christian Pluralism in the United States: The Indian Immigrant Experience* (Cambridge, 1996), pp. 255–6.

The Namesake,[22] Jumpha Lahiri deftly portrays the inter-generational clash of cultures between first-generation Indian immigrants and their US-born children. The reader is introduced to these issues through the eyes of Lahiri's young protagonist, Gogol, and his fraught relationship with his parents as he tackles family expectations while attempting to forge his own identity. Encounters with first-generation Indian Catholic parents and their US-born children reveal some of the factors, including language and theological education that may impact the survival of Indian Catholic traditions in North America.

It is impossible to over-emphasize the degree of the attachment on the part of parents to the languages in which their Syro-Malabar and Syro-Malankara worship services are typically conducted, or to determine exactly what and how much is lost when the children of immigrants begin to lose a connection with the native language and culture of their parents. However, in his 1988 study Williams noted that the children of immigrants from India and Pakistan who had reached the ages of 15–25 were largely absent from temples, mosques and churches, and that in part this may have been because the children of immigrants were gaining only marginal ability in spoken and written forms of the languages central to their religious ceremonies.[23] It is perhaps inevitable that children will feel less attachment to religious and cultural services conducted in a language many are less comfortable with, or in some cases completely unfamiliar with. And it is possible that one way to cultivate a loyalty to the Indian Catholic rites among the younger generations born and raised in North America is to make services available to them in English. Steps are today being taken in this direction. Most communities now conduct the Holy Qurbana in English one Sunday (often the first) in every month. Catechism classes most often also take place in English (though with the added complexity that often the only catechism materials available for instruction – due to budgetary constraints – are those prepared by local dioceses, and thus according to the Latin rite). The preparation of Catechism instructional materials according to the Syro-Malabar and Syro-Malankara rites, not to mention incorporating Indian Catholic traditions into the religious instruction that takes place in Catholic parochial schools, might further enhance appreciation for Indian Catholic traditions among the younger generation. Some of the teenagers I interviewed favoured the offering of more services and Catechism materials in English, though several also spoke with fondness of the more traditional service conducted in Malayalam. One individual expressed more affinity to Latin churches than to the Indian church of his parents. In addition to the language hurdle, the length of the Indian mass, and some of the gender components that do not fit with his 'American' way of viewing male and female relationships, were the main reasons given for his preference.

The allusion to 'American' in the above points to the other significant difference for young persons who are born and raised in North America, namely that unlike their parents, for them North America and not India is home. This idea of North

22   Jumpa Lahiri, *The Namesake: A Novel* (Boston, MA, 2003).
23   Williams, *Religions of Immigrants*, p. 288.

America as home and India as somewhere one visits comes across in a recent informal transcript provided by a group of East Coast teenagers sharing Christmas reflections. One individual mentions feeling very alone during a Christmas in India since everyone this individual loved was back in the US. This young person signed off, 'no place like home'. Another commented: 'it feels kinda funny when you wake up Christmas morning and it's 90 degrees outside and sunny with the palm trees decorated with Christmas lights – somehow the effect is lost … so basically waiting to get back and celebrate a wonderful Christmas with friends'. Yet this same transcript also indicated a clear sense of community between these young people, who shared stories about carolling, Christmas trees, the giving of gifts (including to strangers in need) and gorgeous new Indian outfits for Christmas. One individual even commented on attending a Jacobite (Orthodox) service on Christmas Eve. As more and more Asian Indian Catholics immigrate to North America, it seems likely that the inevitable increase in the numbers of Asian Indian youth born and raised in the United States may in fact help elicit more of a 'youth community' connection to their Indian roots.

This notion is borne out in a brief article prepared for one of the Syro-Malankara conventions. In this article, a young adult notes that she only began to embrace Malayalee culture as more Malayalee families gravitated toward her home city in the US, thus making available other children to whom she could relate. Clearly, a sense of community is as significant for these young people as it is for their parents. The same young woman applauds the efforts her parents have made to preserve the Indian culture and instil in her and her siblings traditional values. Another speaks of the time in her late teens when she began to embrace the meaning of Syro-Malankara traditions and the way in which they have moulded her religious identity.

Despite the hurdles to be faced, herein lies the hope for the immigrant Indian Catholic communities in North America – that as the youth mature into young adults, their own versions of Syro-Malabar and Syro-Malankara identities will emerge within their American selves, reminding them that they are both Indian and American, and transnational in the best sense of that word, as the admittedly much more flawed hero appears to discover at the end of Lahiri's novel.

The Syro-Malabar and Syro-Malankara Catholic Churches are slowly but surely fashioning a home for themselves in North America, one replicating much from India, and one that will of necessity in the long run be moulded significantly by its immigrant experience. These Indian churches have much to teach North American Catholic churches about the diversity that exists within the unity of Catholicism; they also provide one of the many great examples of the dynamic of globalization in religion.

References

Andrews, K.P. (ed.), *Keralites in America: The Community Reference Book* (Glen Oaks, NY: Literary Market Review, 1983).

Flannery, Austin (ed.), *Vatican Council II: Constitutions, Decrees, Declarations* (Northport, NY: Costello Publishing, 1996).

Gilman, I. and H.J. Klimkeit, *Christians in Asia before 1500* (Ann Arbor, MI: University of Michigan Press, 1999).

Kanichikattil, F., *To Restore or to Reform? A Critical Study on Current Liturgical Renewal in the Syro-Malabar Church in India* (Bangalore: Dharmaram Publications, 1992).

Lahiri, Jumpa, *The Namesake: A Novel* (Boston, MA: Houghton Mifflin, 2003).

Neill, Stephen, *A History of Christianity in India: The Beginnings to AD 1707* (Cambridge: Cambridge University Press, 1984).

Podipara, Placid, 'Hindu in Culture, Christian in Religion, Oriental in Worship', in George Menachery (ed.), *The St. Thomas Christian Encyclopedia of India*, vol. II (Trichur, India: BNK Press, 1973), pp. 107–11.

Vattakuzhy, Matthew, 'The Three Rites in Malabar', in George Menachery (ed.), *The St. Thomas Christian Encyclopedia of India*, vol. II (Trichur, India: BNK Press, 1973), pp. 52–6.

Williams, Raymond Brady, *Religions of Immigrants from India and Pakistan: New Threads in the American Tapestry* (Cambridge: Cambridge University Press, 1988).

Williams, Raymond Brady, *Christian Pluralism in the United States: The Indian Immigrant Experience* (Cambridge: Cambridge University Press, 1996).

Chapter 10

New Land, New Challenges: The Role of Religion in the Acculturation of Syro-Malabar Catholics in Chicago[1]

Selva J. Raj

Introduction

Subsequent to the United States Immigration Act of 1965, there was a tidal wave of emigration from India which brought many Indian groups – including various Christian communities – to several US metropolitan areas such as Chicago.[2] Of the various Indian Christian groups in the Chicago area, the Syro-Malabar Catholic community from the state of Kerala in south-west India occupies a unique position because it is by far the largest homogenous Christian group.[3] In addition, while

[1] I am grateful to Albion College for a Hewlett-Mellon research grant that provided funds for field research in Chicago in the summer of 1997. This chapter results from this field research as well as from my personal knowledge of and familiarity with a large segment of the Syro-Malabar Catholic population in Chicago over a fifteen-year period (1985–2000). Special thanks to Liberty Kyser and Tamara Parish who assisted me during the field research. The names of interviewees have been changed to protect their privacy.

[2] According to the 1991 Census of India, Indian Christians, who constitute a tiny minority of the Indian population (2.3 per cent, or approximately 19.6 million), belong to various Christian denominations, with Roman Catholics forming the single largest group, numbering 13.8 million. The bulk of the Christian population is concentrated in the Indian states of Goa in the west, Kerala and Tamil Nadu in the south, and Nagaland in the north-east; J. Heitzman and R.L. Worden (eds), *India: A Country* (Washington, DC, 1996), p. 170.

[3] The Catholic Church in India is configured and structured along three liturgical rites (Syro-Malabar, Syro-Malankara and Latin) that are in use today, giving rise to three distinct episcopal administrative bodies as collectively held auspices of the Catholic Bishops Conference of India (CBCI). While the Syro-Malabar rite is mainly confined to the state of Kerala in southwest India with a few mission dioceses in north India, the Latin rite is the major liturgical rite observed in the rest of the country. The liturgy of the Syro-Malabar rite belongs to the Chaldean liturgical family. From around the fourth to the sixteenth century, Aramaic (East Syriac) was the official liturgical language for the Syro-Malabar rite. After the Daimper Synod in 1599, the Syriac liturgy was modified to conform to the Latin rite. In the wake of post-Vatican II liturgical renewal in India, the Syro-Malabar Church restored the pre-Daimper liturgy, paving way for the vernacularization of Syro-Malabar liturgy with

most Indian Catholics belong to the Latin liturgical rite which makes for easy acculturation to the predominantly Latin rite American Catholicism, the Syro-Malabar Catholic community possesses a distinctive liturgical rite that sets it apart from other Christian immigrants from India.[4] This has produced among its members both a sense of distinct identity and just religious pride as well as a certain alienation from American Catholicism and a corresponding feeling of urgency to develop ways and means to preserve its distinctive religious and cultural heritage. In light of a brief overview of the history of the Syro-Malabar congregation in Chicago, this chapter explores the role and function of religion in the acculturation of its immigrant members to the US landscape.

Target Group and Methodology

In order to ascertain the role of religion in the immigrant experience of Syro-Malabar Catholics in Chicago, in the summer of 1997 I conducted a month-long intensive field research project with the congregation. The field study took the form of extended interviews with 20 Syro-Malabar Catholic families – chosen as representative sample of a cross-section of the community – of diverse social, economic, professional and immigration backgrounds. In addition to these 20 households, I also interviewed the resident pastor of the congregation and some lay leaders. Except for two families that lived in the city, others lived in the various suburbs of Chicago such as Downers Grove, Darien, Woodridge, Libertyville, Oakbrook, Forest Park, Lisle and Skokie.

Both structured and unstructured interviews were conducted in the homes/residences of interviewees when all members of the family, including young adults, were present. All 20 households had two careers and dual incomes.

Malayalam as the official liturgical language. Based on <http://www.stthomasdiocese.org/liturgy.htm>, accessed 15 February 2005.

[4]   The Syro-Malabar Church is the second largest Oriental Catholic church, with a membership of more than 3.5 million Catholics, of which about 100,000 are said to live in North America (United States and Canada). Commonly known as St Thomas Christians, its members trace their origin to St Thomas the Apostle, who, according to church tradition, came to India in 52 CE and established the church, which is said to be 'Christian in faith, Oriental in worship, and Indian in culture'. Based on information at <http://www.stthomasdiocese.org/diocese/mission.htm>, accessed 15 February 2005. The Syro-Malabar Church enjoys the status of a Sui Juris Particular Church headed by a Major Archbishop, who has general jurisdiction over four archdioceses, 21 suffragan dioceses and approximately 3000 parishes and mission stations. Currently, Cardinal Varkey Vithayathil occupies this position. At present, there are 50 bishops from the Syro-Malabar rite working in Kerala and outside: 31 serving in Syro-Malabar dioceses and 19 serving in other dioceses and apostolic offices. There are about 7000 Syro-Malabar priests and 30,000 nuns working in India and outside. Based on <http://www.stthomasdiocese.org/diocese/mission.htm>, accessed 15 February 2005.

Professionally, nursing and allied professions in the medical field were the most popular career options for the women I interviewed: of the 20, 13 were either registered nurses (RN) or licensed practical nurses (LPN), two were physicians, and the remaining five were physical and respiratory therapists. All the women were gainfully employed, often earning much higher wages than their spouses, which had occasionally led to domestic tensions, strained relationships and power struggles.[5] The men I interviewed held diverse professions: two were business entrepreneurs, two physicians, two university professors, one was a vice-president and managing director of a major corporation, two were engineers, two medical supervisors, two chartered public accountants (CPA) and bankers, two technicians, three clerks, and one was a real estate agent. In terms of immigration history, in nine cases, women – all of whom were nurses – preceded their husbands, while in eight, men came first and their spouses followed them later. In the remaining three cases, both husband and wife migrated at the same time through sponsorship by a family member living in the US. At the time of the interview, all 20 families had been in the US for several years, ranging from four to 36 years.

As to their socio-economic mobility pattern, each of these families began their immigrant life in rented apartments in the city of Chicago. After saving enough money, they purchased two-unit apartments in the city, living in one and renting out the other unit. When they had accumulated sufficient wealth, they moved to single houses in relatively safe suburbs. The more successful among them finally moved to very large houses in exclusive, affluent suburbs. Ordinarily, these immigrants had been in the US for twenty years or more with highly lucrative and successful professional careers and greater economic wealth. Of the 20 families I interviewed, two of them – both recent immigrants – lived in the city, 12 had their homes in the suburbs, and the remaining six lived in very affluent suburbs like Oakbrook, Illinois. The two recent immigrant families were green card holders, while the remaining 18 had one or more naturalized citizens in their household. In terms of linguistic proficiency, with the exception of the elderly grandparents who regularly commuted between India and the US, most of them had good fluency in English, though the children frequently commented on their parents' Indian 'accent'. Overall, the level of acculturation to mainstream American culture these families demonstrated – as discussed below – was generally commensurate with the number of years spent in the US and the socio-economic and professional success they were able to achieve. This fact also determines the extent of their dependence on and involvement in church activities.

As noted above, my field research also entailed extended formal and informal conversations with the resident pastor of the Syro-Malabar Church, which occurred in his official residence. Jointly appointed by the Bishops of Kerala and the Archbishop of Chicago, the Rev. Thomas, who in 1996 began a three-year tenure

---

[5]   For a fuller discussion of this reality in the wider Indian immigrant community, see J. Lessinger, *From the Ganges to the Hudson: Indian Immigrants in New York City* (Boston, MA, 1995).

as the resident pastor, had completed one year at the time of my interview. Fluent in both English and Malayalam – the language of Kerala – in his dress, demeanour, and pastoral approach, Rev. Thomas resembled any Catholic priest in South India. The long white cassock he wore at all times was one external sign of his strong ties to the clerical culture in the native country. A relatively recent immigrant, he seemed more at ease with Keralaite food and customs than local cuisine and customs. In addition to the pastor, I also interviewed several male and female lay leaders who acted as musicians, song leaders, liturgical assistants, teachers and lay church administrators. A notable feature of Syro-Malabar immigrant church life in Chicago is the prominent role accorded to women. A set of prepared questions provided the general framework and parameters for the interviews. The interviews themselves covered such topics as the role of religion in immigrants' lives, patterns of change and continuity in the domestic and religious spheres, inter-generational conflicts and gender roles. However, in this chapter I will confine my observations to the role religion and religious institutions play in the social, cultural and religious life of Syro-Malabar Catholics in Chicago.

The History of the Syro-Malabar Church in Chicago: An Overview

The origins of the Syro-Malabar Catholic Church in Chicago are traced to the initiatives of a handful of university students from Kerala who were pursuing advanced degrees in the city in the late 1950s. Isolated from their native cultural and social contexts, these students periodically met for social hour at the Crossroads Student Center located near the University of Chicago. Their number grew rapidly after the passage of the 1965 Immigration Act. The immigrant Catholics from Kerala attended local Latin rite churches and sent their children to the archdiocesan schools for education and religious instruction. These families periodically met together for social fellowship. However, 'in the seventies non-Catholic ... groups and Hindus ... organized several of their religious organizations – the Marthoma Church, Jacobite and Orthodox Churches'.[6]

This led to the formation in 1977 of a Kerala Catholic fellowship comprising members of the three Kerala liturgical rites: Syro-Malabar, Syro-Malankara and Latin. Members met every first Sunday of the month at Loyola University campus, for mass and social fellowship. Besides services in Malayalam, 'other cultural, social, and recreational activities ... [were] organized to protect and enhance the traditional values of the Kerala Syro-Malabar Community'.[7] Among others, these included the observance of the St Thomas celebration in July and an annual retreat. The fellowship also organized receptions to visiting bishops from Kerala, who recommended the formation of separate Catholic groups on the basis of the

---

[6]   K.S. Antony, 'The Development of Syro-Malabar Mission of Chicago', in *Syro-Malabar Catholic Mission Souvenir* (n.p., 1988).

[7]   Ibid.

three rites found in Kerala. Thus in 1983, the Archbishop of Trivandrum, Kerala, sent a priest to serve as chaplain for the Syro-Malankara Catholics in the Chicago area. The same year, the Bishop of Kottayam appointed a separate chaplain for the Knanaya Catholics.[8] Both ministries operated with the approval of the Archdiocese of Chicago. This necessitated the formation of the Syro-Malabar Catholics into a separate organization in September 1984 under the leadership of the Rev. Anthony Kurialachery. The congregation met every fourth Sunday at St Bernandine's Catholic Church in Forest Park for mass and a social hour. The Syro-Malabar bishops of Kerala offered official approval for Kurialacherry's pastoral leadership by appointing him as chaplain for the Syro-Malabar community. Thus the Syro-Malabar Mission in Chicago was solemnly inaugurated in August 1985 by Cardinal Joseph Bernardine of Chicago in the presence of Bishop Joseph Pallickaparambil, who represented the Syro-Malabar Bishops' Conference in Kerala.

In September 1987, Rev. Zacharias Elappunkal succeeded Rev. Kurialacherry as chaplain. In early 1988, the Archdiocese of Chicago offered to lease to the Syro-Malabar congregation for a nominal fee the St John Chrysostum Church and its school building in Bellwood, Illinois, which was scheduled to close. Since July 1988, St John Chrysostum, renamed Mar Thoma Schlecha Church, became the official church for the Syro-Malabar Catholics in the Chicago area. Subsequently, the parochial school was remodelled as a multi-purpose hall and re-dedicated as Alphonsa Hall in 1994 in honour of Sister Alphonsa, a Clarist nun of Kerala currently being considered for canonization.[9] The members proudly stated that this was the first full-service Syro-Malabar Catholic Church outside India. A Syro-Malabar priest from Kerala was assigned to the congregation as its resident pastor by a joint appointment by the Syro-Malabar hierarchy in Kerala and the Archbishop of Chicago.

Thus the congregation, which began with about 150 families, has witnessed steady numerical growth, an institutional base and structural stability, with the laity assuming increasing control of the temporal administration of the church. The increased lay participation in church governance is a distinctive feature

---

[8]   The Knanaya Catholics – also known as 'southists' since most of them lived in the southern part of Kerala – constitute a sub-group within the Syro-Malabar Church. While the group shares the Syriac liturgy of the Syro-Malabar Church, it is an endogamous ethnic group with its distinct traditions, customs and culture. Spread throughout the world, this 200,000-plus strong community is under the Bishop of Kottayam in Kerala, who enjoys personal jurisdiction over the group. Members of this group trace their origin back to 72 Mesopotamian Christian families who immigrated to India and settled in Kerala in 345 CE. Thomas Kinayi, a merchant by occupation, is said to have organized these immigrant families into a separate cultural and ethnic group. Known as 'Kananites' because of their ethnic ties to Thomas Kinayi, descendants of this group strive to preserve to this day its ancient ethnic roots and cultural traits.

[9]   For a concise and analytical treatment of the life and cult of Sister Alphonsa, see Corinne G. Dempsey, *Kerala Christian Sainthood: Collisions of Culture and Worldview in South India* (New York, 2001), pp. 115–55.

of Syro-Malabar Church life in the US. Of particular note is the visible and prominent leadership role exercised by women as music leaders and catechism teachers, who in the native country were generally excluded from participation in church governance. In 2001, Pope John Paul II created the first transnational Syro-Malabar Catholic Diocese of Chicago with jurisdiction over the entire United States, appointing Mar Jacob Angadiath as its first bishop, who also serves as the permanent Apostolic Visitator to Canada. The newly erected St Thomas Syro-Malabar Catholic Diocese of Chicago is the 25th Syro-Malabar Catholic diocese, the other 24 being located in India. With the creation of the diocese and the appointment of a resident bishop, Mar Thomas Sleeha Church in Bellwood, Illinois, which served as the parish church for the Syro-Malabar Catholics of Chicago for over a decade, was declared the cathedral of the new diocese in 2001. The cathedral now functions as the nerve centre of all the activities of the Syro-Malabar Catholics living in and around the city of Chicago.[10] According to the church's official Website in February 2005, there were over 800 registered families in the congregation. The diocese now has four parishes and 29 missions. The diocesan Website claimed that the total families registered under different parishes and missions numbered approximately 8500, of which 1400 were Knanaites.[11]

The Role of Religion in Acculturation

Recent studies have highlighted the crucial role religion plays in the ethnic identity formation and the acculturation of new immigrants living on alien soil. What role does religion play in the identity formation and social cohesion of Syro-Malabara Catholic immigrants as they seek to protect and preserve their cultural and religious heritage on American soil? Conversely, has immigration significantly altered the character, function and structure of the church? Stated briefly, although the Chicago church resembles a typical Kerala church in liturgy and language, the specific challenges and needs encountered by its immigrant population have necessitated significant changes in the church's roles, functions, programmes, structure and administration. Consequently, the Syro-Malabar Church in Chicago has assumed multiple – frequently non-religious – roles and functions. In the remainder of this chapter, I will focus on four specific functions, and reflect on their implications.

The Church as the Locus of Culture Transmission

In his landmark work on Indian Christian immigrants in the United States, Raymond Williams observes that 'a major reason immigrants give for establishing churches and religious institutions is to assist them in socializing their children as Indian

---

[10]   Based on information available at <http://www.stthomasdiocese.org/cathedral.htm>, accessed 18 January 2008.
[11]   Ibid.

Christians in American society'.[12] Elsewhere in the same work, he writes: 'Parents and leaders grapple with the question of how to transmit effectively the Christian tradition they learned in India to the children raised in America to enable them to mature as Asian-Indian Christians.'[13] The Syro-Malabar Catholics of Chicago are no exception. To immigrant parents grappling with the issue of effective transmission of their cultural heritage and religious identity to their US-born children, the church serves as a viable and necessary institution. A variety of church programmes have been devised to help immigrant parents realize this goal.

The two principal modes of transmission of tradition which the Syro-Malabar Catholics have effectively adopted are ritual and language, which frequently work in tandem – a pattern which Williams also discerns among other Asian-Indian Christian and Hindu[14] immigrants in the United States. At the ritual level, conscious and concerted efforts are being made to preserve the Syrian liturgical heritage. The Sunday liturgy is conducted in Malayalam according to the traditional Syro-Malabar rite, which many youth find painfully 'too long and too boring'.[15] However, for elderly grandparents, who spend several months a year with their US-based children providing childcare to their grandchildren, the weekly worship service in the native language is a vital need. This is because most of them do not speak English. Besides, many wear the traditional dress commonly worn by the elderly in Kerala, which makes them self-conscious when attending mass in an Euro-American Catholic parish. Added to this is their feeling of social isolation, since they do not have the kind of social network available to them in the native village. Not surprisingly, therefore, these senior citizens look forward to the weekly church services and events with much anticipation, because for many of them these serve as the primary – if not the sole – social and religious outlet. Given these realities, the vernacular mass in a vernacular church fulfils a vital social and religious need of the senior citizens in the community. For first-generation immigrant parents, the Malayalam liturgy also instils a sense of nostalgia for the native country. The common language shared by its members acts as an identity marker, serving to simultaneously create external boundaries, internal cohesion, and group bonding and commitment.[16]

---

[12] Raymond B. Williams, *Christian Pluralism in the United States: The Indian Immigrant Experience* (Cambridge, 1996), p. 208. In her recent study entitled *A New Religious America: How a 'Christian Country' has Become the World's Most Religiously Diverse Nation* (San Franciso, CA, 2001), Diana Eck discerns this pattern among other immigrant religious groups in North America, including Buddhists and Muslims of different stripes and nationalities.

[13] Williams, *Christian Pluralism in the United States*, p. 190.

[14] Raymond B. Williams (ed.), *A Sacred Thread: Modern Transmission of Hindu Traditions in India and Abroad* (Chambersburg, PA, 1992).

[15] Interview with Manju Puthenveetil, 30 June 1997.

[16] Williams, *Christian Pluralism in the United States*, p. 190.

Besides the Syrian rite liturgy, the congregation celebrates several popular religious festivals observed in Kerala. For example, the feast of St Thomas is celebrated for three days with much fanfare and the usual trappings of religious festivals in Kerala, including colourful processions with canopies and a golden cross. However, in order to accommodate the members' hectic work schedules, the festival is observed during the 4 July long weekend in lieu of the date prescribed in the official liturgical calendar. The community also celebrates the feasts of the blessed Alphonsa and Chavara Kuriakose – two Malayalee candidates for canonization – as well as the feasts of Saints George and Sebastian, who command the religious devotion of a large number of Catholics in Kerala.

In addition, ten years ago the Bellwood church instituted a school of language where US-born children can learn the native language and receive religious instruction in Malayalam. Furthermore, its youth have a diverse social and immigration history. The children of recent immigrants who have limited fluency in English are more at ease with Malayalam and native pop culture. By contrast, the US-born children, who self-identify themselves as Americans, are more at ease with American pop culture. To facilitate easy social exchange among the youth with different social needs and immigration history, the church has established two separate youth organizations, one for Malayalam-speaking youth, and another for English-speaking youth. In addition, the church patronizes two dance classes for girls, considered essential for the cultural formation of young girls. Girls trained in these classes have opportunities to perform Indian dances at cultural and religious events regularly organized by the church, such as the Onam festival and St Thomas Day celebrations. The church also sponsors Malayalam music festivals (Ganamela) featuring popular artists and singers from Kerala. These music concerts yield dual benefits. While they help the first-generation immigrants to keep abreast with popular culture in Kerala, they also act as fundraisers for the church and other charitable causes in Kerala.[17] Spiritual retreat in Malayalam by well-known preachers from Kerala is another annual event.

Several church-sponsored activities and organizations, including the Syro-Malabar Youth Movement and CYM (Catholic Youth Movement), are geared towards instilling in the US-born children pride in their Syro-Malabar religious heritage and Indian culture. To this end, the church regularly conducts discussions and debates on certain vital social themes such as dowry, arranged marriage, dating and inter-generational conflicts. They even hold Indian cooking classes. The Rev. Thomas explained the rationale for these non-religious programs and events:

> We are doing these things with a definite goal and outcome in mind. When they [youth] mingle among themselves, may be they will choose their life-partner from the Syro-Malabar community, instead of going out and getting married in other communities.

---

[17] A fuller discussion of the impact of transnational communities like the Syro-Malabar Church in Chicago and its leaders on the native country would require a separate chapter.

Instead of saying 'don't marry Vietnamese or Filipinos or African-Americans', we give opportunities to our youth to mingle, and even date, which itself is unheard of in India.[18]

Towards this end, the church also patronizes and organizes on its premises several beauty pageants and disco evenings for the youth. In this regard, the Bellwood church also functions as a 'dating service', not unlike the Singles' Club in some American Catholic parishes.

The Church as a Cultural Comfort Zone

In response to the changed cultural context of North America, the Syro-Malabar Church in Bellwood, as noted above, has made several adjustments and modifications in its temporal, pastoral and institutional administration. These modifications notwithstanding, in many respects the church serves as a microcosm of Kerala. Its liturgy, language, music, customs, practices, and even the food served at church socials, replicate the material and religious culture of Kerala. The various programmes mentioned above are deliberate attempts to preserve this microcosm. As such, the church serves as a vehicle for cultural reminder, pride and nostalgia.

Although most Syro-Malabar immigrants regard the church as a valuable and necessary institution, the extent of dependence on the church and its activities is commensurate with the level of professionalism, the age of children, parents' initial experience in the US and their cross-cultural experience prior to immigration. Reliance on the church for cultural survival and social network is particularly high among lower economic groups, unskilled workers and recent immigrants, for whom the church serves as an 'extended family' in the US, providing networking, counselling, employment opportunities, cultural outlets and financial stability. These immigrants exhibit a deep attachment to native culture, language and food, and conversely, a strong resistance to mainstream American popular culture and values. For others who feel threatened by or alienated from mainstream American social values, customs, practices and their perceived ills, the church provides a cultural 'comfort zone' and 'safety net'. These immigrants take their children to the church, as one lay leader put it, 'to safeguard them from the moral dangers and social ills' plaguing mainstream American society. Both groups view the church as a religious safe haven and cultural asylum that guarantees certain short-term and long-term cultural dividends. This explains why these immigrants feel deeply invested in the church and its activities. However, dependence on the church for their cultural needs is minimal among those immigrants who have achieved some degree of cultural assimilation through education, marriage or professional life. These immigrants view the church primarily as a religious institution, since their social, cultural and professional needs are adequately fulfilled in mainstream American society. Their marginal interest in matters Syro-Malabar is impelled

---

[18]   Interview with the Rev. Thomas, 28 June 1997.

solely by religious needs. Once active leaders in the community, many of them have become disinterested in and disenchanted with church affairs because they are, as one put it, 'sick and tired of group politics'.[19]

These facts suggest that while the church serves as the locus and agent of transmission of culture and tradition, it also fosters – some might say self-consciously – a climate of cultural insulation helping to create an insular community, isolated and removed from the fears and ambiguities of the mainstream American culture. Its insular character is evident in the pastor's self-admission. He said: 'Though I have been here for two years, I never felt I have been in America … The language I speak, the food I eat, and the homes I visit are all from Kerala … I am living in Kerala in America!'[20] Sunday sermons and pastoral exhortations warn parents of the moral and social ills plaguing American culture and society, and constantly remind parents of their responsibility to protect and safeguard their children from the 'evil one'. In this regard, the Syro-Malabar Church in Chicago functions as a 'countercultural' group.

The Church: Agent of Assimilation or De-assimilation?

While the church has vigorously promoted the preservation of Syro-Malabar religious and cultural heritage, what role does it play in the assimilation of immigrants into mainstream culture? Does it act as an agent of assimilation, or de-assimilation? When asked about this, the pastor noted:

> The church has not done anything as yet … In fact, we don't have to do anything in this regard since they [youth] are already exposed to it [American culture] in their daily life, in the school, and the media. There is no particular need for me to help them blend into the American society.[21]

The perceptive remarks of a layman are worth noting:

> If the church does that, it will lose me and my children, meaning, we would not need the Syro-Malabar church any more … By perpetuating immigrants' fear of mainstream American culture the church legitimizes its own existence and survival.[22]

Another stated very directly:

> No, it does not and it won't and that is the problem. They [the church and immigrants] do not want the children to intermarry but rather marry among themselves.[23]

---

[19]   Interview with Molly Thomas, 7 July 1997.
[20]   Interview with the Rev. Thomas in Bellwood, 20 June 1997.
[21]   Ibid.
[22]   Interview with George Palamattam on June 15, 1997.
[23]   Interview with Molly Thomas, 7 July 1997.

The insular culture of the Syro-Malabar Church is also evident in its limited interest and engagement in local civic life. While other South Asian immigrant religious groups have developed various outreach initiatives in an effort to assimilate to the larger American religious and social landscape to gain goodwill among native-born Euro-Americans and other ethnic groups,[24] the Syro-Malabar Church in Chicago is largely, if not totally, inward-looking, insulated, with their primary interest among themselves and their native church. In some ways, church leaders are at the forefront of the silent resistance to full cultural assimilation. Through sermons and counselling, the clerics perpetuate immigrants' fear of and ambivalence towards mainstream popular culture and values. According to some lay leaders within the group, the clergy's protectionist strategy is more inspired by a desire to legitimize their privileged position and relevance, and less by a genuine desire to preserve native cultural and religious heritage.

The Church as a Contesting Site for Status Elevation

Increased lay participation in pastoral and temporal administration distinguishes the Bellwood church from its counterparts in Kerala, where the laity has only marginal involvement and minimal input in the temporal administration of the church. Many compete for leadership roles in the church. Competition for leadership positions in church organizations and boards is particularly high among those immigrants who have spent several years in the US and have achieved considerable economic and professional success but lack social and civic recognition. Strangely, a good number of these men were either inactive or indifferent to church affairs in India. Several factors seem to contribute to this shift in interest. First, whereas the church is economically self-sufficient in Kerala, the church in Chicago relies heavily on the financial contributions of the laity for general upkeep and the priest's salary. Because the laity provides financial support, it feels more invested in the governance of church funds and activities. A related factor is the influence of the American core values of democracy and free speech. Notwithstanding the proverbial Keralite deference to clerical authority, Syro-Malabar immigrants feel that they have a legitimate say and role in the administration of their church.

Perhaps the most important factor is the status elevation which church involvement provides for those immigrants struggling with what I call the 'Nobody–Somebody Syndrome'. The church provides the context, platform and opportunity for Syro-Malabar immigrants, particularly the men, to gain status, power and leadership that are either unavailable or denied to them in the mainstream society. In other words, gnawed by the feeling of 'nobody' in mainstream society, the immigrant men see the church as an institution where they can become 'somebody'. This is especially true of immigrants who have achieved economic and professional success but not social recognition. These men are deeply invested in church and community affairs, often marshalling personal

---

[24]   See Eck, *A New Religious America*, pp. 68, 179.

resources for community events. Many of them compete for leadership positions in the church administrative and governing boards. To them, the church serves as the primary locus for leadership opportunities. In his recent study of Indian Christian immigrants, Williams alludes to this phenomenon. He writes: 'The church is one institution in which immigrant men can seek to gain status and ego-satisfaction denied to them in other social contexts.'[25] Rev Thomas corroborated this fact:

> In India there are clubs, movie theatres, political parties and so many other opportunities to meet people and display talents. But here there is no other opportunity. So the church is the only place where they can talk in their language. The church provides a platform to exercise leadership; this is a natural, psychological need and not always a selfish need.

A female doctor, who has chosen not to be active in church events and affairs, emphatically asserted: 'Besides the mass and social gatherings, there is a lot of politicking in the church ... doctors and the wealthy men try to buy power in the church.'[26]

Conclusion: The Cultural Liminality of Syro-Malabar Catholics

A sense of liminality is characteristic of both the first- and second-generation Syro-Malabar Catholic immigrants, though the types of liminality they experience are quite distinct. Let me begin with the parents. Like many Indian immigrants, Syro-Malabar immigrants also grapple with the feeling of 'liminality', of being between and betwixt, of being neither here nor there. The early years of the immigrant experience are spent in pursuit of the American dream. Once that is attained, thoughts of returning to India occur to the immigrants, especially when they have to address such important social issues as dating and marriage in the lives of their teenage children. At such moments, some entertain the idea of sending their children to expensive boarding schools in India in an effort to protect them from the moral dangers and the perceived negative influences of American life. While some do choose this option, many find it emotionally too difficult and painful. When confronted by these issues, they begin to feel that they do not really belong in the US. A similar sentiment overwhelms them during their periodic visits to India, which convinces them they are not the Indians they used to be before they moved to the US. Having spent many years in the US, they feel alienated and strangers in the native country. But returning permanently to India has a serious complication, since their children consider the US their real home. Added to this, Indian bureaucracy, inefficiency, corruption and a host of other problems render returning to India an impractical option. Put differently, when in the US they see themselves as Indians, and when in India they see themselves as Americans.

---

25   Williams, *Christian Pluralism in the United States*, p. 205.
26   Interview with Mrs Mary Jose, 25 June 1997.

They cope with their liminality in the US by romanticizing Indian culture. And when in India, they tend to idealize and extol the virtues of American life, such as material prosperity, affluence, comfort and hard work. Whereas the parents' cultural liminality concerns the world, culture and society outside, their children's liminality concerns the world inside – the world of identity, values, practices and expectations – that affect them at a profoundly personal level. These children constantly wrestle with questions like: Why are certain practices and customs such as dating and sleepovers a taboo for them at home although these are acceptable and a way of life among their American peers? Why aren't girls allowed to go for prom, while their brothers may be permitted?

There is another type of liminality which the immigrant parents and their children experience in relation to each other. They regard each other as 'ambivalent others'. This has led the two generations to develop their own mechanisms to cope with the 'other', the 'alien' within the family. We may describe this as the Indianization versus Americanization dialectic, in which the parents try very hard to Indianize their US-born children, who in turn try to Americanize their India-born parents. What is ironic is that while the Indianizing process concerns the internal world of identity, values, perspectives and world view, the Americanization process concerns the external world of dress (avoiding Indian dress), habits (food), speech (Indian accent) and social skills (dancing, manners, etiquette, cocktail conversations, and so on). The collision of these two types of liminality experienced by these groups and their diametrically opposed coping strategies inevitably produces intense domestic conflicts and inter-generational tensions that occasionally lead to fatal results.

Admittedly, all immigrant groups – irrespective of ethnic origins – wrestle with these and similar issues in the early stages of immigration. The mechanisms and strategies devised by the Syro-Malabar leaders – both ecclesiastical and lay – suggest that like their immigrant predecessors, the Syro-Malabar Catholics of Chicago are also negotiating the growing pains of immigration. Perhaps they too will grow out of the pangs of acculturation and assimilation to an alien soil and landscape. Even as they struggle to make the United States their new-found cultural and religious home, some gnawing questions still linger: Will the church lose its appeal as these immigrants enter the third- and fourth-generation phase and become fully assimilated into the American mainstream culture, as happened with their European and other Asian immigrants? Is there something intrinsic to the Indian cultural and religious ethos that precludes total assimilation into a culture that is as radically different from its native cultural and value system as mainstream American culture? Would the creation of the North American Syro-Malabar diocese in Chicago which seeks to transplant Kerala religious culture and structure to the US alleviate or perpetuate this cultural liminality? These are difficult questions that defy simplistic answers. Only time and future research will shed light on these difficult yet pertinent questions.

References

Antony, K.S., 'The Development of Syro-Malabar Mission of Chicago', in *Syro-Malabar Catholic Mission Souvenir* (n.p., 1988).

Dempsey, Corinne G., *Kerala Christian Sainthood: Collisions of Culture and Worldview in South India* (New York: Oxford University Press, 2001).

Eck, Diana, *A New Religious America: How a 'Christian Country' has Become the World's Most Religiously Diverse Nation* (San Francisco, CA: HarperSan Francisco, 2001).

Heitzman, James and Robert L. Worden (eds), *India: A Country Study* (Washington, DC: Federal Research Division Library of Congress, 1996).

Lessinger, Johanna, *From the Ganges to the Hudson: Indian Immigrants in New York City* (Boston, MA: Allyn and Bacon, 1995).

Williams, Raymond B. (ed), *A Sacred Thread: Modern Transmission of Hindu Traditions in India and Abroad* (Chambersburg, PA: Anima Publications, 1992).

Williams, Raymond B., *Christian Pluralism in the United States: The Indian Immigrant Experience* (Cambridge: Cambridge University Press, 1996).

Chapter 11
Indian Christians and Marriage Patterns

Farha Ternikar

Introduction

This chapter seeks to describe and examine changing marriage patterns of Indian Christian immigrants in the United States. It is based on a review of current literature and in-depth interviews with 15 Indian Christian immigrants, Catholic and Protestant, in the greater Chicago area. Indian Christian immigrants in the US, like other Indian immigrants, try to maintain endogamy. Historically, there has been little out-marriage among Indian immigrants in comparison to other Asian immigrant groups.

My research findings conclude that there is some change in how Indian Christian immigrants marry, but small change in who they marry. Looking at endogamy amongst this group is significant, as it gives us an indication of both assimilation and racial tolerance. However, it is important to first understand how and when Indian immigrants arrived in the US, as the immigrant experience shapes the way that religious, racial and ethnic minorities develop their group identities.

Indian Immigration to the United States

There are nearly two million Indian immigrants in the United States.[1] These immigrants have come in two main waves.[2] The first wave consisted of approximately 6800 Punjabi Sikhs who immigrated to rural California between 1899 and 1920 to work as manual labourers on farms and on the railroad.[3] A large portion of this group returned to India eventually.[4] Many of those Sikhs who did remain in the US married Mexican women.[5] However, inter-racial and

---

[1]   P. Kurien, 'Gendered Ethnicity: Creating a Hindu Indian Identity in the United States', *American Behavioral Scientist*, 42/4 (1999): 648–70.

[2]   R.B. Williams, *Christian Pluralism in the United States: The Indian Immigrant Experience* (Cambridge, 1996).

[3]   Kurien, 'Gendered Ethnicity'.

[4]   J.Y. Fenton, *Transplanting Religious Traditions: Asian Indians in America* (New York, 1988).

[5]   Williams, *Christian Pluralism in the United States*; K. Leonard, *The South Asian Americans: New Americans Series* (Westport, CT, 1997).

inter-faith marriage has occurred more infrequently with the post-1960 South Asian immigrants.

The majority of post-1965 South Asian immigrants settled in metropolitan cities such as Chicago and New York.[6] This new South Asian immigration can itself be divided into two waves. The first South Asian new immigrants were part of the 'brain drain' – educated, professionals who immigrated to the US for educational and economic reasons. Many of these immigrants were scientists, physicians and engineers who, because of their education and technical skills, quickly found jobs and became successful. While some of these immigrants came with their families, others – especially men – came alone and returned to South Asia to marry.[7] The second group began to come in 1980, largely through family reunification programmes or in search of better educational and employment opportunities, higher standards of living, and political and religious freedoms. These South Asians often had lower education levels than their predecessors, and as a result, they have also had a lower median income and higher unemployment rates in the United States.[8] There have been some changes in this pattern, however. A substantial group of recent South Asian immigrants are small business owners, and there has also been an increase in the number of computer-related professionals and physical therapists.[9]

An important difference between the two waves of post-1965 immigrants is the number of immigrants completing graduate and professional degrees. Although both post-1965 Indian immigrant groups had the same percentage of bachelor's degrees, the 1965–80 group had a larger percentage of post-bachelor degrees, including master's, doctoral and medical degrees.[10] Bachelor's degrees from India are not always recognized in the US for jobs or advanced degrees. As a result, in addition to religion and region, there is also class diversity among South Asian immigrants.

However, religion has been a key factor in developing a group identity for South Asian immigrants. Scholars have noted that South Asians have been able to construct an identity as an ethnic group – often by using religion – rather than as a racial group.[11] This identity has allowed South Asian immigrants to incorporate into 'mainstream' American society rather than being racialized and marginalized in a manner similar to African Americans. Religion is not only used to construct ethnic identities, but religion remains a significant factor in choosing mates for Indian immigrants.

---

[6]   S. Maira. *Desis in the House: Indian American Youth Culture in New York City* (Philadelphia, PA, 2002).

[7]   Fenton, *Transplanting Religious Traditions*; Williams, *Christian Pluralism in the United States*.

[8]   Kurien, 'Gendered Ethnicity', B.B. Lawrence, *New Faiths, Old Fears: Muslims and Other Asian Immigrants in American Religious Life* (New York, 2002).

[9]   P. Rangaswamy, *Namaste America: Indian Immigrants in an American Metropolis* (University Park, PA, 2000).

[10]   Ibid.

[11]   Rangaswamy, *Namaste America*; Kurien, 'Gendered Ethnicity'.

Importance of Marriage

Marriage is the cornerstone of Indian family life and community life. Married individuals are given a higher status in Indian community than those that are unmarried. In addition, immigrant children are not looked at as adults until they have married, regardless of age and professional accomplishments. The importance of marriage is reinforced by both families and Indian immigrant and ethno-religious communities.

Ethnic communities make great efforts to find appropriate mates for single Indian immigrants, and have developed a 'marriage economy.' Marriage bureaus, matrimonial advertisements and matchmakers catering to the Indian immigrant community are quite common in urban metropolises such as Chicago or New York. These services often put immigrants in touch with families of potential mates. Parents take out advertisements for their children in Indian periodicals. Matchmakers also organize formal and informal social events for young single Indian immigrants. These events and institutions signify the importance of marriage in the Indian American community.

Within the Indian immigrant community, there are also many informal networks that assist in making introductions. Some of these networks are loosely based in religious congregations or college campus organizations; others are through groups of family friends

Marriage Typologies among Indian Christians in the United States

Indian Christians, like other Indian immigrants, rely on traditional as well as popular methods in how they get married. Williams categorizes Indian Christian marriages into three groups: arranged marriages by returning to India, arranged marriages within the Indian immigrant community and inter-racial marriages with white Christians.[12]

My research on Indian Christian immigrants in Chicago found variations of these marriage types, as I categorize them into four types: (1) returning to India, (2) arranged, (3) semi-arranged 'introductions' and (4) 'love' or romantic marriages with another Indian or white Christian.

The arranged marriage is between individuals of the same ethnicity and religious background. Arranged marriages are arranged by family members or respected members in the religious or ethnic community. Arranged marriages in my sample were sometimes between first- and second-generation immigrants as well. My interviews and marriage advertisements also provide evidence for the continued practice of arranging marriages for Indian immigrants living in the US with Indians abroad, as Williams also suggests.

---

[12] Williams, *Christian Pluralism in the United States*.

Semi-arranged marriages include self-initiated marriages, but also include those marriages where parents and community members make the initial introductions, sometimes via the Internet. In a semi-arranged marriage, parents or family friends usually 'introduce' potential mates. After the initial introduction, the individuals usually have a courting period, which can consist of emails and phone calls or actual dates. Successful 'introductions' usually result in an engagement or marriage within a year.

Lastly, love marriages are those marriages that are self-initiated and include dating in the marriage process. Family members are not involved in this process. Love marriages vary, and can be divided into two sub-categories: endogamous and exogamous. Indian Catholic immigrants that find a mate through this process usually find an Indian Catholic mate, but sometimes Indian, and other times white. Indian Catholic immigrants try to maintain endogamy in terms of both ethnicity and religion. But in the second generation we do see a small increase in exogamous marriages because of the slowly growing acceptance of 'love marriages'. However, there were two instances in my study where college-age immigrants where involved in relationships with non-Christians as well. One male college student and one female college student both spoke of being engaged to Muslims. But they also spoke of stress and conflict related to being in an exogamous relationship.

The Arranged Marriage

The characteristics of the ideal marriage partner are a common topic of discussion for single Indian immigrants. Many of these immigrants choose to have arranged or semi-arranged marriages with the assistance of relatives or community members. As a result, they have given quite a bit of thought to what they are looking for because they have been asked this question numerous times. Fenton (1988) identifies key factors for Indian immigrants in marriage selection as language, caste, religion and immigration status. My respondents agreed with these, and also indicated that choice of profession, educational level, physical appearance, ethnicity, region of origin and years lived in the United States affect marriage choice as well. An arranged marriage often seeks to fulfil these ideals.

Although the thought of an arranged marriage may seem strange and backwards to most in the West, it is still a common phenomenon in many Indian immigrant families. There are several reasons for this. Some individuals and their families believe that the arranged marriage is the key to maintaining religious and ethnic tradition. This is often tied to the idea that the arranged marriage functions as a safeguard, and protects youth from sexual promiscuity and premarital relations. Some Indian immigrants place great importance on their parents' wishes, often over their own personal preferences. Other immigrants see it as a final way of finding a marriage partner; if they do not find their own spouse by a certain age, they would rather let their parents find them a mate than remain single. This often happens after a slew of unsuccessful dating relationships, or with those immigrants who feel too shy or introverted to look for their own mates. These themes were found among Indian Christians as well as Indian Muslim and Hindu immigrants. However, the factors that influence individual choices include family involvement and ties to the ethnic community. For Indian Christian minorities such as the Knanaya, religious ideology also plays a role in maintaining endogamy through arranged marriages. Endogamy and arranged marriages are closely tied to maintaining traditions.

My interviews and conversations with Indian Christian immigrants indicate that the arranged marriage is still a common option for finding marriage partners in Indian immigrant communities. The reasons supporting the arranged marriage as cited in my interviews were to maintain ethnic and religious ties for those tied to family and community and as a last option for those immigrants in their late twenties or thirties. Indian Christian second-generation immigrants spoke of the arranged and semi-arranged marriage as ways to maintain ethnic and religious traditions. One Christian Indian second-generation woman claimed that she saw arranged marriages as a last resort if they had not found partners before their late twenties.

Each of the Christian Indians in my study also spoke of the continued practice of arranging marriages in the American context. Conservative Christian Indian theology further promotes the arranged marriage as it advocates chastity until marriage. Indian Christians also mentioned the maintenance of ethnic ties as a reason for choosing arranged marriages. As Nita, an Indian Christian woman, explained:

> Arranged marriage is the thing. If you have a love marriage you need to make sure that the guy is from a good family or he's from the same religion as you are the same denomination as you are. Make sure your parents know about it. You know how it is with a love marriage. They go crazy. And mainly they should see how the family is. That makes a big difference. The guy if he's settled, the guy he's fine and the family if they've got a big name, and stuff like that. Arranged marriages are more common. (personal interview, 2002)

Nita explained that in her family's Indian community, love marriages were accepted if the marriage was endogamous and the family was respected. Obviously, parents had more control in making sure their children had suitors from a 'good family' and of their religion if the marriage was arranged. Another Indian Christian woman, Sapna, mentioned that she was comfortable with having her parents find a marriage partner for her because she wanted to marry within the Malayalam ethnic group and the Catholic faith. For her, there was not a strong possibility that she would be able to find a partner without her parents' assistance and community ties. In addition, she mentioned that she trusted her parents' judgement in finding her a partner, and they had allowed her to reject suitors in the past.

Williams writes of the prevalence of the arranged marriage among Indian Christian churches, and specifically among the Knanaya Christians.[13] The Knanaya

---

[13]   Ibid.

Christians have strict rules regarding racial and religious endogamy. The arranged marriage helps preserve endogamy within the Indian Knanaya community. He does note the exception of the Christian Brethren, who allow dating if it is within the congregation. My informal conversations with Indian youth at the Brethren congregation also reflected the prevalence of both arranged marriages and dating. Several of the youth that I spoke with explained that they could date or marry non-Indian members of the Brethren congregation.

Race and ethnicity, class and religion all play significant roles in the marriage equation in arranged and non-arranged marriages. Although often discouraged, 'love marriages' and semi-arranged marriages are increasing in the Indian community.

The Love Marriage

The alternative to the arranged marriage has historically been the 'love marriage'. 'Love marriage' is the term used by Indian immigrants and Indians to describe dating to find a marriage partner. However, as mentioned previously, dating is still somewhat looked down upon, especially when Indian immigrant women are involved. Dating is somewhat more acceptable for men. One of the reasons that first-generation parents from all Indian religions discourage dating is because it is equated with sexual promiscuity. Dating practices are contingent on family, religious ideology and ethno-religious community.

Dating is prevalent in some Indian Christian communities if it is endogamous racially and religiously. One Catholic Indian woman, Mary, explained that arranged marriages are still common in her community, but that some more liberal families such as hers did allow dating: 'In the community it's mostly arranged, but like some parents are more liberal than others, like mine, like my parents are like as long as the guy is Indian Christian.'[14] Mary added that her family's Indian community is conservative and does not promote dating. Her parents have made an individual decision to allow her to date as long as she dates another Indian Christian. Another Catholic man, Joseph, talked about his dating process as well. Joseph said that his parents did try to arrange his marriage, and they were not successful. He eventually met a white Catholic woman at his church, and they dated before marrying. Joseph's parents were pleased that he had at least married a Catholic woman.

None of the Christian immigrants I interviewed favoured or were married through a strictly arranged marriage. More than half of the Christian immigrants preferred or had been married through a semi-arranged marriage, while less than a third of the Christian immigrants favoured or had undertaken dating before getting married.

---

[14]   Personal interview, 2001.

Semi-arranged Marriages

Are the alternatives to the arranged marriage, such as 'arranged introductions', replacing tradition? With the increase of Indian immigrants in the United States since 1965 and the popularity of the Internet, new alternatives to the arranged or love marriage are possible. The most popular options that my respondents spoke of included arranged introductions or 'semi-arranged marriages' and online services.

Arranged introductions, also known as semi-arranged marriages, include those situations where parents, relatives, family friends or community members are involved in introducing their children to suitable or appropriate mates. The daughter or son can get to know the potential mate by talking on the phone, through exchanging emails, and/or via group dates with chaperones. The semi-arranged marriages are encouraged by the children themselves because they do not necessarily want to date; yet they do not want parents strictly arranging their marriages. Those immigrants who want a semi-arranged marriage want to know their potential mates before they get married. But the semi-arranged marriage process does not promote any premarital sexual relations. Partners in this process do not develop any physical relationship at all before their wedding, often for religious reasons, and sometimes for cultural ones.

The semi-arranged marriage was always between two people of the same pan-ethnic and religious background. It is a way for second-generation immigrants to find like-minded partners. The semi-arranged marriage allows for some level of freedom, romance and self-selection without any physical intimacy before marriage. The semi-arranged marriage was the most popular option in my sample. The semi-arranged marriage is popular among second-generation immigrants because it satisfies parents' requirements of endogamy, and it gives children a sense of autonomy. The semi-arranged marriage also results in endogamous marriages. Therefore, it also helps maintain ethnic and religious traditions while also giving children agency in the marriage process. The semi-arranged marriage pacifies both parents and children.

Matrimonial online services are an option for Indian immigrants as well. Online services often help facilitate arranged and semi-arranged marriages. Parents and siblings look online also for mates for single family members. Single individuals also initiate relations through these sites. Popular matrimonial Websites for Indian immigrants include <http://www.godblessmatrimonials.com>, <http://www.malayalimatrimonial.com>, <http://www.indianmarriages.com> and <http://www.suitablematch.com>. Through these sites, Indian singles are able to search databases for ideal matches. Characteristics most often mentioned in these singles ads include ethnicity, religion, age, immigration status and education level. Another appeal of online marriage services is that they often decrease the involvement of parents and family in the marriage process, where single people can look for appropriate matches on their own and make initial contact with potential partners without a chaperone. This alternative continues to grow in popularity as new online dating and marriage sites targeting Indian immigrants continue to develop. One of my respondents, a

Christian Indian, mentioned that he used an online dating service, <http://www. match.com>, in the hope of finding a marriage partner. More second-generation Indians are dating or semi-arranging their marriages. However, the truly 'arranged marriage', where parents select a mate for their children, is still a practice in immigrant communities in the United States. In Rangaswamy's 2000 study of Chicago Indian immigrants, 71 per cent of her respondents approved of arranged marriages.[15] However, the majority of Rangaswamy's sample were Hindu. This most likely will remain a practice in Indian immigrant communities because it allows parents to have great involvement in the selection of their children's spouse, while ensuring the maintenance of ethnic and religious tradition and racial purity. In my study, Christian immigrants preferred the semi-arranged marriage, with a 78 per cent approval rating over the arranged marriage or love marriage

Endogamy and Exogamy: Inter-marriage in the Indian Immigrant Community

Ethnic traditions, family and religion play a part in both how Indian Christian immigrants marry and who they marry. This section takes a closer look at who Indian Christian immigrants marry. I examine current inter-marriage patterns among Indian immigrant Christians in the greater Chicago area, with an emphasis on race, ethnicity and religion as significant variables in the inter-marriage equation. Just as religion and ethnicity play important roles in how Indian Christian immigrants get married, we see how these same factors influence who Indian immigrants marry.

Indian Immigrants and Inter-marriage

I mentioned in the previous section that among Asian immigrants in the United States, Indian immigrants have the lowest rate of inter-marriage.[16] In addition to cultural and religious traditions, Fenton found that the key reason for endogamy among Indian immigrants was the maintenance of traditional Indian values as opposed to liberal 'Western' ideals.[17] Indian values are associated with traditional family values. Religion is another reason that respondents cited for low rates of inter-marriage among Indian immigrants. Specifically, Knanaya Catholics have strict religious rules on inter-faith marriage.

I argue that Indian values are often reinforced by religion, and religion is a significant reason for immigrants to maintain both ethnic and religious endogamy. In the case of Knanaya Catholicism, ethnic endogamy is closely tied to religious

---

[15]   Rangaswamy, *Namaste America*.

[16]   L.H. Shinagawa and G.Y. Pang, 'Asian American Panethnicity and Intermarriage', *Amerasia*, 22/2 (1996): 127–52.

[17]   Fenton, *Transplanting Religious Traditions*.

endogamy. Indian immigrants are influenced by Indian immigrant society in reinforcing these perceptions. The majority of Indian immigrants tend to be Hindu or Muslim, rather than Christian. However, even Indian Christians emphasize endogamy in immigrant congregations because of the strong link between Indian Christianity and specific South Indian cultural practices.

Inter-marriage rates are low for Indian immigrants, but in the second generation there are some changing patterns. Fenton's research[18] showed that first-generation Indian men married non-Indians more than did Indian women. First-generation men who arrived in the late 1960s and early 1970s either came with Indian spouses or as single students. Single Indian male students often met non-Indian mates in the college setting. With the exception of the Indian Christian women, most Indian women who came to the US before 1985 came with their husbands. This trend may be reversing in the second generation, as Indian immigrant women are given more autonomy through access to education and economic success.[19] More independence from family and societal restriction often accompanies higher rates of education. Kalmijn's 1991 research concludes that individuals with higher education tend to be more individualistic rather than familial.[20] Higher rates of education are also associated with higher rates of inter-marriage.[21]

Jethwani highlights two main reasons for inter-marriage among second-generation Indian women: that Indian men tend to be traditional and patriarchal, and that Indian immigrant women are attracted to American standards of masculinity, often defined as rugged and individualistic.[22] The idea that Indian immigrant men are perceived as more conservative and traditional than Indian immigrant women was a recurring theme in my research as well. This behaviour is often a result of Asian men's response to emasculating images in the media.[23] Several Indian female college students talked about their perception of Indian men as macho, patriarchal and domineering. This perception of Indian men is incompatible with second-generation Indian women who are highly educated and individualistic.

Although more Indian immigrant women may inter-marry when compared with their male counterparts, inter-racial marriage is still strongly discouraged within the Indian American community, especially with African Americans. Racial prejudice against African Americans in particular was mentioned frequently in

---

[18]   Ibid.

[19]   Ibid.

[20]   M. Kalmijn, 'Shifting Boundaries: Trends in Religious and Educational Homogeny', *American Sociological Review*, 56 (1991): 786–800.

[21]   S. Lieberson and M. Waters, *From Many Strands: Ethnic and Racial Groups in Contemporary America* (New York, 1988).

[22]   T. Jethwani, 'Revisioning Boundaries: A Study of Interracial Marriage among Second-generation Asian Indian Women in the U.S.' (unpublished Ph.D dissertation, Rutgers University, 2001).

[23]   D.L. Eng, *Racial Castration: Managing Masculinity in Asian America* (Durham, NC, 2001).

my interviews. In an informal conversation, one Indian Catholic man told me he was open to marrying a white American woman, but had specified in his online advertisement that he did not prefer African American women. Race is definitely an important factor in the inter-marriage equation. Indian immigrants remain aware of the American system of racial stratification in their own assessment of race relations.[24]

In summary, Indian immigrants do have a low rate of inter-marriage, and this is because of cultural traditions, societal pressure, religion and prejudice. Qian asserts that 'interracial marriage, however, occurs far less frequently than inter-ethnic or inter-faith marriage'.[25] However, my data show the contrary. Among my sample, inter-racial marriage was more common that inter-faith marriage.

There are similar views on inter-racial marriage in Catholicism and Protestantism. In theory, Christian doctrine does not forbid or dissuade inter-racial marriage. However, in practice, the Indian Knanaya Church is an exception, as it promotes strict endogamy. My Knanaya respondents explained that Knanaya Catholics who do not marry within the church, even if a spouse converts, are no longer considered part of the church.

Other Indian Christians varied in their support of inter-racial marriage. Thirty-three per cent of the Indian Christian immigrants that I interviewed approved of inter-racial marriage. In an interview with Joseph, an Indian Catholic, the issue of inter-racial marriage was not so contentious. Joseph talked of his parents' overall support of his marriage to a white Catholic. He emphasized that religion, not race, was the criterion that he took into account when selecting a marriage partner. Perhaps his gender and age also made this choice easier for him. As a 30-year-old Indian man, he probably received less resistance from his family than had he been a 20-year-old woman:

> F: How did your family react when you got married to somebody who was a white Catholic?
> J: We had been dating three or four years before we got married. In the beginning they were not too sure if it was the right thing. And I was in communication with them. But then they came around … They were not totally opposed to it as long as she was Christian or Catholic.
> F: For your parents, her being Catholic was more important than being Indian?
> J: Same religion.
> F: When you told your parents about her, were they trying to introduce you to other people?
> J: They did not do any of that, but when I was in India they tried about seven years ago – I think it's kind of characteristic of my family. (personal interview, 2003)

---

[24]   Kurien, 'Gendered Ethnicity'.

[25]   Z. Qian, 'Breaking the Racial Barriers: Variations in Interracial Marriage Between 1980 and 1990', *Demography*, 34: 263–76, p. 269.

Joseph's experience is reflective of the American Catholic experience, where inter-racial marriage is not a religious taboo in theory. Maria, a 28-year-old Indian Catholic, had a similar experience. She explained:

> Even if he wasn't Indian, at least Catholic. Like that's their big thing, I don't even think, I mean, of course, they would prefer Indian but they would be okay with Catholic regardless of their culture. (interview, May 2006)

In my interview with Maria, she went on to reveal that she was currently engaged a Pakistani Muslim. Their relationship was inter-ethnic and inter-faith. However, she did not see any real conflicts between Islam and Catholicism:

> So, I'm like I don't think that this is impossible, I think that we could do it and [Islam and Catholicism] actually are very compatible in some respects. Um, so, what we decided is that, um, we would get married in the church we would find and imam, he did agree to have the children baptized and I don't even push religion so much in early childhood 'cause that could be confusing. But we will expose them like to it like when we go to church we'll take them to mass and then – to mosque – and as they get older and they're mature enough and have enough knowledge to make a decision for themselves, they'll choose. (interview, May 2006)

This pattern of dating or marrying outside the Christian tradition was small in number in my research. However, the few Christian immigrants that spoke of it had some graduate education and were second-generation immigrants.

Conclusion

This research on Indian Christian immigrants in Chicago suggests that how Indian Christian immigrants marry is changing. However, these changes are contingent on family, community, Christian denomination and generation. Most significant in this research is the conclusion that there is a slight increase of inter-marriage among Indian Christians, particularly among Indian Catholics and Brethren.

In both of these traditions, there seems to be greater acceptance of inter-racial marriages if both partners are of the same Christian denomination. However, there continues to be reluctant support of inter-faith marriages among all the Indian Christian communities I had contact with.

Lastly, members of the Knanaya denomination continue to maintain strict ethnic and religious endogamy. More in-depth studies of the Knanaya community in the United States should explore both dating and marriage trends among their second- and third-generation youth.

208 *South Asian Christian Diaspora*

References

Eng, D.L., *Racial Castration: Managing Masculinity in Asian America* (Durham, NC: Duke University Press, 2001).

Fenton, J.Y., *Transplanting Religious Traditions: Asian Indians in America* (New York: Praeger, 1988).

Jethwani, T., 'Revisioning Boundaries: A Study of Interracial Marriage among Second-generation Asian Indian Women in the U.S.' (New Brunswick, NJ: unpublished Ph.D dissertation, Rutgers University, 2001).

Kalmijn, M., 'Trends in Black/White Intermarriage', *Social Forces*, 72 (1990): 119–46.

Kalmijn, M., 'Shifting Boundaries: Trends in Religious and Educational Homogeny', *American Sociological Review*, 56 (1991): 786–800.

Kurien, P., 'Gendered Ethnicity: Creating a Hindu Indian Identity in the United States', *American Behavioral Scientist*, 42/4 (1999): 648–70.

Lawrence, B.B., *New Faiths, Old Fears: Muslims and Other Asian Immigrants in American Religious Life* (New York: Columbia University Press, 2002).

Leonard, K., *The South Asian Americans: New Americans Series* (Westport, CT: Greenwood Press, 1997).

Lieberson, S. and M. Waters, *From Many Strands: Ethnic and Racial Groups in Contemporary America* (New York: Russell Sage Foundation, 1988).

Maira, S., *Desis in the House: Indian American Youth Culture in New York City* (Philadelphia, PA: Temple University Press, 2002).

Mukhi, S., *Doing the Desi Thing: Performing Indianness in New York* (New York: Garland Publishing, 2000).

Qian, Z., 'Breaking the Racial Barriers: Variations in Interracial Marriage Between 1980 and 1990', *Demography*, 34 (1997): 263–76.

Rangaswamy, P., *Namaste America: Indian Immigrants in an American Metropolis* (University Park, PA: Pennsylvania State University Press, 2000).

Sherkat, D., 'Religious Intermarriage in the United States', unpublished paper presented at American Sociological Association, Toronto, August 2003.

Shinagawa, L.H. and G.Y. Pang, 'Asian American Panethnicity and Intermarriage', *Amerasia*, 22/2 (1996): 127–52.

Williams, R.B., *Christian Pluralism in the United States: The Indian Immigrant Experience* (Cambridge: Cambridge University Press, 1996).

Chapter 12

Doing Friendship, Making Contacts and Building Trust: Christian Indian Responses to Religious Diversity

Nori Henk

Introduction

The South Asian Fellowship Center (SAFC) is open for a Sunday evening service. As I enter, I notice that the bookstore has been transformed. The tables and books have been removed, and in their place there are three rows of chairs split almost in half by an aisle. Up front, an overhead projector sits atop the administrative desk. Jack, a white, middle-aged man, is hunched over, quietly playing a Christian hymn on his new guitar. I am early, and only a few people are there, mostly older men and a few older Indian women. Zohra, an older Indian woman, greets me almost immediately with a warm welcome, and she points out a seat for me on the right side of the room. As more people enter, women and children sit on the right and men sit on the left. By the time the service begins, there are 25 people, 15 women, 7 men, and 3 children. All the children are white, all but two women are Indians, and the other two women are white. There are three white males and four Indian males. All the men are dressed in slacks and long- or short-sleeve dress shirts, whereas the women vary, wearing saris, long tunics with pants, dresses, and long pants and blouses. Most, however, wear long tunics with pants. A young college-age Indian woman stands out, wearing shorts and a tank top.

Zohra passes out three song sheets. Jack plays chords on his guitar more loudly, indicating the beginning of the service. He stops mid-stroke and is quiet for almost a half a minute. He announces that he will open the service in prayer. Five Indian women cover their heads with veils. The prayer is very short. When finished, Jack starts strumming his guitar and declares that we are to sing 'This is the Day'. On the song sheet, the song is in English and Hebrew. We sing through the song twice in English and twice in Hebrew. The congregation claps along, and Jack plays the tambourine. Zohra asks Jack why we have not sung it in Hindi. Jack says that the song is not written in Hindi on the paper. She insists that everyone knows it, and some people grunt or nod their heads in agreement. We proceed to sing the song again twice through in Hindi. The white, female congregants do not sing. The next song is a Hindi song, 'Deep Jale'. The words are:

Deep Jale Prabhu Naam Rahe
Meure Mundir Mein, Mundir Mein
Keep the lamp burning so the Lord's name will remain
Remain in the temple, remain in the temple
(×2)

Verse 1
Naam Rahe Mun Mein
Prabhu Naam Rahe Mun Mein
Let your name remain in my soul
Lord for your name to dwell in me
(×2)

Verse 2
Aan Bason Dil Mein
Prabhu Aan Baso Dil Mein
Come dwell in my heart,
Lord, come dwell in my heart
(×2)

The white women do not sing along, but the Indian women do. The worship ends with the song leader saying, 'Hallelujah, Hallelujah. Praise the Lord.'

The service at SAFC, rich with religio-cultural amalgamation, segregation and synthesis, reveals the bi-culturalism of the Indian and American religious community in Chicago. I argue that the relationship between religion, ethnicity and bi-national influences create a new and distinct Christian community. This argument addresses two research questions: (1) How are Christian Indians creating community within the larger Indian immigrant population? (2) How is religious identity negotiated with and influenced by ethnic constraints and opportunities? I attempt to answer these questions in three ways: informal and formal networks, the relationship between ethnicity and Christianity, and religious identity reformulation.

Methods, Sample and Research Design

I conducted an interview-based and participant-observation study over the course of three months. I participated in and observed activities and programmes at three sites, including prayer groups, holiday celebrations and church services. I made a total of three or four visits to each of the sites. A typical event was three to four hours long. In most cases, I was treated like a congregant or a participant in the activity. However, in one instance, I was asked to help out with an activity.

Towards the end of my observations, I formulated an interview schedule. I then used the interview schedule to conduct ten audio-taped interviews (eight men and two women). Of the ten interviewees, seven were Indian and three were white.

I used a snowball sampling method, and I recruited by the suggestion of site leaders. I interviewed three people from the SAFC, two people from St Luke's Lutheran-Missouri-Synod Church, and five people from the Christ Mennonite Congregation.

While each interview followed a basic format, I also allowed for variance in what experiences, meanings or explanations interviewees used to answer these questions. In fact, I was using the interviews in a twofold manner: to fill out existing themes found in my field notes, and to obtain detailed accounts of past religio-cultural events. These interviews gave content to the basic theoretical frames of informal networking, the relationship between Christianity and ethnicity, and becoming and being Christian. In particular, although I used an interview schedule, through the observation process I picked up on language and symbols that I asked the interviewees to expand on, such as 'doing friendship', 'fellowship' and 'going native'. The meanings behind these phrases given in interviews will be further explored and analysed in the following section.

Community-building and Evangelization

A common thread found across my Christian Indian sites was the process of community-building and evangelization. In all the sites, informal networks, the intentional connections that bridge ethnicity to Christianity, and the meaning of being and becoming Christian for Indian immigrants informed and shaped the theological imperative to share Christ with others.

Part I: Informal Networks

The New Immigrant Survey Pilot (NIS-P) found that religious preference reflected social and economic connections between the US and other parts of the world.[1] This shared religious identity is one of many paths in which new immigrants link up to social networks in the US. Although I did not collect explicit data on the impact of religious preference on immigrant experiences, interviewees discussed religious conversion strategies pertaining to informal networks with Indian immigrants. Rangaswamy explains that once Indians accept the US as their new home, they begin to cultivate family ties, religious and cultural traditions, and new connections to their immediate environment.[2] Informal networks function in the third sense: how Indians might make new connections to their immediate environment. This section outlines how informal networks form through social appeal.

---

[1]　Guillermina Jasso et al., 'Exploring the Religious Preferences of Recent Immigrants to the United States: Evidence from the New Immigrant Survey Pilot', in Yvonne Haddad, Jane Smith and John Esposito (eds), *Religion and Immigration* (Walnut Creek, CA, 2003).

[2]　Padma Rangaswamy, *Namaste America: Indian Immigrants in an American Metropolis* (University Park, PA, 2000).

Inviting Strategies

Bringing together the Indian community into a Christian sphere for social purposes is an intentional process. The members of the immigrant congregations I visited sought to bring other non-Christian immigrants into their church through passing out tracts, inviting colleagues from work, and a strategic casual conversation in public.

The minister, Saraj (Indian male, age 52), at the Telugu church developed a series of tracts using non-Christian religious terms to make a case for Christianity. He stated:

> I created one or three gospel tracts, that is 'The Great Guru that is Jesus Christ,' The Great Guru is Jesus Christ … And one more tract is 'Moksha, the Kingdom of God'. How to attain moksha … our moksha is the Kingdom of God … Even though it is different meaning for them, but I can explain the Christian way of thinking.

Part of his friendship evangelism training was to pass out the tracts to start a religious conversation. His tracts, however, are specific to the religious and cultural background by using particular religious symbols and Indian language. Furthermore, the uniqueness of the US as a free country gives Saraj confidence to make new friendships and discuss his religious beliefs.

The minister of missions, Tanveer (Indian male, age 52), at the Mennonite church discussed a threefold strategy to announce non-religious activities and social get-togethers. His first and preferred strategy is person-to-person contact. This strategy entails encouraging a family to invite their friends. The second approach is putting up advertisements in Indian/Asian stores. However, he states: 'Most of the time, I meet them on the road like public libraries, stations, airports and I will introduce myself that I am so and so. And I get their addresses, phone numbers, and I'll invite the new contact to the group [Indian Fellowship].' The last time he did this was when he went to the airport to pick up his brother. He says that often he will go to public places with two purposes: to pick up someone or read a book, and to concentrate on any new person he can meet. All three are making a conscientious effort to bring people with similar cultural backgrounds into the church. From the public space of the street corners, libraries or airports, Saraj, and Tanveer are using public spaces with a religious impetus.

Social Events

Doing friendship is categorized as a social activity primarily through invitations to non-religious activities, relationship-building events and the Christian community. Interviewees expressed that because of shared language and culture, their religious organizations have events that appeal to non-Christians. For example, the Lutheran church organized an India Independence Day celebration that brought together the Indian community. On this day, 22 people arrived at the church to play games, share a meal and hear speeches about this important event. In actuality, this was a co-national, inter-religious and multi-cultural event where white Christian Americans and Hindu and Christian Indian immigrants shared the table. Co-nationality was represented physically by an American flag and an Indian flag, one women dressed in a sari with the Indian flag colours, the American head pastor sat at the head of the table, and the Indian minister sat to his right. In the speeches themselves there was a collective sense of what independence meant, including mutual freedom from Britain.

Culturally this was a complex event, but religiously this event also represented the pluralism and diversity of the Christian church. One of the organizers would tell me later that not all of the participants were Christians. Some were Hindu friends from work. Due to the shared cultural symbol of independence, religious differences were played down, or rather, Christianity was accepted for the sake of the event. The head pastor emphasized the role of Christianity in shared cultural experiences in terms of the body of Christ, but none of the Indian participants alluded to Hindu symbols. Finally, Christian diversity within the Lutheran church played an interesting role in this event. This was one of the rare events when the head pastor joined the Telugu minister in his activities. Along with the head pastor was his wife, the church secretary and her family, and the school principal, all of whom were white. The church also holds a Sudanese service. The following day would bring together all of the congregations in their annual pan-Lutheran service. This event, like many others, would show how the Christian church becomes a shared space for social gatherings in a complex, multi-dimensional way.

From Socializing to Converting

Organizational structures facilitate the formation of informal networks where Indian Christians can share their spiritual lives. My participants felt compelled to seek out other Indians and bring them into the Christian community. Non-Christian Indians and Christian Indians share a common nationality, cultural backgrounds, the immigrant experience, and they are a racial minority. Friendship evangelism works from these common assumptions and embraces the possibility of an Indian sub-culture in a foreign place. Still, I would not downplay the significance of religion in this explanation, because as every interviewee expressed, sharing Christ with non-Christians is a moral imperative.

Conversion itself is a product of organizational structures, including both Indian and white Christian churches and organizations. Training and accountability are examples of organizational procedures that assist conversion. Where the 'how' question gets murky is who in the organization facilitates conversion practices and training. At the SAFC, both Christian Americans and Christian Indians share organizational responsibilities. The Bethesda Telugu Church and the Asian Christian Fellowship are a part of larger American denominations. On the local level, Americans and Indians share responsibilities in their respective church, but of course, beyond this level Americans dominate decision-making.

On a more specific level, most conversion practices, as noted in the data, are actually non-evangelical practices, in that Indians are not directly asking other Indians to become Christians; rather, they are sharing their faith to raise religious interest. Another term that can be categorized as non-evangelical is 'seeker-friendly activities'. The Mennonite church stated that its mission was to reach non-Christians, and the SAFC expressed similar sentiments: 'The service is really designed for seekers to be open for people from Hindu and Muslim backgrounds to be there and to feel comfortable.' Sharing and seeking are two sides of the same coin for friendship evangelism. The centre of both of these methods is the relationship that exists between the Christian and the non-Christian. At this initial analysis, the non-Christian is a stranger, a business colleague or a newly made friend. Relationship-based, informal networks facilitate both the organizational goals and the individual imperative to share their faith and bring in seekers. This is not to say that more traditional strategies are not occurring, such as passing out tracts, but largely, Christian Indians are using friendship evangelism to convert others to Christianity.

Part II: Ethnicity and Christianity

Friendship evangelism has cultural and ethnic implications. For instance, the evangelistic technique contextualizes or shapes Christian theology to Indian culture. Cultural contextualization involves the construction of ethnic boundaries and the 're'-construction of Christianity to fit within these boundaries. For the immigrant community, the church has historically been a place where newcomers could 'regroup' with people from similar backgrounds.[3] Joane Nagel argues: 'Ethnicity is not simply an historical legacy of migration or conquest, but is constantly undergoing redefinition and reconstruction.'[4] Likewise, the immigrant church adapts Christian beliefs to ethnic practices. In this section, I will use the data to answer the analytic questions that Nagel asks herself: 'What are the processes that motivate ethnic boundary construction? What is the relationship between culture and ethnic identity?'[5]

Ethnic Boundary Construction

Of particular interest to this research is how ethnic communities change due to contact with other ethnic communities. Barth argues that three possible changes will occur for ethnic minorities: the ethnic minority will become incorporated into the normative or dominant culture; the ethnic minority will accept its minority

---

[3]   Robert Harney, 'Religion and Ethnocultural Communities', in G. Pozzetta (ed.), *The Immigrant Religious Experiences* (New York, 1991).

[4]   Joane Nagel, 'Constructing Ethnicity: Creating and Recreating Ethnic Identity and Culture', *Social Problems*, 41/1 (1994): 153.

[5]   Ibid.

status but reduce negative implications in this position, or ethnic minorities will emphasize ethnic identity to develop new positions and patterns to organize activities not formerly found in the normative or dominant culture.[6] Both theorists pose an important question about ethnic boundary construction: How do ethnic minorities deal with marginality?[7] In the sites I observed, Indian immigrants are incorporated into, segregated from and disassociated from an American Christian culture.

One way to argue for ethnic reconstruction within the normative or dominant culture is by examining cultural institutions. In this case, the cultural institution is the Christian community. I found that Christian Indian organizations in Chicago both incorporate into and segregate from the larger Christian community. An instance of incorporation into the larger Christian community is the multi-cultural project of the Mennonites. The Mennonite church pastor shared the newsletter, *Mennonite Weekly Review*, where several articles alluded to the church's mission and vision towards multi-cultural diversity. Their harvest festival, involving both Christian music and Indian food, exemplified this new-found purpose. Tanveer expressed that this particular Mennonite church puts on several bi-cultural outreach events. Again, like the other sites, Tanveer and his church are making an effort to be inclusive of Indian culture within the Christian sphere. The church itself supports Tanveer's ministry with an office, supplies, church space and mutual support.

Whereas the Mennonite church represented incorporating Indian immigrants into the larger Christian community, the Lutheran church was an example of segregation from the larger Christian community. The Lutheran church houses three separate services: Sudanese on Sunday afternoon, Telugu Indian on Saturday nights, and American on Sunday morning. From the outside, a wooden sign designates these three services, with pastors for each. The pastor of the Telugu congregation, Saraj, is also a pastor of another Chicago Telugu congregation, also sharing a space with other ethnic congregations. This is an interesting trend, where multiple ethnic congregations use church space for their services and events, but do not actually worship together. This church is not entirely ethnically segregated, however, since all three congregations come together three or four times a year for a multi-cultural service.

Another variation on the same theme is partial integration and partial segregation. For example, the SAFC clearly integrates both Indian leadership and Anglo leadership, but white males give sermons and lead music. Both Indian families and white families attend events and services, but in formal settings, Indians and whites typically sit separate from one another. Music is in Hindi and in English, but the remainder of speaking is in English. One event that brought together both white and Indian families was the annual block party, which

---

[6]   Fredrik Barth, *Ethnic Groups and Boundaries: The Social Organization of Culture Difference* (Boston, MA, 1969), pp. 32–3.

[7]   Samir Dayal, 'Minding the Gap: South Asian Americans and Diaspora', in Lavina Dhingra Shankra and Rajini Srikanth (eds), *A Part, Yet Apart: South Asians in Asian America* (Philadelphia, PA, 1998).

formed the exception to white primacy, quasi-Indian/white integration. An Indian leadership prevailed in this case, largely because the focus was to bring Indian families into the SAFC. The purpose behind the block party might point to why leadership structure changed to accommodate the event. The goal of the party was to 'break down religious barriers' between Christians, Muslims and Hindus in the Indian community. Through Indian music, multiple games for children, movies and informal discussions, religious differences were played down. Highlighting the cultural elements of the party advertised the SAFC as a place where Indian families are welcome and a place of belonging. How, then, do places like the SAFC move from belonging culturally to belonging religiously? In other words, starting from a common cultural position initiates relationships, but religious differences remain. What are the other ways that religious barriers are broken? The following section on culture and ethnicity will attempt to answer this question.

Culture and Ethnic Identity

For all the sites, there was a vision of commonality and unity within the church. As the head pastor of the Mennonite church, June, put it: 'Christ is the head of the family making us one ... All walls of partition are broken down and there is no this or that or the other, we are one.' This was especially true of the Mennonite church because of its interaction with non-Christian groups and a characteristically diverse congregation. Similar to other sites, this church encouraged inter-religious dialogue by mutual connections between Christianity and Hinduism or Islam. The pastor observed these kinds of connections made in the store. In this way, the Mennonite church has made a concerted effort to unify diverse groups of people in informal and non-intrusive ways. They sell items made from international artisans for a fair wage. Those looking for a church are welcomed, and those who are just there for the shopping are treated respectfully. Finally, it is important to note that this Mennonite church explicitly encouraged unity while respecting diversity in its inception. As June stated:

> From the very, very beginning our church was designed to be multicultural and multi-racial, and from the very first public service, we have been a real mix of people. We value that and so it is for our church, I don't think it is a huge leap to also be friends to ... to reach out to people of different religions, different faiths, or people who are not Christians. And of course we use the Bible, we preach it, and we teach it.

In other words, non-Christians are welcome, but the primacy of Christian authority, namely the Bible and its teaching, is held firmly.

Moreover, Pastors at all three sites sought to make Christianity relevant to the audience to which they spoke. The idea of *de facto* congregationalism is applicable to the formulation of Christian Indian community.[8] *De facto* congregationalism theoretically describes the role of sub-cultural influences on congregational identity beyond prescribed denominational values. The active agents in bringing Indians into the Christian community are other Indians. This may point to assimilation, but how Indians are strategizing is culturally based. As the director of women's ministry, Zohra, stated:

> We try to do things in an ethnic way ... we dress like the community does. We dress very modestly. We are all things to all people for the sake of the Gospel, like Paul said, 'Without compromising the Gospel ...'. So we make it as easy as possible for them, so that the outer does not disgust them, that sort of offences are kept to a minimum.

Indians are sensitive to how other Indians might perceive their practices, their organization and how they interact with the Indian community. Another interviewee used the phrase 'going native' to describe how Christianity is introduced to the community in order to work against common perceptions that Jesus is the god of white people. The 'de-Europeanization' of Christianity becomes a form by which ethnic identity is negotiated and structured.[9]

The next logical area to examine in the Christian Indian community is the larger Christian organization. Integration of Indian Christians into the Christian community not only changes the 'Christian' culture, but it also provides grounds for conflict and accommodation in light of the evangelistic thrust of this particular sub-culture. The following section will address these issues.

Part III: Becoming and Being Christian

Conflict and community coexist in immigrant religious organizations. On one level, as discussed above, immigrants are negotiating and constructing ethnic identity, but on the other hand is the religious imperative to share the Gospel. Ethnicity and religion are not mutually exclusive processes, but for the sake of this study, religion will be treated separately from the ethnic constructs discussed earlier in the chapter. The main focus of this section is to develop the meaning of religious identity for Indian Christians in the US, and the conflict and community implications that American religion has for this Christian immigrant community.

---

[8]   R. Stephen Warner, 'The Place of the Congregation in the American Religious Configuration', in James P. Wind and James W. Lewis (eds), *American Congregations, Volume 2: New Perspectives in the Study of Congregations* (Chicago, IL, 1994), pp. 54–99.

[9]   Laurie F. Maffy-Kipp, 'Eastward ho! American Religion from the Perspective of the Eastern Rim', in Thomas Tweed (ed.), *Retelling US Religious History* (Berkeley, CA, 1997).

Religious Identity in the US

As Indians begin to participate in social, economic and political life, they are becoming active agents in every arena.[10] This new and engaging concern is a salient issue for Christian Indians. The opportunity to share their faith is constructed differently in the US. For example, Saraj commented:

> We want to talk to people to share the Gospel to non-Christians because God gave us a challenge to talk to them in America. In India, we don't have this chance to talk like that, now we do. So, in our case, in this free country, we are able to talk. So we have a lot of friends with me to go and talk about Christ to Hindus.

Because of religious freedom, the US is seen as a new mission field. Within this new cultural context, Christian Indians have an opportunity to reformulate Christian identity.

For Christian Indians, being open to share about multiple faiths is about the opportunity to learn, to be open and to feel good about the religious differences that exist. At the same time, non-Christians are prayed for, invited to community activities, and offered non-religious services such as counselling, legal advice and immigrant-related information. As Imran (Indian male, age 47) put it: 'One should respect individuality, but be firm in their gift to God.' In other words, the American ideal of liberalism and free choice is respected, but there is something universal and important about Christianity that should be respected more. Christian Indians are helping other Indians in their daily lives, especially issues that pertain to their immigrant status, but the end goal is to offer Christianity as the ultimate choice.

Religious diversity views orient around the subject of religious sensitivity. For example, a volunteer at the SAFC, Ranchi, articulated:

> I think we need to be aware of religious diversity in America now. And the response is not to condemn, the response is to love and accept them. And we need to be different to show them that there is a difference in us ... We shouldn't be condemning and saying that you are wrong, no, but we should love them.

Respecting differences is the basis for which Christians gain an audience in which to share their own faith. As an interviewee at the Mennonite church, Imran, stated: 'Religious diversity is the reality of the world. One cannot deny it. The most appropriate response is Jesus' mandate: Go out and preach. Churches should understand that mandate contextually and apply it the best they can.' The idea of plurality is the starting place for many Christian Indians, an idea that should be considered contextually, but at the same time, the distinctions of Christianity ought to be made clear. This is a response to religious pluralism that is a 'yes,

---

[10]   Lavina Dhingra Shankar and Rajini Srikanth (eds), *A Part, Yet Apart: South Asians in Asian America* (Philadelphia, PA, 1998).

but' answer. There is acknowledgement of diversity, but there is also an exclusive claim for Christianity that gives it authority above other religious traditions. This is different than a pluralist position where all religions have equal authority and therefore take an inclusive claim over divine truth.

American Religion and the Immigrant Christian Community

Finding new churches in the US that resemble churches in their host churches means that new immigrants are both relocated and dislocated within the American religious organization.[11] The immigrant church represents both a reassertion of familiar rituals and an accommodation to an American religion. As a gathering place, the church often represented a home away from home.[12] The complex nature of the immigrant church, however, is to be both pseudo-home and not at all like home. Religious identity, like ethnic identity, is renegotiated and restructured into an American context.[13] In Christian Indian congregations, religious identity is structured by evangelistic methods and activities. The imperative to evangelize is critical to highlight. As Tanveer put it: 'The first object is going into this mission field, evangelizing each person to know that God is significant in their life.' Within this purpose to share Christ is the hope that non-Christians will convert.

Herein lies the conflict within Christian Indian organizations. Most disagreement centres on how to approach non-Christians in terms of aggressiveness. One plausible solution is to base the approach on the type of relationship that the Christian has with the non-Christian. Another is the context in which one shares one's faith. Still, there is considerable debate and variation regarding the appropriate method.

What does being Christian mean to Indian Christians in an American context? It ultimately means changing their life to serve God's purpose and loving those who are not yet Christians. Simply put by Saraj, being Christian is 'to love the Lord with all of their heart, mind, soul and strength'. The necessity of the Christian life is that Christians 'must have a passion present, transform their life, must love, and must understand the supremacy of God's word' (Saraj). Experiencing the power of God is personally transformative, but at the same time compels Christians to change others as they themselves were changed.

The process from becoming Christian to being Christian is a step towards evangelical commitment. For example, Tanveer from the Mennonite church stated: 'Once they understand God and God's presence and the importance of God, they are part of the third group, the core group. The third group is evangelists, sharing

---

[11] Jon Gjerde, 'Conflict and Community: A Case Study of the Immigrant Church in the United States', in G. Pozzetta (ed.), *The Immigrant Religious Experiences* (New York, 1991).

[12] Harney, 'Religion and Ethnocultural Communities'.

[13] Kenneth Jones, 'The Negative Component of Hindu Consciousness', in Geoffrey Oddiee (ed.), *Religious Traditions in South Asia: Interaction and Change* (Padstow, UK, 1998).

what they believe.' The last step, being Christian, opens up the likelihood that others will become Christian. The process of becoming and being Christian is the substance and core to religious identity for Christian Indians in this study. Without the religious identity that Christian Indians hold dear to their life, ethnic sensitivity and social cohesion fall by the wayside.

Conclusions and Future Research

A few conclusions can be drawn from this initial study on Christian Indians. There are twin goals in this project that were examined and analysed in the findings: access to community in a non-Indian society, and the contextual influences on ethnic and religious identity. With considerable support from interview and field note data, Christian Indians support the new Indian immigrant community with frequent events and services as well as shape the Christian message to the perceived American context of religious liberalism and pluralism. The link between these two important conclusions is the identity transformation and reformulation that occurs in the process of inviting non-Christians into the Christian community. Through the interaction with non-Indian Americans and non-Christian Indians, Christian Indians are reshaping Christianity in a distinct fashion, albeit strongly affirming their evangelistic heritage.

By starting with network analysis and moving towards ethnic considerations, religious identity becomes better understood. These are not Christian groups simply evangelizing to non-Christians, but rather groups that are sensitive to the bi-culturalism that exists in their respective organizations. Had I begun with religious identity, this may not have been as clear. In other words, the inter-connection between networking, ethnic construction and American religion produces a unique and interesting religious immigrant community.

In this study, I explored the nuances of this inter-connection, but I admit to the shortcomings of my method. For example, this study does not purport to be generalizable for the greater Indian immigrant community. In order to achieve a deeper and broader understanding of this community, future research should go in a number of different directions. First, there should be ethnographic studies of non-Christian Indians' impressions of Christian Indians, with particular attention to exclusion or inclusion at Christian Indian activities, views of or impact of evangelistic strategies, and exclusion or inclusion of Christian Indians within the Indian community at large. Capturing how non-Christians are reacting to Christian Indians or whether they are even aware of their activities would add to the significance to this study.

I also think that white and Indian relations within the Christian sub-culture should be explored further. For example, what are white Christians' perceptions of Indian Christians, how are they impacted by their presence in the church, and what is the future of the immigrant churches in light of non-immigrant relations? Finally, I would like to explore the Christian Indian community in India. How is it similar or different, what ideas or strategies are carried over from the Indian context, and what are the transnational ties between the American and Indian communities? These are a few of the many questions that should influence future studies on Indian immigrant communities in the US and India.

This study refines prior research done on new immigrants in the US. In particular, my research reinforces research on Indian new immigrants and the importance of religion for new immigrants. For instance, the role of friendship evangelism or 'doing friendship' is made explicit, and the informal backbone of the Christian Indian community. While the term 'friendship evangelism' is used in theological circles, a sociological study on the term and its meaning has not been carried out. Furthermore, the indigenous leadership issue present in India fused with a new context presents a new set of conflict and change for the community. This was noted in the organizational structure of the various sites. Finally, and most importantly, my research continues to affirm the position that religion plays a significant role in immigrant communities. It is without a doubt that at least three American Christian organizations are intentionally bringing in and developing a new and distinct Christian community with Indian immigrants.

References

Barth, Fredrik, *Ethnic Groups and Boundaries: The Social Organization of Culture Difference* (Boston, MA: Little, Brown, 1969).

Dayal, Samir, 'Minding the Gap: South Asian Americans and Diaspora', in Lavina Dhingra Shankra and Rajini Srikanth (eds), *A Part, Yet Apart: South Asians in Asian America* (Philadelphia, PA: Temple University Press, 1998).

Gjerde, Jon, 'Conflict and Community: A Case Study of the Immigrant Church in the United States'. in G. Pozzetta (ed.), *The Immigrant Religious Experiences* (New York: Garland Publishing, 1991).

Harney, Robert, 'Religion and Ethnocultural Communities', in George Pozzetta (ed.), *The Immigrant Religious Experiences* (New York: Garland Publishing, 1991).

Jasso, Guillermina et al., 'Exploring the Religious Preferences of Recent Immigrants to the United States: Evidence from the New Immigrant Survey Pilot', in Yvonne Haddad, Jane Smith and John Esposito (eds), *Religion and Immigration* (Walnut Creek, CA: Altamira Press, 2003).

Jones, Kenneth, 'The Negative Component of Hindu Consciousness', in Geoffrey Oddiee (ed.), *Religious Traditions in South Asia: Interaction and Change* (Padstow, UK: Curzon Press, 1998).

Maffy-Kipp, Laurie F., 'Eastward ho! American Religion from the Perspective of the Eastern Rim', in Thomas Tweed (ed.), *Retelling US Religious History* (Berkeley, CA: University of California Press, 1997).

Nagel, Joane, 'Constructing Ethnicity: Creating and Recreating Ethnic Identity and Culture', *Social Problems*, 41/1 (1994): 152–75.

Rangaswamy, Padma, *Namaste America: Indian Immigrants in an American Metropolis* (University Park, PA: Pennsylvania State University Press, 2000).

Shankar, Lavina Dhingra and Rajini Srikanth (eds), *A Part, Yet Apart: South Asians in Asian America.* (Philadelphia, PA: Temple University Press, 1998).

Warner, R. Stephen, 'The Place of the Congregation in the American Religious Configuration', in James P. Wind and James. W. Lewis (eds), *American Congregations, Volume 2: New Perspectives in the Study of Congregations* (Chicago, IL: University of Chicago Press, 1994), pp. 54–99.

Chapter 13

From Hinduism to Christianity, from India to New York: Bondage and Exodus Experiences in the Lives of Indian Dalit Christians in the Diaspora[1]

Rachel Fell McDermott

The resurrection occurred in my life. The missionaries resurrected my life. I was dead in my culture. (The Rev. Gideon Jebamani)[2]

In June of 2007, a number of Indian pastors and lay people from various Protestant denominations gathered at Princeton Theological Seminary for a Consultation on Multiplying Asian Indian Ministries in North America. The topic of discussion was the challenges of pastoring in the New York/New Jersey area. Only one speaker addressed the subject of caste prejudice directly.[3] He called it 'the elephant in the room', and exhorted his colleagues both to address the atrocities going on in India by supporting local and transnational efforts on behalf of Dalits and to be sensitive to caste discrimination in their own churches. It was clear from the comments and questions following his paper that most people in the room considered ill treatment of Dalits an Indian issue, not an American one.

The fact that not a single other chapter on North America in the present volume treats caste as a central diaspora problem is also indicative. For many Dalits, this silence is a good thing, as they too would like to forget.

---

[1]   I wish to thank all those who gave of their time to speak with me: those mentioned in note 12 below, as well as Professors Raymond B. Williams, Eleanor Zelliot, and John C.B. Webster. Special thanks go to the Rev. Gideon Jebamani, who helped me get started on this project, and to my husband Scott, who went with me every Sunday in the spring and summer of 2007 to a different Indian church.

[2]   Interview, 4 April 2007.

[3]   The Rev. Prince Singh, 'Issues of Social Justice, Mission and Evangelism in the Context of Developing Asian Indian Ministries: What Constitutes Mission and Evangelism for Asian Indian Ministries/Churches in the United States?'; this draft essay, along with a number of others referenced below, comes out of the Princeton Consultation on Church Union 2007, and will be published in a volume entitled *Communities of Pilgrims: Christians from India at the North American Frontier*.

But, as this chapter attests, there is ample evidence of the elephant, of discrimination in American contexts and beyond,[4] and Dalit activists, following the lead of trauma experts, aver that true healing cannot occur 'unless the wound is identified and uncovered in each individual Dalit .... Failure or denial of acknowledgment cannot bring transformation and liberation.'[5] What follows is an examination of the complexities involved in daring to hope for such a liberation.

The Academic Context of Absent Dalits

My context for this discussion of Dalit Christians is metropolitan New York. No book on South Asian Christians resident in North America and Europe can omit consideration of the New York/New Jersey area, which is home to more than 25 per cent of the total Asian Indian population in the United States. And no book on Indian Christians written early in the twentieth-first century can, or should, fail to include focus on the experiences of those who make up at least 75 per cent of the Indian church, those at the very bottom of the caste hierarchy, Dalits.[6]

There is a sort of silence about Dalits in the published literature on, and even by, Indian churches in North America. This was true in the mid-1990s, in Raymond B. Williams's landmark study, *Christian Pluralism in the United States:*

---

[4]   Apart from the material presented in this chapter, see, for examples of caste discrimination in the UK, *Dalit International Newsletter*, 11/3 (October 2006); the Appendix to Sabrina Mahtani, 'Work and Descent-based Discrimination in the South Asian Diaspora: A Briefing for the Sub-commission on the Promotion and Protection of Human Rights' (draft, December 2003), and Jasvinder Sanghera, *Shame* (London, 2007). The *New York Times* (3 January 2008) recently featured a story about a Chicago Hindu man, Subhash Chander, who burned alive his daughter, her husband and two children because she had married below her caste.

[5]   The Rev. Gideon Jebamani, 'Dalit Christians: From Submission to Liberation' (DMin. Demonstration Project, New York Theological Seminary, 2004), p. 119.

[6]   The word 'Dalit' comes from the Marathi verb 'to hit or strike'; Dalits are therefore those who have been hit, struck down or oppressed. The great social reformer and Untouchable leader Dr Bhimrao Ramji Ambedkar (1891–1956) popularized this term as an alternative to Untouchable, Harijan ('child of God', Gandhi's term) or someone of the 'Depressed Classes' (British legal nomenclature). The term 'Scheduled Castes', or those on a schedule for reservation benefits, also came into usage through the efforts of Amebedkar after the 1931 Round Table Conference. Many Untouchables do not like the term 'Dalit', and many Christian Untouchables feel that 'Christian' and 'Dalit' together are a contradiction. For an excellent set of references on this issue, see John C.B. Webster, 'Dalit Identity and Dalit Theology' (unpublished paper presented at Andover Newton Theological School, Spring 2006), p. 2 n. 1. In this short chapter, I retain the word 'Dalit', as most of my informants also used it in their conversations with me. Approximately 2.2 per cent of the Indian population, currently at 1.136 billion, is Christian. Approximately 16 per cent of the total population is Dalit.

The Indian Experience (1996),[7] and the silence hangs in the air even today. In a forthcoming book of essays by Indian Christians on the challenges facing their North American churches, fewer than a quarter mention caste as an issue, and only one author squarely addresses the experience of Dalit Christians in the Indian church as a whole.[8] This omission of Dalit concerns is not to be taken as deliberate or malicious; it is, first of all, a symptom of the ambivalence of the Dalit community itself with regard to identity formation; Dalits do not always wish to draw attention to themselves, in any forum. Second, the absence of sustained academic attention to Dalit church experience in the US is a result of the lack, in general, of diaspora studies of South Asian Christians, as opposed to Hindus or Muslims. But third, and equally important, the United States Census Bureau does not keep data on Asian Indians by religion, and certainly not by caste, so it is extremely difficult to estimate how many Dalit Christians there are in the country, where they live, and from what part of India they hail. My gathered impression of the New York area is that Protestant Christian Dalits tend to be from South India, and that Dalits form a significant percentage of Christians originally from the Protestant Church of South India (CSI),[9] since many dioceses of Tamilnadu, in particular, are Dalit-majority, and since the missionary-founded educational and medical institutions there, such as the Christian Medical College and Hospital (CMCH) at Vellore, provide the sort of training that enables emigration. The Church of North India (CNI),[10] by contrast, a self-proclaimed Dalit church, is able to send fewer people overseas because of the generally lower educational and socio-economic status of their parishioners, as well as their fewer connections to jobs abroad.[11] The Indian members of North American Pentecostal and other non-sectarian Protestant churches are, I am told, mainly Dalit, and the Roman Catholic Church there is home to many Dalits – some interviewees estimated that as many as half of the Dalits in the New York metropolitan area are Catholics – although their numbers are, again, difficult to

---

[7]   In e-mail correspondence (2 May 2007), Williams said that Dalits did not appear on his radar screen as a significant community when he was conducting his research in the early 1990s.

[8]   See note 3 above.

[9]   The Church of South India was formed in 1947 as a union of Anglican, Presbyterian, Methodist, Reformed and Congregational churches, all of which ceased to exist as independent denominations thereafter. The American Methodists withdrew at the last moment, and today are an autonomous denomination in India.

[10]   The Church of North India followed the example of the CSI in 1970, joining together the Anglicans, the United Church of Northern India, the Church of the Brethren, the British and Australian Methodists, the Presbyterians, the Disciples of Christ and various Baptist churches.

[11]   The Right Rev. Dr A. George Ninan, formerly Bishop of Nasik (1994–99) in North India, told me that 95 per cent of the North Indians in the United States are Hindus and Muslims; only a small number are Christian. That is because 98 per cent of the CNI is Dalit. He could think of only one pastor from the CNI in the US, and he is a Mahar, or Dalit, now living in New York; telephone interview, 7 July 2007.

access because the Catholic Church does not allow separate congregations to be established on the basis of ethnicity. Churches with demonstrably few Dalits in their congregations are the Mar Thoma and Orthodox Syrian immigrant churches, mostly from Kerala, who are very high-caste in their composition and tend to form separate congregations, with pastors being sent on rotation directly from India. How many of the Dalits in the United States are Christian, as opposed to Hindu, Sikh, Buddhist or Muslim, is almost impossible to tell. But because of their comparatively higher educational status – in general, most Dalit Christians in New York and New Jersey came to the US either through the hospital industry, as nurses, administrators or chaplains, or through the church, as seminary students, doctoral students or ordained priests or pastors – it is possible that Christians predominate. Accordingly, the Dalits in the US, even among Christians, are the 'cream' of the total Dalit pool.

Given all of these imponderables and statistical lacunae, it is a daunting task to try to characterize the experience of 'Dalit Christians' even in one urban area, and this chapter is not intended to be exhaustive. The research undertaken for this project began in April 2006, but was intensified from April 2007 through January 2008, and involved interviews with 23 Indian Christian priests, pastors, scholars or students,[12] visits to ten different churches, and as much relevant reading as possible. My *entrée* into the project was mainly through Protestant congregations affiliated, in India, with the CSI, and most but not all of the people with whom I spoke were from South India. Again, most but not all were Dalit. I tended to initiate contact with the leaders of congregations, and since not everyone wants to be known by his or her caste background, to speak with individual congregation members only upon the directive or introduction of the priest or pastor. I also interviewed three very helpful second-generation church members, who were able to give me insights into caste issues from the perspective of the emerging youth leadership.

Although, in terms of coverage, the limitations of my research are therefore obvious, I have learned several lessons about Dalit Christian experience in New York and New Jersey that are almost certainly generalizable. Indeed, they make for interesting, sometimes hopeful, and always sobering reading.

---

[12]   I spoke, on the telephone or in person or both, sometimes multiple times, with the following people: Sarah Anderson-Rajarigam (Lutheran); the Rev. Dr S. Wesley Ariarajah (Methodist), Father Bala (Roman Catholic); Father Benjamin Chinnappan (Roman Catholic); the Rev. Dr Sathianathan Clarke (CSI); Rev. Sundar Devaprasad (Lutheran); the Right Rev. Dr V. Devasahayam, current Bishop of Chennai; the Rev. Dr Jacob David (CSI); Divya Gideon (CSI); the Rev. Dr Gideon Jebamani (CSI); the Rev. B.B.C. Kumar (CSI); the Rev. Anandsekhar Joseph Manuel (CSI); Jeremy Mathews (Mar Thoma); the Right Rev. Dr A. George Ninan (CNI); the Rev. Dr Abraham David Purushottaman (CSI); the Rev. Paulsson Rajarigam (CSI); the Rev. Christopher Sigamani (CSI); the Rev. Dr Prince Singh (CSI), Dr Roja Singh (CSI), the Rev. Christopher Solomon (CSI), the Rev. Dr Nehemiah Thompson (Methodist), Nithin Thompson (Methodist) and the Rev. Dr Anand Veeraraj (CSI). Many of these people knew each other, and had a history together in the New York area.

In what follows, I survey the Indian contexts of my informants, including their experiences of caste discrimination in their country of origin, describe their lives in the north-eastern United States, particularly concerning responses to their caste identity, discuss important competing factors that impact the Indian churches of North America and that may influence the recognition of caste issues, and conclude with a question: What will the experiences of American Dalits likely become in twenty years, and why?

The Indian Context: A 'Hidden Apartheid'

Every Dalit I interviewed, whether Protestant or Catholic, told me poignant, sometimes hair-raising stories of caste discrimination in India. Several were born into families that had converted fairly recently, and the strains of that transition were marked in their memories.

The situation was worst for those in villages, for the Dalit section, called *cheri* in the Tamil context, was still is demarcated and segregated from that of the caste Hindus. Said the Rev. Gideon Jebamani to my students in a guest lecture at Barnard College on 25 April 2006: 'We were almost like slaves, to look after caste people's cattle. We cannot go to their houses. We are always physically divided. Our houses have no water, no roads.' The Rev. David Purushottaman corroborated this picture of village life: 'When you visit a Christian *cheri* in another village, you have to pass through the caste section. Whoever you are, you have to take off your shirt, shoes, and dhoti below the knees.'[13] In the Reverend B.B.C. Kumar's case, it was his grandfather who converted. As a little boy the grandfather was forced to fetch water and deal with dead bodies, and even though the fastest way to the cremation ground was through the caste Hindus' section of the village, he was not allowed to take the bodies through. One day a missionary came by and asked him if he wanted to go to school. He was sent to a boarding school, and studied up to eighth grade. He accepted Christ, along with his father, the Rev. Kumar's great-grandfather. This was traumatic, as the boy and his father were driven out of the village, and their house burned down. Later, when the new Christian had become an evangelical preacher in another village, his house was burned down again and he was forced to flee.[14] The Rev. David Purushottaman tells a similar biographical narrative. The very night that his grandfather, a Dalit Hindu priest, converted to Christianity through the efforts and care of a missionary, the villagers burned down their house, killed all their livestock, and kidnapped his grandmother:

> We do not know what became of her. That is why I am involved in this kind of ministry. I know what is starvation. We walked. My grandfather said, we will never go back ....

---

[13]   Interview, 10 May 2007.

[14]   Telephone interview, 21 July 2007.

No one accepted us. To be Christian is worse than being a Dalit. Finally my grandfather
went to a native Indian pastor, and he helped us.[15]

Christian Dalits living in Indian urban areas have a slightly easier time,
as city life prevents such easy geographical definition. Both Sarah Anderson-
Rajarigam and Divya Gideon described how their parents tried to keep their
Dalit identity from them, and did so successfully into their early teens, at which
point the necessity of filling out school forms or some other precipitating factor
made them confront their parents and demand full disclosure.[16] The particular
city in which one lives also makes a difference, due to caste demographics. Dr
Roja Singh commented that her parents were both prominent members of the
CSI church in (then) Madras, and her father, the Rev. Ponnu A. Sathiasatchy,
was a noted Dalit theologian. But when they moved to a Nadar-majority area
in Madurai, 'the difference was night and day. He wasn't asked to preach in
a single church in Madurai.'[17] Several of the non-Dalit pastors and priests I
interviewed who came from city contexts stated that caste was not an issue they
thought much about during their upbringing: 'It is possible to live in India and be
unaware,' said Rev. Prince Singh, who described a dawning consciousness only
on a field trip to a village, where one of his co-workers at a tea stall was served
tea in a different type of cup.[18]

It is important to underline the role of the missionaries, from whatever
denomination, whose witness brought many Dalits to Christianity. The point was
most forcefully made to me by the Right Rev. V. Devasahayam, Bishop of Chennai,
on a pastoral visit to New York in April 2007 (see Figure 13.1). The missionaries
brought us mass education, he said, and this led to social revolution: 'Education is
a sacrament; it is a sign of grace that really transforms people.'[19] The Rev. Gideon
Jebamani concurred:

> We wanted to escape this onslaught of slavery, so Christianity came. There is something
> in Christianity that gives us a space, a space to be a community. The education
> (previously, we were not allowed to learn) opened our eyes to see our situation. For
> example, the creation story in Hinduism leaves no room for Dalits. No, the Christian

---

[15]   Interview, 10 May 2007.

[16]   Sarah Anderson-Rajarigam, interview, 27 June 2007; Divya Gideon, telephone
interview, 29 August 2007.

[17]   Telephone interview, 7 May 2007. Nadars are an upwardly mobile jati in contemporary
Tamilnadu who have successfully 'moved up' from Dalit to 'upper-caste' status. Their history,
however, is one of persecution. For an excellent survey of this history, see Eliza F. Kent,
Converting Women: Gender and Protestant Christianity in Colonial South India (New York:
Oxford University Press, 2004). The Rev. Nehemiah Thompson, a Nadar, spoke of the pain of
this oppression, even though it had been before his own time; interview, 7 May 2007.

[18]   Telephone interview, 27 June 2007.

[19]   Interview, 28 April 2007.

Figure 13.1   The Right Rev. V. Devasahayam, Bishop of Chennai, and the Rev.
Gideon Jebamani, April 2007. (Photo: Rachel Fell McDermott)

preachers told us; you are in the image of God. This was something unique for us ....
Education causes us to disturb the social order. Now we don't work in the fields, we
own property.[20]

The Rev. David Purushottaman (see Figure 13.2) preaches every Sunday, he
says, about the missionaries: 'If it weren't for them ...'. Such sincere praise for
people who are today typically maligned in the context of South Asian studies is
worthy of note.[21]

Persecution of Dalits in India, of course, is not a thing of the past, a bad memory
in the lives of middle-aged immigrants in the United States. It is ongoing. One only
has to watch the recently released documentary *India Untouched: The Story of a
People Apart*, directed by K. Stalin (2007), access any news medium or read the
reports of human rights organizations such as *Broken People: Caste Violence against
India's 'Untouchables'* (1999) to be made viscerally aware of how, in India's 'hidden
apartheid', entire villages remain segregated by caste, their occupants unable to use
the same wells, visit the same temples, drink from the same cups at tea stalls or
lay claim to land that is legally theirs. Whole communities are made to perform
degrading tasks, and when complaints are lodged, under the Scheduled Castes
and Scheduled Tribes Prevention of Atrocities Act of 1989,[22] it is found that the

---

[20]   Class presentation, Barnard College, 26 April 2006.

[21]   Telephone interview, 28 April 2007.

[22]   The list of offences punishable by this Act testifies to the indignities endured in
the daily life of Dalit communities: causing someone to drink or eat urine/faeces; dumping

Figure 13.2   The Rev. David Purushottaman and the Tamil Christian Congregation,
                April 2007. (Photo: Jim Prajesh)

police stations are in the upper-caste sections of villages, and represent upper-caste interests. Dalits who have tried to contest political office in seats 'reserved' for them have been threatened with abuse and even death to get them to withdraw. In other words, attempts to alter village customs or demand land, increased wages or political rights lead to violence and economic retaliation by those threatened. These atrocities and inhumane treatments are endured by Dalits of whatever religious affiliation.

Unfortunately, the Indian church has also frequently been complicit in such discriminatory behaviour. Because the Roman Catholic Church early on, from the sixteenth century, took the view that caste was a social not religious custom, and hence could be tolerated, Catholic Dalits have long suffered the stigma of caste inequalities in church. Even today in some places, they are segregated in the liturgy, do not serve at mass, read the readings or sing in the choir. Their dead are buried separately. They do not get their feet washed on Maundy Thursday. The decorated cars in parish festivals do not go through their streets.[23] Father Bala

---

such in their neighbourhood; parading them naked or with painted faces; forcing them into bonded labour; taking away their land; corrupting their water; denying rights of passage to a public place, and sexually exploiting a Dalit woman.

[23]   Poornam Daniel SJ, 'Dalit Christian Experiences: Some Reflections on Dalit Christians' Struggle for Liberation and its Implications for Doing a Dalit Theology', in

remarked to me that although in theory the Catholic Church is a universal church based on equality, in practice it discriminates, all the way up into the leadership. Speaking of Tamilnadu, where 70 per cent of the Catholic Church is Dalit, he said: 'There are 130 priests in our diocese, but only six or seven are Dalits. They purposely avoid Dalit seminary candidates .... I am the first Dalit priest in my diocese. I was allowed in because of the prominence of my family's devotion.'[24]

A scathing recent denunciation of caste prejudice in the church is the Tamil autobiography, *Karukku* (1992), of a former nun who calls herself Bama.[25] Bama is a Paraiyar, and from an early age she experiences the humiliation of caste oppression. She joins a Catholic order in order to show kindness to Dalit children, but finds that the nuns denigrate Dalits, both inside and outside the order:

> Far worse is the attitude in our own church. ... In the churches, Dalits are the most, in numbers alone. In everything else, they are the least. It is only the upper-caste Christians who enjoy the benefits and comforts of the church. Even amongst the priests and nuns, it is the upper castes who hold all the high positions, show off their authority and throw their weight about. And if Dalits become priests and nuns, they are pushed aside and marginalized first of all, before the rest go about their business. It is because of this that even though Dalits like me might wish to take up the path of renunciation, we find there is no place for us there.[26]

Recognizing such problems, many church theologians and activists have agitated for reservations for Dalits in all church institutions and parish councils, and in 2000 the Dalit Christian Liberation Movement prepared a memorandum for Pope John Paul II on his visit to India, demanding redress.[27]

The Protestant Church of South India has its own problems. Although the prominent Chennai diocese now has a Dalit bishop, Bishop Devasahayam himself

---

Xavier Irudayaraj SJ (ed.), *Emerging Dalit Theology* (Madras, 1990), pp. 22–3, citing *SAR News* (12–18 January, 1987), pp. 37–8. For more on Roman Catholic Church-related discrimination against Dalits, see *Dalit International Newsletter*, 5/3 (October 2000): 6–9.

[24] Telephone interview, 19 June 2007. At the national level, the numbers are equally dismal: as of 2007, only 6 per cent of the clergy and nuns in India, and only 6 out of 156 bishops in India, were Dalit.

[25] Bama, *Karukku*, trans. from Tamil by Lakshmi Holmström, ed. Mini Kirshnan (Chennai, 2000).

[26] Ibid., p. 69.

[27] This memorandum, as well as one presented at the meeting of the Catholic Bishops Conference of India in January 2000, called for the eradication of caste in the church, the banning of all forms of division (separate paths in graveyards, separate burials, separate places in festivals), the goal of 75 Dalit bishops in India, ten of whom would be based in Tamilnadu, the appointing of a Dalit cardinal, the establishment of a Cell or Secretariat for Dalit Christian Affairs in the Vatican, the institution of reservations within the church, and the closing of churches in which caste priests and nuns continue to oppress and marginalize Dalit congregation members.

admits that 'still we have not faced the real caste issue. Ninety-nine percent of marriages are along caste lines. So is employment, even renting a house.'[28] The Rev. Anandsekhar Joseph Manuel admitted that 'as a priest in India, I was ashamed of my Dalit background and never mentioned it'.[29] In Dalit-majority dioceses, such as Vellore, a traditional Dalit stronghold, Dalits face fewer prejudices in church. But I was repeatedly told that in dioceses dominated by Brahmans, Nadars or Vellalas, Dalits had a more difficult time realizing the equality that they believed the Gospel to promise. Asserted the Rev. Gideon Jebamani: 'The church is still the only hope [for me and my people], but it is not perfect.'[30]

Can Context Change Thought? The American Experience

Given the fact that caste is presumably absent from normative American culture, one would expect Dalit Christians to find the United States a land of religious and social freedom and opportunity. Do they?

Most of the priests, pastors and lay people whom I interviewed were deeply involved in the church, seminary or university education, the hospital world, social services outreach, or a combination thereof, and they had often achieved fairly visible positions. Some were hired by all-white or mixed white, black and Hispanic congregations, where they and their families were the sole Indians in the worshipping community. A sub-set among these chose at the same time to respond to a vision of felt need in the Indian community and to initiate their own church or service organization 'on the side'. Many such Indian immigrant groups began in a modest way, meeting on Sunday afternoons or evenings, but some of them became regular churches, even growing to own their own property. The two oldest and best examples in the New York area are the Tamil Christian Congregation, started in 1977 by the Rev. David Purushottaman and conducted in Tamil,[31] and the Christhava Tamil Koil, a Tamil-worshipping congregation that soon split off from the Tamil Christian Congregation over caste differences and has been served ever since by the Rev. Sundar Devaprasad, who has built up the church to such a degree that they have their own building.[32] This church has been responsible

---

28   Interview, 28 April 2007.

29   Interview, 24 July 2007.

30   Class presentation, Barnard College, 26 April 2006.

31   For eighteen years this church met in Astoria, Queens, first in a Reformed church and then in a United Methodist church. Now they meet at the Totowa Methodist Church in Totowa, New Jersey. See their Website, <http://www.tamilchristiancongregation.org>. For an overview of the splintering of the original Tamil Christian Congregation and its daughter groups, see the Rev. Gideon Jebamani, 'Dalit Christians: From Submission to Liberation'.

32   The Rev. Sundar Devaprasad was approached by a number of Christians to start a church where the worship could be conducted in Tamil. He responded to their request, and the church was started in 1978 in Old Bergen, Jersey City, New Jersey, although they quickly shifted

Figure 13.3   The Rev. B.B.C. Kumar and the Rev. Christopher Solomon at the Asian Indian Christian Church, March 2008. (Photo: Rachel Fell McDermott)

for sponsoring the immigration of many Indian pastors and priests, such that the Koil now has a number of spin-off groups: the Asian Indian Christian Church, jointly pastored by the Rev. Christopher Solomon and the Rev. B.B.C. Kumar and featuring English-language services for Protestant Indian Christians of varied linguistic, ethnic and caste backgrounds (see Figure 13.3);[33] the combined South Asian and non-South Asian congregation of St Paul's, Woodside, Queens since 1994 under the direction of Rev. Anandsekhar Manuel, who has also started a school, a daycare centre and St Paul's Multiethnic Ministries,[34] and the New Jersey

---

to Queens. In 1991, they moved to Richmond Hill and gave the church its current name. In 2002, they bought the present building, in Middle Village, New York, after raising $1.2 million from the congregation of 75 families. See <http://www.christhavatamilkoil.org>.

[33]   This group had its roots in the Christhava Tamil Koil, but separated out under the leadership of the Rev. B.B.C. Kumar to form its own group in 1989, principally to serve people living in Jersey City and also to worship in English, not Tamil. They moved several times, from Old Bergen to Maplewood in central New Jersey to the present facility in Roselle Park, New Jersey. In the late 1990s, the Rev. Kumar, who was burdened with a full-time job as the Director of Social Services in East Orange, New Jersey, invited the Rev. Christopher Solomon, then an associate pastor at the Christhava Tamil Koil, to join him as the senior pastor. See <http://www.aiccnj.org>.

[34]   This church too began as a breakaway group from the Christhava Tamil Koil. The church also hosts the Romanian Orthodox, the Korean Presbyterians and the Bangladeshi Pentecostals, all of whom the Rev. Anandsekhar Manuel brings together annually into one service.

Indian Church under the leadership of the Rev. Anand Veeraraj, whose church was initiated in 1995 as an outreach project of the Christhava Tamil Koil to minister to those in South and Central New Jersey.[35] While most of these congregations have a sizable percentage of Dalit members, this fact is not advertised in the churches themselves, and I did not attempt to do much interviewing of lay members.[36]

Those who were willing to speak to me candidly about caste and their experiences of it spanned a spectrum between those who were frank in acknowledging their Dalit birth but who thought of their Christian identity in more pietistic or universalistic terms, and those who were social activists regarding their Dalit Christian self-understanding. Many expressed great pain. Bishop Devasahayam described the inferiority complex, self-hate, self-negation and withdrawal that Dalits experience from an early age;[37] the Rev. Gideon Jebamani repeatedly in his conversations with me brought up the 'untold pain' of being a Dalit, such that he worries he cannot truly express Christian joy. One pastor, fearing that some upper-caste congregation members might leave were his caste background to be publicized, admitted that he was a Dalit, but asked me not to speak of it when I came to his church.

A minority, those of an activist frame, were generally more positive in their self-description: 'I have no hesitation in saying that I am a Dalit,' said the Rev. Anandsekhar Manuel.[38] Similarly, affirmed Father Benjamin Chinnappan: 'I am open-minded about my identity. I am precious in the eyes of God. I do not need to live by the prejudices of others.'[39] The Rev. David Purushottaman told me that the greatest advice his father ever gave him was never to be afraid to tell people his background: 'Tell them that God has lifted you up. Be a witness.'[40] The Rev. Christopher Solomon, of the Asian Indian Christian Church, takes a slightly different approach. Many people spoke to me of his wonderful pastoral care, describing him as an inspirational shepherd of his people. Although not afraid to speak of his background and that of many in his church, he nevertheless does not make caste an issue. Speaking of caste in the United States, he told me: 'Unless we Dalit pastors create confusion by separating people, there is no problem.'[41]

Many of the more outspoken Dalit Christians were critical of their brothers and sisters who were unwilling to face the impact of caste on their lives. The Rev. Gideon Jebamani has made it his passion to encourage people not to hide, put on

---

[35]   They currently meet in Kendall Park, New Jersey, in the Community Presbyterian Church of the Sands. See <http://www.njic.org>.

[36]   I was warned by several of my informants that while it was a luxury, or a necessity, for Dalit pastors to be open about their caste identity, congregational members often preferred to keep their family origins private, and hence would be uncomfortable talking about caste issues.

[37]   Interview, 28 April 2007.

[38]   Interview, 24 July 2007.

[39]   Telephone interview, 14 June 2007.

[40]   Interview, 10 May 2007.

[41]   Interview, 9 July 2007.

false masks or evade Dalit pain: 'This is my breathing,' he told me.[42] Rev. Prince and Dr Roja Singh have become very involved at the national and international level in Dalit causes, but claim that it is easier to raise funds in non-Indian churches than it is in mostly Dalit ones. Roja Singh narrated the sorts of responses she got from Dalits in the local Indian congregations to whom she appealed for help: '"Why are you bringing Dalit issues up here?" "We came here [to the United States] to forget and get away from all this." "None of this exists any more."'[43]

Whether they want to admit it or not, however, the overwhelming impression I gained through nine months of research was that Dalit Christians continue to experience caste discrimination in the United States. The US does indeed present a new geographic context, for it lacks the physical boundaries of the *cheri* and the obvious identity cues of occupation, clothing and pronunciation of the local language; in addition, the opportunities for identity construction in a context that is 99 per cent outside the ambit of caste are numerous. Everyone I spoke with welcomed these opportunities and celebrated the new freedoms that they were experiencing. But in the north-eastern seaboard, where there are so many South Asian immigrants, it is nearly impossible, even if it were desirable, to avoid mixing to a greater or lesser degree with other South Asians. And here is where the accounts of prejudice arise. Indeed, in a place one informant described as just 'like India',[44] the majority of advertised matrimonials demonstrate that Indians still practice caste preferences.[45] 'We are very caste-minded, though none of us says it out loud,' conceded the Rev. Sundar Devaprasad.[46] According to Rev. Gideon Jebamani, discrimination is very visible in the upper-caste churches: 'It is unsaid that I cannot walk into just any Indian Christian church.'[47] Even in mixed congregations, people will not participate in social interactions if Dalits are known to be the hosts. Since some dioceses of the church in India are known to be Dalit-majority, the caste of newcomers is quickly found out by probing questions about geographic origin. Recounted the Rev. David Purushottaman:

> Even the most sophisticated Indians ask about [my] background. They start by asking about the region, and then narrow it down by that. Most of the time I am not recognized. They feel better if I tell them that I am Jamaican or Guyanese. Caste, colour and culture: these are the first things we pack in our suitcases.

Most Indians, he says, talk more readily to his wife, because she is light-skinned and not a Dalit. 'Sometimes I feel that. It hurts. ... Coming away from our country

---

[42]   Interview, 4 April 2007.

[43]   Interview after the church service at St Alban's Episcopal Church, Oakland and Franklin Lakes, New Jersey, 28 July 2007.

[44]   The Rev. Gideon Jebamani, interview, 13 April 2007.

[45]   Others painted a less dismal picture, giving instances of Christian inter-caste marriages in the United States.

[46]   Interview, 2 August 2007.

[47]   Interview, 13 April 2007.

has not changed us.'[48] One of the younger Dalit Christians to whom I spoke was vocal, ironic and critical of the ways in which university students express caste prejudice. Not knowing the caste background of their friend, whom they think to be upper-caste because 'I tell them that I am a Christian, and I do not "look" Dalit', they feel free to make snide remarks about other Indians in the student body known to be Dalits: 'Prejudice? I experience it every day! They know their caste identity more than their Tamil!'[49] Even the Rev. Christopher Sigamani, who does not serve an Indian-majority church and works full-time as a chaplain in an inner-city hospital that does not cater to South Asians, feels what he calls the 'scars' of discrimination: 'Once you come here, you do not expect caste. There *is* a lessening, but it does not disappear. There will always be some mark, especially at marriage.'[50] As the Rev. Gideon Jebamani concluded at the end of his DMin. thesis for the New York Theological Seminary in 2004: 'The fact is that the change of geographical location, however far, does not alter the mindset of the Indian community regarding caste.'[51]

Many Indian Christians in the New York area, Dalit or not, feel compelled to take some action to alleviate the suffering they perceive, especially among Dalits in India. Some send money home to needy relatives or friends, sponsor Dalit children in the Ramabai Mukti Mission[52] or found an institution, such as a school, an orphanage or a hospital, to which they return year after year in their vacations.[53] Other activists prefer to work through their contacts in India to pressure the Supreme Court to award Christian Dalits the same reservation and affirmative action benefits currently enjoyed by Hindu, Sikh and Buddhist Dalits.[54] And some

---

[48]   Interview, 10 May 2007.

[49]   Telephone interview, 29 August 2007.

[50]   The Rev. Sigamani works at the Interfaith Medical Center, Brooklyn, New York. While 50 per cent of the doctors are South Asian, the client population served is nearly entirely African American; telephone interview, 17 August 2007.

[51]   The Rev. Gideon Jebamani, 'Dalit Christians: From Submission to Liberation', p. 23.

[52]   The Asian Indian Christian Congregation is currently sponsoring two such girls. The Pandita Ramabai Mukti Mission was founded by the famed Christian convert Ramabai (1858–1922) in 1889. The mission supports orphanages, schools, medical services, homes for the unwanted, and churches.

[53]   The Rev. Prince and Dr Roja Singh formed a companion parish relationship between St Peter's, Morristown, New Jersey, where they were posted from 1997 to 2000, and a very poor church in Kothapallimitta, near Chitur, Tamilnadu, where they had served for five years while in India. Eventually, St Peter's built a school for the village. The inauguration of the school occurred in August 2007, and the Singhs took a group of parishioners from St Peter's and St Alban's, where they are currently serving, to India to participate in the celebrations. To further cement the relationship, St Alban's and the church at Kothapallimitta are conducting Bible studies on the same verses, video-taping them, and then exchanging them.

[54]   The Indian Constitution awarded such benefits to Scheduled Castes belonging to the Hindu tradition in 1950. Dalit converts to Sikhism were added in 1956, and Buddhist converts in 1990. Christians have yet to be included.

work at the highest, most global level by lobbying churches, Congress and the United Nations for the purpose of getting descent-based discrimination formally declared a human rights abuse. In such a campaign, all consciousness-raising is useful; examples include the fostering of ties between American and Indian dioceses for information sharing and fund-raising, the founding of newsletters[55] and the creation of Websites.[56] That these sorts of campaigns have been somewhat successful in bringing Dalit concerns to the attention of policymakers and legislators in the United States is proven by the facts that the 2002 United Nations World Conference Against Racism in Durban produced a Draft Program of Action in which 'caste practices of distinction' were declared to be 'hidden apartheid',[57] and that in May 2007 the US House of Representatives passed a historic resolution requesting that the American government work with India through diplomatic channels and encourage American businesses, USAID, the State Department and other US programmes to take every possible measure to ensure that Dalits are included, and not discriminated against.

The experience of discrimination has made many Dalit Christians turn to social outreach in general as a tool of compassion, extending their concern for the downtrodden to include African Americans, Mexicans and Appalachians, taking youth members of congregations on service missions and working in local neighbourhood projects such as daycare facilities, food pantries or shelters. The Rev. David Purushottaman is an excellent example of this drive to serve. He was instrumental in founding Christian Approaches to Urban and Suburban Encounter (CAUSE), an ecumenical organization with Reformed, Episcopalian, Roman Catholic and Methodist participation, the purpose of which is to encourage wealthy churches in New Jersey to help the poor in Jersey City. He is the director, and I visited him in Jersey City to see the ministry. None of his clients is Indian, and most of them are young men with alcohol or drug-related problems, in addition to abuse and poverty.

Sometimes 'mission' even extends to local Hindus in the metropolitan New York area. Indeed, in the course of my interviews with Indian Christians in the New York/New Jersey area, I encountered a variety of different attitudes towards Hindus and Hindu organizations. Some did not seem to think much about

---

[55]   Although the editors of the *Dalit International Newsletter* – Owen Lynch, Eleanor Zelliot and John C.B. Webster – were not Indian or Dalit, their point in bringing out the newsletter in 1996 was to bring Dalit issues to international notice. The inaugural issue went to 1800 people in 42 countries.

[56]   See, for example, Father Benjamin Chinnappan's Website <http://www.dalitchristians. com>, which serves as a platform for news updates and other services. In 1996, he told me, there were no Websites devoted to Dalits: 'Then I took training, and launched my own, in 1997–98.' He got a lot of feedback from all over the world from people who had previously never heard of such caste-related cruelties; telephone interview, 14 June 2007.

[57]   See <www.ncdhr.org.in/>, the official Website of the National Campaign on Dalit Human Rights.

Hindu–Christian relations or antagonisms, and felt a call to embrace all persons, no matter the background. Others who did not distinguish between Christians and Hindus sought to forge a common bond across Dalits of all religious affiliation, and did not want lines of religion to separate potential activism and uplift. But the fact that Hindus predominate in the South Asian community of New York and New Jersey does bring its own opportunities and challenges. Indian Christians are at pains to show that they are not Hindu, naive local assumptions notwithstanding. In the late 1980s, American misconceptions about the religious distinctions between South Asians caused the Christian community acute distress; members of the Asian Indian Christian Church, which had first settled in Old Bergen, a part of racially divided Jersey City, were 'harassed by the neighbouring community. Our cars were broken into by people calling themselves dot-busters. "You Hindus go back!"'[58]

Thus to many, Hindu–Christian differences do matter. Several pastors and lay people with whom I spoke felt a call to minister to or evangelize the Hindus in their communities. The Princeton Consultation of June 2007 was partly convened with this in mind: how to understand the Gospel in this new multi-ethnic context, where our neighbours are not only white or black Americans, but South Asian Hindus and Muslims? Do we need to spread the Gospel in a Western or in an Indian mode?[59] The day's events were started off with an introduction by Dr David Chigurupati, who prayed for the large South Asian population in the United States: 'Right in our own back yards we have a mission field. Reaping has to be done every day.' Some Indian churches do precisely that. The youth members of the Asian Indian Christian Congregation take regular trips to Edison, New Jersey, a city with a high concentration of South Asians, to hand out religious tracts in English, Hindi and Gujarati. Several interviewees also told me, some with evident satisfaction, that they had lobbied successfully to prevent local Hindus from gaining permission to build Hindu temples in their neighbourhoods. A story from the Rev. David Purushottaman is paradigmatic. In 1983, he said, Hindus brought 22 acres in Jersey City to build a temple. He objected, calling them a cult, and testified in court in front of a judge, Mayor Edward Koch and 23 Hindus. He asked the Hindus: 'How many missionaries have you driven out? How many churches have you burned down? How many caste barriers have you built up?' The judge tabled the issue and denied the request.[60]

The Rev. Nehemiah Thompson (see Figure 13.4) is passionately critical of what he calls the 'Hindutva' brand of Hinduism in India and the United States.[61] After the

---

[58]   The Rev. B.B.C. Kumar, interview, 21 July 2007.

[59]   The Rev. Anand Veeraraj, convener and organizer of the Consultation; telephone interview, 3 May 2007.

[60]   Interview, 10 May 2007.

[61]   Hindutva (lit. 'Hindu-ness') refers to the ideology first expounded by Hindu nationalist V.D. Savarkar is his book, *Hindutva*, published in 1923. According to Savarkar, all true Indians share, or should share, a core Hindu identity defined as a geographical, cultural and religious loyalty to the land of India. This ideology is frequently perceived to

Figure 13.4   The Rev. David Purushottaman and the Rev. Nehemiah Thompson, October 2006. (Photo: Jim Prajesh)

church burnings in 1999,[62] he began to spend his summers giving educative seminars about the dangers of the Hindutva position at Christian College, Marthandam, in Tamilnadu. In his chapter to be published in the forthcoming Princeton Consultation volume, he writes that the same Hindutva forces that are attempting to increase caste divisions in India are also 'active in the U.S. The ecumenical Indian Christian communities are needed to reach out to the Hindutva groups and preach the gospel to them.' Responding less directly and less personally to Hindutva-coloured critiques that Indian Christianity is a colonial legacy or a vehicle for neo-colonial interference, the Rev. Sundar Devaprasad's Christhava Tamil Koil hosted an international conference in 2005 on 'The History of Early Christianity in India'. The main thrust of the conference was to prove that Christianity has been in India

---

exclude Muslims, Christians and 'secular' Hindus. Hindutva ideology today is espoused by many groups, the three most prominent being the Vishwa Hindu Parishad (VHP), the Rashtra Swayamsevak Sangh (RSS) and the political Bharatiya Janata Party (BJP).

[62]   The year 1999 was one of attacks against churches, priests and nuns, laity and missionaries all across North India. The most grisly incident involved the burning alive of Australian missionary Graham Staines and his two young sons in a tribal area in Orissa, in January 1999.

for two thousand years and that many elements of South Indian culture were likely influenced by the Christian community's early presence.[63]

A few of my conversation partners were much more optimistic about Hindu–Christian understanding emerging here in the United States. Paulsson Rajarigam and Sarah Anderson-Rajarigam agreed that America is the ideal context in which Indian Christians, even low-caste or Dalit, can engage Hindus: 'Here we are in a better position to talk to them; the playing field is even when we come here.'[64] Perhaps the most astounding testimony of this benefit – the changed geographic context – for Dalit self-esteem comes, again, from the life story of the Rev. David Purushottaman. In 2003, twenty years after he had successfully prevented the construction of one Hindu temple, another was built in Perth Amboy, New Jersey. The organizers invited him to the inaugural function: 'I thought at the time that they had confused me with someone else,' he said, 'as my last name is not a Christian one.' When he got to the temple, the organizers asked him to bless them and the temple. He replied that he could do so only in the name of Jesus Christ. 'Yes; that is what we want,' they assured him. He prayed for them, and then they seated him in a place of honour on the dais, next to the Brahman priest. At that point, Rev. Purushottaman stopped the flow of his conversation and looked at me: 'I could never imagine this,' he said quietly.[65]

Caste prejudice may be alive and well in the United States, but so are opportunities for its alleviation and potential healing.

Additional Reasons for the Unnoticed Elephant

In the course of my research for this project, I gained the strong impression that Indian churches, or churches catering to Indians, have a distinct array of issues they must face in the coming years. And caste is not always central in the minds of Indian Christians, even those from Dalit backgrounds, as they think about their future in the United States.

Challenges that appear very pressing include the following. Firstly, what kind of church environment is best suited for the average Indian Christian? Should we be creating what the Rev. Nehemiah Thompson calls 'enclave churches',[66] meaning congregations that consist of tightly bound communities who worship in their regional Indian languages, are pastored by Indians sent from India and retain diocesan or organizational ties to Indian prelates? The various Syrian and Orthodox branches of the Keralite churches take this approach, and in so doing they have

---

[63]   This was held at the Bronxville, New York campus of Concordia College, 13–16 August 2005.

[64]   Joint interview, 27 June 2007.

[65]   Interview, 10 May 2007.

[66]   See his forthcoming essay, 'The Common Journey: Living by the Ecumenical Spirit'.

built versions of India in American cities. Recently, in 2003, the Church of South India shocked many of its affiliated priests and pastors here by agreeing to create a North American branch that would, in effect, allow congregations to be overseas branches of the Indian CSI rather than to join local denominations here. For those who envision a church that is accommodative to both Indian and American concerns and that attempts to build upon the unity of all believers, such ethnic and linguistic enclaves are to be deplored.[67] There is nevertheless a certain comfort in worshipping with one's birth community and in one's native language. The Christhava Tamil Koil is a case in point. The church is beautiful, with candlesticks, altar pieces, paintings and crucifixes all brought lovingly from India by the Rev. Sundar Devaprasad. The outside church bell tower is being constructed in the shape of a lotus, the national Indian flower, with materials brought from India, and during the crowded all-Tamil services, the men and women sit on opposite sides of the church, the women almost uniformly dressed in brightly coloured saris with flowers in their hair.

As mentioned above, other pastors, while sensitive to the needs of both 'American' and 'Indian' Christians, tend to separate the two in their lives, pastoring two churches, one 'mainstream' in the morning and the other Indian in the afternoon or evening. Still more bold are those clergy who are endeavouring to build multi-ethnic congregations that are responsive to Indian and non-Indian parishioners, and hence that worship together and in English. The Rev. Jacob David, rector of St Paul's and Resurrection, Wood-Ridge, New Jersey, and Bishop George Ninan, rector of All Saints Episcopal Church – CSI Congregation in Valley Cottage, New York are both engaged in merging separate Indian and non-Indian congregations under the same roof and in the same service. The hardship presented by this type of mixing is illustrated by an anecdote told me by Bishop Ninan.[68] The two congregations (Malayali and English) tried to merge their Sunday schools, but quickly asked to be allowed to separate again. To explain to children what 'God is love' means, the Malayali teacher asked the children to memorize Bible verses, whereas the Caucasian teacher asked them to explain the meaning of the words in terms of analogies from everyday life. Both sets of teachers felt that the others were denying the children true learning.

In terms of caste, the enclave churches tend to be least accepting, unless they are all-Dalit, which brings its own stigma, as upper-caste Indians tend to avoid

---

[67]   There are currently 32 such congregations in the United States. In the eyes of Bishop Ninan, this arrangement is theologically unsound and very undemocratic, for the Indian CSI Synod gives no effective episcopal or pastoral support to the American churches, and the CSI Council of North America has no representation in the Synod, which means they have no vote to elect officers or make decisions affecting the life of the CSI , including their own. E-mail communication, 24 January 2008. The Rev. Dr S. Wesley Ariarajah, a Methodist from Sri Lanka who teaches about India at Drew University, told me that on principle he goes to a local, not ethnic, church. Telephone interview, 27 April 2007.

[68]   Interview, 29 July 2007.

such congregations. Dalit Christians feel most welcome either in 'mainstream' congregations, where they are known as 'Indian' rather than as 'Dalit', or in mixed congregations, where the effort to unite rather than discriminate on the basis of difference is the reigning principle.

Secondly, another pressing concern of Indian Christian pastors and lay people are the challenges of adapting to the 'salad bowl' of American culture. Most of the chapters submitted for the volume to come out of the 2007 Princeton Consultation focus on facets of what Catholic theologian Peter C. Phan has called the 'betwixt and between' reality of immigrant communities.[69] What this means is less the discomfort of mingling with other Indians than the tension of being differently Christian in a nominally Christian country where people expect one to be Hindu, and hence alien.[70]

Thirdly, the social and cultural effects of living in the United States can also be deleterious to community health. The Rev. Dr David K. Ravinder, a counsellor who has worked in the New York metropolitan area with the Asian Indian community for 27 years, writes in his chapter in the Princeton Consultation volume, 'Pastoral Care and Counseling in the Asian Indian Christian Community: Some Observations and Reflections', that the main problems besetting the community are marital, inter-generational, and involve bereavements and accidents. In the eyes of the Rev. Anand Veeraraj and Rev. Jacob David, spousal abuse, care of parents and even dowry are additional prime worries for the community.[71] In these written and oral reflections, caste is nowhere mentioned as an issue requiring counselling.

Fourthly, the fate and future of the second and third generations produce a special kind of anxiety on the part of all Indian Christians, no matter what the caste background. First-generation immigrants worry that their children will fall away both from church and from an India-derived commitment to family and culture. Those in linguistic congregations find that their children are not interested in all-Malayalam or all-Tamil services, and when given the opportunity to read in the service, prefer to use English. Indian Christians whose services are already in English worry that the style of worship is not relevant or interesting to the second generation: 'The youth leave for Pentecostal churches. We are too traditional.'[72] Some first-generation pastors try to compensate for this gap by involving the youth

---

[69] See Peter C. Phan, *Christianity with an Asian Face: Asian American Theology in the Making* (Marknoll, NY, 2003). Phan's work is discussed in Glory Thomas's forthcoming essay 'Trading Churidhar for Jeans: Challenges facing Asian Indian Christian Women in the United States of America'.

[70] The same focus occurs in Sam George, *The Coconut Generation: Ministry to the Americanized Asian Indians* (Niles, IL, 2006), and Prema A. Kurien, 'Christian by Birth or Rebirth? Generation and Difference in an Indian American Christian Church', in Tony Carnes and Fenggang Yang (eds), *Asian American Religions: The Making and Remaking of Borders and Boundaries* (New York, 2004), pp. 160–81.

[71] Telephone interview, 22 June 2007, and interview, 26 June 2007, respectively.

[72] Bishop George Ninan, telephone interview, 7 July 2007.

– either incorporating rock-style music in church or special youth presentations in the service context, or outreach activities that cause bonding between the youth and the pastor. Two young Indian Christians, Nithin Thompson and Jeremy Mathews, both seminary students at the Alliance Theological Seminary in Nyack, New York, spoke with me about their perspectives on the issues facing the church.[73] What concerned them most was creating a ministry to second-generation youth that would keep them involved in and committed to the churches of their parents: 'The harsh reality is that the majority of second-generation youths who attend first-generation events find camaraderie in complaining about boredom. ... Second-generation ministry will require spiritual formation processes outside of the church walls.' Not surprisingly, caste was nowhere on their minds. When pressed on the point, both replied that birth-based discrimination was a problem mainly confined (1) to India or (2) to first-generation Indian Christians in the United States. Said Mathews, a Syrian Christian whose parents hail from Kerala:

> The average second-generation Indian is totally ignorant, uninterested and uninformed about the Dalit situation in India, not intentionally, but simply because it is not a part of life here in America. ... If I may be quite frank, asking established Indian Christians to accept Dalits as equals in their congregations is the same as asking established homogeneous American churches to accept American inner-city minorities into their churches as equals. It is unfortunate that it is this way. Of course, there are many in the bunch who are filled with Christ's servant-hearted love such that they can cross boundaries within their own culture .... [But] caste issues are first-generation issues. A second-generation worshipper could care less [about] the caste or race of someone he/she is worshipping with.

That the opinions of Thompson and Mathews, neither of whom is Dalit, regarding the irrelevance of caste in the United States may not be entirely universal is proven by recalling the student referred to earlier who spoke of caste discrimination in the university context.

A fifth reason that discussion about caste may appear less prominent in North American churches is the lack of resources for its promulgation. Where caste is a fact of life, as in India, its negative effects are obvious. But also available for utilization in India are the exhortations of countervailing voices, particularly outspoken champions of what has come to be known, since 1978, as Dalit Liberation Theology.[74] Proceeding from the assumption that Dalits in general

---

[73] They co-authored a paper presented at the Princeton Consultation that they entitled 'Calling First Generation Missionaries to Second Generation Ministry: A Concise Anthropological Assessment and Praxis Guide to Providing Culturally Relevant and Meaningful Ministry to Second Generation Indians in First Generation Indian Churches', and they agreed to discuss caste with me via e-mail (27 and 28 July, 2007).

[74] Dalit Theology grew out of a meeting of the first National Consultation on the Plight of Christians of Scheduled Caste Origin, in Bangalore in 1978, although the first national

suffer from six oppressions (economic deprivation, political minoritization, social marginalization, cultural mutilation, religious ostracization and physical segregation), and that Christian Dalits contend with four additional alienations (from the state, from non-Christian Dalits, from upper-caste Christians and from their own deep divisions), Bishop Masilamani Azaraiah speaks of the Dalit's 'wound in the soul' or 'wounded psyche',[75] for which a humanized, suffering Jesus is the healing antidote. In a classic essay, 'Towards a Dalit Theology', Arvind P. Nirmal describes the Dalit Christians' 'Exodus Experience' as coming out from Hinduism into a tradition where God, and Jesus, are Dalits: 'Servitude is innate in the God of dalits. Servitude is the sva-dharma of our God.' He interprets Isaiah's prophecy – 'he had no form or comeliness, no beauty. He was despised and rejected of men, a man of sorrow, and acquainted with grief' – as referring to Jesus in his Dalitness, and praises Jesus' cleansing of the temple as a radical action on behalf of temple-entry rights for the downtrodden. Implicit in Dalit theology is a critique of the Hindu tradition. Noting that Rama kills Shambuka the Untouchable because he has dared to undertake a life of *tapas*, Nirmal states: 'Rama is a killer God – killer and murderer of dalits.'[76]

Dalit Theology as it has developed over the last three decades in India is distinct from the Euro-centric theological approach to Christianity, which is speculative, kerygmatic, logos-centred, individualistic, other-worldly, dichotomistic, underestimates social evils, and associates women with the body and emotion.[77] By contrast, Dalit Theology celebrates an engaged, even subversive God whose concern is the field of human action. Like the Israelites, who are commanded not to forget their sojourn as slaves in Egypt, Dalits need, says Bishop Azaraiah, to come out of the 'sickness of Amnesia'. He calls 'this forgetting of the past'

---

conference of Christian Dalits did not occur until March, 1985. For seminal volumes that treat Dalit theology, see, in order of publication: M.E. Prabhakar (ed.), *Towards a Dalit Theology* (Delhi, 1988); Xavier Irudayaraj SJ (ed.), *Emerging Dalit Theology* (Madras, 1990); Arvind R. Nirmal and V. Devasahayam (eds), *A Reader in Dalit Theology* (Madras, c. mid-1990s); V. Devasahayam (ed.), *Frontiers of Dalit Theology* (Madras, 1996); James Massey (ed.), *Indigenous People: Dalits. Dalit Issues in Today's Theological Debate* (Delhi, 1998), and Bishop Masilamani Azaraiah, *A Pastor's Search for Dalit Theology* (Delhi, 2000). A new seminar on Dalit Theology, to plan for a 'second wave' of Dalit theological thinking, was held on 13–17 January 2008, in Kolkata.

[75]   Bishop Masilamani Azaraiah, *A Pastor's Search for Dalit Theology*, p. xix.

[76]   See Arvind R. Nirmal, 'Towards a Dalit Theology', originally delivered as a lecture on 3 November 1987, and reprinted in Xavier Irudayaraj SJ (ed.), *Emerging Dalit Theology*, (Madras, 1990), pp. 123–42. The quotations come from pp. 135 and 136.

[77]   Franklyn J. Balasundaram, 'Dalit Theology and Other Theologies', in V. Devasahayam (ed.), *Frontiers of Dalit Theology* (Madras, 1996), p. 252. For a similar argument, see M.E. Prabhakar, 'The Search for a Dalit Theology', in James Massey (ed.), *Indigenous People: Dalits. Dalit Issues in Today's Theological Debate* (Delhi, 1998), p. 206.

the worst obstacle to the liberation of the Dalit population. The second worst, he opines, is fatalism and resignation, due to the belief in karma.[78]

Is this type of theology relevant in the New York area? My interviewees were mixed in their responses, but most felt that Dalit theology was of interest only to academics and pastors, and even then, that the American context of Indian Christians militates against Dalit Theology's pertinence, since most pastors there are – whether comfortably or not – accustomed to preaching in a Western theological tradition that is therapeutic rather than aggressive in its attention to social justice. Bishop George Ninan, in his forthcoming essay 'Asian Indian Ministries in the United States',[79] writes succinctly on this point:

> The immigrant community does not have the confidence to involve itself in societal issues. There is also the great influence of the 'prosperity Gospel' and of emotional expressions of faith which are very consoling and comforting to a timid, new immigrant in unfamiliar circumstances. So the immigrant community holds on with fervency to the old home style expression of faith, and this is reinforced by the conditions here.

Sathianathan Clarke phrases the issue this way: perhaps the same impetus that makes Dalit theology relevant in India today can be translated into the American context by thinking of a theology for 'subalterns', as opposed just to Dalits, who are, after all, a minority in the American churches.[80]

In short, the challenges of creating the most appropriate worship style in a majority culture that is not entirely welcoming to the immigrant, of adapting to a social setting where all types of family problems and inter-generational gaps can arise, and of preaching in a theological milieu that is not conducive to the raising of liberation theology – these are additional demands upon the lives of Indian Christians that add to the silence surrounding Dalit issues in their transnational churches.

In conclusion, what lies ahead for the Dalit members of Indian churches in New York? Increasing liberation, or renewed shame? I asked two young Indian Christians, both in their early twenties, what they foresaw. Both pinned their hopes on the churches eventually planted and/or led by second-, third- and fourth-generation Indian Americans. Jeremy Mathews felt that caste discrimination, if present among first-generation churches, would completely disappear in second-generation churches, though this would be a long time in coming. 'Since second-generation churches have not been established yet, it is difficult to bring lower-caste Christians into established first-generation churches. It will take a long time before purely second-generation churches emerge.'[81] Divya Gideon was far less sanguine about prospects for the

---

[78]   Azaraiah, *A Pastor's Search for Dalit Theology*, p. 147.

[79]   This essay will also appear in the forthcoming volume deriving from the Princeton Consultation of June 2007.

[80]   Sathianathan Clarke, telephone interview, 5 June 2007. Clarke is the author of *Dalits and Christianity: Subaltern Religion and Liberation Theology in India* (New Delhi, 1999).

[81]   E-mail correspondence, 28 July 2007.

future. Yes, she agreed, if no more Indian immigrants come to the United States, and if the communities here now are left to develop on their own, then caste consciousness will decrease in the churches of the second generation and beyond. However, if, as is much more likely, the South Asian population only increases in the United States, such that more and more 'little Indias' with their enclaves and India-centric ways of thinking and living are created, then caste-consciousness, inherent in transplanted Indian communities, may only harden and flourish.[82] Bishop Devasahayam told me that Ambedkar had warned overseas societies not to accept Indians, as they would bring caste with them. This is the source of Divya Gideon's fear for the future: caste *is* a diaspora problem now, and will only become more so in the coming years. But she, like many Indian Christians passionate for social justice in the world, also believes in a God who blesses the exodus from bondage, and in this belief lies her hope.

References

Azaraiah, Bishop Masilamani, *A Pastor's Search for Dalit Theology* (Delhi: Society for Promoting Christian Knowledge, 2000).

Balasundaram, Franklyn J., 'Dalit Theology and Other Theologies', in V. Devasahayam (ed.), *Frontiers of Dalit Theology* (Madras: Gurukul Summer Institute, 1996).

Bama, *Karukku*, trans. from Tamil by Lakshmi Holmström, ed. Mini Kirshnan (Chennai: Macmillan India, 2000).

Broken People: Caste Violence against India's 'Untouchables' (New York: Human Rights Watch, 1999).

Clarke, Sathianathan, *Dalits and Christianity: Subaltern Religion and Liberation Theology in India* (New Delhi: Oxford University Press, 1999).

Dalit International Newsletter, 5/3 (October 2000).

Dalit International Newsletter, 11/3 (October 2006).

Daniel SJ, Poornam, 'Dalit Christian Experiences: Some Reflections on Dalit Christians' Struggle for Liberation and its Implications for Doing a Dalit Theology,' in Xavier Irudayaraj SJ (ed.), *Emerging Dalit Theology* (Madras: Jesuit Theological Secretariat, 1990), pp. 18–54.

Devasahayam, V. (ed.), *Frontiers of Dalit Theology* (Madras: Gurukul Summer Institute, 1996).

George, Sam, *The Coconut Generation: Ministry to the Americanized Asian Indians* (Niles, IL: Malls Publishing, 2006).

Irudayaraj SJ, Xavier (ed.), *Emerging Dalit Theology* (Madras: Jesuit Theological Secretariat, 1990).

Jebamani, Rev. Gideon, 'Dalit Christians: From Submission to Liberation' (DMin. Demonstration Project, New York Theological Seminary, 2004).

---

[82]   Divya Gideon, telephone interview, 29 August 2007.

Kent, Eliza F., *Converting Women: Gender and Protestant Christianity in Colonial South India* (New York: Oxford University Press, 2004).

Kurien, Prema A., 'Christian by Birth or Rebirth? Generation and Difference in an Indian American Christian Church', in Tony Carnes and Fenggang Yang (eds), *Asian American Religions: The Making and Remaking of Borders and Boundaries* (New York: New York University Press, 2004), pp. 160–81.

Mahtani, Sabrina, 'Work and Descent-Based Discrimination in the South Asian Diaspora: A Briefing for the Sub-commission on the Promotion and Protection of Human Rights' (draft, December 2003), Appendix.

Massey, James (ed.), *Indigenous People: Dalits. Dalit Issues in Today's Theological Debate* (Delhi: ISPCK, 1998).

Mathews, Jeremy and Nithin Thompson, 'Calling First Generation Missionaries to Second Generation Ministry: A Concise Anthropological Assessment and Praxis Guide to Providing Culturally Relevant and Meaningful Ministry to Second Generation Indians in First Generation Indian Churches' (Princeton, NJ: Princeton Consultation on Church Union, forthcoming).

Ninan, Bishop A. George, 'Asian Indian Ministries in the United States' (Princeton, NJ: Princeton Consultation on Church Union, forthcoming).

Nirmal, Arvind R., 'Towards a Dalit Theology', in Xavier Irudayaraj SJ (ed.), *Emerging Dalit Theology*, (Madras: Jesuit Theological Secretariat, 1990), pp. 123–42.

Nirmal, Arvind R. and V. Devasahayam (eds), *A Reader in Dalit Theology* (Madras: Gurukul Lutheran Theological College and Research Institute, *c.* mid-1990s).

Phan, Peter C., *Christianity with an Asian Face: Asian American Theology in the Making* (Marknoll, NY: Orbis Books, 2003).

Prabhakar, M.E. (ed.), *Towards a Dalit Theology* (Delhi: Christian Institute for the Study of Religion and Society, 1988).

Prabhakar, M.E., 'The Search for a Dalit Theology', in James Massey (ed.), *Indigenous People: Dalits. Dalit Issues in Today's Theological Debate* (Delhi: ISPCK, 1998).

Ravinder, Rev. David K., 'Pastoral Care and Counseling in the Asian Indian Christian Community: Some Observations and Reflections' (Princeton, NJ: Princeton Consultation on Church Union, forthcoming).

Sanghera, Jasvinder, *Shame* (London: Hodder and Stoughton, 2007).

Singh, Rev. Prince, 'Issues of Social Justice, Mission and Evangelism in the Context of Developing Asian Indian Ministries: What Constitutes Mission and Evangelism for Asian Indian Ministries/Churches in the United States?' (Princeton, NJ: Princeton Consultation on Church Union, forthcoming).

Thomas, Glory, 'Trading Churidhar for Jeans: Challenges facing Asian Indian Christian Women in the United States of America' (Princeton, NJ: Princeton Consultation on Church Union, forthcoming).

Thompson, Nehemiah, 'The Common Journey: Living by the Ecumenical Spirit' (Princeton, NJ: Princeton Consultation on Church Union, forthcoming).

Webster, John C.B., 'Dalit Identity and Dalit Theology' (unpublished paper presented at Andover Newton Theological School, Spring 2006).

Williams, Raymond B., *Christian Pluralism in the United States: The Indian Experience* (Cambridge: Cambridge University Press, 1996).

Conclusion
South Asian Christians in the West

Raymond Brady Williams

Gods and religions travel on the shoulders of migrants. Migrations of various types give religions their geographic and social place in the world. Immigration over time has impacted the religious and ethnic profiles of countries, their competing group and national identities, and the resulting ethos of individual national cultures. Current migration patterns that developed in the last half of the twentieth century create new religious realities in Europe and North America. Migrations of Indian Christians documented in this book are a relatively recent, largely unnoticed and significant aspect of recent population movements and resulting cultural adaptations.

Immigration is a primary factor in American history, shaping the current religious and ethnic demography of the United States. A foundational story for the country and for most families and groups starts with the theme that the United States is a country of immigrants. That is the reason that the United States is by many measures – including attendance at religious observance, private acts of piety, and profession of beliefs – the most religious of Western industrialized countries. Each new immigrant group has had to establish its social and cultural identity and space. Religion has been a powerful and accepted marker that empowers identity, place and negotiation with the larger society through a transcendent allegiance that enables the individual and group to resist both marginalization and forced assimilation. The latent function is creation of social capital through social networks and associated norms of reciprocity and trustworthiness necessary for the creation of the common good.[1]

The American foundational story emphasizes the open door, and the lines of Emma Lazarus, copied beneath the welcoming light of the Statue of Liberty: 'Give me your tired, your poor, your huddled masses yearning to be free ...'. That is one truth, but another is that the opening has been a swinging door, welcoming some and excluding others at various times. The early arrival of Protestants from northern and western Europe, the forced arrival of African Americans, the belated welcome of Catholics and Jews from central and eastern Europe, the exclusion of Asians, the closed door from roughly 1920 to 1970, and the current open door for a brain drain and family members of all the world's religions have created the

---

[1]   Robert D. Putnam, '*E Pluribus Unum*: Diversity and Community in the Twenty-first Century. The 2006 Johan Skytte Prize Lecture', *Scandinavian Political Studies*, 30/2 (2007): 137–74.

diverse religious and ethnic American patchwork quilt that is the heritage and the current American reality.

European foundational stories contrast with the American experience in so many different ways – so many doors, so many cultures, distinct histories, different colours and designs of patchwork quilts. Immigration has not been the foundational story of European countries, unless it is way back and way deep. Contemporary immigration is primarily into secularized societies with vestiges of a Christian heritage by people from deeply religious cultures, people who often become more religious and more observant in their new locations. Distinct migrations from South Asia and the presence of diverse religious groups are relatively recent. Christians among these immigrants to European countries arrive from locations where Christians are small minorities, sometimes oppressed, especially those who arrive as refugees. These new immigrants are changing the religious face of European countries in ways analogous to the American experience. Research shared in this book contributes to understanding of the new religious and ethnic realities in Western countries.

Recent Migrations of South Asian Christians

Detailed analyses of diverse Christian immigrant groups in several countries from several academic perspectives highlight how diverse the experiences of Indian Christian migrants to the West have been. Each sending and receiving country in each time period in the past half-century has created distinct religious and ethnic groups. Even though migrations have been shaped and powered by invisible hands – economic, political, bureaucratic and others – that move migrants in various constellations across the globe, the results are visibly concrete in lives, neighbourhoods, politics and culture throughout Europe and the United States.

A partial unveiling of those invisible hands requires a focus on the push/pull factors that result in recent migrations. Indian Christian migration to the United States has been part of the brain drain created by the new immigration law passed in 1965 that reopened the door to the United States for scientists, physicians and engineers, not 'your tired, your poor, your huddled masses yearning to be free …'. Administrators later added nurses to the preference lists at a time when women in the United States turned away from nursing to pursue other occupations recently opened to them. That happened when government funding of Medicare created a need for more nurses, especially in inner city hospitals, and the military siphoned off nurses for service in military hospitals in Vietnam. The preference category permitting family reunification dictated that future immigrants duplicate the national, ethnic and religious identities of the earlier immigrants.

Colonial administration and decolonization shaped migration to several European countries. Many migrants, some Christians among them, moved from the colonies to Europe to help rebuild following the Second World War and then to fuel the subsequent economic revival. Students followed colonial networks, and some 'stayed on' to build distinguished careers. The Roman Catholic Church in Germany had also recruited nurses and nuns to serve in hospitals and other Catholic agencies, providing the basis for subsequent developments of Indian Christianity in Germany. Rapid-fire decolonization in Africa and Asia in the 1960s caused many to exercise rights to immigrate that had been granted with Commonwealth or national citizenship. Continuing ethnic and religious conflicts around the world created refugees who found new homes in various countries. Christians with ties to India have been caught up in these movements, as portrayed in the chapters of this book.

These migrations are multi-layered, with different migratory groups representing distinct movements in response over time to an array of push/pull factors. Christians with ancestral or personal heritage in churches in India arrive from India, Sri Lanka, Indonesia, Suriname, Africa, Pondicherry, Goa and other locations, some of whom may never have visited India or spoken an Indian language. Roman Catholics from Goa and Pondicherry arrive from areas where Portuguese and French colonial rulers supported Catholicism, whereas those from Sri Lanka came from a location where the Dutch and British did not favour Catholicism, which has affected adaptation in South Asia and the West. France is home to Christians from Pondicherry, Sri Lanka and Tamil Nadu, each group with a potentially distinct ethnic and religious identity. Catholics from Pondicherry arrived in France in the 1950s following Indian nationalization of Pondicherry, to be joined by Pondicherrian refugees from Viet Nam following American withdrawal in the 1970s. Distinctions are noted in the Netherlands by references to those from Suriname as 'Hindustanis' and those directly from India as 'Indians'. Moreover, each country has those who were Christian prior to migration and those who converted after immigration. South Asian Christians in the West have no strong sense of comprising a single community.

Delineation of the generations becomes analytically significant only in relation to immigration. The pioneers, who established ethnic and religious organizations, are the first generation; those who arrive as small children form an important first-and-a-half generation; the second generation is the first socialized in the new context; the third generation is just beginning to reach adulthood in the West. As long as the door to immigrants is open, these several generations coexist and are refreshed by new first generations. Relations with the majority societies and cultures develop at different rates influenced by status, size, age and generational identities of the immigrant Christian community in each country. Recent research on Indian Christian groups in the West is providing data and perspectives that illumine a more complex, multi-layered migration history and contemporary reality.

Unfortunately, we possess neither the statistical data nor accurate timelines. Government statistics regarding these migrations, especially regarding religious affiliation of migrants, is very sketchy. Christians are hidden in the midst of large migrations. Statistics of religious bodies are notoriously unreliable. It is impossible to determine the number of immigrants who grasp the opportunities provided by migration to change or abandon religious affiliations. Some vanish from view as nominal Christians. It may not even be wise in the current world climate of ethnic and religious conflict to encourage governments to carefully identify and track religious affiliation or participation. Imagine what a new Hitler might do with contemporary computer databases! Nevertheless, a future challenge for research is to develop a careful timeline of the movement of Indian Christians around the globe, and to create a reliable demography of Indian Christians in various locations. The chapters in this book provide important information in response to basic questions about Indian Christian migrations: Who? What? When? Where? How? and Why?

Transnational Experience of South Asian Christians

Christians with roots in South Asia are part of a new transnational reality created by historical movements and by more rapid current mobility and communication. Transnational occupational networks are as diverse as movement of nurses from southern India to the urban hospitals in the United States and Catholic hospitals and social agencies in Germany, to movement of Sri Lankan fishermen and refugees to Norway. Some Western countries admitted refugees from turmoil and conflict in locations where South Asian Christians resided and where some suffered persecution or deprivation. Family ties and religious affiliations helped shape those occupational and refugee networks. These factors determined to a large extent the economic and social status of the immigrants, along with caste and denominational affiliations – many of which are new in the West.

The resulting transnational networks maintained by past migrations and shaping contemporary movements are busy highways of mobility and communication. 'Transnational' is a technical designation of the experience of recent immigrants in maintaining many associations that span several societies, developing identities and communicating through social networks that connect them with two or more societies simultaneously.[2] South Asian immigrants established themselves in several countries, and marriage negotiations, economic transfers, new ideas and customs, implied legal and moral obligations, and viable options for mobility move along these new networks. Religious organizations are primary mediating institutions for these networks.

'Transnational' is a better term for describing this phenomenon than 'globalism', because the networks are discrete. Networks are different for people in diverse religions and ethnic groups. Christians create networks that reach back to distinct locations in India and other countries different from those cultivated by Muslims,

---

[2]   Nina Glick Shiller, Linda Bash and Christina Blanc-Szanton (eds), *Towards a Transnational Perspective on Migration: Race, Class, Ethnicity, and Nationalism Reconsidered*, Annals of the New York Academy of Sciences no. 645 (New York, 1992), pp. 1–24.

Hindus or Sikhs. These distinct networks rarely cover the globe, rarely intersect or have much interaction. US Senator Barack Obama describes visiting Google company headquarters, where he saw a large monitor displaying a vibrant network of lights modelling real-time traffic patterns throughout the Internet system.[3] The image is never uniformly light, but has huge dark or grey spots. The lights trace networks of communication that are analogous to social networks created by transnational families and religions that are dynamic, not static, and transnational, not global. Christians from South Asia do not migrate everywhere, but only along well-established transnational networks.

The new transnational reality for Christian individuals and denominations with roots in South Asia is a relatively new phenomenon in Western countries. The chapters of this book are organized along national lines, but transnational networks, movements and communication are evident. Roman Catholics of the Latin, Syro-Malabar and Syro-Malankara rites, representing various caste-level backgrounds, reside in Goa, East Africa and the United Kingdom. Nurses and physicians from Kerala, both Protestants and Catholics, reside in North and South India, in Europe, Canada and the United States. The largest city of Sri Lankans is now Toronto. The occasions when the complex networks become physically embodied are when people living in several countries and continents gather for religious festivals or for elaborate wedding ceremonies, often uniting those from different countries. Priests and other religious specialists move across these networks on tours or for temporary residence, to instruct and serve migrant populations. The networks are officially recognized in some cases by the formation of dioceses uniting North American and European countries in a single diocese under a synod of bishops in India.

Omnipresent Internet access among the well-educated and well-to-do creates virtual transnational religions in the twenty-first century – virtual Hinduism, virtual Islam, virtual Buddhism and virtual South Asian Christianity – that affect religious identities in every location. The prominence of scientists and computer specialists among immigrants and the growth of the information technology industry in India result in sophisticated sites for the transmission of tradition, presentation of revised forms of religious teaching and devotion, and assistance in identity formation, especially for children and youth. Technological modernization and free access to new modes of communication mean that religious knowledge is no longer mediated or controlled by parents, teachers, priests or pastors, but shifts into the hands of technologically skilled editors of Web pages and those who gain their allegiance and service. Marriage advertisements on Websites discriminate through a hypertext organization so that a South Asian Christian family interested in marriage negotiations can explore potential candidates by denomination, ethnicity, language facility, caste, residence and a multitude of other factors. The messages that a church group wants to transmit, either internally to instruct

---

[3]   Barack Obama, *The Audacity of Hope: Thoughts on Reclaiming the American Dream* (New York, 2006), p. 140.

or inspire or externally to establish identity and status, are available any time and everywhere to any person who has Internet access. The growth of virtual religion and virtual Christianity in the twenty-first century is a powerful and little understood phenomenon.

A complex web of reciprocal influences affects South Asian and European Christianity both here and there, wherever 'here' or 'there' may be. In earlier periods, the missionary influence moved primarily from west to east as people, funds, ideas and structures moved eastward. Then, in the past half-century, the reality has become primarily a reverse movement from east to west when missionary activity was restricted and new immigrants entered Europe and North America, often retracing old missionary paths. One fairly common poignant experience of immigrants is in visits to retirement centres, monuments or graves to honour Christian missionaries who served in South Asia. A new transnational reality is reciprocal influences across communication and mobility networks shaping new manifestations of European and American Christianities. Monetary remittances from non-resident Indians and other South Asians are a major boon to families, neighbourhoods, villages, religious institutions and churches. Family prayers and financial gifts support migrants as they move across transnational networks, and then resources return from migrants to support others. Priests, nuns and evangelists travel in many directions to visit individuals and congregations. Although changes take place at a pace dictated by local circumstances, changes in customs, theology, ritual and polity are shaped by reciprocal influences moving, like telephone messages, in many directions across new networks.

Study of contemporary South Asian Christianity involves analyses of the nature and impact of transnational networks, internal to the United States or European countries and connecting to specific groups and neighbourhoods in other nations. Christians in an American church, for example, relate to centres in other American cities and maintain regular contact with those in Canada, Britain, Western Europe, East Africa and stretching back to regional, linguistic, ethnic and caste groups in India. Individuals, families, religious leaders, ideas, rituals, money and all kinds of familial, economic and political negotiations move rapidly through the network in multi-dimensional communication. Peggy Levitt refers to 'social remittances' of ideas, behaviours, identities and social capital flowing along such networks.[4] Religions in America are transnational in ways not possible or even imagined fifty years ago. The shape and size of future migrations, and resulting transnational realities, will be determined by legislative and administrative changes in immigrations laws in many countries influenced by unforeseen political and economic forces impossible to predict.

---

[4]   Peggy Levitt, 'Social Remittances: Migration-driven Local-level Forms of Cultural Diffusion', *International Migration Review*, 32/4 (Winter 1998): 926–48.

Function of Religion for Immigrants

Religion is a powerful force for immigrants in the formation and preservation of personal and group identity because it provides a transcendent grounding for identity. That is the reason religion is potentially either one of the most conservative or the most radical aspects of culture. Basic religious affirmation and commitment pit the individual and group against external forces that would precipitate either chaos or homogeneity. They provide bases for resistance to mainstream values. Many immigrants affirm that they are more religious following immigration than in their native place, even though the style of their participation and their religious roles in Western countries are substantially different. When everything is changing, religion provides a firm, transcendent base from which to negotiate those changes.

Countries in the West are becoming more religiously diverse. That is one reason that the first decade of the twenty-first century is witnessing a more conservative move, more religious tensions, and more intense negotiations among religious groups, calling into question hypotheses of secularization and assimilation dominant in earlier decades. Conservative moves and intense negotiations will be transnational, as well, because of established and expanding networks of transnational ethnic and religious groups, including Christian groups. Immigrants and the religious groups they establish exist both here and there in ways not previously possible. Indeed, immigrants are balancing worlds, merging them and creating something new.

South Asian Christian identities are important to parents in trying to maintain coherence between the here and now and the then and there. The transmission of markers of identity is essential to maintaining communication and empathy with their children and grandchildren. Each generation has to gain competence in the syntax of several possible identities to facilitate their negotiations with those in the majority population and with those in other minorities. Fortunately, identities are malleable within limits, and individuals are able to emphasize more than one element of their identity in different contexts as circumstances dictate. Immigrants must be adept at integrating elements of several identities and using them to their best advantage in different social settings. It may be advantageous to identify oneself as Christian in one context, Indian in another, Mar Thoma Christian, Malayalee, or German, Canadian, Norwegian or American in appropriate contexts. Movement from one to the other requires diverse sets of knowledge and skills, the acquiring and maintenance of which require enormous investments of energy (which is why the tendency is for individuals to become monocultural – it is easier). At the very least, some coherence and compatibility of elements of personal identity are essential to personal health and social effectiveness. The relationship between these potential individual identities is reflected in the establishment of churches and other organizations that reinforce different elements of identity.

Personal identity is malleable in a free society in ways that institutional identity is not. Therefore, potentials for personal identity are reflected in the intricate relationships and competition that exist among ethnic, religious and professional organizations. Immigrants are not being deceitful when they respond to the boundaries imposed on them internally and externally by selecting or stressing designations for themselves in their own best interest; it is simply an aspect of the greater freedom for re-creation and self-identification than is generally the case in the place of origin. Firm boundaries are essential to identity; malleability is essential for migrants; the tensions and negotiation between potential identities are determinative for new immigrants and their children.

Formation and preservation of Christian and ethnic identity are at one level rhetorical moves. Rhetoric of representation is continually changing in a larger syntax of communication shared by many groups defined in a variety of ways. Rituals, festivals, modes of dress, language or accent, cuisine, calendar, gesture, art and ritual communicate intricate messages an individual or a group transmit of itself. These constitute the ritualizing of personal and group identity – if one accepts Edmund Leach's definition of ritual as the communicative aspect of customary behaviour. The audience for such rhetorical acts is the group itself, as well as those outside. Socialization and individuation for new residents and those in the settled population, especially the youth, require increased facility in verbal and non-verbal communication in rituals and language newly created or refined to enable understanding between individuals and groups. Dangerous and potentially fatal mistakes result from communication failure, so the challenge and responsibility are great on the shoulders of leaders in education, politics and religion.

The rhetoric of representation preserves distinctions within society as well as essential unity, and is refined, with sharper ability to reveal nuanced differentiations and finer distinctions. In the use of such refined rhetoric, a society develops greater sophistication in inter-personal and group relations. Individuals are able to express a range of identities and loyalties in a wide variety of contexts and among different groups. Both individuals and groups are able to position themselves with greater clarity and to greater advantage among diverse groups. Such sophistication contributes to the orderly and creative development of society.

The move of Indian Christians to establish new congregations and organizations in the West is not an act of separation. The latent function is not to maintain isolation from the rest of society, but to get a footing and build a firmer foundation from which to engage in intricate negotiations with other social, political, economic and religious structures regarding place and power in society. The desire is to be part of society on mutually acceptable terms, if possible. That is easier in some ways and more difficult in others, because Indian Christians are a small immigrant group among larger movements of adherents of other religions to Europe and North America.

Relations with Other Religious Groups

Indian Christians are part of a new religious diversity in the West, along with Hindus, Sikhs, Muslims, Jains and Buddhists from South Asia and from secondary outposts in South-east Asia, Africa and other continents. In most instances, Christians moved from the experience of being in the minority to where they are in a putative majority or in a new kind of minority in secularized cultures. Migration transforms the dynamics of inter-religious relations. Christian immigrants with roots in South Asia have had more experience living cheek by jowl with Hindus, Muslims, Sikhs or Buddhists than have Christians, Jews and secularized populations in Western countries. Contacts between Christians and other South Asian religions continue in neighbourhoods (such as Flushing, New York), in language-based ethnic groups (Gujarati or Tamil Associations), in professional groups (Gujarati Motel Owners Association, Indian Physicians Association), and in national groups (such as India Cultural Associations).

Two aspects of these relationships in both South Asia and in Western countries are (1) evangelism and conversion, and (2) inter-religious/inter-cultural marriage and conversion. Chapters in this book provide evidence that some immigrants with roots in South Asia convert to Christianity after immigration. The primary impetus for conversation is evangelistic initiatives undertaken by individuals, congregations and organizations formed by Christian immigrants, not by institutions of the majority populations, many of which have accepted an interpretation of multi-cultural tolerance that discourages evangelism and conversion in favour of dialogue. Immigrants reinforce the evangelistic heritage of Christianity. Pentecostal Christians have been very active in India and in the West in evangelistic efforts among fellow immigrants and their families. Catholic and Eastern Orthodox churches accuse some evangelistic groups of 'sheep stealing'.

Conversions also result from inter-religious and inter-cultural marriages, especially in those communities that expect the bride to adopt the religious affiliations of her spouse. The desire of immigrant parents to protect the religious and ethnic identities of their children becomes acute at the point when the second generation begins dating, which many families discourage, and faces marriage negotiations. Different valuations of 'arranged marriage' conducted by parents, 'semi-arranged marriage' initiated by the couple, or 'love marriage', which often implies parental objections, are evident in different Christian groups and the generations. These two aspects create tensions within families and communities and provide an important component of negotiations between religious and ethnic groups, sometimes within the larger Christian community as well as between religions.

Tensions and pressures between Christians and other religions are analogous to magnets with positive and negative poles that have the potential for both attraction and repulsion. Christians carry into their new neighbourhoods negative valuations of Hinduism or Islam, depending upon the nature of inter-religious relations and ethos in their native places. In some cases, it depends upon the caste experience and economic status of the immigrants. Thomas Christians from Kerala claim a Syrian heritage and a relatively high caste status in India, and have negotiated a fairly harmonious relationship with Hindus and Muslims. Latin rite Catholics and Protestants with roots in Dalit communities see their conversion and that of their ancestors as escape from the deprivations of Hinduism and its caste culture. Positive evaluations of Hindu or Muslim cultures and practices stressed in Western society, churches and schools are not appreciated by many new Christian immigrants. Moreover, many view teaching about Hinduism and Islam in the schools as an unwelcome threat to the religious identity and commitments of their children.

The attraction field of the magnet is evident in common rituals and many aspects of devotion (*bhakti*) that create similarities of worship, weddings, festivals and personal behaviour between Christians, Muslims, Hindus and others. Many years ago, my Hindu tutor in Madras was eager to take me to view the St Thomas Day festival at which a relic from the Apostle Thomas was carried in procession around the cathedral. As we watched, he commented to me: 'It is just the same as the Sri Vaishnava processions that we have been visiting!' Indeed, many of the ritual gestures and devotional activities seemed multi-religious, and it was unclear how many in the procession were Christian and how many were Hindu. Parallels in the West are most evident in Christian devotion to the Virgin Mary and in festivals and pilgrimages to Marian shrines. Festivals related to the 'Tamil Virgin' create national and transnational pilgrimages in Europe, but they also attract Hindus and a few Muslims, for whom the power and salvific acts of the Virgin are parallel, if not identical, to those of female deities or saints. Hindus are more likely to include Christian artefacts in their home shrines, but many images, gestures and rituals are multivalent and function within diverse immigrant communities.

The positive and negative charges that create attraction and repulsion are aspects of establishing the inter-relation of religious and cultural characteristics in the identity of immigrant individuals and groups. It is especially difficult to separate cultural markers from religious commitments and activities in India and in other South Asian countries. Hence, it is difficult for scholars to determine what aspects of customary behaviour by immigrants and their children are parts of ethnic heritage, national heritage or religious heritage. Because migrations have taken place over time, especially in the past two centuries, and because they skipped across several transnational locations, it is a complex matter to distinguish the multi-layered religious and cultural influences that shape new identities in Western countries. They certainly influence our experience and interpretations of the new multi-religious reality and potentials in Western countries.

Models of Immigrant Christian Experience

Scholars and society at large create models of analysis, evaluation and even prediction to critique levels of adaptation to the majority culture by new immigrants and their descendents. Two models dominant in interpretation of immigrant groups in the late nineteenth and early twentieth century were assimilation and secularization. Assimilation of Christians, Jews and others from southern and eastern Europe meant the loss of regional languages, shedding of distinctive ethnic gestures and symbols, and the transformation of religious rituals and practices to make them congruent with those of earlier immigrants from northern and western Europe. Public schools were the primary socializing agency of the second and third generations, whereas churches and synagogues were the primary location outside the homes for preservation of ethnic and religious markers of distinction. The evolution of the American Catholic Church and its move toward many aspects of the dominant Protestant model shows the power of the assimilation model, especially in the second quarter of the twentieth century. Many expected that to be the experience of the descendents of immigrants in the twenty-first century.

The concomitant model was secularization and the interpretation and/ or expectation that the experience of the Christians in America would be a progressive move towards secularization of political, social and personal lives. The expectation was that American society and churches would follow European models of secularization. The mid-twentieth century marked a homogenization of American society accompanied by a decline of ethnic languages and markers, along with liberalization and an ecumenical movement that muted Christian theological and ritual differences. *The Secular City: Secularization and Urbanization in Theological Perspective* marked the high-water mark of that interpretation just at the point when American doors were opened to new immigrants whose experience seems to require a re-evaluation of old models.[5]

The major movement towards assimilation and secularization in the United States came during a lull in immigration in the half-century from 1920 to 1970, a peculiar period in American history when the doors were effectively shut and when in some years more people left the United States than arrived. What was absent during the lull was the revitalization of religious and ethnic groups by a constant flow of new immigrants that had characterized the nineteenth century and that characterizes North America and Europe in the twenty-first century. That experience of immigration and the vitality of religious and ethnic identities necessary to establishing footholds by immigrants had been largely absent in many European countries until the second half of the twentieth century. Some of the tensions between the majority populations and new residents are related to analyses, evaluations and expectations shaped by older models of assimilation and secularization. However, some scholars now refer to the post-secular city to characterize the urban religious organizations of new

---

[5]   Harvey Cox, *The Secular City: Secularization and Urbanization in Theological Perspective* (New York, 1965).

immigrants in Europe and question interpretative categories of pluralism, multi-culturalism, assimilation and secularism.

Cultural and religious negotiations propelled by recent immigration in both Europe and North America are complex and diverse, and it is unlikely that one model of interpretation will be adequate for diverse migrations throughout an extended period. Networks for migration and protocols of relationships were established during periods when European countries governed colonies in South Asia and elsewhere. Decolonization in the second half of the century brought Christians from both the primary and secondary colonial locations to European cities. Adaptation to some aspects of Western culture had already taken place in the colonies, in part to enable Christians to establish and preserve identities separate from those of the majority non-Christian populations. Canada and Britain established Commonwealth ties with previous colonies that facilitated recent migrations of labourers, students and refugees. Each of the Christian groups – national, ethnic and denominational – has a different array of grievances or gratitude from the past, and a distinct set of hopes and fears for the future. These affect the adaptation in the new settings and the types of adaptive strategies that are encouraged or permitted by the majority society or by other minority groups. It is difficult for mediating institutions – such as schools, hospitals, government agencies, the media and religious organizations – to agree on desired or acceptable models of adaptation and interpretation, which confuses the missions of these institutions in relation to immigrants and their families.

Christians in South Asia accepted or rejected enculturation as both a theological and a social challenge. How much of culture dominated by Hindu, Muslim or Buddhist world views and practices should or could be accepted by Christians? Distinct Christian groups in various countries responded differently to the issues posed. Some groups, including Roman Catholics who followed instruction regarding enculturation from Vatican II, adopted elements of the dominant South Asian cultures, including regional languages, ethnic customs and religious gestures in liturgy. Other Christian groups attempted to distinguish themselves from Hindus, Muslims and Buddhists by rejecting, in so far as possible, dominant cultural, ethnic and religious markers. The struggle of embodiment of Christianity between 'Christ in culture' and 'Christ against culture' in H. Richard Niebuhr's *Christ and Culture*, reflecting the past experience of earlier immigrants, makes more complex the strategies of adaptation in Western Christian or post-Christian and multi-cultural societies. It raises the issue of the appropriate, expected or permitted adaptations for Christians in South Asia and of their compatriots in Western societies. Some political and religious leaders, particularly in the United States and Canada, propagate a multi-cultural vision that encourages new residents to preserve essential ethnic and religious markers, especially those of Hindus, Muslims and Buddhists. A few even understand and encourage preservation of diverse Christian markers. Others encourage assimilation and/or secularization, even though the previously dominant ethos has so weakened in many countries as not to be compelling.

Christian immigrants are often disappointed in the moral and religious reality they discover in what they had idealized as Christian countries and in Christian churches in the West. One reason for establishing South Asian Christian churches in Western countries is a desire to protect their children from contemporary moral dangers, social ills and decadence. A result is that it is impossible for new immigrants to fit a generally accepted model; it is certainly impossible for them to satisfy the varied expectations of majority populations; it is increasingly difficult for recent immigrants of the first and later generations to agree upon or implement effective and successful strategies of adaptation. Tensions, strained relationships and conflicts erupt between Christian groups, between the generations, between new Christian groups and the majority population, and between minority religious groups. Some of those tensions are visible in the analyses in this book.

Tensions and Conflict

Tensions and some conflict are concomitant with negotiations of new immigrants and their organizations as they attempt to establish social and cultural identity and social space. Religion has been a powerful and accepted marker that empowers identity, place and negotiation with the larger society through a transcendent allegiance that enables the individual and group to resist both marginalization and forced assimilation. The greater diversity in both Europe and North America may lead to a breakdown, at the least in the short term, in social capital needed to preserve constructive negotiations among ethnic and religious groups and to create the common good. Robert D. Putnam called attention to 'social capital', and defined it as 'social networks and the associated norms of reciprocity and trustworthiness'. His most recent research is on the effects of diversity on social capital.[6] Analysis of current diversity in the United States, resulting largely from immigration since 1965, leads him to the disturbing conclusion that 'diversity seems to trigger *not* in-group/out-group division, but anomie or social isolation'.[7] He notes:

> Rather, inhabitants of diverse communities tend to withdraw from collective life, to distrust their neighbours, regardless of the colour of their skin, to withdraw even from close friends, to expect the worst from their community and its leaders, to volunteer less, give less to charity and work on community projects less often, to register to vote less, to agitate for social reform *more*, but have less faith that they can actually make a difference, and to huddle unhappily in front of the television. Note that this pattern encompasses attitudes and behavior, bridging and bonding social capital, public and private connections. Diversity, at least in the short run, seems to bring out the turtle in all of us.[8]

---

6   Putnam, '*E Pluribus Unum*', p. 137.

7   Ibid., p. 49.

8   Ibid., pp. 150f.

One might have expected in-group/out-group conflict and division, but not anomie, breakdown of social capital, or internal tensions and conflict. It is risky to generalize from experiences in the United States to other Western countries. Nevertheless, the research does point to challenges in the short term in preserving and reconstituting social capital in multi-cultural and multi-religious contexts. Chapter 12 in this book has the title 'Doing Friendship, Making Contacts and Building Trust', which is closely related to building social capital.

Putnam's research highlights two aspects that provide a basis for optimism his for the long-term future. First, religious activity is the one aspect of social capital and civic engagement that is essentially uncorrelated with diversity.[9] The finding relates to the hypothesis mentioned above that many immigrants are more religious after immigration than in their native place because religion provides a transcendent basis for personal and group identity and a firmer footing from which to negotiate space and social location in a new context. Putnam summarizes a basis for some optimism: 'Bonding social capital can thus be a prelude to bridging social capital.'[10] Religious affiliation and activity are components in maintenance and re-creation of social capital. Second, Putnam notes the power of religion to deconstruct divisive racial and ethnic identities. He reports finding among younger people in evangelical mega-churches and in large Catholic parishes a construction of religiously based identities that cut across (while not effacing) conventional racial and ethnic identities.[11] This second point permits hope that immigration is not only inevitable, but can become a positive force in strengthening society. Christians might contribute to that outcome.

Recent Christian immigrants from South Asia occupy a unique position in several contemporary Western countries with potential to mediate between other South Asian religious groups and the majority populations. The short histories in this book recount the beginnings of the process of adaptation and social negotiations. South Asian Christians share aspects of world view and many commitments and characteristics with the majority populations. They also have shared experiences of living in religiously and ethnically diverse countries and, in India, a democratic political system. It is a challenge for religious leaders of all recent immigrant groups and majority communities to increase social capital, rather than reduce it, and to help redraw social lines that transcend ancestry and reduce conflict and tension. That is a hopeful note on which to conclude a book on South Asian Christianity and the common good in the West and in the transnational world.

---

[9]   Ibid., p. 150.
[10] Ibid., p. 165.
[11] Ibid., p. 161.

Conclusion

These research reports mark an advance in the study of South Asian Christians in the West. Careful national studies of discrete Christian groups are essential foundations for future research on the changing face of Christianity and religion in Europe and North America. A new, diverse group of scholars with transnational ties is prepared to conduct future research. Several trajectories for that research emerge from these studies. A historical atlas of migration of Christians in relation to migration of other South Asian religions is needed in order to put current migrations in appropriate historical contests. A timeline of migrations and a careful analysis of geographical distributions will provide the statistics needed to analyse Christian diversities. Additional national studies, more comprehensive ethnically and denominationally than these chapters, dealing with internal migrations and residence patterns, will help to fill out the patchwork quilt of contemporary religions. Transnational networks form the skeleton of contemporary Christianity and religions, and these have grown exponentially over the past few decades and cry out for detailed analyses. Longitudinal studies of strategies of adaptation of Christian groups, including conversions and transitions in affiliations, are needed to understand the function of religion and Christian affiliation in diverse settings. Caste affiliation and rejection of caste remain embarrassing, hidden factors within invisible migrations. Prospects for research on South Asian Christians provide a hopeful note regarding the academy and its contribution to understanding Christianity and religion in the contemporary world.

References

Cox, Harvey, *The Secular City: Secularization and Urbanization in Theological Perspective* (New York: Macmillan, 1965).

Glick Shiller, Nina, Linda Bash and Christina Blanc-Szanton (eds), *Towards a Transnational Perspective on Migration: Race, Class, Ethnicity, and Nationalism Reconsidered*, Annals of the New York Academy of Sciences no. 645 (New York: New York Academy of Sciences, 1992), pp. 1–24.

Levitt, Peggy, 'Social Remittances: Migration-driven Local-level Forms of Cultural Diffusion', *International Migration Review*, 32/4 (Winter 1998): 926–48.

Obama, Barack, *The Audacity of Hope: Thoughts on Reclaiming the American Dream* (New York: Crown Publishers, 2006).

Putnam, Robert D., '*E Pluribus Unum*: Diversity and Community in the Twenty-first Century. The 2006 Johan Skytte Prize Lecture', *Scandinavian Political Studies*, 30/2 (2007): 137–74.

Index